# Eurojihad

## *Patterns of Islamist Radicalization and Terrorism in Europe*

Throughout history, radicalization has involved social and economic conditions and issues of identity. Patterns of Islamist radicalization in Europe reflect the historical experience of European Muslim communities, particularly their links to their home countries, the prevalence of militant groups there, and the extent to which factors of radicalization in Muslim countries transfer to European Muslim diasporas. *Eurojihad* examines the sources of radicalization in Muslim communities in Europe and the responses of European governments and societies. In an effort to understand the scope and dynamics of Islamist extremism and terrorism in Europe, this book takes into account recent developments, in particular the emergence of Syria as a major destination of European jihadists. Angel Rabasa and Cheryl Benard describe the history, methods, and evolution of jihadist networks in Europe with particular nuance, providing a useful primer for the layperson and a sophisticated analysis for the expert.

Angel Rabasa is a senior political scientist at RAND whose research and analyses address problems of international security, extremism, and terrorism. His 2003 book, *The Muslim World after 9/11*, received wide acclaim for its comprehensive synthesis of the trends across the different regions of the Muslim world. Rabasa is the lead author of the 2006 book *Beyond al-Qaeda*, *Building Moderate Muslim Networks* (2007) with Cheryl Benard, *Ungoverned Territories: Understanding and Reducing Terrorism Risks* (2007), and *Deradicalizing Islamist Extremists* (2010).

Cheryl Benard is the president of Metis Analytics, a Washington, DC–based research company. From 2003 to 2012, she was a senior analyst with the RAND Corporation, where she worked primarily on methods for understanding and countering radical extremism. Benard's career has spanned two continents. Her focus has been on published results with a high degree of accessibility for policy makers, media, and the interested public. She has been the recipient of several awards in recognition of her work, including the Theodor Kery Prize for Socially Relevant Research and the Donauland Prize for Nonfiction Writing. Her books, including *Civil Democratic Islam*, have been translated into several languages.

# Eurojihad

*Patterns of Islamist Radicalization and Terrorism in Europe*

ANGEL RABASA

CHERYL BENARD

CAMBRIDGE
UNIVERSITY PRESS

32 Avenue of the Americas, New York, NY 10001-2473, USA

Cambridge University Press is part of the University of Cambridge.

It furthers the University's mission by disseminating knowledge in the pursuit of education, learning, and research at the highest international levels of excellence.

www.cambridge.org
Information on this title: www.cambridge.org/9781107437203



First published 2015

Printed in the United States of America

*A catalog record for this publication is available from the British Library.*

*Library of Congress Cataloging in Publication Data*
Rabasa, Angel.
Eurojihad : patterns of Islamist radicalization and terrorism in Europe / Angel Rabasa, Cheryl Benard.
pages cm
ISBN 978-1-107-07893-2 (hardback) – ISBN 978-1-107-43720-3 (pbk.)
1. Islamic fundamentalism – Europe.
2. Radicalism – Religious aspects – Islam. 3. Terrorism – Religious aspects – Islam.
4. Muslims – Europe – Social conditions. 5. Jihad. 6. Terrorism – Prevention – Government policy – Europe.
I. Benard,
Cheryl, 1953– II. Title.
BP166.14.F85R34 2014
363.325094–dc23 2014018139

ISBN 978-1-107-07893-2 Hardback
ISBN 978-1-107-43720-3 Paperback

## Contents


*List of figures* page vii
*List of tables* viii
*Preface* ix
*Acknowledgments* xi
*List of abbreviations* xv

1 Introduction 1
2 Europe's Muslim Populations 8
France 9
Germany 12
Great Britain 15
The Netherlands 17
Spain 18
Other Countries 19
Demographic Trends 21
3 Salafism and Radical Islamism in Europe 23
Evolution of Radical Islamism 26
Jihadi Ideology and Strategy 27
Themes and Messages 33
Strategy 35
4 Origins of Radical Islamist Networks in Europe 41
Gateways to Violent Extremism 50
Pool of Radical Sympathizers in European Muslim Communities 54
5 Radicalization Patterns 56
Second-Generation Extremists 56
Radicalized Middle Eastern and North African Immigrants 72

East Africans 83
Turks: A Traditional Community on the Path to Radicalization? 86
Converts 89
Conclusion 101

6 Radicalization and Recruitment Nodes 103
Radical Mosques and Social Centers 103
Prisons 110
The Internet and Social Media 117

7 Evolution of Radical Networks in Europe 123
Recent Evolution of Islamist Terrorist Networks in Europe 124
The Global Dimension of Europe-Based Islamist Terrorism 131

8 Terrorist Operations and Tactics 154
The European Environment 154
Attacks on Commercial Aviation 156
Attacks on Ground Mass Transportation Systems 159
Jihadist Adaptation 162
The Jihadists' Search for Weapons of Mass Destruction 163

9 New European Approaches 169
"Illegal" vs. "Subversive" Activities: The Divide in European Threat Assessment 174
Reaching Out to Muslim Communities 179
Building Effective Anti-Terrorism Legal Tools 181
Enhanced Cooperation within the EU 188

10 Key Judgments 192
Europe's Lessons for the United States 194

*Bibliography* 197
*Index* 217

# Figures


5.1 Age Range of Second-Generation British Terrorism Suspects of South Asian Ancestry *page* 66
5.2 Marital Status of Second-Generation British Terrorism Suspects of South Asian Ancestry 67
5.3 Educational and Occupational Status of Second-Generation British Terrorism Suspects of South Asian Ancestry 68
5.4 Education and Occupation of Converts Linked to Terrorism 96
5.5 Nationalities of Converts Linked to Terrorism 96
5.6 Age Range of Converts Linked to Terrorism 97
5.7 Marital Status of Converts Linked to Terrorism 98

# Tables


5.1 Second-Generation British Terrorism Suspects of South Asian Ancestry *page* 60
5.2 Hofstad Group 81
5.3 Converts Linked to Terrorism 93

# Preface

The terrorist attacks in Madrid in March 2004 and in London in July 2005, the assassination of Dutch filmmaker Theo Van Gogh in November 2004, the killing of U.S. soldiers at Frankfurt airport in March 2011, and several major foiled attacks throughout Europe such as the so-called Europlot – al-Qaeda's plan, uncovered in 2010, to attack targets in several European countries – erased any doubt that Europe has become a central theater of Islamist terrorist operations. The 9/11 Commission listed European cities with Muslim communities, along with the Afghan-Pakistani border, the Horn of Africa, and Southeast Asia, among the places where terrorists seek sanctuary and operating bases. Indeed, investigations after 9/11 uncovered extensive terrorist networks in the United Kingdom, France, Spain, Germany, Belgium, and Italy. The threat of Islamic radicalism has also become a central contentious issue of domestic and European politics, influencing elections and policy at all levels from the municipal to the European Union.

To understand the shape and dynamics of the Islamist extremist and terrorist challenge in Europe, it is necessary to examine the sources of Islamist radicalization in Europe; jihadist ideology and strategy; radicalization patterns, nodes, and networks; terrorist operations and tactics; and the response of European governments and societies. We can then draw the implications and lessons from the European experience with Islamist extremism and terrorism.

This book builds on research at the RAND Corporation on Islamist radicalism and terrorism in Europe over the past several years. It integrates work from several projects as well independent research conducted by the authors. The first project was part of the RAND Corporation's continuing program of self-initiated independent research. Support for such research is provided, in part, by donors and by the independent research and development provisions of RAND's contracts for the operation of its U.S. Department of Defense federally funded research and development centers. The second project was sponsored by the Office of the U.S. Under-Secretary of Defense for Policy, and the third project was sponsored by a private foundation. The work was conducted within the International Security and Defense Policy Center of the RAND National Security Research Division (NSRD). NSRD conducts research and analysis on defense and national security topics for the U.S. and allied defense, foreign policy, homeland security, and intelligence communities and foundations and other nongovernmental organizations that support defense and national security analysis. NSRD includes the RAND National Defense Research Institute, a federally funded research and development center sponsored by the Office of the Secretary of Defense, the Joint Staff, the Unified Combatant Commands, the Navy, the Marine Corps, the defense agencies, and the defense intelligence community.

# Acknowledgments

The authors wish to thank those who made this study possible: The RAND Corporation, which provided the funding for the initial phase of the research and under whose auspices the work was conducted, and former Under Secretary of Defense Eric Edelman, who took a personal interest in this project. We also wish to acknowledge the invaluable contributions of Brian Jenkins, senior adviser to the president of the RAND Corporation; Thomas Rid, who made a significant contribution to the study as a Transatlantic Post-Doctoral Fellow for International Relations and Security at the RAND Corporation; Lorenzo Vidino, currently a Fellow at the Swiss Federal Institute of Technology (ETH Zurich); and Jeffrey M. Bale, Director of the Monterey Terrorism Research and Education Program at the Monterey Institute of International Studies, as well as Ambassador Daniel Benjamin, Director of the John Sloan Dickey Center for International Understanding at Dartmouth College and former U.S. Coordinator for Counterterrorism, and John Horgan, Director of the Center for Terrorism & Security Studies, University of Massachusetts Lowell.

Our most important sources of information were European intelligence analysts, terrorism experts, policy practitioners, and members of civil society who shared their insights with us. Particular thanks are due to M. Gilles de Kerchove, EU Counter-Terrorism Coordinator; Peter Neumann, Director of the International Centre for the Study of Radicalisation and Political Violence at King's College London; Alan Johnson, Edge Hill University, United Kingdom; Ghaffar Hussain of the Quilliam Foundation, London; Shiraz Maher, now a Senior Research Fellow, International Centre for the Study of Radicalisation and Political Violence; Alexander Meleagrou-Hitchens, Policy Exchange, London;

Jamie Bartlett, Demos, London; Robert Lambert and Jonathan Githens-Mazer, University of Exeter, United Kingdom; Michael Whine, London; Jonathan Paris, London; Fernando Reinares, Real Instituto Elcano, Madrid; Javier Jordán, University of Granada, Spain; Oscar Jaime Jiménez, University of Navarra, Spain; Fernando Marco and José Antonio Gutiérrez, Athena Intelligence, Spain; Doron Zimmermann, Swissgrid, Switzerland; Markus Kerber, Johannes Urban, and Jürgen Merz, formerly of the Federal Ministry of Interior, Germany; Alexandra Schäfer-Borrmann, Bundeskanzleramt, Germany; Guido Steinberg, SWP, Germany; and Yassin Musharbash, Der Spiegel.

In relation to the earlier RAND research, we thank Franz-Michael Skjold Mellbin of the Danish Ministry of Foreign Affairs; Marianne van Leeuwen, Roel Willemse, and Paul Dercon of the Netherlands Ministry of the Interior; Georg Witschel, Anti-Terrorism Division of the Ministry of Foreign Affairs of Germany; Karlheinz Fiedler, Richard Rösener, and Eva Maria Sand of the Austrian Ministry of Education; Cosima Eggers, Emil Brix, and Florian Haug of the Austrian Ministry of Foreign Affairs; analysts at the Centro Nacional de Inteligencia (CNI) of Spain; Petter Nesser of the Norwegian Defense Establishment (FFI); Tore Bjørgo, Norwegian Police University College; Michael Taarnby, Danish Institute of International Studies; and Rafael Bardají of Fundación FAES, Spain.

We also benefited from participation in conferences hosted by Robert Leiken of the Nixon Center; the Center on Islam, Democracy, and the Future of the Muslim World at the Hudson Institute; the Jamestown Foundation; and the Foundation for the Defense of Democracies; as well as the annual conferences of the International Institute for Counter-Terrorism in Herzliya, Israel.

Within RAND, we thank President and Chief Executive Officer Michael Rich, Senior Fellow and former Vice President and director of Project AIR FORCE Natalie Crawford, and Senior Vice President for Research and Analysis Andrew Hoehn for their support for the initial research; Jane Ryan, Office of External Affairs; David Shlapak for his tough critique of the initial draft; and Ambassador James Dobbins, former Director, International Security and Defense Policy Center (ISP), under whose auspices this report was prepared. We are indebted to Julie DaVanzo and Clifford Grammich for developing the demographic data that laid the foundation for the analysis; Diana Dunham-Scott, who has done important work on radical groups in the United Kingdom; Lindsay Clutterbuck of RAND Europe; and Francisco Walter for his help in developing the report's bibliography. Finally, Kai-Moritz Keller, formerly a student assistant at the Brandeis University Center for German and European Studies, contributed valuable research on Islamist extremism in Germany and the German government's counterterrorism posture. Those being thanked are not responsible for the content of this book. Any errors or omissions are entirely the responsibility of the authors.

# Abbreviations

| | |
|---|---|
| AIVD | Algemene Inlichtingen- en Veiligheidsdienst (General Intelligence and Security Service, The Netherlands) |
| AQAP | Al-Qaeda in the Arabian Peninsula (Yemen) |
| AQIM | Al-Qaeda in the Islamic Maghreb (formerly GSPC) |
| BfV | Bundesamt für Verfassungsschutz (Office for the Protection of the Constitution, Germany) |
| CNCA | Centro Nacional de Coordinación Anti-Terrorista (Spain) |
| CNI | Centro Nacional de Inteligencia (Spain) |
| DCRI | Direction Centrale du Renseignement Intérieur (France) |
| DGSE | Direction Générale de la Sécurité Extérieure (France) |
| DGSI | Direction Générale de la Sécurité Intérieure (France) |
| DNAT | Division Nationale Anti-terroriste (France) |
| DST | Direction de la Surveillance du Territoire (France) |
| FFI | Forsvarets Forskningstitutt (Norwegian Defense Research Establishment) |
| GIA | Armed Islamic Group (Algeria) |
| GICM | Moroccan Islamic Combatant Group |
| GSPC | Salafist Group for Preaching and Combat (Algeria) |
| ICI | Islamic Culture Institute (Milan, Italy) |
| ICU | Islamic Courts Union (Somalia) |
| IJU | Islamic Jihad Union (Central Asia, Pakistan, and Germany) |
| IMU | Islamic Movement of Uzbekistan |
| ISIS | Islamic State of Iraq and al-Sham (Iraq and Syria) |
| MCB | Muslim Council of Britain |
| MI-5 | Security Service [Internal] (United Kingdom) |

| | |
|---|---|
| RG | Direction Centrale des Renseignements Généraux (France) |
| RICU | Research, Information, and Communications Unit (United Kingdom) |
| SITCEN | Situation Centre (EU) |

# 1

# Introduction

In recent years, Europe has become a main theater of Islamist terrorism, with major terrorist attacks in Madrid and London and dozens of foiled plots throughout the Continent. The 9/11 Commission listed European cities with Muslim communities (along with the Afghan-Pakistani border, the Horn of Africa, and Southeast Asia) among the places where terrorists seek sanctuary and operating bases. The U.S. perception of the problem of Islamist extremism in Europe is primarily one of radicalization as a stage in the progression toward terrorism. While also concerned about the radicalization and recruitment of European Muslims into terrorist groups, Europeans see radicalization in the context of the broader social problem of integration of the Continent's Muslim communities. In Paris, Berlin, London, and Madrid, the integration problem is seen, first and foremost, in terms of inadequate economic, social, and political participation; high unemployment rates; criminality; and other social issues.

Europe is home to at least 15 million Muslims (not counting Turkey's 68 million). Immigration and above-average birthrates make immigrants of Middle Eastern origin one of the fastest-growing demographic groups in European societies. But most of these Muslims lag behind the average in education, income, economic opportunities, and political participation. Integrating these communities, with their very different cultural backgrounds, is one of Europe's most challenging social problems.

Conservatives in many European countries are disturbed by the resistance of Muslim immigrants or their descendants to integration and express fears about the development of parallel societies. The left is more willing to advocate multicultural approaches. Still, many draw a causal link between inadequate integration and marginalization of Muslims in Europe and the upsurge in Islamist terrorism after 9/11. While the subject is highly contentious, both sides agree that the lack of integration is at the heart of the problem of Islamic radicalization. But is such a generalization correct?

The research on Islamist extremism in Europe supports the view that the integration of Muslim populations into European societies and the radicalization of sectors of those populations are distinct phenomena, although there may be an indirect relationship, to the extent that extremists are embedded in communities where they find some degree of support, tolerance, or indifference. The broad literature that examines the various social, economic, and political root causes of terrorism[1] – to include, for example, the political rights available to immigrants and their socioeconomic status – largely concludes that while the presence or absence of these types of variables helps shape the conditions under which radicalization is more or less likely, structural variables rarely bear out as proximate causes of terrorism.[2]

The ringleaders of the Madrid train bombings, three of the four 7/7 London bombers, Theo Van Gogh's assassin Muhammad Bouyeri, and others involved in Islamist terrorist plots in Europe appeared on the surface to be well integrated. These individuals spoke their new home countries' languages – Spanish, English, or Dutch; they were born and educated in European countries or, as in the case of the Madrid bombers, long-time residents; and some of them were economically successful and had attained middle-class status. But they still turned to violence against the societies of which they were part. A 2010 report published by the Center for Studies in Islamism and Radicalization at Aarhus University, *House of War: Islamic Radicalization in Denmark*, based on interview with 1,113 young Muslims residing in Denmark showed that 5.6 percent were radicalized and 17.8 percent sympathized with radical Islamism but did not support it directly. According to the study, the most radicalized are well educated, speak Danish well, watch Danish television, work and earn money.[3] More recently, Johannes Kandel, an expert on radical Islamism

[1] For an extensive review of the literature on the root causes of terrorism, see Darcy Noricks, "The Root Causes of Terrorism," in Paul K. Davis and R. Kim Cragin, eds., *Social Science for Counterterrorism: What Do We Know That Should Affect Analysis?* Santa Monica, CA: RAND Corporation, 2009.

[2] The exception to this general rule is government repression of a politically active group, which has regularly been found to correlate with the adoption of violent tactics by the persecuted group. (See, e.g., Callaway and Harrelson-Stephens (2006); Crenshaw (1994, 2001); Della Porta (1985); Gurr (1970); and Weinberg (1991).

[3] Marco Goli and Shahamak Rezaei, *House of War: Islamic Radicalisation in Denmark*, Center for Forskning i Islamisme og Radikaliseringsprocesser), Aarhus University, 2010.

with the Friedrich Ebert Stiftung, warned that in his estimation, almost a third of Muslim youths in Germany hold radical Islamist views.[4]

The psychology of relative deprivation may have some explanatory value. A UK study found that although those involved in terrorism are more likely to be well educated, they are almost all employed in unskilled or low-skill jobs.[5] This corresponds to the view of some scholars that the most aggrieved, and therefore the most likely to be recruited into radical groups, are not those at the lowest end of the socioeconomic scale, but those in the middle, whose expectations exceed their opportunities.[6] Of course, there are cases that do not fit the pattern, for instance, the July 2007 UK "doctors' plot," which resulted in the arrest four medical doctors (one of whom subsequently died from injuries suffered in a terrorist attempt) for their role in failed car bomb attempts in London and Glasgow. All of the suspects had ties to Britain's National Health Service and worked in two hospitals in England and Scotland.[7]

Clearly, the intricate relationship between integration and radicalization in Europe's Muslim communities needs to be analyzed more rigorously. But first, what do we mean by radicalization and its ideological manifestation among Muslims, radical Islamism? Most dictionaries define *radicalization* as the process through which individuals or groups adopt extreme ideas. Radical or extreme variations are inherent in any society and what is considered radical depends on social and historical context. In some societies, there is broad acceptance of behavior that in the West is considered extreme, such as draconian punishments for deviations from religious orthodoxy, adultery, or homosexuality, whereas what is regarded in the West as normative, for instance, gender equality and the liberalization of sexual norms, is considered socially subversive.

Radicalization, therefore, is very much context dependent. Since the context of this study is Europe, *radicalization* is defined as "the rejection of the key dimensions of modern democratic culture that are at the center of the European value system." The values include support for democracy and internationally recognized human rights, gender equality and freedom

[4] Johannes Kandel, *Islamismus in Deutschland*, Zwischen Panik und Naivitaet, Herder 2011.

[5] "MI5 report challenges views on terrorism in Britain," *The Guardian*, August 21 2008, http://www.guardian.co.uk/uk/2008/aug/20/uksecurity.terrorism1/print.

[6] Gurr (1970).

[7] Raffaello Pantucci, "Doctor's Plot" Trial Examines Unexpected Source for UK Terrorist Attacks," Jamestown Foundation, *Terrorism Focus*, Vol. 5 Issue 36, October 22, 2008, at http://www.jamestown.org/single/?no_cache=1&tx_ttnews%5Btt_news%5D=5226.

of worship, respect for diversity, acceptance of nonsectarian sources of law, and opposition to violence as a means to attain political ends. A radical organization may not be a violent one, although the attitudes of even ostensibly nonviolent organizations toward violence are often ambiguous and these groups can function as "conveyors belts" to violent extremism.

The ambiguous role of integration in the radicalization process can be better understood if the phenomenon of Islamist extremism in Europe is disaggregated into three separate, but related components:

- The problem of integration of members of European Muslim communities into the national societies;
- The radicalization of sectors of these communities; and
- The recruitment of radicalized individuals into extremist and terrorist groups.

Violent extremists, it should be noted, are extreme exceptions among Europe's Muslims. The combination of a lack of integration and the absence of radicalization seems to be the norm for the majority of Muslims in Europe. Large numbers, if not the majority of Muslims in Europe, are neither well integrated nor radicalized. For the minority that becomes radicalized, the trajectories toward extremism and violence begin with a condition of disaffection or alienation. These feelings may lead an individual to seek out and join radical groups to find companionship, establish an identity, or take action to address perceived grievances.[8]

The circumstances that generated these feelings of disaffection provide a cognitive opening into which radical ideas are more readily introduced.[9] Scholars such as Olivier Roy (2004) argue that some second-generation Muslims find it difficult to live within either the traditional culture of their parents or the modern Western culture of the countries where they reside. Extremist Salafi ideologies offer a new identity that allows the individual to identify with an imagined worldwide Muslim community.

[8] See March Sageman, *Understanding Terror Networks*. Philadelphia: University of Pennsylvania Press, 2004; Thomas Hegghammer, "Terrorist Recruitment and Radicalization in Saudi Arabia," *Middle East Policy*, Vol. 13, No. 4, 2006, pp. 39–60; Aidan Kirby, "The London Bombers as 'Self-Starters': A Case Study in Indigenous Radicalization and the Emergence of Autonomous Cliques," *Studies in Conflict & Terrorism*, Vol. 30, No. 5, 2007, pp. 415–428; and Todd Helmus, "Why and How Some People Become Terrorists," in Paul K. Davis and R. Kim Cragin, eds., *Social Science of Terrorism and Counterterrorism: What Do We Know That Should Affect Analysis?* Santa Monica, CA: RAND Corporation, 2009.

[9] Quintan Wiktorowicz, *Joining the Cause: Al-Muhajiroun and Radical Islam*, Rhodes College, Department of International Studies, 2004, p. 7, at http://www.cis.yale.edu/polisci/info/conferences/Islamic%20Radicalism/papers/wiktorowiczpaper.pdf.

Extremist groups and ideologies contribute to the radicalization of its members by first creating what Juergensmeyer (2003) calls a "culture of violence." In this context, the use of violence by members is not only permitted but also encouraged, ostensibly in defense of the community. Threats to the community are often interpreted in a very expansive way, weaving international events into the narrative of the community's persecution. Radical groups, for example, create a culture of violence through regular viewing of carnage tapes from Chechnya, Ambon, and Iraq, as well as discussions about the approved parameters of violent jihad in the context of broader religious discussions and of appropriate rationales, targets, and means. When these discussion groups are supplemented with pseudo-military or actual military training, locally or abroad, it reinforces the culture of violence and complements the theory with the development of practical skills.[10]

For those in the technologically adept generation born in the 1980s and 1990s, the propensity to radicalization is increased by the easy access to radical material through the digital media. The role of the Internet in the radicalization process is at the core of the argument that "self-radicalization" is taking place in the sheltered confines of private homes, and that jihad has become "leaderless," driven by users who have access to bomb-building manuals and poison handbooks, wirelessly accessed while hiding in the suburbs of European cities.[11] But such a view of the Internet is likely to be misleading. Many individuals today use the web to socialize and to make and maintain contact – a novelty that applies to an entire generation of "digital natives."[12]

Such activity is all about turning online contact into off-line action, dissolving the dividing line between online and off-line. For younger generations, the web is accessed more and more through smartphones first and computers only second. The cell phone is not used in social isolation, but to break out of social isolation. Smartphones and social networking services are the fastest-growing segments of the new media industry today, not only in Europe, but also throughout the world. The view that lone-wolf militants self-radicalize secretly and in isolation through the Internet needs to

[10] Alan Travis, "The making of an extremist," *The Guardian*, August 20, 2008, at http://www.guardian.co.uk/uk/2008/aug/20/uksecurity.terrorism.

[11] See, for instance, Marc Sageman, *Leaderless Jihad: Terror Networks in the Twenty-First Century*. Philadelphia: University of Pennsylvania Press, 2008.

[12] John Palfrey and Urs Gasser, *Born Digital: Understanding the First Generation of Digital Natives*. New York: Basic Books, 2008; Marc Prensky, "Listen to the Natives," *Educational Leadership*, Vol. 63, No. 4, 2005.

be updated to take account of the importance of networks, both digital and off-line.

One of the objectives of this book is to identify patterns of Islamist radicalization and terrorism in Europe. A generational distinction is at the center of our argument. First-generation Muslim immigrants to Europe arrived either for political or more frequently economic reasons. The political activists among them, and the few who were leaning toward extremist views by and large had a local (e.g., Middle Eastern) agenda, not a global one, shaped by their experiences in their countries of origin.

Europe's second- and third-generation Muslims do not possess the same ties to their ancestral countries of origin, neither positive in the form of social contacts with families and friends, nor negative in the form of political grievances. Their home countries are now France, Germany, the United Kingdom, or the Netherlands. For the small number with a political impetus, the immediate source of grievance, logically, is not the government of their country of ancestry, but Europe, or more broadly "the West." Europe, the Continent that was an economic or political refuge for their parents, has become for them a source of grievance and marginalization or a party to the perceived global conflict between the secular West and Islam. For a very small group among these youths, in a biographical and personal way, the "far enemy" has become the "near enemy."[13]

First-generation extremists shared a background in Middle Eastern political movements that turned violent. Some took part in veritable insurgencies against their own ruling regimes. These movements touted a cause, tapped into widespread grievances, and sometimes succeeded in mustering significant popular support. Europe's second- and third-generation Islamist extremists are markedly different: they do not share their ideological predecessors' experience of life under authoritarian Muslim regimes; the number of fellow Muslims who share a strong grievance and a willingness to act is comparatively small; and their goals are not related to concrete national or local concerns. The new Islamist terrorists do not share a background in local political movements – they turn first global and then violent.

The surprisingly large number of converts who get involved with Islamic extremism in various European countries illustrates this trend.

[13] An analysis of radical Islamic francophone websites, for example, reflects a younger generation in a constant search for identity; social issues are dominant, unlike the dominance of politics found in radical Arab websites. Deborah Touboul, "Francophone Internet Forums Shed Light on Concerns and Issues of Islamists in Europe," Global Research in International Affairs (GLORIA) Center, Vol. 3 No. 5 (September 2005) at http://www.e-prism.org/images/PRISM_no_6_vol_3_-_Islamic_sites_in_French.pdf.

Ethnic German, French, or British citizens turn to Islam for various reasons, but those reasons do not include failed integration into an alien recipient society. The attraction of Islam might be that the new faith, strictly interpreted, provides a sense of order, belonging, spirituality, and duty that is largely absent from liberal and largely secular European societies. This book will provide some detail on European converts with a history of radicalization.

Extremists may build on an underlying alienation and grievances, but the real driver of Islamist radicalization, recruitment, and ultimately violence lies elsewhere. It lies, we argue, not in a cause with a broad political potential, but in groups and ideologies that tilt to the extreme – extreme taken literally, as deviating from the mainstream and therefore bound to remain a fringe movement within the extremists' communities. Latter-day Eurojihad is therefore self-limiting, but also stable and probably more difficult to eradicate than the violence rooted in Middle East politics that affected Europe in the 1990s.

## 2

# Europe's Muslim Populations

The nature of the radical Islamist presence in every European state is specific to the particular demographics of each country. There are also significant variations in the composition of European Muslim communities.[1] "Muslim," in Europe, denotes ethnicity as well as religion. As Jytte Klausen notes, individuals balance this in different ways. For some, faith is the key source of identity. For others, faith takes a backseat to origin.[2]

Because the availability of data on religious identification varies by country, determining the total number, much less the composition, of Muslim communities in Europe is difficult. Nevertheless, a conservative estimate is that at least 17 million Muslims live in the countries that constitute the European Union, with some sources estimating higher numbers still.[3] Regardless of the source one uses to estimate the number of Muslims in Europe, there is a broad consensus on the nations where these populations are most concentrated. These nations include France, Germany, the United Kingdom, the Netherlands, Belgium, Italy, and Spain. The Muslim population in each of these nations varies in its composition. Generally, the ethnic composition of these populations

[1] Julie DaVanzo and Clifford Grammich of the RAND CORPORATION contributed to the demographic analysis of European Muslim population in this chapter.

[2] Jytte Klausen, "Counterterrorism and the Integration of Islam in Europe," Foreign Policy Research Institute, *Watch on the West*, Vol. 7, No. 1, July 2006.

[3] "Europe's Muslim Population," 2008, at http://www.islamicpopulation.com/Europe/europe_islam.html. The Pew Research Center estimates the European Union's Muslim population at 18,267,000 in 2010. The Pew Forum on Religion & Public Life, "The Future of the Global Muslim Population," January 27, 2011, at http://www.pewforum.org/future-of-the-global-muslim-population-regional-europe.aspx#1.

reflects historical ties between their countries of residence and their home countries or their geographic proximity, as in the case of Spain and Morocco.

## FRANCE

France is considered to have the largest Muslim population in Europe – 4 to 6 million persons, which corresponds to approximately 6 to 10 percent of the French population.[4] This population is composed mostly of persons of North African descent. France also has a growing population of Muslims from sub-Saharan Africa, as well as nearly 250,000 Turkish nationals.[5] The percentage is likely to grow as a result of future immigration – legal or not – and a higher birthrate among Muslims. This figure reflects the number of persons in France with a likely Muslim background and not necessarily of persons who regard themselves as Muslim. According to a 2005 survey conducted by the Institut National d'Etudes Démographiques (INED) and Institut National de la Statistique et des Études Économiques (INSEE), 5 percent of people in France age 18–79 defined themselves as Muslim.[6]

When Algeria achieved independence from France in 1962, about half a million Muslims lived in the metropolitan territory of France.[7] Independence left the many Algerians who had cooperated with the French with well-justified fears for their safety. France admitted its former loyalists, beginning a period of large-scale migration driven by the boom in the automobile industry and other labor-intensive sectors of the French economy. In 1974, an attempt to limit immigration from Algeria and other parts of previously French-ruled North Africa motivated Muslims already in France to bring their families before the window for immigration closed.

[4] Estimates by RAND demographers. The Pew Research Center estimates the French Muslim population in 2010 at 4.7 million. Pew Forum on Religion & Public Life, "The Future of the Global Muslim Population," January 27, 2011, at http://www.pewforum.org/future-of-the-global-muslim-population-regional-europe.aspx#1.

[5] In the 2009 census of France, persons of foreign nationality included, from predominantly Muslim countries, 468,000 Algerians, 440,000 Moroccans, 144,000 Tunisians and 222,000 Turks. Institut National de la Statistique et des Études Économiques (INSEE), *Recensement de la population, Répartition des étrangers par nationalité*, at http://www.insee.fr/fr/themes/tableau.asp?reg_id=0&ref_id=etrangersnat.

[6] Arnaud Régnier-Loilier and France Prioux, "Does Religious Practice Influence Family Behaviours?" *Population & Societies*, Vol. 447, July-August 2008, at http://www.ined.fr/fichier/t_publication/1366/publi_pdf2_pesa447.pdf.

[7] Not including France's overseas departments and territories.

Estimates indicate that immigration, together with high birthrates, doubled the Muslim population to 1 million by 1973, doubled it again by 1981, and then doubled it again to 4 million in 1995.[8]

The 2005 riots in France have re-opened the debate on the current size of the Muslim population, for which there still are no official statistics. The French secularist tradition limits the government's capacity to collect census data on religious practices and dictates that no religious data be collected in the National Census, which is carried out every 10 years. Despite a flurry of statistical studies, private polling companies have also failed to reach convincing results, mainly because of the lack of scientific and officially recognized standards for measuring an individual's religious identification.

Until recently, nonscientific and often highly politicized estimates of the Muslim population prevailed. A variety of semiofficial figures have been floated publicly in the decade after 2000, most of them in the range of 5 to 8 million. The first comprehensive statistical estimate of the Muslim population was conducted in 2001 and 2002 by the French government's INED on a sample of 380,000 adults, and on the basis of the data collected during the 1999 census about "family history," the closest the French government had come to gathering data on religion in more than a century.[9] Based on the country of origin of both first- and second-generation immigrants, demographer Michèle Tribalat estimated the Muslim population in France at between 3.65 and 4 million in 1999,[10] including 1.7 million first-generation, 1.7 million second-generation, and 300,000 third-generation descendants of immigrants from countries where Islam is the majority religion.[11]

Estimates for 2008 indicate that about 1.8 million people living in France were descendants of immigrants from Maghreb states, that is, former French colonies in North Africa. The descendants of immigrants are a young population. Their average age is about 31.9 years, significantly lower than that of the population as a whole (40.5 years).[12] Of the population older than age 15, only 1.7 percent of Turkish nationals,

[8] Estimate by RAND demographers.

[9] INSEE-INED, *Etude de l'Histoire Familiale*, 1999.

[10] A 10 percent margin of error was calculated to take into account various unknown quantities, such as converts.

[11] Michèle Tribalat, "Le nombre de musulmans en France: Qu'en sait-on?," *Cités*, July 2003.

[12] Ministère de l'intérieur, *Immigrés et descendants d'immigrés en France*, Insee Références – Édition 2012, at http://www.interieur.gouv.fr/Actualites/L-actu-du-Ministere/Immigres-et-descendants-d-immigres-en-France.

4.2 percent of Moroccans, 4.3 percent of Algerians, and 5.0 percent of Tunisian were age 60 or older (compared to 21 percent for all persons). The Turkish population is younger than the others; 9.6 percent of persons of Turkish nationality, 7.7 percent of Moroccans, 5.7 percent of Algerians and 5.2 percent of Tunisians are between ages 15 and 25.[13]

Muslims in France are largely concentrated in a few quarters of large cities such as Paris and Marseilles and even more in the *banlieues or cités*,[14] the close-in suburbs where they occupy huge tracts of high-rise apartment houses and which were the epicenter of the rioting in November 2005. Almost 8 percent of the population in the department of Seine-Saint-Denis, for example, is composed of persons of Algerian, Moroccan, Tunisian, or Turkish nationality. Within Seine-Saint-Denis, the proportion of the population of these predominantly Muslim nationalities is twice as high (15.67 percent) in the commune of Clichy-sous-Bois, where the riots began, than it is in either Seine-Saint-Denis as a whole or metropolitan France.[15]

Algerian, Moroccan, Tunisian, and Turkish populations are predominantly male and younger than the general population. According to 2008 statistics, 54.45 percent of persons of these populations are male, with males outnumbering females in each age group.[16] Unemployment disproportionally affects immigrants from predominantly Muslim countries, particularly those between ages 15 and 29. Algerian immigrants and youth of Algerian origin younger than age 30 who held a high school diploma had an unemployment rate of 32 percent, in contrast to a rate of 15 percent for French youths in the same age category.[17] Members of these communities are also concentrated in a few occupational categories and, moreover, are less likely to hold managerial or professional

[13] INSEE, *Population immigrée, population étrangère en 2008, Tableau CD-A2, Immigrés actifs, dont chômeurs, selon le sexe, l'âge quinquennal et le pays de naissance détaillé* at http://www.insee.fr/fr/themes/detail.asp?reg_id=0&ref_id=pop-immigree-pop-etrangere-2008.

[14] A term that in this context means low-income suburban areas with high concentrations of immigrants or descendants of immigrants.

[15] INSEE, *Étrangers en 2009: comparaisons départementales*, at http://www.insee.fr/fr/themes/tableau.asp?reg_id=99&ref_id=t_0405D;. *EPCI de la CA de Clichy sous Bois – Montfermeil – 249300070*, at http://www.insee.fr/fr/bases-de-donnees/esl/comparateur.asp?codgeo=epci-249300070.

[16] INSEE, *Population immigrée, population étrangère en 2008, Tableau CD-MF3, Étrangers selon le sexe, la catégorie de population et la nationalité détaillée at* http://www.insee.fr/fr/themes/detail.asp?reg_id=0&ref_id=pop-immigree-pop-etrangere-2008.

[17] Jonathan Laurence and Justin Vaisse, *Integrating Islam: Political and Religious Challenges in Contemporary France*. Washington, DC: Brookings Institution Press, 2006, p. 34 at http://www.brookings.edu/press/books/chapter_1/integratingislam.pdf.

positions. Among all French workers in 1999, 34 percent held managerial or professional positions, but only 14 percent of Algerian, 12 percent of Tunisian, 10 percent of Moroccan, and 5 percent of Turkish workers did so.[18]

## GERMANY

Germany has the second-largest Muslim population in Europe, with estimates ranging up to 5.2 percent of the total German population of 82.4 million, or between 3.8 and 4.3 million persons.[19] Of the more than 7 million permanent residents of Germany who do not hold German citizenship, by far the largest group, between 2.5 and 2.6 million Muslims, are of Turkish origin, including some 500,000 Turkish Kurds.[20] Beginning with the post-war economic boom of the 1950s, Germany began attracting "guest workers." Many of those from the former Yugoslavia and nearly all from Turkey were Muslim. Guest workers, originally, also came in large numbers from non-Muslim countries that today are part of the European Union, such as Spain, Italy, Greece, and Portugal.

In a 2008 study that used official micro census data, Turks were identified as the least integrated group among of the approximately 15 million people in Germany with "immigration backgrounds": only 5 percent marry Germans; only 14 percent have college education; and their unemployment rate is far higher than the national average, between 23 and 28 percent. The micro census data, the most comprehensive available, bear out that Turks who hold German citizenship are indeed better integrated than those who do not.[21]

Germany's Turks are extraordinarily diverse and include ethnic Turks and Kurds as well as smaller ethnic subgroups. The largest number, 63 percent of the Muslim population, are of Turkish descent. Around

[18] Figures from 1999 census. The subsequent census does not appear to include these data. INSEE, *Recensement de la population 1999 Exploitation complémentaire*, Tables NAT2 and NAT3, at http://www.recensement.insee.fr/EN/ST_ANA/F2/NATALLNAT3ANAT3A4F2EN.html.

[19] Sonja Haug, Stephanie Müssig, Anja Stichs, Muslimisches Leben in Deutschland – im Auftrag der Deutschen Islam Konferenz, Forschungsbericht 6, Bundesamt für Migration und Flüchtlinge (2010), at http://www.bmi.bund.de/cae/servlet/contentblob/566008/publicationFile/31710/vollversion_studie_muslim_leben_deutschland.pdf.

[20] Federal Republic of Germany, Federal Statistical Office, 2005.

[21] The study's dataset includes 800,000 individuals. Berlin-Instutit für Bevölkerung und Entwicklung, "Ungenutzte Potenziale," January 2009, at http://www.berlin-institut.org/publikationen/studien/ungenutzte-potenziale.html.

14 percent have their family roots in Bosnia, Bulgaria, or Albania; another 8 percent come from the Middle East and 7 percent are from North Africa, with Moroccans predominating. The remainder originated in Central Asia, Iran, South Asia, Southeast Asia, and Africa. Almost two-thirds of the group are Sunni. Alevis make up 13 percent, and Shi'ites are in third place with 7 percent.[22]

Although a large majority of Turks in Germany have been living there for eight years or longer, as of 2008 more than two-thirds were still Turkish citizens and therefore constituted a significant political constituency from the standpoint of Turkish domestic politics. The Turkish government is heavily involved in regulating religious affairs among German Turks. The Diyanet İşleri Başkanliği (Directorate of Religious Affairs), an office that reports to the prime minister of Turkey, and has a budget larger than most ministries, administers hundreds of Turkish mosques in Germany, including the training of imams. Imams are sent from Turkey to Germany and work in assigned mosques affiliated with the Turkish-Islamic Union for Religious Affairs (DITIB) – an ostensibly independent association of nearly nine hundred Turkish mosques, but in fact an arm of the Diyanet in Germany – for a period of four years under the supervision of the Attachés for Religious Affairs at Turkish consulates in Germany. In 2006, some 530 imams were employed in Germany, in addition to 130 imams sent for one-year tours jointly funded by the local mosque and the Diyanet. Until recently, the sermons for the imams were drafted by the Diyanet staff in Ankara and distributed in and outside of Turkey. In addition, the Diyanet provides theological training in Turkey to students from Germany with a Turkish background.[23]

Violent Islamist extremism in Germany is, in contrast to demographics, largely concentrated among non-Turkish Muslims in Germany, although investigations since 2007 have shown a growing number of German converts and ethnic Turks recruited into terrorist networks. A survey of 1,011 people of Turkish heritage between ages 15 and 29 conducted in 2012 indicated a trend toward greater religiosity, but also greater willingness to integrate into German society. The proportion of those who identified themselves as strictly religious increased from 33 percent in 2009 to 37 percent in 2012. While 63 percent identify as Turks even if they live in Germany and 62 percent prefer to be exclusively with Turks, 78 percent

[22] Haug, Müssig, and Stichs, Muslimisches Leben in Deutschland.

[23] Kerstin Rosenow-Williams, *Organizing Muslims and Integrating Islam in Germany: New Developments for the 21st Century*. Leiden: Brill, 2012, p. 194.

indicated that they wanted to integrate into German society absolutely and without reservations and 95 percent that they wanted children with Turkish backgrounds to go to day care facilities and learn German prior to entering school. At the same time, 95 percent agreed that it was important to preserve Turkish culture in Germany.[24]

A 2011 study of Muslim youth attitudes in Germany found a relationship between naturalization and identity, with only 20 percent of young people who obtained German citizenship expressing mixed loyalties toward their country of origin, compared to 50 percent of those who did not hold citizenship. This finding is open to different conclusions. For example, it is conceivable that those who felt more drawn to their German identity were more likely to seek German citizenship. However, the authors interpreted it conversely and argued that naturalization had a positive effect on loyalty.[25]

In 2007, the Ministry of the Interior published a study of Germany's general Muslim population. The report found that a minority, between 8 and 12 percent, has attitudes that are "clearly distant to democracy." For half of that group, 6 percent, the skepticism toward democracy was allegedly combined with a "fundamentalist-religious orientation." The religious and political attitudes of 12 percent of the total Muslim population in Germany were classified as "Islamic-authoritarian." These findings, however, need to be put into context. The factors that determine these attitudes vary significantly. Neither religious orientations nor social exclusion (i.e., lack of integration) can explain radicalization, the ministry cautioned. Conversely, among the non-Muslim German youth, 14 percent had xenophobic attitudes and German adolescents in comparable socioeconomic conditions were equally prone to authoritarian and "democracy-resistant" attitudes. "This is not a phenomenon that is specific to Muslims," the authors wrote.[26]

Empirical research brought to light that the 12 percent of potentially radicalized Muslims in Germany fall into three quite different subsets: the first group is composed of highly educated and generally integrated

[24] INFO GmbH and Liljeberg Research International, Ltd., "Deutsch – Türkische Lebens – und Wertewelten 2012," at http://liebbu.files.wordpress.com/2012/08/wertewelten-2012-pressemitteilung.pdf.

[25] W. Frindte, K. Boehnke, H. Kreikenborn, W. Wagner, "Lebenswelten Junger Muslime in Deutschland," Bundesministerium des Innern, 2012.

[26] Katrin Brettfeld and Peter Wetzels, *Muslime in Deutschland: Integration, Integrationsbarrieren, Religion sowie Einstellungen zu Demokratie, Rechtsstaat und politisch-religiös motivierter Gewalt*. Berlin: Bundesministerium des Innern, 2007, p. 495.

Muslims with potentially high participation who yet perceive the Muslim community as victimized, oppressed, and under attack, internationally as well as domestically (although they personally might not have had that experience). A second group of less educated Muslims has had personal negative experiences in Germany and show generally low levels of social and economic participation. A third group are the "traditionalists" who deliberately do not want to integrate and instead retreat into isolated communities. The ministry identified the urgent need for more empirical research into the causes of Islamic radicalization in Germany.

German authorities have expressed concerns about the more random forms of radicalization. They have been particularly alarmed by plots that involved individuals who did not fit the usual patterns that their security apparatus was better geared to detect: those who had not gone abroad for training or indoctrination and did not belong to a known network of cells.[27] The large Turkish community shows signs of incipient radicalization (see Chapter 5). Turkish Kurds have joined jihadist groups in greater numbers in recent years. The same holds true for members of the sizeable Palestinian community, which might have been influenced by the radicalization of the Palestinian diaspora in the Middle East.[28]

## GREAT BRITAIN

From the legacy of empire through to the twenty-first century, the United Kingdom has had a rich and diverse Muslim community, now the third largest in Europe: newly arrived immigrants and second- or third-generation descendants of immigrants, mostly South Asians and East Africans, asylum seekers and thriving middle-class entrepreneurs. In recent decades, Britain's Muslims have become very much a part of British society. The interwoven strands of the Muslim South Asian population of Britain particularly have left a greater permanent impact on Britain's society and culture than any other ethnicity.

Great Britain's Muslim communities consist of three main groups: those born in the UK as second- or third-generation Muslims (the vast majority of whom originated in South Asia, in particular Pakistan and

[27] "Gotteskrieger" als Familienersatz," n-tv, September 8, 2011, at http://www.n-tv.de/politik/119/Gotteskrieger-als-Familienersatz-article4245691.html.

[28] Guido Steinberg, "The Threat of Jihadist Terrorism in Germany," Real Instituto Elcano, June 11, 2008, at http://www.realinstitutoelcano.org/wps/portal/rielcano_eng/Content?WCM_GLOBAL_CONTEXT=/elcano/elcano_in/zonas_in/international+terrorism/ari142-2008.

Bangladesh, as well as India), those recently arrived as new immigrants or asylum seekers (generally from North Africa and other parts of the Muslim world not traditionally resident in the UK), and converts to Islam. The United Kingdom includes religion in its census for England and Wales. The 2011 census enumeration found 2.7 million Muslims or 4.8 percent of the resident population of 56.1 million.[29] This represented a 74 percent increase over the 2001 census figure of 1.55 million or 2.97 percent of the population of 52.04 million. The Muslim population in Britain grew at more than six times the rate of the overall population.[30] The increase was attributed to immigration, a higher birthrate, and conversion to Islam.[31]

The British Muslim population was predominantly of South Asian origin. As of 2011, it included 1,125,000 of Pakistani, and 447,000 of Bangladeshi origin.[32] The largest Muslims populations were in London and Birmingham, with Birmingham having more than 177,000 Muslims (19.5 percent of a total estimated population of 908,000 in 2011).[33] Outside of London and Birmingham, the largest Muslim communities are in the North-West around Leeds-Bradford, and in the Yorkshire and Humber region.[34] Compared to other religious groups in the UK, Muslims rank as the second-largest religious population and, according to some accounts, Muslims now outnumber Anglicans as active adherents.

[29] Office for National Statistics, Census 2011, "Religion in England and Wales 2011," at http://www.ons.gov.uk/ons/rel/census/2011-census/key-statistics-for-local-authorities-in-england-and-wales/rpt-religion.html.

[30] Office for National Statistics, "Census 2001 Key Statistics, Local Authorities in England and Wales Part 1," Table KS07, Religion, at http://www.ons.gov.uk/ons/rel/census/census-2001-key-statistics/local-authorities-in-england-and-wales/index.html.

[31] "Muslim Population 'Rising 10 Times Faster Than Rest of Society," *Times*, January 30, 2009, at http://www.timesonline.co.uk/tol/news/uk/article5621482.ece.

[32] United Kingdom, Office for National Statistics, QS201EW Ethnic group, 2011, at http://www.ons.gov.uk/ons/data/web/explorer/dataset-finder?p_auth=u2nxi7lQ&p_p_id=FOLeftPanel_WAR_FOLeftPanelportlet&p_p_lifecycle=1&p_p_state=normal&p_p_mode=view&p_p_col_id=column-2&p_p_col_count=1&_FOLeftPanel_WAR_FOLeftPanelportlet_context=Census&_FOLeftPanel_WAR_FOLeftPanelportlet_collectionId=QS201EW&_FOLeftPanel_WAR_FOLeftPanelportlet_geoTypeId=2011WARDH&_FOLeftPanel_WAR_FOLeftPanelportlet_javax.portlet.action=ipcDatasetDetail.

[33] BRAP, "Census 2011: Religion and Ethnicity Data Overview" at http://www.brap.org.uk/component/docman/doc_download/96-brapcensus2011?Itemid=.

[34] United Kingdom, Office for National Statistics, "Religion in England and Wales 2011," at http://www.ons.gov.uk/ons/rel/census/2011-census/key-statistics-for-local-authorities-in-england-and-wales/rpt-religion.html.

## THE NETHERLANDS

Almost 1 million Muslims live in the Netherlands, comprising nearly 6 percent of the population.[35] Of these, more than two-thirds are from Turkey (389,000) and Morocco (356,000). The next largest Muslim communities by origin are from Suriname, a former Dutch colony, and more recent immigrants from Afghanistan, Iraq, and Somalia, many of them asylum seekers.[36] The Muslim population is growing and is concentrated in the four largest urban centers of Amsterdam, Rotterdam, The Hague, and Utretch.[37] An estimated two-thirds of Turkish and Moroccan immigrants and the large majority of second-generation residents of Turkish and Moroccan origin – 94 and 93 percent respectively –hold Dutch and often dual citizenship.[38] Immigrants in general (not just those who are Muslim – about half of the immigrants to the Netherlands are non-Muslim) tend to be clustered in ethnic neighborhoods in urban areas. They form nearly half of the population of Rotterdam, which along with Amsterdam is expected to have a nonnative Dutch majority within a few years. Sixty-five percent of schoolchildren at the secondary level in both cities are from immigrant families.[39]

[35] The Pew Research Center's Forum on Religion & Public Life estimated the Muslim population in 2009 at 946,000. Pew Research Center's Forum on Religion & Public Life, "Mapping the Global Muslim Population," October 2009, p. 22, at http://www.pewforum.org/2009/10/07/mapping-the-global-muslim-population. A Netherlands Central Bureau of Statistics study of religion in the Netherlands estimated that there were 825,000 Muslims in 2007/2008. Centraal Bureau voor de Statistiek, *Religie aan het begin van de 21ste eeuw*, Den Haag/Heerlen, 2009, p. 35, at http://www.cbs.nl/NR/rdonlyres/953535E3-9D25-4C28-A70D-7A4AEEA76E27/0/2008e16pub.pdf.

[36] According to Central Bureau of Statistics data, in 2012 there were 168,214 first-generation and 194,740 second-generation Dutch residents of Moroccan background and 197,107 first-generation and 195,816 second-generation residents of Turkish background. Centraal Bureau voor de Statistiek, StatLine, "Population; key figures," April 5, 2013 at http://statline.cbs.nl/StatWeb/publication/?DM=SLEN&PA=37296eng&D1=0-51,56-68&D2=0,10,20,30,40,50,%28l-1%29-l&LA=EN&VW=T.

[37] Euro-Islam.Info, "Islam in the Netherlands," at http://www.euro-islam.info/country-profiles/the-netherlands/.

[38] Maurice Crul and Liesbeth Heering, editors, *The Position of the Turkish and Moroccan Second Generation in Amsterdam and Rotterdam: The TIES study in the Netherlands*, Amsterdam University Press, 2008, pp. 35, 45. Dutch citizenship is acquired through birth to a Dutch parent, naturalization, or for children of immigrants born in the Netherlands, the "option" procedure, a less demanding naturalization process.

[39] Christopher Caldwell, "The Dutch Rethink Multiculturalism," *The Weekly Standard*, December 27, 2004, and expatica.com, "Netherlands Islamic Community to Hit 1 Million in 2006," September 20, 2004, at http://www.religionnewsblog.com/8727-.html.

## SPAIN

Like France and Germany, Spain does not include religion in its census, but rough estimates can be made on the basis of national origin data. According to an immigration survey, 606,105 immigrants came from the Maghreb countries and 161,484 from sub-Saharan Africa in 2007.[40] Immigration statistics for the 2000–2009 period reported 698,000 Moroccans, as well as large contingents from other Muslim majority countries.[41] Because Spanish census figures undercount the actual immigrant population, other estimates of the actual Muslim population range up to well more than 1 million, or 2.5 percent of the country's population of 47 million.[42] A demographic study of the Muslim population released in 2013 by the Union of Muslim Communities in Spain (Unión de Comunidades Islámicas de España [UCIDE]), a Muslim organization that may have an interest in inflating the number of people that it claims to represent, provides a higher estimate, at 1.67 million.[43]

As in most other European countries, the Muslim population of Spain was expected to grow substantially between 2010 and 2030.[44] However, the economic crisis in Spain – which as of 2013 had the second-highest unemployment rate in the European Union – is beginning to reverse the pattern of the past two decades. About half of the Moroccan immigrants in Spain are reported to have lost their jobs and about 100,000 have indicated a desire to return to their home country. The Spanish government is

[40] Instituto Nacional de Estadística (INE), Encuesta Nacional de Immigrantes 2007: una monografía, Table 7, Madrid 2009, at http://www.ine.es/ss/Satellite?L=es_ES&c=INEPublicacion_C&cid=1259924957585&p=1254735110672&pagename=ProductosYServicios%2FPYSLayout¶m1=PYSDetalleGratuitas.

[41] Instituto Nacional de Estadística (INE), "Residential Variation Statistics, Data Decade 2000–2009," at http//www.ine.es. Immigrants from Muslim majority countries other than Morocco include 60,000 Senegalese, 35,000 Algerians, and 45,000 Pakistanis.

[42] For instance, the respondents in INE statistics on immigrants are those who are at least age 15 and have lived in Spain for a year or have the intention to stay in Spain for at least a year. One million is the figure usually cited by Spanish Muslim leaders and Spanish intelligence sources.

[43] This figure includes 514,000 Spanish citizens and 1.16 million noncitizens. Unión de Comunidades Islámicas de España (UCIDE), Observatorio Andalusí, "Estudio demográfico de la población musulmana," Madrid: 2013, p. 7, at oban.multiplexor.es/estademograf.pdf.

[44] The Pew Forum on Religion & Public Life estimated that the Muslim population in Spain would reach 1,859,000 or 3.7 percent of the population in 2030. Pew Forum on Religion & Public Life, "The Future of the Global Muslim Population," January 2011, at http://features.pewforum.org/muslim-population/.

seeking to encourage their repatriation by providing financial compensation to those leaving the country if they forfeit their residence cards.[45]

The predominantly Moroccan character of the Spanish Muslim community is the result of large-scale Moroccan migration since the 1990s. The first wave of migration, in the 1970s and 1980s, was composed of Syrians and Palestinians. Despite Spain's colonization of northern Morocco (a Spanish protectorate until 1956) and the Western Sahara and the continued Spanish presence in the enclaves of Ceuta and Melilla on the North African coast, relatively few Moroccans settled in Spain before the 1990s because of the underdeveloped condition of the country before its accession to the European Union. Spain was, therefore, a country of transit rather than settlement for North African migrants seeking jobs in more affluent parts of Western Europe.[46] During the 1990s, the Spanish economy grew at a higher rate than that of the European Union as a whole, and the country became a magnet for immigration – from both North Africa and Latin America. Spain's Muslim population grew from approximately 100,000 at the beginning of the 1990s to approximately 1 million in 2005, that is, tenfold. In 2005, there were 380 authorized mosques in Spain and an unknown number of informal mosques and praying halls. The majority were in Barcelona, Madrid, and the region of Andalusia.[47]

## OTHER COUNTRIES

Notable Muslim concentrations can be found in Italy, Belgium, Austria, and Switzerland, and smaller populations in the Scandinavian countries. Estimates of the Muslim population in Italy range up to 2 percent. The most recent estimates of the foreign population in Italy indicate that as of January 2010, there were 4.2 million foreign residents in Italy, totaling 7.0 percent of the population. Almost half were from Eastern Europe. Those from predominantly Muslim nations included 466,684 from Albania, 431,529 from Morocco, 103,678 from Tunisia, 82,064 from Egypt, and

[45] Mohamad Sharki, "Thousands of Moroccan Migrants Return from Europe," *Al-Hayat*, June 27, 2012 at http://alhayat.com/Details/413852 and http://www.al-monitor.com/pulse/business/2012/06/thousands-of-moroccan-migrants-r.html.

[46] However, Moroccan troops played an important role in the Spanish Civil War, fighting on the nationalist side. After the Civil War, Generalissimo Franco established the first Islamic communal prayer center in modern Spain, the Morabito de los Jardines de Colón in Cordoba, for the use of his Moorish troops. Jordi Moreras, "Musulmanes en España," at http://www.flwi.ugent.be/cie/moreras2.htm.

[47] Agenzia Fides, "Spain and Islam," at: http://www.fides.org/en/news/3953-EUROPE_AND_RELIGIONS_SPAIN_AND_ISLAM#.U3ozEC9woSA.

73,965 from Bangladesh. The combined population from these five nations is 1,177,920, out of a total population of 60 million.[48] The Muslim population is concentrated in northern and central cities that have attracted immigrants over the previous decades. The heterogeneity of national origin of the Italian Muslim communities complicates the formation of civic and religious organizations. Despite these differences, common elements can be found among Muslims in Italy. They are overwhelmingly Sunni and disproportionately male. Italian Muslims also tend to be noncitizen first-generation immigrants, and many reside in the country illegally. Surveys of Muslims in Italy also find that only a small proportion are devout adherents. Most Muslims observe Ramadan and celebrate Eid al Fitr (the feast marking the end of Ramadan) but do not regularly attend mosques.[49]

Precise estimates of Belgium's Muslim population are complicated because Belgium has not conducted a national census in two decades (when it did, questions about religious affiliation were not included). Most estimates place the number of Muslims in Belgium at between 300,000 and 450,000.[50] More than half of the Muslims in Belgium are naturalized Belgian citizens. Thirty-seven percent are nationals of predominantly Muslim countries, whereas 10,000 to 15,000 are converts. The rest are children from Muslim families who acquired Belgian nationality at birth. Moroccans and Turks are the predominant ethnic groups within the Belgian Muslim population. Together they represent some 88 percent of the Muslims who are naturalized citizens and 67 percent of the nationals from predominantly Muslim countries.[51]

Switzerland includes questions on religion in its census. According to the most recent census in 2010, Muslims constituted 4.5 percent of the resident population of 7,955,000.[52] Most Swiss residents of foreign nationality come from EU countries. Turks (71,400) comprise the single

[48] L'Istituto nazionale di statistica, "La popolazione straniera residente in Italia," October 12, 2010, at http://www3.istat.it/salastampa/comunicati/non_calendario/20101012_00/testointegrale20101012.pdf.

[49] Lorenzo Vidino, "Islam, Islamism, and Jihadism in Italy," *Current Trends in Islamist Ideology*, Vol. 7. Washington, DC: Center on Islam, Democracy and the Future of the Muslim World, Hudson Institute, August 4, 2008.

[50] "Islam in Belgium," http://www.euro-islam.info/country-profiles/Belgium/.

[51] Open Society Institute, EU Monitoring and Advocacy Program, "Muslims in the EU: Cities Report – Belgium, 2007," at http://www.opensocietyfoundations.org/sites/default/files/museucitiesbel_20080101.pdf.

[52] Confédération suisse, Office fédéral de la statistique, *Relevé structurel du recensement fédéral de la population 2010. Un cinquième des habitants de la Suisse n'a pas d'appartenance religieuse*, June 19, 2012, at http://www.bfs.admin.ch/bfs/portal/fr/index/news/medienmitteilungen.html?pressID=8091.

largest group from a Muslim majority nation, followed by Bosnians (27,100).[53] As in most other European countries, the Muslim communities are concentrated in the major cities: Zürich, Bern, Basel, Lausanne, and Geneva. Turks and nationals of the former Yugoslavia have gravitated to the German-speaking cantons; the bulk of the North Africans live in French-speaking areas.[54]

Austria likewise includes religion in its decennial census. In 2001, there were 338,988 Muslims in Austria (4.2 percent), more than double the figure of 158,776 of 1991.[55] By region, Muslims are most prevalent in Vienna (121,149, or 7.6 percent of the city's population of 1.6 million), though seven of the nine regions of the nation have Muslim populations of at least 20,000. The majority of Austria's Muslims are of Turkish descent, followed by Bosnians.[56]

Sweden has the largest Muslim population in Scandinavia, estimated at 250,000 to 400,000, or 1.8 percent to 4.4 percent of the Swedish population of 9 million. Most of the Muslim populations live in major cities, with about half residing in Stockholm. There are also large Muslim communities in Göteborg and Malmö. The Swedish Muslim population is very diverse, with most coming from Turkey, Iraq, Iran, and Bosnia, as well as Pakistan, and Middle Eastern and African countries.[57] Denmark and Norway do not include religious affiliation in demographic data. An estimated 175,000 to 200,000 Muslims live in Denmark and Norway, respectively. Most are first-generation and second-generation residents. The majority in both countries are ethnic Turks, but important contingents also come from Lebanon, Pakistan, Bosnia, and Somalia.[58]

## DEMOGRAPHIC TRENDS

Demographic data suggest that even absent further immigration, Muslim populations will likely grow faster than other European populations in

[53] Confédération suisse, Office fédéral de la statistique, *Population résidante permanente étrangère selon la nationalité*, 2011, at http://www.bfs.admin.ch/bfs/portal/fr/index/themen/01/07/blank/key/01/01.htm.

[54] Jørgen S. Nielsen, *Muslims in Western Europe*, Edinburgh University Press, 2004, p. 90.

[55] Statistics Austria, 2002, *Volkszählung, Hauptergebnisse I*, at ftp://www.statistik.at/pub/neuerscheinungen/vzaustriaweb.pdf.

[56] David Motadel, "Islam in Austria," at http://www.euro-islam.info/country-profiles/austria/.

[57] Open Society Institute, "Muslims in the EU: Cities Report – Sweden, 2007," at http://www.opensocietyfoundations.org/sites/default/files/museucitiesswe_20080101_0.pdf.

[58] Iben Helqvist and Elizabeth Sebian, "Islam in Denmark," at www.euro-islam.info/country-profiles/denmark/.

coming years because of their younger age structures (meaning more of this population is or will soon be of childbearing age), and also because their fertility rates tend to be higher than those of European non-Muslim populations. For instance, in France, the combined Moroccan, Tunisian, and Turkish populations are concentrated among younger age cohorts more than other populations. In the United Kingdom, Muslim families were both the most likely to have children and to have the largest families.[59]

Long-term projections are difficult because emigrants are not necessarily representative of their countries of origin (they may have lower fertility rates than those who remain).[60] Furthermore they tend, over time, to adopt the fertility patterns of those they join at the destination (because of a combination of social and economic factors – for instance, the higher costs of raising children), though their fertility rates may remain higher than those of native communities for a period of time that could be as long as two or three generations. For example, fertility rates among immigrant women in France have tended to converge with the French norm, though they remain higher than that for other French women.[61] The fertility rate of South Asians in the United Kingdom is down to 2.5 children per family, lower than Pakistan (3.65) and closer to the British norm of 1.88.[62]

[59] Nearly three in four (73 percent) Muslim families in the United Kingdom have at least one dependent child, compared to about two in five Jewish (41 percent) and Christian (40 percent) families. More than one in four (27 percent) Muslim families have at least three children, compared to less than one in fourteen (7 percent) Christian families. Pakistanis and Bangladeshis in the United Kingdom also say they desire more children than whites say they desire. See United Kingdom, Office for National Statistics, "Muslim Families Most Likely to Have Children," in Focus on Families 2005 Summary Report, at http://www.ons.gov.uk/ons/index.html.

[60] For the 2005-2010 period, the total fertility rate (TFR) in Bangladesh was 2.40 children per women and that in Pakistan was 3.65; in the United Kingdom, it was 1.88. (A TFR of about 2.1 is considered necessary for population replacement or for a subsequent generation to have about the same population as the previous generation.) The TFR was 2.38 in Morocco, 2.05 in Tunisia, 2.16 in Turkey, and 1.97 in France. See United Nations Population Division, *World Population Prospects, The 2012 Revision*, File FERT/4, at http://esa.un.org/wpp/Excel-Data/fertility.htm.

[61] Justin Vaisse, "Unrest in France, November 2005: Immigration, Islam and the Challenge of Integration," presentation to congressional staff, January 2006, online at http://www.brookings.edu/research/testimony/2006/01/12france-vaisse. Vaisse estimates that without immigrant births, the fertility rate "would drop by 0.05 children per woman." This, he claims, means that "one can hardly speak of a 'demographic time bomb,' 'colonization in reverse,' or the 'Islamicization of France.'"

[62] See United Kingdom, Office for National Statistics, "Muslim Families Most Likely to Have Children," in Focus on Families 2005 Summary Report.

# 3

# Salafism and Radical Islamism in Europe

All of the major categories of Muslim belief can be found in Europe. This diversity reflects the religious practices in the countries of origin of Europe's Muslim population. The difference between Muslim communities in Europe and those in the Muslim world, of course, is that in Europe, Muslims are a minority in non-Muslim majority countries; therefore, the practice of Islam takes place in a social context where Islamic norms do not always fit comfortably with, and sometimes clash with, the norms and social practices of the majority society.

This tension has generated two parallel and opposite phenomena within Europe's Muslim communities: one, on the part of liberal Muslims, is the effort to construct a "European Islam" that harmonizes the core principles of Islam with modern Western values. The second phenomenon is the rejection of both secular Western values and the traditional, culturally bound beliefs of the majority of Europe's Muslims in favor of a reconstruction of what its followers regard as a more authentic practice of Islam known as Salafism. The combination of the increasing secularization of Western society with the globalization of religion has led to the liberalization of the religious marketplace – in which religions and ideologies compete to meet the demands of consumers – and the emergence of new religious ideologies and practices formerly unknown in Europe.[1] Because of its potent elucidation of the alienation felt by Muslims in Western

[1] This analysis is laid out by Laurence Iannaccone in "Vodoo Economics? Reviewing the Rational Choice Approach to Religion," *Journal for the Scientific Study of Religion*, Vol. 34, No. 1, 1995, pp. 76–89. This framework was applied to the transformation of the religious phenomenon in France by Gérard Donadieu in his essay, "Vers un marché du religieux, le nouveau paysage du croire," Futuribles, n° 260 (January 2001). Olivier Roy

societies and its emphasis on their empowerment through the reaffirmation of the basic tenets of Islam, Salafism has been one of the major beneficiaries of this phenomenon.

Salafism is a religious concept in Sunni Islam. Islamism is a religiously based ideology that has political ends. Islamist extremists in Europe generally adhere to a Salafist interpretation of Islam, but not all Salafis are Islamists. Some eschew politics and make their religious practices the focus of their work.[2] Indeed, some Salafis oppose Islamist groups because they believe that parties (*hizbiyah*) undermine the unity of the Muslim community, the *umma*. Within the universe of Sunni Islamism are various Islamist groups – for instance, Jamaat-i-Islami in the Deobandi movement, which adheres to the Hanafi school of Islamic jurisprudence; the Muslim Brotherhood in its great variety; groups derived from the Brotherhood; and the violent extremists or jihadists who are the subject of this text.[3]

Salafis claim that only the model and example of those first Muslims are authoritative in Islam. Although present-day Salafis reject modernity, they are themselves the product of modernity. The genesis of Salafism as a modern intellectual movement within Islam can be traced to the nineteenth-century reformers Jamal al-Din al-Afghani (1839–1897) and Muhammad Abduh (1849–1905) whose ideas were influenced by Auguste Comte and the French positivists. The core of their teachings was the rejection of the authority of the established schools of Islamic jurisprudence (*mazhab*) and the practice of *ijtihad*, or independent judgment, in legal or theological questions by applying the principles of deduction and analogy to the interpretation of the Quran and the Sunna, the tradition of the Prophet Muhammad, to meet the demands of science and the modern age.[4] Al-Afghani and Abduh protested against certain traditional patterns in Islam that they deemed to be deviant from the original Islamic model and at the same time responsible for the stagnation of the Islamic world.

states that the globalization of religion (or, rather, religiosity as a personal experience) involves the detachment of religion from culture. Roy (2004), pp. 25–29.

[2] Many Salafis eschew political allegiances or organization because they believe that parties (*hizbiyya*) undermine the unity of the Muslim community, the *umma*. The term *hizbiyya*, in particular, is used as a derogatory term by some conservative Salafis to describe followers of the Muslim Brotherhood.

[3] See Angel Rabasa, "Ideology, Not Religion," in Richard C. Martin and Abbas Barzegar, *Islamism Contested Perspectives on Political Islam*. Stanford: Stanford University Press, 2009.

[4] Mohamed Selim El-Awwa, "A return to the centre," *Al-Ahram Weekly*, December 9–15, 1999, at http://weekly.ahram.org.eg/1999/459/ramadan.htm.

This school of thought bifurcated in later years. One branch of the movement developed into the liberal modernist tendency within Islam that stresses the compatibility of the original teachings of Islam with progress and democracy.[5] The second branch moved closer to more conservative interpretations of Islam. Rather than seeking accommodation with modern Western values, conservative Salafis regarded them as sources of decadence and decay. Muhammad Rashid Rida, Abduh's most prominent disciple, represented this conservative Salafi movement.[6] Rida and his associates popularized the concept of Salafism in the 1920s through the al-Manar press and the Salaffiya bookstore in Cairo and passed it along to Hasan al-Banna, the founder of the Muslim Brotherhood.

As formulated by Rida and his associates, Salafism converged conceptually with Wahhabism, the conservative revivalist religious movement founded by Muhammad ibn Abd al-Wahhab in the eighteenth century in the Nedj region of what is today Saudi Arabia. This movement became the official interpretation of Islam in Saudi Arabia after the establishment of the Saudi state in the 1920s. (Wahhabis consider the term pejorative and prefer to call themselves *Ahl al-Sunna*, or *Ahl al-Tawhid*, "the people [who uphold] the unity of God.") Nevertheless, despite their areas of convergence – particularly their hostility to modernity – Wahhabism differs in some respects from Salafi movements: strict Salafis reject all schools of Islamic jurisprudence, relying on direct interpretation of the Quran and the Sunna, whereas Wahhabis subscribe to the Hambali *mazhab*, the strictest of the four schools in Sunni Islam. More importantly, the sect is closely associated politically with the House of Saud, although at various times Wahhabi extremists have challenged the regime, notably in

[5] Among the liberal modernists were Rifa'at Rafi al-Tahtawi (1801–1873), who sought to develop a new educational system in Egypt that incorporated both Islamic and European elements; Shihab al-Din Marjani (1818–1889) and Ahmad Makhdum Danesh (1827–1897), who worked to reform the curriculum in Bukhara schools by introducing secular subjects; Muhammad Tahir Jalaluddin (1867–1957), Haji Ahmad Dahlan (1869–1923), and Ahmad Surkati (1872–1943), who established reformist schools in Southeast Asia; and Sayyid Muhammad Tabataba'i (1843–1921) and Sayyid Abdullah Behbehani (1846–1910), supporters of the Persian constitutional movement. Charles Kurzman, ed., *Liberal Islam: A Sourcebook*. New York and Oxford: Oxford University Press, 1998.

[6] Henri Lauzière differs from this generally accepted view of the origins of Salafism and argues that the concepts associated with modern Salafism did not originate until the 1920s. Henri Lauzière, "The Construction of Salafiyya: Reconsidering Salafism from the Perspective of Conceptual History," *International Journal of Middle East Studies*, Vol. 42, Issue 3, August 2010.

the Ikhwan rebellion of 1927 to 1930 and the seizure of the Grand Mosque in Mecca in November 1979.

## EVOLUTION OF RADICAL ISLAMISM

Islamist extremism in Europe has two ideological sources. One is the militant trend in the Muslim Brotherhood represented by Sayyid Qutb and developed by subsequent Egyptian ideologues such Muhammad abd al-Salam Faraj, Sukri Mustafa, and Ayman al-Zawahiri. The other is rooted in a violent branch of the Wahhabi movement represented by Saudi, Yemeni, and Kuwaiti members of al-Qaeda and some of the movement's religious authorities.[7]

The seminal figure in the development of radical Islamist ideology was Sayyid Qutb, the editor in chief of the Egyptian Muslim Brotherhood's weekly *Al-Ikhwan al-Muslimin* and a member of the Guidance Council, the organization's highest body. In his influential book *Milestones Along the Road*, Qutb argued that the Muslim world was in a state of *jahiliyya*, the state of ignorance that prevailed before the Prophet Muhammad's revelation and that Muslim rulers were apostates. Contrary to the Muslim Brotherhood's gradualist approach to the establishment of an Islamic state, Qutb advocated the seizure of power by a revolutionary vanguard that would then impose Islamic rule from above. Egyptian President Gamal Abdel Nasser's government executed Qutb in 1966.[8]

Muhammad abd al-Salam Faraj founded the al-Jihad organization, the group responsible for the assassination of President Anwar Sadat. Faraj's most important treatise, *Jihad: The Neglected Obligation*, sets forth two main goals: to replace secular law with Islamic law, even if that meant killing Muslims who resist, and to kill the leaders of governments who adopt secular ways. Faraj emphasized the individual duty of jihad and rejected interpretations of the jihad other than violent confrontations with the enemy. Faraj developed his revolutionary theory in opposition to another Qutb disciple, Shukri Mustafa, leader of *Takfir wal-Hijra* (Excommunication and Exile), who also rejected the Muslim Brotherhood's gradualist approach but argued that the Muslims were

[7] Reviewer's comments.

[8] John Calvert, *Sayyid Qutb and the Origins of Radical Islamism*. New York: Columbia University Press, 2010; William E. Shepard, "Sayyid Qutb's Doctrine of 'Jāhiliyya,'" *International Journal of Middle East Studies*, Vol. 35, No. 4, 2003, pp. 521–545; A. B. Soage "Hasan al-Banna and Sayyid Qutb: Continuity or Rupture?" in *The Muslim World*, Oxford: Blackwell Publishing Ltd, 2009.

too weak to overthrow the established order and therefore needed to separate themselves from infidel society until they were strong enough to launch a jihad.[9]

Ayman al-Zawahiri, the current leader of al-Qaeda, is in the same tradition. He was a member of the Muslim Brotherhood who came in contact with Muhammad Qutb, Sayyid Qutb's brother, and Abdullah Azzam, a Palestinian who was one of the founders of al-Qaeda. He appears to have been associated with Faraj's al-Jihad organization and was arrested after Sadat's assassination. He emerged from prison in 1984 as the leader of the Egyptian Islamic Jihad.[10] In his book *Bitter Harvest*, al-Zawahiri articulates a view of democracy as a new religion that must be destroyed. He characterizes the Muslim Brotherhood as *kuffar* (infidels) for sacrificing Allah's authority by accepting the notion that the people are the ultimate source of authority. He also condemns the Brotherhood for renouncing jihad as a means to establish the Islamic State.[11]

## JIHADI IDEOLOGY AND STRATEGY

The role of ideology and ideologically driven narratives is a contested issue in the analysis of Europe-based Islamist extremism. One school of thought argues that the factors driving individuals to join terrorist groups are independent of the ideology. In this view, the properties of group cohesion, including the creation of personal relationships that precede recruitment into a terrorist group, have particular relevance for understanding radicalization.[12] On the other hand, a plausible argument can be made that ideology is a central component of Islamist extremist groups and movements. In this regard, it is worth noting the high priority that radical Islamists themselves attach to ideology. According to Stephen Ulph, at least 60 percent of the materials circulated in jihadi forums and specialist

[9] Calvert, *Sayyid Qutb and the Origins of Radical Islamism*; PWHCE Middle East Project, "Muhammad abd al-Salam Faraj," Perspectives on World History and Current Events," at http://www.pwhce.org/faraj.html.

[10] PWHCE Middle East Project, "Dr. Ayman al-Zawahiri," Perspectives on World History and Current Events," at http://www.pwhce.org/zawahiri.html; Mark Erikson, "Islamism, fascism and terrorism," Part 4, *Asia Times Online*, December 5, 2002, at http://www.atimes.com/atimes/Middle_East/DL05Ak01.html.

[11] Mark Erikson, "Islamism, fascism and terrorism.".

[12] Marc Sageman, *Understanding Terror Networks.*, Philadelphia: University of Pennsylvania Press, 2004, p. 14; Carol Williams, "German terror cells link to 9/11 detailed" *Los Angeles Times*, August 30, 2002, at http://articles.latimes.com/2002/aug/30/world/fg-hijack30.

sites were not located in the sections devoted to news commentary or audiovisual propaganda, but in the "doctrinal" and "cultural" sections.[13]

It is important to understand that al-Qaeda's strategy is to tap into sectors of the broader Salafi movement that are susceptible to the ideological appeal of jihadist militancy. This argues for a focus on the ideological and political rather than on the physical aspects of the terrorist and extremist networks and on targeting the linkages – as strategist, propagandist, and vanguard – that al-Qaeda has established with other sectors of the radical Salafi universe. These linkages have been forged through the axioms of radical religious ideologies shared by many of these groups. A plausible argument can be made that ideology is the center of gravity of jihadist and radical Islamist movements. It is a central component of the recruitment and motivation of militants. To sustain themselves, militant groups require the revolutionary "software" that helps convince militants that their mission is worth the sacrifices and to induce new members to join. If the ideology continues to spread and gain greater acceptance, it will produce more militants. If the ideology is countered and discredited, the jihadist movement will find it difficult to recruit and sustain its momentum.[14]

Jihadi ideology has two core elements that are common to Salafism. The first is the purification of Islam by returning to the uncorrupted form that Salafis believed was practiced in the time of the Prophet Muhammad and his companions and an insistence on the unmediated authority of the Quran and the Sunna. So even though much of contemporary radical Salafi ideology is based on the writings of medieval Islamic theologian Ibn Taymiyya, the thrust of the ideology is to reject or disregard the body of Islamic jurisprudence that developed in the 14 centuries since Muhammad's revelation. In this insistence on a return to the original texts of the religion, the religious methodology of the Salafis resembles that of Protestant groups that rejected the authority of the Catholic Church and its tradition in favor of the personal, unmediated interpretation of the scriptures. In the present context, when people in the West speak about the need for an Islamic reformation, it is worth noting that such a reformation has in fact occurred and that the results have not been favorable to Western liberal concepts.

[13] Stephen Ulph, Testimony to the Open Hearing of the Senate Select Committee on Intelligence, June 12, 2007, at http://www.gpo.gov/fdsys/pkg/CHRG-110shrg40579/html/CHRG-110shrg40579.htm. This is generally true of comparable ideological movements. For instance, the extreme left has always been embroiled in massive ideological debates.

[14] Angel Rabasa et al., *Beyond al-Qaeda*, Vol. 1: *The Global Jihadist Movement*, Santa Monica, CA: RAND Corporation, 2005.

The second element is *tawhid*, the unity of God. This is the founding principle of Islam and is a belief shared by all Muslims, but Salafis, especially radical Salafis, have taken this concept and given it a radical interpretation; for instance, as God alone is the source of law, no human being or legislature could alter in any way God's law, the *shari'a*, because that would mean that human beings would set themselves in the place of God. Democracy, therefore, in the radical Salafi view, is a false religion.[15] Salafis are unwilling to accept the interpretations of other Muslim schools of thought, seeing their pure return to fundamentals as the legitimating factor of the superiority of their beliefs.

Radical Salafis also reject the concept of freedom because it would permit what God has forbidden, conduct that is viewed as tied to Western ideas of freedom and secularism, and not what God has commanded.[16] As freedom culturally denotes licentious conduct, most Salafis do not connect good governance with liberty but instead with justice. (Note that many Islamist parties include the word *justice* in their names.) Also, as God alone is worthy of worship, in the Salafi view, any devotions directed at intermediaries amounts to idolatry. This is at the root of the Salafis' intense hostility to traditionalist Muslims,[17] Sufis, and Shi'ites.

One of the factors that facilitates the movement from mainstream to radical Islam is the unifying vision of the *umma*, the universal Muslim community. This conception resonates very strongly among Muslims and has two effects: first, it facilitates recruitment into radical and jihadist groups that purport to represent the vanguard of Islam and speak with the authentic voice of the religion; second, it inhibits moderates from strongly confronting the radicals for fear of being accused of siding with infidels against Muslims. Among radicalized young Diaspora Muslims, identification with the *umma* provides an alternative source of identity to the traditional culture of their families' countries of origin from which they feel detached, and to Western culture from which they feel alienated.[18] Related to this is the political expression of the universal *umma*, the caliphate, the common goal of most of the politically oriented Salafi groups.

Although mainstream Salafis and Islamist may not support the extremists' expansive concept of jihad as armed struggle, it is difficult for them to refute it on religious grounds because it is grounded in the texts and axioms

[15] As Abu Musab al-Zarqawi stated in opposition to the Iraqi elections.

[16] Mary Habeck, *Knowing the Enemy: Jihadist Ideology and the War on Terror*, New Haven and London: Yale University Press, 2006, pp. 78–79.

[17] Defined as those whose practice in Islam is informed by historical and cultural traditions.

[18] Oliver Roy (2004).

that they share. The ideological transition from Salafism to violent extremism has a great deal to do with the choice of texts, that is to say, with the hermeneutics, the methodology for textual interpretation used by Muslims to understand and apply the teachings of the Quran. This is important because a Muslim must justify his or her political worldview by an appeal to the sacred texts.

Mainstream Muslims rely on the whole body of the Quran, the Sunna, and Islamic tradition to develop their positions, whereas many Salafis, particularly the more radical sector of the movement, make selective use of the Quran to support their militant views. Radicals, for example, make extensive use of abrogation (*naskh*) – which is the practice by which an earlier text in the Quran is superseded by a later, more authoritative text. Radicals generally consider that earlier (more peaceful and tolerant) verses of the Mecca period are abrogated by later (more militant and intolerant) verses of the Medina period –the so-called Sword Verses.[19] Islamic hermeneutics scholar Joseph Kickasola found a total of eight abrogations in the approved Saudi translation and commentaries on the Quran. Although Islamic scholarship accepts the practice of abrogation, there is no consensus on the hierarchy of texts and the method of abrogation. Some moderates take the opposite approach from the radicals: that it, is the earlier, more tolerant message of the Quran and not the later, more militant one that is normative today.[20]

The main area of discrepancy between mainstream Salafis and jihadists is, of course, the definition of jihad. Salafis and jihadists agree that in the absence of the caliph, the armed jihad can only be defensive, but there are disagreements over the meaning of "defensive." Most Salafis, and even other Muslims, are equivocal on the issue of terrorism. There is no blanket

[19] One example of abrogation is the following: Quran 2.109 states "Many of the followers of the Book wish that they could turn you back into unbelievers after your faith, out of envy from themselves, (even) after the truth has become manifest to them; but pardon and forgive, so that Allah should bring about His command; surely Allah has power over all things" is abrogated by Quran 9.29 "Fight those who do not believe in Allah, nor in the latter day, nor do they prohibit what Allah and His Apostle have prohibited, nor follow the religion of truth, out of those who have been given the Book, until they pay the tax in acknowledgment of superiority and they are in a state of subjection." Joseph N. Kickasola, "The Clash of Civilizations Within Islam: The Struggle Over the Qu'ran between Muslim Democrats and Theocrats," The Center for Vision and Values, Grove City College, August 18, 2006, at http://www.visionandvalues.org/docs/The%20Clash%20of%20Civilizations%20WITHIN%20Islam.pdf.

[20] That is the view, for instance, of Mahmoud Taha, *The Second Message of Islam*, Syracuse, NY: Syracuse University Press, 1996. Taha was executed for apostasy by the Sudanese government in 1985.

denunciation of violent jihad, but they tend to define it narrowly, relegating to areas where Muslims are under attack.[21] For jihadists, the meaning of "defensive" extends to striking at the enemies of God wherever they are. They see themselves as a vanguard who are willing to fulfill the religious obligations of jihad, even if other Muslims do not.

Mainstream Muslim opinion can be mobilized against jihadist violence particularly when the victims are Muslim. For instance, al-Zarqawi's excesses in Iraq alienated many Salafis who were otherwise sympathetic to his goals and provoked a break with Abu Muhammad al-Maqdisi, his one-time mentor. Al-Maqdisi wrote a lengthy treatise, *The Thirtieth Letter on Cautioning Against Excesses in Rendering the Verdict of Unbelief*, in which he criticized al-Zarqawi's overindulgence in employing suicide bombers; he puts suicide bombers in the category of "exceptional" and not "original" in jihad.[22]

The radicals' willingness to declare Muslims who do not share their views apostates, is a major area of discrepancy. Some establishment Salafis (in Saudi Arabia, for instance) say that the radicals have accepted Kharijite teachings on *takfir*, the practice of declaring other Muslims unbelievers (kuffar).[23] Differences between jihadist and other Salafis also relate to strategy and tactics, although, like everything else, the positions of the groups are justified in religio-ideological terms. In his January 5, 2006, videotape, al-Zawahiri mocks the Brotherhood's success in the Egyptian parliamentary elections, accusing them of serving as fig leaves for corrupt regimes.[24]

Despite these differences, the lack of firebreaks between mainstream Salafist and Islamist groups and movements and their radical fringes means

[21] For instance, asked his opinion about a jihad to defend Muslims under attack in the Moluccas, Yemeni Salafi Sheikh Muqbil bin Hadi al-Wadi laid down the following conditions: (1) that Muslims have the capacity to fight the kafirs, (2) that the jihad not lead to conflicts within the Muslim community, (3) that mobilization for the jihad be based purely on religion, (4) that the jihad be based on Salafi principles and not be conducted under *hizbiyya* [party] flags, (5) that it not distract Muslims from studying the true religion, and (6) that it not be used for personal gain or to obtain political positions. International Crisis Group (ICG), "Indonesia Backgrounder: Why Salafism and Terrorism Don't Mix," ICG Asia Report No. 83, September 13, 2004.

[22] Nibras Kazimi, "A Virulent Ideology in Mutation: Zarqawi Upstages Maqdisi," Hudson Institute, *Current Trends in Islamist Ideology*, Vol. 2, 2005, at http://www.hudson.org/content/researchattachments/attachment/1368/kazimi_vol2.pdf.

[23] The Kharijites (Arabic plural *Khawārij*, literally "those who have left") were a heretical sect that emerged during the caliphate of Ali. They waged war against other Muslims, whom they accused of apostasy.

[24] "Muslim Brotherhood Challenges al Qaeda for Jihadi Primacy," DEBKA-Net Weekly, Vol. 5, Issue 237, January 13, 2006.

that these groups and movements can become gateways to violent extremism. The Polish-German convert Christian Ganczarski told authorities that he was recruited by al-Qaeda while attending the Islamic University of Medina in Saudi Arabia. Ganczarski was reportedly referred to the university by Nadeem Elyas, an official in the Islamic Center of Aachen, one of the nine Muslim Brotherhood–affiliated organizations in the Central Council of Muslims in Germany (Zentralrat der Muslime in Deutchsland – ZMD). Although Elyas does not appear to have directly indoctrinated or recruited Ganczarski, his influence in steering Ganczarski and hundreds of others to the Islamic University of Medina, which was replete with radical activists and al-Qaeda sympathizers, appears to have contributed to Ganczarski's involvement with extremists that eventually led to his terrorist training in Afghanistan and his involvement in the 2002 bombing of the Djerba synagogue in Tunisia.

Some of the most extreme radical Islamists depart from the practice of other Muslims in their willingness to practice *takfir*. Declaring *takfir* provides the necessary justification to fight and kill those who do not adhere to the radicals' interpretation of Islam. Radicals have extended the scope of *takfir* beyond the traditional definition of apostasy – denying the unity of God or the authenticity or finality of Muhammad's revelation – to a much broader range of alleged deviations, including insulting the Prophet or adhering to secular or liberal ideas, or even participating in elections.[25] Omar Bakri Mohammed, founder of the now disbanded UK-based extremist organization Al-Muhajiroun, defended the practice of declaring *takfir* as follows:

> We worship Allah (subhana wa Ta'ala) by making takfeer – declaring a person to be Kafir. At-takfeer is an obligation upon all Muslims. Those who do not make takfeer are Mushriks [polytheists] as the first pillar of Tawheed [Islamic monotheism] requires one to make takfeer by declaring those who Allah calls Kafir to be Kafir.[26]

Unlike mainstream Muslims, who make a distinction between the greater jihad (striving for self-improvement) and the lesser jihad (armed struggle in the path of God), violent radical Salafis regard armed struggle as the only true jihad and as a personal religious obligation on the same level or higher

[25] Shmuel Bar, *Warrants for Terror: The Fatwas of Radical Islam and the Duty to Jihad*. Lanham, MD: Rowman & Littlefield, 2006, pp. 80–81.

[26] Quoted in James Brandon, *Virtual Caliphate: Islamic Extremists and Their Websites*. London: Centre for Social Cohesion, 2008, p. 12, at http://www.civitas.org.uk/pdf/VirtualCaliphate.pdf.

than the five obligatory duties of Islam.[27] Moreover, contemporary radical interpretations have taken the jihad well beyond its traditional conception to erase all limits on warfare. Fatwas issued by radical sheikhs justify the killing of persons protected under Islamic law such as Muslims, non-Muslims who have treaties with Muslims, travelers with safe passage, *dhimmis* (protected non-Muslim minorities), monks and clergy, women, children, and aged persons; the killing of prisoners and hostages; the use of weapons of mass destruction (WMD); and other deviations from the classical Islamic law of war. The radical Islamist worldview is also marked by the cult of martyrdom, what the scholar Shmuel Bar has referred to as thanatophilia.[28]

## THEMES AND MESSAGES

A British study of UK-based extremist websites found that martyrdom and paradise are important themes. A description of paradise by the medieval writer Ibn al-Qayyim al-Jawziyya published on an extremist website describes the tangible rewards that await the martyrs. In his martyrdom video, Shazad Tanweer, one of the 7/7 bombers, stated, "You cling inherently to the earth and you believe in the life of this world rather than the hereafter. But little is the enjoyment of this world as compared to the hereafter."[29]

The common message of violent Islamists is that the United States and the West are leading a crusader-type campaign against Islam, and that

[27] The professions of faith are prayer five times a day, almsgiving (zakat), fasting during Ramadan, and the pilgrimage to Mecca (hajj). There is an extensive literature on Jihad. See Bar, *Warrants for Terror*; Youssef H. Aboul-Enein and Sherifa Zuhur, "Islamic Rulings on Warfare," SSI, Army War College, October 2004, at http://www.strategicstudiesinstitute.army.mil/pdffiles/pub588.pdf; Bassam Tibi, "War and Peace in Islam," and Sohail Hashmi, "Interpreting the Islamic Ethics of War and Peace," in Hashmi, ed., *Islamic Political Ethics: Civil Society, Pluralism, and Conflict*. Princeton: Princeton University Press; James Turner Johnson, "Jihad and Just War," *First Things*, 124 (June/July 2002); Patricia A. Martinez, "Deconstructing Jihad," in Kumar Ramakrishna and See Seng Tan, *After Bali: The Threat of Terrorism in Southeast Asia*. Singapore: Institute of Defence and Strategic Studies, 2003.

[28] Bar, *Warrants for Terror*. Suicide is forbidden in Islam, as it is in all monotheistic religions. A hadith states that whoever commits suicide shall be punished in Hell forever by the same means that he used to kill himself (Sahih Bukhari 2.446, 2.445), but some scholars such as Yusuf al-Qaradawi, have justified suicide bombing under certain circumstances. See "Al-Qaradhawi Speaks in Favor of Suicide Operations at an Islamic Conference in Sweden," MEMRI Special Dispatch Series, No. 542, July 24, 2003, at http://www.memri.org/bin/articles.cgi?Area=sd%26 ID=SP54203.

[29] Cited in Brandon (2008), p. 25.

armed jihad is a *fard ayn* (personal duty) because of the occupation of Muslim lands by infidels. Jihadi literature typically used certain episodes in Muslim history as points of reference, portraying a vision of armed jihad as rooted in historical precedents. Large sections of Abu Mus'ab al-Suri's 1,600-page book, *Da'wat al-muqawamah al-islamiyyah al-'alamiyyah* (*The Global Islamic Resistance Call*) offer a historical overview of the reasons for the decline of the Arab world, setting the stage for his prescription of armed jihad as the solution. Similarly, in his book *Idarat al-Tawahhush* (Management of savagery), Abu Bakir Naji dwells on humiliating historical events such as the Sykes-Picot Agreement of 1916 that resulted in the division of the Arab world. Like al-Suri, he believes that jihad offers the only means of liberation.

A common theme is the corruption of Western societies – a view shared by mainstream and radical Islamists alike. In an article entitled "Broken Britain," Iftikhar Ahmad of the London School of Islamics, a British educational trust that advocates state funding of Muslim schools, presented this view of contemporary Britain:

> Britain has a broken society. This is a dark portrait but it is very true. Children are left to rot and they grew into animals. Binge drinking, drug addiction, a culture of disrespect and antisocial behavior, teenage pregnancies and abortions, knife and gun culture are part and parcel of every day life in all big city centers. The teenage pregnancies and the sheer madness of sex education teach nothing about morality. British society is suffering from unprecedented social decay and societal breakdown.[30]

Homosexuality, the article averred, was once regarded as mental illness, "but now blue eyed western educated elites are its defenders and promoters."[31] In response to proposals to ban the *burqa* in some European countries, the German Taliban Mujahideen, in a statement released on February 8, 2010, stated:

> How long will you keep insisting that the Muslim woman is oppressed? In Western countries, women are being abused, prostituted, enslaved and humiliated! The uncovered women are the oppressed because they have no protection against the dirty looks of men.
>
> And you dare to say that Muslim women are oppressed? You, who do live in a society that lives by the motto "sex sells." Your whole dirty marketing industry is built on the abuse of female charms. How do you dare to say even a single word

[30] Iftikhar Ahmad, "Broken Britain," February 4, 2010, at http://world.mediamonitors.net/content/view/full/71201.

[31] Iftikhar Ahmad, "Broken Britain," London School of Islamics, March 21, 2010, at http://world.mediamonitors.net/content/view/full/71201.

about the honorable sisters, mothers and women of the Ummah of the Prophet Muhammad, peace and blessings be upon him, when you are the oppressors?[32]

These themes are prominent in the discourse of Europe-based extremists. In a 2001 talk entitled "Islam Under Siege," Sheikh Abdullah Faisal, a Jamaican convert to Islam who became an influential extremist preacher in Britain and was said to have played a key role in radicalizing some of the 7/7 London bombers, argued that Islam is in an inevitable struggle with Christians and Jews:

The unbelievers ... are enemies of Allah and his messenger and are enemies of the Muslims. Allah tells us the struggle between Islam and the kufr [unbelief], between Muslims and the kaffirs, the unbelievers, is a never ending struggle ... The Christians and the Jews will never be contented until you follow their evil and corrupted evil way of life.[33]

The way forward, according to Abdullah Faisal and other extremist preachers, is jihad. Even if Muslims do not want jihad, he says,

The kaffirs are going to bring it to your doorstep ... they are killing you in Chechnya, killing you in Palestine, killing you in Iraq, every day, 24 hours a day, every day. So the days of soft Islam are over. Because the kaffirs, even if you don't want to wake up, they are making sure you wake up, by killing your men, putting your scholars in prison, raping your women, robbing you of your natural resources.[34]

Some radical Salafist thinkers, such as Anjem Choudary, the former deputy leader of Al-Muhajiroun, and the London-based jihadi theoretician Abu Bashir al-Tartusi (who retracted some of his earlier positions after the 7/7 London bombings) have criticized the use of violence against civilian targets in Britain. Their argument rests on the idea of a covenant between Britain and its Muslims inhabitants that makes terrorist attacks against British targets *haram* (forbidden by Islam).[35]

## STRATEGY

In most radical movements, ideology and strategy are closely intertwined. In al-Qaeda's view, Muslim apostate regimes survive because of U.S. and

[32] "German Taliban Mujahideen Commander Abu Ishaq al-Muhajir Responds to Proposed European Burqa Ban," Released February 8, 2010, NEFA Foundation, Charleston, SC

[33] Brandon (2008), p. 7.

[34] Ibid., p. 8.

[35] Choudary argued that Muslims in Britain live under a covenant of security, where in return for the security of their lives and wealth, they are not allowed to take the lives or wealth of anyone. Ibid., p. 21.

Western support. Therefore, undermining foreign support for these governments will lead to their collapse. The withdrawal of such support, al-Qaeda leaders believe, can be accomplished through acts of mass-casualty terrorism. The presumption is that the United States and its Western allies are materially strong but morally weak and, therefore, could be driven out of the Muslim world if the terrorists inflicted enough punishment.

In his final videotape before his arrest in Pakistan in October 2005, responding to the July 2005 London bombings, al-Suri lays out the argument for terrorism in Europe:

> Throughout the past decade, Shaykh Usama [Bin Laden] and Dr. Ayman [al-Zawahiri] have both pleaded with the U.S in particular – as well as the Western world in general – to stop their aggression on our countries and stop the ongoing occupation of our land. As we all know, our pleas went unanswered, and no one heeded our warnings. Consequently, the war began and the *mujahideen* resorted to using their weapons as the preferred means of communicating with the enemies.[36]

Britain, according to al-Suri, is the first to blame among European countries, both because of the British government's alleged harsh measures against supporters of jihad at home and because Britain joined the United States in invading Afghanistan and Iraq. In al-Suri's view, France is also a legitimate target. "I advised the commander of the Armed Islamic Group (GIA)," he stated, "to strike deep inside the French mainland in order to punish her and deter her from supporting the dictatorial military government [in Algeria] . . . I added that we had a right to strike France and that we were at war – [we were not] just playing around. It was about time for our enemies to understand that."[37]

Al-Suri called on militants within and outside Europe to act quickly and strike Britain, Italy, Holland, Denmark, Germany, Japan, Australia, Russia, France, and all other countries that have a military presence in Iraq, Afghanistan, or the Arabian Peninsula:

> If Blair, Berlusconi, and their counterparts insist on continuing this war, they should know the strategic principles that guide us, and according to which we formulate our policy . . . We consider the battle to be against a single entity that is comprised of all the allies. As far as we are concerned, America is the same as Israel, Britain, Poland, Italy, and the others. They are an alliance, and as such, they are all accountable for their actions. Each and every enemy country will be treated as a part of a larger entity, and the military and civilian components of each nation will be treated as a unified

[36] "Message to the British and the Europeans," August 2005, Global Terror Alert, at http://www.globalterroralert.com.

[37] "Abu Musab al-Suri's Final 'Message to the British and the Europeans,'" August 2005, Global Terror Alert, at http://www.globalterroralert.com.

entity. We will practice our right to strike civilians in order to deter soldiers, in light of the military and technological disadvantages that we face.[38]

In prioritizing the theaters of the global jihad, al-Suri places Europe after the Muslim world and American and allied interests in third world countries, but ahead of the U.S. homeland (even though, he says, America is "the viper's head" and "the origin of scourge and the head of the alliance"). Al-Suri cites the presence of large Muslim communities in Europe, as well as its closeness to the Arab and Islamic world and the transportation links between the two as a reason to give it priority over the United States and goes on to say,

The Muslims in those countries are like Muslims everywhere, the religious duty of jihad, of repelling their enemy and resisting him, rests in their shoulders in exactly the same way as for Muslims in their own countries. AAction in Europe and those countries must be subjected to the rules of political benefits versus political harms, judged against the positions of the European governments. At the same time, one has to adopt a strategy of winning the support of the people, and avoid harming them. I will present this in detail in the political theory of the Resistance, God willing.[39]

Al-Suri's reference to the "positions of the European governments" is revealing. Jihadi strategy seeks to exploit policy differences between the United States and its allies. A confluence of developments in recent years widened the gap between the United States and European governments and peoples on a broad range of policy issues, particularly those relating to the Middle East and counterterrorism. The reasons for the drifting apart of the United States and Europe – and rising anti-Americanism in Europe – are complicated, contested, and for the most part beyond the scope of this book. What is relevant here is that the war in Iraq and discrepancies over broader U.S. policy toward the Middle East created opportunities for Islamists to drive wedges between the United States and Europe.

On the same day as the Madrid bombings, an analyst at *Forsvarets Forskningstitutt* (FFI, the Norwegian Defense Research Establishment) found a document on an Islamic website that was thought to be a terrorist roadmap. This document was prepared by the Media Committee for Victory of the Iraqi People and was entitled "Jihadi Iraq: Hopes and Dangers." The document stated that although the insurgency would

[38] Ibid.

[39] Abu Musab al-Suri, "The Global Islamic Resistance Call (Key Excerpts)," in Brynjar Lia, *Architect of the Global Jihad: The Life of Al-Qaida Strategist Abu Mus'ab al-Suri*. New York: Columbia University Press, 2008, p. 395.

not be able to overcome the coalition forces of the United States, coalition members such as the United Kingdom, Spain, and Poland could be persuaded to drop out of the war in Iraq. The document focused on the removal of Spain from Iraq and stated that the upcoming elections in Spain had to be strategically used to force Spain out of Iraq.[40] FFI researchers consider it likely that the terrorists responsible for the Madrid bombings were familiar with the contents of the strategy document.[41]

If, in fact, the terrorists' strategy was to shape Spanish public opinion, it succeeded. Spain's Popular Party government was one of the staunchest supporters of the U.S. decision to go to war against Saddam Hussein, despite the fact that by and large the Spanish population did not support military action in Iraq. The parliamentary election, held just a few days after the Madrid bombings, ushered in a Socialist government that withdrew Spain from the U.S.-led Iraq coalition.[42]

According to Spanish analysts sympathetic to the Popular Party, the Socialist Party (PSOE) leaders brilliantly exploited the information that the bombing was the work of Islamist terrorists, while the Popular Party government was paralyzed by its belief that the Basque terrorist organization ETA was responsible. Although the Popular Party was leading in the polls just prior to the bombing, the Spanish people turned out the ruling party in large part because of the widespread belief that the government had deceived the public.[43]

The Madrid terrorists successfully targeted the fracture line between the Popular Party government and Spanish public opinion on Iraq. Rabei Osman Sayed Ahmed, alias El Egipcio, convicted in Italy in 2006 of being a member of a terrorist organization, did not hide his satisfaction with the political results of the bombing:

> In my opinion all of the countries that support the United States will end like [Spanish Prime Minister] Aznar ... I am immensely happy that the government of the dog Aznar has fallen, but my brothers, whoever supports the dog [Bush] will only reap an earthquake, and Madrid is the proof... Let us give thanks to God that

[40] Brynjar Lia and Thomas Hegghammer, *FFI Explains Al-Qaida Document.* Kjeller, Norway: Norwegian Defence Research Establishment, 2004.

[41] Petter Nesser, "Jihad in Europe: A Survey of the Motivations for Sunni Islamist Terrorism in Post-millennium Europe," FFI/RAPPORT-2004/01146, Kjeller, Norway, 2004, at http://www.ffi.no/no/Rapporter/04-01146.pdf, p. 73.

[42] John Vinocur, "Some in Europe See Spain's Turnabout as Al Qaeda Victory," *New York Times*, March 17, 2004, at http://www.nytimes.com/2004/03/17/news/17iht-a8_12.html.

[43] Discussion with Spanish terrorism analysts, Madrid, August 2005.

we have eliminated Aznar. Madrid is a lesson for Europe, that must understand that it should distance itself from the Americans.[44]

Nevertheless, it does not appear that policy on Iraq was the only reason for the attacks. Spain was explicitly designated as a target by al-Qaeda even after the election of a socialist government that pledged to withdraw Spanish forces from Iraq. Al-Qaeda spokesmen made aggressive references to al-Andalus (the medieval Muslim state in Spain) and to the Spanish enclaves of Ceuta and Melilla, which al-Zawahiri compared to the Russian occupation of Chechnya and the Israeli occupation of the Palestinian territories.[45] Spain continues to be a target of terrorists with links to militants in the tribal areas of Pakistan.

As in the case of the Madrid bombings, the London bombings could have been meant to widen the gap between the United States and its European allies. In an analysis of the London bombings, published on the evening of July 7, 2005 on the jihadi website "Barbarossa," probably Abu Abd al-Aziz, a Saudi who commanded Arab volunteers in the Bosnian war, revealed that the London attacks were meant to bring the issue of the war in Iraq once again to the core of the public debate in Britain, even though the British elections had been held two months before. According to Barbarossa, the attacks were also designed to influence an environment in which European unity had become increasingly fragile, following the rejection of the European Constitution in the referendum in France. Finally, the attacks were timed to occur in the midst of the meeting of the leaders of the G-8 in Britain. Above all, the bombings were to remind the Muslim world, not only the West, that the global jihad had a long-range strategy, and that its leaders choose the targets and the timing of the attacks.[46]

Denunciations of France in jihadi forums; at least four foiled terrorist plots in Spain since the Zapatero government withdrew Spanish troops from Iraq;[47] a train bomb plot in the fall of 2006 and the 2007 Sauerland

[44] Juzgado Central de Instrucción Número 6, Audiencia Nacional, Madrid, 75/09 (DP 263/08), Auto de Procesamiento, February 24, 2010, pp. 1325–1326.

[45] Fernando Reinares, Presentation at Terrorist Threats in Europe Panel, International Institute for Counter-Terrorism, 8th Annual International Conference, Herzliya, Israel, September 10, 2008, at https://www.youtube.com/watch?v=HgEvbDIb-9Y.

[46] Reuven Paz, "From Madrid to London: Al-Qaeda Exports the War in Iraq to Europe," GLORIA/PRISM, Occasional Papers, Vol. 3 No. 3, July 2005.

[47] Javier Jordán and Robert Wesley, "After 3/11: The Evolution of Jihadist Networks in Spain," *Terrorism Monitor*, The Jamestown Foundation, Vol. 4, Issue 1, January 12, 2006, at http://www.jamestown.org/single/?no_cache=1&tx_ttnews[tt_news]=640#.U4pj1C9woSA.

plot in Germany;[48] and plots in Italy, Belgium, and Denmark suggest that extremists are treating Europe and the West, as al-Suri averred, as a unified theater of jihad. Of course, individual terrorists threaten specific countries and may not be motivated by strategic-level considerations, but from the point of view of al-Qaeda strategists, the struggle is global and attacks in individual countries fall into a larger pattern.

[48] "Train bomb plot brings fear of terrorism to Germany," *The Times*, August 21, 2006, at http://www.thetimes.co.uk/tto/news/world/europe/article2599763.ece.

# 4

# Origins of Radical Islamist Networks in Europe

Europe's experience with Islamist terrorism started decades ago when Middle Eastern terrorist organizations established networks in Europe. The first generation of Islamist extremists in Europe consisted of asylum seekers and refugees. These were individuals who had been politically active before they arrived in Europe and brought their experience and, in some cases, their battles and political agendas with them. Some of the leading ideologues of radical Islamism in Europe fall into this category. In some cases, recent refugees turned against the host country and its culture because that country's government supported the regime they opposed or took a foreign policy stance that was inimical to their broader political values or because they became exposed to a more global agenda while in the West.

France was the first Western country to be targeted by international Middle East–based Islamist terrorist networks. France's intimate involvement in Algerian affairs caused it to be targeted by Algerian Islamist networks after the Algerian government canceled the elections in 1992 that the Islamist coalition Islamic Salvation Front (FIS) was on the verge of winning, and Algeria entered a cycle of massive terrorist and counter-terrorist violence.

The Algerian networks were built around a small group of former Algerian volunteers in the Afghan war in the 1980s and organized in the Armed Islamic Group, known as GIA, the acronym for its French name, Groupe Islamique Armé. Beginning in 1993, the GIA started to assassinate French expatriates in Algeria, 42 in all between 1993 and 1996. The French government, which closely monitored exiled Algerian Islamists on its territory, quickly responded by unleashing an all-out war against these networks. In a chilling prelude to the September 11, 2001, attacks, a GIA team hijacked an Air France flight in Algiers in December 1994. The hijacking was foiled when French special forces stormed the aircraft in Marseilles, and it was later revealed that the hijackers were planning to crash the plane in Paris, possibly into the Eiffel Tower.

In 1995 and 1996, the GIA carried out a series of bombing attacks in public squares and the transportation system, which left 12 dead and 290 injured. By this time, French counterterrorism authorities had gained substantial experience and knowledge of Islamist movements and were able to roll up these cells in short order, while tracing their funding back to prominent Algerian exiles in London such as accused terrorist financier Rachid Ramda and criminal gangs such as the Roubaix Gang, which provided financing to some GIA networks by robbing banks. The investigation into the GIA's international connections is credited with leading to the arrest on December 14, 1999, of Ahmed Ressam at the U.S.-Canadian border in Washington State with a trunk full of 120 pounds of explosives and four detonators that he planned to use in an attack against the Los Angeles airport.[1]

In the mid-1990s, French security services started collecting information on the international connections of French and Algerian GIA militants, including those with the jihadist underground in London, and they noticed the departure of many militants to Bosnia, Afghanistan, and Chechnya for military training. The interrogation of the people belonging to the Lyon cell, responsible for the terrorist acts of 1995, also revealed that they had been sending recruits to Afghanistan well before the arrival there of Osama bin Laden from Sudan in 1996. At that time, the training was provided by international elements linked to two major Afghan Islamist factions, Gulbaddin Hekmatyar's Hezb-e-Islami and Abdul Rasul Sayyaf's Ittihad-e-Islami.[2]

The tapering off of the Algerian civil war, the breakup of the GIA into several rival factions, and successful counterterrorism operations in Algeria and France essentially ended the Algerian conflict as a source of terrorism. It has, however, been replaced by a loose confederation of networks and organizations with small footprints that present increasingly difficult challenges to the counterterrorism community.

[1] Jeremy Shapiro and Suzan Bénédicte, "The French Experience of Counter-Terrorism," *Survival*, Vol. 45, No. 1, Spring 2003.
[2] Ibid.

In the 1990s, new cells with links to al-Qaeda, but operating independently, established themselves in Germany and Italy. One was the so-called Meliani cell, based in Frankfurt. Mohamed Bensakhria, the leader of this group, fled to Spain after the arrest of other cell members in Germany. He was arrested in Spain in June 2001. Four coconspirators were convicted in Germany of planning to bomb the Christmas market in Strasbourg and sentenced to prison terms of 10 to 12 years.[3] Another was the Italian cell headed by the Tunisian Essid Sami Ben Khemais and composed largely of North Africans.[4]

Djamel Beghal, a London-based Algerian Takfir wal-Hijra operative, was arrested in Dubai in September 2001 as he returned to Europe from Afghanistan on false French documents. Beghal was believed to be returning to France to give the go-ahead for a suicide attack on the U.S. embassy in Paris, using a truck bomb or even a helicopter.[5]

French intelligence has increasingly come across a new and disturbing profile: French-born Islamic militants who were recruited into jihadist networks through a strong ideological and social infrastructure. These new profiles came up in operations against the Salafist Group for Preaching and Combat (GSPC )and Takfir wal-Hijra networks that in 1998 were planning to conduct terrorist attacks against the Soccer World Cup in France.[6]

While France was battling North African terrorist groups, lenient asylum laws in the United Kingdom fostered the growth of the largest and

[3] Assaf Moghadam and Metthew Levitt, "Radical Islamist Groups in Germany: A Lesson in Prosecuting Terror in Court," February 19, 2004, at http://www.washingtoninstitute.org/templateC05.php?CID=1712.

[4] Shapiro and Bénédicte, "The French Experience of Counter-Terrorism." Khemais was arrested in Milan in April 2001 and convicted in February 2002 of criminal association with the intent to obtain and transport arms, explosives, and chemicals; he was sentenced to five years in prison.

[5] "The Secret War, Part 2" *The Observer*, September 30, 2001, at http://observer.guardian.co.uk/focus/story/0,6903,560658,00.html.

[6] Pascal Ceaux et Fabrice Lhomme, "Le procès de 24 islamistes soupçonnés d'appartenir au Takfir s'ouvre à Paris," *Le Monde*, September 28, 2001, at http://scholar.lib.vt.edu/Chronicles_Ingest/InterNews_bag/data/InterNews/LeMonde/issues/2001/monde.20010929.pdf; Alexandre Garcia, "A Paris, première audience du procès de l'affaire Mamache," *Le Monde*, October 4, 2001, at http://scholar.lib.vt.edu/Chronicles_Ingest/InterNews_bag/data/InterNews/LeMonde/issues/2001/monde.20011005.pdf; C. D., "Nos banlieues représentent un vivier de volontaires" [Interview with Alain Chouet, former DGSE official], *Le Parisien*, December 10, 2003 at http://www.leparisien.fr/une/nos-banlieues-representent-un-vivier-de-volontaires-10-12-2003-2004602162.php; Jean-Louis Bruguière, "Terrorisme; Le juge Bruguiere parle," *L'Express*, December 12, 2002, at http://www.lexpress.fr/actualite/monde/le-juge-bruguiere-parle_497342.html.

most overt concentration of Islamist political activists outside of Taliban-ruled Afghanistan.[7] Islamist radicals were attracted to London because of its role as an international financial and transportation hub, its large Muslim population, the freedom to carry out political activities, and Britain's tradition of taking in refugees and asylum seekers. Moreover, the British legal system rendered it exceedingly difficult for the authorities to extradite undesirables – even violent militants – to their home countries. British courts have repeatedly ruled that militants could not be sent back to countries where there is a death penalty or where they could not be assured fair trials.[8]

London became the international headquarters for Takfir wal-Hijra; Hizb ut-Tahrir; the Movement for Islamic Reform in Arabia (MIRA), an extreme neo-Wahhabi group that seeks the overthrow of the Saudi government; and the GIA, among others. Lebanese Hezbollah raised funds through its political arms in Great Britain, the Lebanese Welfare Committee (LWC), and the HELP Foundation, as well as through individual activists.[9] Members of the Frankfurt cell, later convicted of plotting to bomb Strasbourg's Christmas market, sought refuge in London from French authorities. An inordinate number of Europe's leading Islamist extremists, many with links to terrorist organizations, populated London during the 1980s and 1990s. More aggressive efforts by British authorities to prosecute or deport undesirable foreigners, including the introduction of new legislation, are beginning to show results. Abu Hamza al-Masri was extradited to the United States in October 2012 to face terrorism charges. In July 2013, after an eight-year legal battle, British authorities finally succeeded in deporting Abu Qatada to Jordan.

For years, Abu Qatada, a Palestinian who, according to the Spanish indictment of al-Qaeda cell members, was appointed as the spiritual leader of al-Qaeda in Europe, GIA, GSPC, and the Tunisian Islamic Combatant Group[10] gamed the system to prevent his extradition to Jordan, where he had been convicted in absentia of terror charges in 1999. In March 2013, the British home secretary lost a legal challenge to a ruling by the Special

[7] Stephen Ulph, "Londonistan," *Terrorism Monitor*, Jamestown Foundation, Vol. 2, Issue 4, February 26, 2004, at http://www.jamestown.org/terrorism/news/article.php?issue_id=2914.

[8] Mohamad Bazzi, "Britain still hub for Islamic militants," *Newsday*, April 14, 2005, at http://williamwebbdotorg.blogspot.com/2005/04/britain-still-hub-for-islamic.html.

[9] Yoni Fighel, "Londonistan," May 1, 2003, at http://212.150.54.123/articles/articledet.cfm?articleid=494.

[10] Juzgado Central de Instrucción No. 005, Madrid, Sumario (Proc. Ordinario) 0000035/2001E, Madrid, September 17, 2003.

Immigration Appeals Commission (SIAC) in November 2012 that prevented his deportation. The SIAC judges had decided there was a "real risk" that evidence from Qatada's former codefendants Abu Hawsher and Al-Hamasher, who were allegedly tortured, could be used against him at a retrial.[11] This roadblock to Qatada's deportation was removed when the UK and Jordan signed a mutual legal assistance treaty that provided that where there were "serious and credible allegations that a statement from a person has been obtained by torture" it would not be used in a court.[12]

Another case is that of Muhammad al-Massari, a Saudi exile who ran an anti-Saudi operation from London in the 1990s. During John Major's government, the British authorities assured the Saudis that al-Massari would be deported, but the authorities have not been able to find a legal way to expel him.[13] Al-Massari approved of the killing of British troops in Iraq and stated that then prime minister Blair was a legitimate target. His associate Saad al-Fagih was accused of involvement in a plot to assassinate then crown prince Abdullah of Saudi Arabia.[14]

The center of radical Islamist activity in Italy has been the Islamic Culture Institute (ICI) of Milan, established in 1988 by Egyptians, many of them members of the terrorist group al-Gama'a al-Islamiyya, who either had received asylum or were living illegally in Milan. The ICI, along with the Sahabah mosque in Vienna, another major bastion of al-Gama'a al-Islamiyya, became a center for the recruitment and logistics of fighters in the Bosnian war. The ICI provided documents, money, transportation, and logistical support for Muslim volunteers, while the mosque's imam, Anwar Shabaan, an Afghan war veteran, became the commander of the Bosnian army's Mujahideen detachment, a unit composed of Arab volunteers.[15] At the International Criminal Tribunal for the former Yugoslavia war crimes trial of former Bosnian army commander General Rasim Delić, the defense

[11] David Barrett, "Government loses latest bid to deport Abu Qatada," *The Telegraph*, March 27, 2013, at http://www.telegraph.co.uk/news/uknews/terrorism-in-the-uk/9956799/Government-loses-latest-bid-to-deport-Abu-Qatada.html.

[12] "Abu Qatada deported from UK," *The Guardian*, July 7, 2013, at http://www.theguardian.com/world/2013/jul/07/abu-qatada-deported-from-uk.

[13] Paul Reynolds, "The last days of Londonistan," *BBC News*, July 27, 2005, at http://news.bbc.co.uk/2/hi/uk_news/politics/4720603.stm.

[14] "Profile: Mohammed al-Massari," History Commons, at http://www.historycommons.org/entity.jsp?entity=mohammed_al-massari__1.

[15] Lorenzo Vidino, "Islam, Islamism and Jihadism in Italy," Current Trends in Islamist Ideology, Vol. 7, 2008, Hudson Institute, Center on Islam, Democracy and the Future of the Muslim World, August 4, 2008, at http://www.hudson.org/content/researchattachments/attachment/1173/20081111_ct7.pdf.

alleged that the Mujahideen detachment cooperated with the Bosnian army but was not under its command and control. Delić's defense told the court that Shaaban was the real authority in the unit and that combat reports were sent to the ICI in Milan and to al-Qaeda.[16]

According to terrorism researcher Evan Kohlmann, French counterterrorism officials concluded that the ICI in Milan served as a command center for a variety of North African armed militant groups including al-Gama'a al-Islamiyya and the GIA. After searching Anwar Shaaban's office at the ICI, Italian counterterrorism police concurred that the institute was involved with Egyptian terrorist organizations, the recruiting of fighters for the Balkan conflict, the establishment of a European network of radical cells, and logistic and operational support to armed cells in Egypt.[17]

After Shaaban was killed in an ambush by Croatian troops in December 1995, the network he had established in Italy and Bosnia-Herzegovina continued to operate under the leadership of Algerian commander Abu el-Ma'ali, aka Abdelkader Mokhtari, and Fateh Kamel, aka "Mustapha the Terrorist," an Algerian who acquired Canadian citizenship in 1993. Kamel is believed to have been a key liaison and coordinator between European terrorist sleeper cells and senior al-Qaeda commanders based in Bosnia and Afghanistan and GIA and GSPC operatives, and he was connected to the masterminds of the 1995 Paris metro bombings.[18]

Algerian and Moroccan groups, particularly the Moroccan Islamic Combatant Group (GICM) and a group that has been labeled Salafiya Jihadia, the groups considered responsible for the Casablanca bombings of May 16, 2003, played an important role in early radical Islamist networks in Spain.[19] In 1997, the Spanish police arrested 15 Algerians linked to the GIA in Valencia and Barcelona. The function of this cell was logistics:

[16] The relevant cases at the International Criminal Tribunal for the Former Yugoslavia are known as "Hadžihasanović and Kubura," "Sefer Halilović," and "Rasim Delić." Delić was convicted of "failing to take the necessary and reasonable measures to prevent and punish the crimes of cruel treatment committed by the El Mujahed Detachment (EMD)... in the village of Livade and in the Kamenica Camp [central Bosnia] in July and August 1995"; he was sentenced to three years in prison. "Bosnian war crimes defendant blames al-Qaeda," October 6, 2008, at http://www.ww4report.com/node/6122.

[17] Evan F. Kohlmann, *Al-Qaida's Jihad in Europe*." Oxford and New York: Berg, 2004, pp. 22, 185–188.

[18] Ibid.

[19] The Casablanca bombings of May 16, 2003, killed 45 people including four Spanish tourists. One of the targets was a Spanish social club, the Casa de España. The majority of the bombers were Moroccans from the Sidi Moumen slums recruited by Salafi radicals. According to one analyst, Salafiya Jihadia is a label given by the Moroccan authorities to various jihadist strands. Alison Pargeter, "The Islamist Movement in Morocco," *Terrorism*

securing funds through petty crime to buy arms and dual-use equipment for militants in Algeria.[20]

Many individuals were recruited in various mosques near Muslim population centers in Spain. Once individuals were recruited, they were sent to training camps in Afghanistan and Indonesia, and later to fight in Chechnya, Bosnia, and Kashmir. There was also a link to the al-Qaeda network in Indonesia. One of the suspected members of an al-Qaeda cell arrested in Madrid in 2001, Luis José Gallant González, aka Yusuf Gallant, a convert to Islam, allegedly received military training at a camp in Indonesia. When Gallant was arrested at his Madrid home, the police found guns, ammunition, knives, a bulletproof vest, forged identification documents, travel documents to Indonesia, and photographs apparently taken at the Indonesian training camp. The camp in question was located near Poso, in Central Sulawesi, an area that was the scene of violent communal conflict from 2000 to 2002.[21]

In 1994, Chej Salah, a Palestinian with a Jordanian passport and a falsified Spanish one, established and led an al-Qaeda cell in Spain. Shortly after the cell was established, Chej Salah was relocated to Pakistan to facilitate the movement of militants from around the world to the training camps in Afghanistan. In 1995, Imad Eddin Barakat Yarkas, aka Abu Dahdah, a Spanish citizen of Syrian origin, was named as Salah's successor to lead the al-Qaeda cell in Spain. He remained in this position until the breakup of the cell and his own incarceration in November 2001. Abu Dahdah was a member of the Syrian Muslim Brotherhood, one of the most radical branches of the organization. He originally came to Spain to attend college but ended up in business as a merchant and began recruiting "like-minded" individuals, who would later fight in Chechnya, Bosnia, and Afghanistan.[22] Salah maintained close contact with Abu Dahdah while in Pakistan, helping new recruits from Spain attend the training camps in Afghanistan and return to Spain for incorporation into the Spanish cell.

*Monitor*, the Jamestown Foundation, Vol. 3, Issue 10, May 19, 2005, at http://www.jamestown.org/single/?tx_ttnews[tt_news]=483#.U4uEWC9woSA.

[20] Jordán, Mañas, and Horsburgh (2008). We do not include in this category attacks by Palestinian groups or state-sponsored terrorism. In 1985, a bomb explosion at a restaurant near the U.S. air base of Torrejón killed 18 persons and injured 100. A group named Jihad claimed responsibility, but there were no arrests and little is known about the parties responsible for the attack.

[21] "Looking for SE Asia's Own Carlos the Jackal," *Jakarta Post*, January 30, 2002, at http://adesiboro.weebly.com/looking-for-se-asias-own-carlos-the-jackal.html.

[22] Daniel Woolls, "Spanish al-Qaida suspect denies helping to plot Sept 11 attacks," *Associated Press Worldstream*, April 25, 2005, at http://www.highbeam.com/doc/1P1-107848802.html.

This Spanish cell is believed to have facilitated a meeting in the Tarragona region of Spain between 9/11 operational leader Mohammed Atta and Ramzi Binalshibh, an Atta associate being held by the United States at Guantanamo Bay.[23]

Although not all of the individuals in the Spanish cell were indoctrinated in Spain, almost all have links to Abu Dahdah. For instance, one of the key figures in the March 11, 2004, Madrid bombings, Amer Azizi, also known as Osman al-Andalusi, is believed to have been one of those who helped organize the meeting between Atta and Binalshibh. Azizi's contact information was found in the possession of Zacarias Moussaoui, the first person associated with the 9/11 attacks who has stood trial in the United States. Azizi is further linked to the late arch-terrorist Abu Musab al-Zarqawi and is known to have had contacts with key figures in the Casablanca bombings who are currently in prison. These include Abdelatif Mourafik, Abdelaziz Benyaich, Salaheddin Benyaich, Mustafa Maymouni, and Driss Chebli.[24] Azizi was killed, together with al-Qaeda's external operations chief Hamza Rabia and three other militants, in a U.S. Hellfire missile strike in North Waziristan on December 1, 2005.[25]

Abu Dahdah also formed an important relationship with Abu Qatada.[26] Dahdah's network also regularly interacted with militants in Germany through Mamoun Darkazanli and Haydar Zammar, two members of the Syrian Muslim Brotherhood, and the Moroccan Said al-Hajji, in Italy through Muhammad the Egyptian, and in Belgium through Tariq al-Maarufi.[27] (Maarufi was allegedly involved in providing falsified Belgian passports to two men who later assassinated Northern Alliance leader Ahmed Shah Massoud on behalf of bin Laden.[28])

[23] The 9/11 Commission Report cites Binalshibh's statement that he and Atta did not meet anyone while in Spain, p. 244. However, Magistrate Garzón's indictment of the al-Qaeda cell in Madrid states that an Algerian member of the Spanish cell, Mohammed Belfatmi, supported the visit of Atta and Binalshibh. The indictment also links Barakat Yarkas (Abu Dahdah) and two other key Spanish cell figures, Driss Chebli and Amer al-Azizi, to the Atta-Binalshibh visit. See Juzgado Central de Instrucción, Sumario, pp. 318–324. The relationship between Atta and Abu Dahdah was verified when Abu Dahdah's contact information was found in Atta's Hamburg apartment.

[24] Juzgado Central de Instrucción No. 005 Madrid, Sumario (Proc. Ordinario) 0000035/2001E, September 17, 2003, pp. 63, 267–268.

[25] Fernando Reinares, "The Madrid Bombings and Global Jihadism," *Survival*, Vol. 52, No. 2, April-May 2010.

[26] Juzgado Central de Instrucción, Sumario 0000035/2001E.

[27] Bale, 2009, p. 41.

[28] Brynjar Lia, *Architect of Global Jihad: The Life of Al-Qaida Strategist Abu Mus'ab al-Suri*. New York: Columbia University Press, 2008, p. 118, footnote 41.

During the mid-1990s, Abu Dahdah also met Mustafa Setmariam Nasar, aka Abu Musab al-Suri, a Syrian settled in Spain who later became the leading theoretician of the decentralized global jihad.[29] While Nasar was living in Madrid, his children and those of Abu Dahdah attended the same school in a nearby mosque.[30] In 1995, Abu Dahdah accompanied Nasar and his Spanish wife Elena when they moved from Madrid to London. In London, Nasar became an associate of Abu Qatada and began to edit the *Al Ansar* magazine, a GIA publication. In January 1997, Nasar founded the Islamic Conflict Studies Bureau. His co-director was Mohamed Bahiah, an al-Qaeda courier for Afghanistan.[31]

Between 1997 and 2001, Nasar moved to Afghanistan to command two al-Qaeda training camps and became a member of the al-Qaeda *shura* or council. After the fall of the Taliban, he fled to Pakistan and went underground. His 1,600-page road map to global jihad entitled *Da'wat al-Muqawamah al-Islamiya al-Alamiya* (Call for international Islamic resistance), which called for international resistance by many unrelated cells, appears to have resonated with Islamist radicals in the West. Nasar was captured in the Pakistani city of Quetta on October 31, 2005.[32] After apparently being held in Diego Garcia, he was transferred to Syria, his country of origin, under the rendition program. In February 2012, there were reports that he was released from prison by the al-Assad government, possibly as a warning to the United States and the West.[33]

Abu Dahdah and other members of his cell were arrested in November 2001 on charges of involvement in the planning of the 9/11 attacks. Around this time, Rabei Osman Sayed Ahmed,[34] an immigrant from Egypt, arrived in Spain and started a group with his fellow North Africans and other individuals with extremist Islamic ideologies.[35] These individuals included Amer Azizi, Jamal Zougam, and Sarhane Ben

[29] Murad Batal al- Shishani. "Abu Mus'ab al-Suri and the Third Generation of Salafi-Jihadists," *Terrorism Monitor*, Vol. 3 Issue 16, The Jamestown Foundation, August 15, 2005, at http://www.jamestown.org/single/?no_cache=1&tx_ttnews[tt_news]=547#.U4uJvi9woSA. See al-Suri's biography in Lia (2008), *Architect of Global Jihad*.

[30] Woolls, "Spanish al-Qaida suspect denies helping to plot Sept 11 attacks."

[31] Nick Fielding and Gareth Welsh, "Mastermind of Madrid is key figure," *The Sunday London Times*, July 10, 2005, p. 5, at http://www.thesundaytimes.co.uk/sto/news/uk_news/article140680.ece.

[32] Lia (2008), pp. 343–345.

[33] Aaron Y. Zelyn, "Free Radical," *Foreign Policy*, February 3, 2012, at http://www.foreignpolicy.com/articles/2012/02/03/free_radical.

[34] Also referred to as Usman Rabay, or "Muhammad the Egyptian."

[35] "Spain asks Italy for bomb suspect," *CBS News from the Associated Press*, June 11, 2004, at http://www.cbsnews.com/stories/2004/11/16/world/printable656001.shtml.

Abdelmajid Fakhet, all known followers of Abu Dahdah and key players in the Madrid train bombings of March 11, 2004.[36]

As in the case of other European countries during this period, Spanish authorities assumed that the purpose of Islamist terrorist cells in Spain was to support operations outside of Spanish territory. The bombing of the Djerba synagogue in Tunisia in April 2002, for instance, was partially financed from Spain by Pakistanis who ran a telephone shop in Logroño.[37] This perception began to change after the Casablanca attacks, when some Spanish intelligence officials and analysts began to suspect that Spain might be a target of terrorism.[38] In a paper published by the Real Instituto Elcano on October 13, 2003, Spanish terrorism expert Javier Jordán wrote that Spain had to assume that terrorists could carry out an attack within the country and that the consequences could be grave.[39] In fact, in a recording released on October 18, 2003, bin Laden explicitly threatened that al-Qaeda reserved the right "to respond at the appropriate time and place against all of the countries that are participating in this unjust war [in Iraq], especially Great Britain, Spain, Australia, Poland, Japan, and Italy."[40]

## GATEWAYS TO VIOLENT EXTREMISM

Beyond terrorist groups, there are ostensibly nonviolent or apolitical organizations and movements in Europe that have functioned as gateways to violent extremism. One of these is Tablighi Jamaat, a *da'wa* (proselytizing) movement founded in India 75 years ago with millions of adherents worldwide. Tablighi Jamaat's goal is the moral improvement of its adherents through a return to original Islamic values.[41] Most Tablighi practice,

[36] CBS News, "The Madrid Bombings" and "Madrid: The Prime Suspect," *The Fifth Estate: War Without Borders*, December 1, 2004, at http://www.cbc.ca/fifth/warwithoutborders/bombing.html; and http://www.cbc.ca/fifth/warwithoutborders/suspect.html.

[37] Fernando Reinares, Presentation at Terrorist Threats in Europe Panel, International Institute for Counter-Terrorism, Eighth Annual International Conference, Herzliya, Israel, September 10, 2008.

[38] Interview with Spanish intelligence analysts, Madrid, September 2005.

[39] Jordán (2003).

[40] Cited in Haizam Amirah Fernández, "El M-11 en la estrategia 'yihadista'," Real Instituto Elcano (Madrid), July 15, 2004, at http://www.belt.es/expertos/HOME2_experto.asp?id=2103.

[41] This practice is criticized by more doctrinaire Salafis, who say that it is not grounded in the Quran and the Sunna.

while conservative, is quietist and apolitical. There are, however, certain segments of the movement that have assimilated a more militant ideology. According to a report on Tablighi Jamaat, the movement "attracts angry people – people who need absolutes, who can't stand the grayness of life."[42] *The Times* of London reported that graduates of Tablighi Jamaat's most influential seminary near Bury expressed deep hatred of *kuffars* (infidels) and Western society, admiration for the Taliban and a zeal for martyrdom. The seminary outlaws art, television, music, chess, and sports and demands complete concealment of women. Bury graduates reportedly have praised the 9/11 attacks and lamented that the "j-word" has become taboo.[43]

José Padilla and John Walker Lindh are two Western converts who were initially influenced by Tabighi Jamaat. Lindh came in contact with the movement and was directed to a madrassa in Pakistan where he fell in with the Taliban. Some individuals in the United Kingdom who transitioned from Tablighi Jamaat to terrorism include two of the London bombers, Mohammed Siddique Khan and Shehzad Tanweer; Assad Arwar and Abdulla Ahmed Ali, ringleaders of the 2006 transatlantic airline liquid bomb plot; and the Glasgow car bomber, Kafeel Ahmed.[44] The extremist Rachid Laoudi, an associate of Pakistan-based European jihadist Moez Garsallaoui, began frequenting a Tablighi mosque in Trappes, near Paris, after being released from prison. German Taliban Mujahideen militant Rami Makanesi also rediscovered Islam at a Tablighi Jamaat seminar in a Frankfurt mosque.

In Spain, segments of the movement assimilated a more militant ideology through contacts in Pakistan and elsewhere. Hamed Abderrahman, a Tablighi from Ceuta linked to the terrorist cell controlled by Abu Dahdah, used the excuse of attending a Tablighi madrassa in Pakistan as a cover to join a terrorist training camp in Afghanistan. Abu Dahdah's cell used the Tablighi network in Madrid to recruit sympathizers, including some of the participants in the March 11, 2004, Madrid train bombings. Aziz el-Bakri, a

[42] Susan Sachs, "A Muslim missionary group draws new scrutiny in U.S.," *New York Times Online*, July 14, 2003, at http://www.nytimes.com/2003/07/14/us/a-muslim-missionary-group-draws-new-scrutiny-in-us.html.

[43] Andrew Norfolk, "Hardliner takeover of British mosques," *The Times Online*, September 7, 2007, at http://www.thetimes.co.uk/tto/faith/article2098578.ece.

[44] Andrew Norfolk, "Muslim group behind 'mega-mosque' seeks to convert all Britain," *The Times Online*, September 10, 2007, at http://www.thetimes.co.uk/tto/faith/article2098589.ece.

Moroccan killed in Iraq in April 2003, was involved with the Tablighi network in Barcelona. Another Tablighi, Mohamed Srifi Nali, was arrested in December 2005 for allegedly recruiting members of the Tablighi communities in Malaga and Seville for suicide bombing missions in Iraq, Chechnya, Kashmir, and other conflict zones.[45]

Hizb ut-Tahrir (HuT), the Party of Liberation, is a global revivalist Islamist movement that seeks to take power in Muslim-majority countries, followed by armed struggles to take control in other states and establish a global caliphate *(Khilafah)*.[46] In the West, the group rejects integration and commands that Western Muslims disengage from mainstream political systems. At the same time, HuT tries to present its worldview as the Islamic norm and as a legitimate alternative to liberal democracy. To do this, HuT seeks to highlight real and perceived failures of Western institutions and offers the caliphate and a *shar'ia*-based legal system as a superior basis for society.[47]

HuT has been banned in Germany for distributing anti-Semitic propaganda, but it is legal in other European countries such as the United Kingdom, the Netherlands, and Denmark. The de facto headquarters of HuT is in London. The British section of HuT, Hizb ut-Tahir Britain (HTB), produces literature for worldwide distribution and hosts branch websites from all over the world. In the United Kingdom, the group has created front organizations and launched single-issue campaigns to propagate its ideology. The group has been particularly active in the greater London area, where it has staged numerous public events, including several anti–Afghanistan war protests in 2009 and 2010 and in the Midlands, particularly in Birmingham. It also conducts aggressive outreach through the Internet and social media.[48] When Germany banned the organization in January 2003, after having kept it under close observation for several years, German Interior Minister Schily explained that in the judgment of

[45] Athena Intelligence, "Movimientos musulmanes y prevención del yihadismo en España: La Yama'a Al-Tabligh Al-Da'wa," Athena Paper, Vol. 2, No. 1, Artículo 3/4, March 27, 2007, at http://www.isn.ethz.ch/Digital-Library/Publications/Detail/?ots591=0c54e3b3-1e9c-be1e-2c24-a6a8c7060233&lng=en&id=47230

[46] Houriyah Ahmed and Hannah Stuart, "Hizb ut-Tahrir: Ideology and Strategy," The Centre for Social Cohesion, London: 2009, at http://henryjacksonsociety.org/wp-content/uploads/2013/01/HIZB.pdf.

[47] Houriya Ahmed and Hannah Stuart, "Profile: Hizb ut-Tahrir in the UK," *Current Trends in Islamist Ideology*, Vol. 10, Hudson Institute, August 2010, at http://www.hudson.org/content/researchattachments/attachment/1293/ahmed_stuart.pdf.

[48] Ibid.

the German courts, "this organization promotes the use of violence to achieve political goals and wants to provoke violence."[49]

Some analysts have called HuT a conveyor belt for terrorism because the ideology that the group promotes is compatible with that of violent extremist groups. Britain's Centre for Social Cohesion reports that a number of violent Islamist groups in the Middle East have been inspired by HuT ideology and that former members have gone on to commit terrorist acts.[50] Omar Khan Sharif, one of the perpetrators of the April 30, 2003, bombing of Mike's Place bar in Tel Aviv, regularly attended HuT meetings while attending King's College in London and was described as "'squarely' with HuT" by a college classmate.[51] Ahmed Omar Sheikh, one of four militants convicted in Pakistan of the murder of *Wall Street Journal* reporter Daniel Pearl, was reportedly involved with HuT as a student at the London School of Economics.[52] An ex-member of HuT said he directly recruited young men to fight overseas. The former Midlands recruiting chief for HuT claims that six of the students that he recruited, including two brothers from Birmingham, went to fight for the Taliban against British forces in Afghanistan.[53]

Al Muhajiroun (the Emigrants), a British splinter of HuT led by Omar Bakri Mohammed, and its successor organizations have been linked to numerous terrorist incidents in the UK and abroad. In 2003, two followers, Omar Sharif (who, as noted earlier, was also associated with HuT) and Asif Hanif, carried out the suicide bombing attack on Mike's Place in Tel Aviv. Sharif and Hanif were also linked to Mohammed Siddique Khan, the ringleader of the 7/7 London bombings. Five Al Muhajiroun members, Omar Khyam, Waheed Mahmood, Jawad Akbar, Salahuddin Amin, and Anthony Garcia, were arrested in connection with Operation Crevice, the first major terrorist plot targeting the UK after 9/11.

[49] Peter Finn, "Germany bans Islamic group; recruitment of youths worried officials," *The Washington Post*, January 16, 2003.

[50] Houriya Ahmed and Hanna Stuart, "Hizb ut-Tahrir: Ideology and Strategy," The Centre for Social Cohesion, London, 2009.

[51] Shiv Malik, "NS Profile – Omar Sharif," *New Statesman*, April 24, 2006, at http://www.newstatesman.com/node/153081 Sharif fled the scene after his bomb failed to detonate and apparently drowned.

[52] "Radical Islam on UK Campuses: A Comprehensive List of Extremist Speakers at UK Universities," London: Centre for Social Cohesion, 2010, p. 4, at http://henryjacksonsociety.org/wp-content/uploads/2013/01/RADICAL-ISLAM-ON-CMAPUS.pdf.

[53] Ben Goldby, "Birmingham brothers fighting for the Taliban," *Sunday Mercury*, December 6, 2009, reproduced in *Birmingham Mail*, December 6, 2009, at http://www.birminghammail.co.uk/news/local-news/birmingham-brothers-fighting-for-taliban-244455.

Mohammed Junaid Babar, the Pakistani American who had helped establish Al Muhajiroun in the United States, identified Khyam and Siddique Khan as having traveled together to al-Qaeda training camps from Al Muhajiroun safe houses in Pakistan.[54]

After the arrest of the fertilizer bomb plotters in March 2004, Al Muhajiroun disbanded but was not officially banned by the authorities. Omar Bakri left Britain for Lebanon after the 7/7 bombings and was subsequently banned from the UK. Two successor organizations, The Saved Sect and al-Ghuraba, were proscribed, but Al Muhajiroun was left off the list because it had already disbanded. Anjem Choudary, one of Omar Bakri's acolytes, revived Al Muhajiroun as Islam4UK in 2008. The group's media exhorted followers to rise up to demand *shari'a* and reject secular law and democracy. Islam4UK achieved great notoriety when it announced a march through Wooton Basset, where the bodies of British soldiers killed in Afghanistan were repatriated. The British government banned the group and a number of its successor organizations in January 2010.[55]

## POOL OF RADICAL SYMPATHIZERS IN EUROPEAN MUSLIM COMMUNITIES

Extremist and terrorist groups do not exist in a vacuum. They are embedded in communities where they can develop the support infrastructure that they require to subsist and operate. They can take advantage of existing networks of mosques and cultural associations. They can also exploit the communities' disconnect from the authorities of the host government and latent sympathies for their agenda to find a safe haven right in the heart of Western Europe. For instance, after the murder of Dutch film maker Theo Van Gogh, it was learned that the members of the Muslim community had been aware of the plans of the assassin, Mohammad Bouyeri, but had not seen fit to warn the authorities and that a trusted translator in the Dutch intelligence service, AIVD (Algemene Inlichtingen- en Veiligheidsdienst

[54] See Raffaello Pantucci, "The Tottenham Ayatollah and the Hook-Handed Cleric: An Examination of All Their Jihadi Children," Studies in Conflict and Terrorism, Vol. 33 No. 3, 2010, at http://www.tandfonline.com/doi/abs/10.1080/10576100903555770.

[55] Raffaello Pantucci, "Ban on U.K. Radical Islamist Group Al-Muhajiroun Raises Free Speech Questions," *Terrorism Monitor* Volume 8 Issue 3, Jamestown Foundation, January 21, 2010, at http://www.jamestown.org/single/?no_cache=1&tx_ttnews[tt_news]=35936.

[General Intelligence and Security Service]), was in cahoots with this cell and had been leaking security information to the group.[56]

The concept of "support" does not necessarily mean active support on the part of the population, but some degree of tolerance or indifference – for instance, an unwillingness to report suspicious activities to the authorities. A degree of tolerance on the part of Muslim communities or some sectors of those communities, therefore, constitutes a critical variable in explaining the growth of Islamist extremism and terrorism in Europe. Extremists are more likely to develop and penetrate a community if the population abides by a set of social norms that are either similar to or at least can be manipulated by the extremists.

Positive attitudes toward extremists vary from country to country, but appear to be highest in the UK. A 2008 survey commissioned by the Centre for Social Cohesion found that 32 percent of the Muslim students polled and 60 percent of those who were active in Islamic societies polled believed that it is acceptable to kill in the name of religion.[57] Even if the pool of sympathizers who agree with the terrorists' goals and methods is small, it could have significant security implications. Even a support level of just 1 percent in a national Muslim community of 3.4 million (Germany) or 1 million (Spain) represents a substantial and potentially dangerous level. (The 1 percent figure is difficult to demonstrate empirically, but it is consistent with the assessments of some European intelligence agencies.)

[56] Marcel Michelson, "Dutch accuse translator of leaking agency secrets," Reuters, January 10, 2005, at http://legacy.utsandiego.com/news/world/20050110-0707-security-dutch-translator.html.

[57] "One third of British Muslim students say it's acceptable to kill for Islam," *Daily Mail*, July 28, 2008, http://www.dailymail.co.uk/news/article-1038953/One-British-Muslim-students-say-acceptable-kill-Islam.html.

# 5

# Radicalization Patterns

Islamist radicalization and recruitment patterns in Europe reflect the ethnic composition of a country's Muslim population. In a way similar to the Algerians in France who link their violence to the legacy of France's colonial occupation of Algeria, Britain's Muslim militants had previously focused their violence on one specific cause: Kashmir. For years, young British Muslim males would travel to Pakistan to take part in the Kashmiri conflict. The specific regional focus on Kashmir and South Asia shifted in the 1990s to include the conflict in Bosnia-Herzegovina as well as other conflicts such as those in Yemen and East Africa, but conflict, nevertheless, remained tied to local causes. That focus has now broadened and converged with al-Qaeda's global agenda.

Within the broader European Muslims communities, certain populations appear to be more vulnerable than others to radicalization and recruitment into terrorist groups. The population segments that have been particularly susceptible to radicalization and recruitment into violent groups include (1) disaffected second- or third-generation British Muslims of South Asian, largely Pakistani, descent; (2) first- or second-generation North Africans settled on the Continent; (3) converts. Until recently, the Turkish community appeared resistant to radicalization, but there are now signs of incipient radicalization among ethnic Turks born in Europe.

## SECOND-GENERATION EXTREMISTS

The propensity of some second-generation Muslims in countries with established Muslim communities to join extremist movements is especially alarming not only because it signals a profound rejection of societal values by individuals raised and educated in the West but also because these homegrown terrorists present a particularly difficult counterterrorism challenge. Unlike foreign extremists who settle in Europe, many of whom have a traceable history of violence and can be monitored by the police and the intelligence agencies, homegrown terrorists tend to be unknown to the authorities until they strike.

But not always. London bomber Mohammed Siddique Khan had come to the attention of the authorities in connection with one of the earlier terrorist plots in the UK, but he was discounted as unimportant. The BBC later interviewed an individual whom it called "Jamal," a close friend of an unnamed "UK-based terrorist suspect." Jamal claimed to have been shown transcripts and photographs (presumably by British intelligence) of a meeting between Khan and the suspect in 2004. Following that suspect's arrest in 2004, Jamal says that Khan contacted him twice. Khan probed Jamal about the information the intelligence services had extracted from the detained individual, apparently in an effort to find out if his own cover had been compromised.[1]

Spanish investigating magistrate Baltazar Garzón told a conference in Florence, Italy, that this second generation of extremists, some of them as young as 16, have in many cases no history of affiliation with al-Qaeda or other established terror groups. Rather than being organized in discrete cells, these second-generation jihadists tended to form loose constellations defined, as Garzón put it, by "the system of personal relationships among the members." For these new, looser networks, "Al-Qaida is an ideological reference point, not a real articulated structure with a command chain." Because these youngsters often have no history of connection to extremist groups, intelligence and law enforcement agencies can remain unaware of their existence.[2] However, closer examination of British-born Muslims

[1] Paul Tumelty, "New Developments Following the London Bombings," Jamestown Foundation, *Terrorism Monitor*, Vol. 3, Issue 23, December 2, 2005, at http://www.jamestown.org/programs/tm/single/?tx_ttnews[tt_news]=622&tx_ttnews[backPid]=180&no_cache=1#.U5JTTiRBxQY.

[2] "Eurojihadis: A new generation of terror," UPI, June 3, 2005, at http://www.upi.com/Business_News/Security-Industry/2005/06/02/Eurojihadis-A-new-generation-of-terror/UPI-25501117712045/. The linkage of the July 7 London bombings to al-Qaeda was established through the last will and testament of Mohammad Sidique Khan, broadcast on al-Jazeera. In a second message on the same tape, al-Qaeda's second in command Ayman al-Zawahiri claimed responsibility for the bombings. "London bomber video aired on TV," *BBC News* (UK edition), September 2, 2005, at http://news.bbc.co.uk/2/hi/uk_news/4206708.stm.

involved in terrorist plots in the United Kingdom almost always show connections to militants in Pakistan.

On the surface, the profile of European second-generation Muslim extremists goes against the stereotype of economically marginalized Muslims. Notably, both Mohammad Bouyeri, the assassin of Dutch film maker Theo Van Gogh, and London bomber Mohammed Sidique Khan had initially taken what appeared to be constructive approaches to the problems of Muslims in European societies: the first by working on youth-mentoring activities, organizing sports events and writing for a community center newsletter; and the second by running youth programs in a local school. Nevertheless, both became radicalized through exposure to extremist preachers and eventually turned to violence. According to a German counterterrorism official, the individuals arrested in connection with the Islamic Jihad Union (IJU) plot in Germany were as well integrated, in some ways, as many Germans.[3] Former German Interior Ministry Planning Director Markus Kerber notes that the most common profile of the terrorist is not the marginalized individual, but the young man of middle-class origin who believes he deserves better.[4]

There is broad agreement among analysts of radical Islam in Europe that radicalization of second-generation Muslims is often driven by social and personal grievances and issues of identity: some second-generation Muslims find it difficult to fit within either the traditional culture of their parents or the modern Western culture of the countries where they reside. Extreme Salafist ideologies offer a new identity that allows the individual to identify with the *umma* or worldwide Muslim community.[5] According to Petter Nesser, some become "born again Muslims" and are radicalized during transitional stages in their lives.[6]

### Second-Generation British Muslims of South Asian Ancestry

Second-generation British Muslims of Pakistani origin are responsible for the majority of terrorist acts by British Muslims outside of Great Britain

[3] Discussion with Federal Chancery official, Berlin, June 2008.

[4] Discussion with Markus Kerber, Berlin, June 2008.

[5] This view is derived from discussions at the RAND Institute for Middle East Youth (IMEY) Conference on Positive Options to Deter Youth Radicalism, Washington, DC, September 22, 2005; and Robert Leiken's presentation at the Washington Institute for Near East Studies 2005 Weinberg Founders Conference, Panel III, "Islamist Threat in and from Europe," September 24, 2005.

[6] Petter Nesser, presentation, IMEY Conference, Washington, DC, September 22, 2005.

and in Great Britain itself. The April 2003 Tel Aviv nightclub suicide bombing was carried out by two British-born Muslims of Pakistani ancestry. The following were also British-born Muslims of Pakistani ancestry: Ahmed Omar Sheikh, implicated in the murder of Daniel Pearl; all but one of the individuals implicated in Dhiren Barot's al-Qaeda-linked plot to bomb targets in the United States and the UK, which included the use of limousines packed with explosives and radioactive "dirty" bombs;[7] eight of the nine men arrested in March 2004 in connection with a plot to carry out massive truck-bomb attacks across London; three of the four suicide bombers implicated in the London transportation system bombings of July 7, 2005; and most of the individuals charged in the transatlantic airline bombing plot of August 2006.

Table 5.1 lists British Muslims of South Asian ancestry linked to terrorist incidents. The sample is not exhaustive. It consists of individuals suspected of involvement in major terrorist events in the UK or organized in the UK on whom there is adequate data on educational, occupational, and social status.[8]

Figure 5.1 represent the overall age range of the individuals in Table 5.1. A total of 30 individuals were included in the assessment with missing data for only one. Two-thirds (67 percent) of the members of this population were in their twenties at the time of their arrest or plotting.

Figure 5.2 shows that this same group of individuals was fairly equally divided between married and unmarried individuals (54 percent to 46 percent). Among those who were married, 71 percent had children.[9] None of those who were unmarried had children.

Figure 5.3 represents educational and employment status for the second-generation British terrorism suspects on our list. Education and occupation are the most difficult details to pin down, primarily because of a lack of or contradictory reporting. Of the 31 individuals in this dataset, we were unable to confirm the education status of about 7. For the 24 about whom we do have information, more than three-quarters (79 percent) had at least begun college, although many never attended for more than one year. Twenty-nine percent received a bachelor's degree.

[7] The exception was Barot himself, a Hindu covert to Islam.

[8] These include the bombing of Mike's Place in Tel Aviv, April 2003; Dhiren Barot's "dirty bomb" plot (police codename "Operation Rhyme"); the 2004 plot to a carry out a series of massive truck-bomb attacks across London (police codename "Operation Crevice"); the London transportation system bombings of July 7, 2005; and the 2006 transatlantic aircraft bomb plot.

[9] Data were missing for two individuals.

TABLE 5.1 *Second-Generation British Terrorism Suspects of South Asian Ancestry*[a]

| Name | Country of Ancestry | Age | Alleged Terrorist Association | Family status/ children | Occupation | Education |
|---|---|---|---|---|---|---|
| 1. Ahmed Omar Saeed Sheikh[b] | Pakistan | 29 | Murder of Daniel Pearl, Jan. 2002 | Married/1 | ISI agent (alleged) | Some college, statistics |
| 2. Asif Mohammed Hanif[c] | Pakistan | 21 | Bombing of Mike's Place, Tel Aviv, April 2003 | Single | Heathrow airport duty free shop (part time) | Some college (Arabic studies at University of Damascus) |
| 3. Omar Khan Sharif[d] | Pakistan | 28 | Bombing of Mike's Place, Tel Aviv, April 2003 | Married/2 | Call center operator | Some college, multimedia information systems |
| 4. Mohammed Naveed Bhatti[e] | Pakistan | 25 | Dhiren Barot's "dirty bomb" plot ("Operation Rhyme") | Unknown | Postgraduate student | First-class degree in systems engineering |
| 5. Junade Feroze[f] | Pakistan | 31 | Dhiren Barot's "dirty bomb" plot ("Operation Rhyme") | Married/ 3 | Car dealer; family owned a garage | Unknown |
| 6. Zia ul-Haq[g] | Pakistan | 28 | Dhiren Barot's "dirty bomb" plot ("Operation Rhyme") | Unknown | Chartered surveyor | Degree in architecture |
| 7. Abdul Aziz Jalil[h] | Pakistan | 34 | Dhiren Barot's "dirty bomb" plot ("Operation Rhyme") | Single | Plasterer | Studied for degree in information systems |

| | | | | | | |
|---|---|---|---|---|---|---|
| 8. Omar Rehman[i] | | 23 | Dhiren Barot's "dirty bomb" plot ("Operation Rhyme") | Unknown | Hotel employee | Studying for degree in graphic information design at time of arrest |
| 9. Qaisar Shaffi[j] | Pakistan | 26 | Dhiren Barot's "dirty bomb" plot ("Operation Rhyme") | Single | Mobile phones sales manager | Some college, business and finance studies |
| 10. Nadeem Tarmohammed[k] | Pakistan | 29 | Dhiren Barot's "dirty bomb" plot ("Operation Rhyme") | Single | Former administrator | Degree in manufacturing engineering |
| 11. Salahuddin Amin[l] | Pakistan | 31 | Operation Crevice[m] | Single | Taxi driver | Bachelor's degree, product design |
| 12. Abu Munthir[n] | Pakistan | U/kn | Operation Crevice | Unknown | Prison, Pakistan | Unknown |
| 13. Mohammed Junaid Babar[o] | Pakistan | 29 | Operation Crevice | Married/1 | Valet parking and other unskilled jobs | Some college, pharmacy studies |
| 14. Jawad Akbar[p] | Pakistan | 22 | Operation Crevice | Married | Student; part-time job Gatwick airport with clearance to work airside | Student at Brunel University, Uxbridge, studying mathematics, technology and design |
| 15. Waheed Mahmood[q] | Pakistan | 34 | Operation Crevice | Married/4 | Subcontractor for national gas company Transco | Some high school |
| 16. Omar Khyam[r] | Pakistan (3rd generation) | 25 | Operation Crevice | Married | Unemployed | High school grad; enrolled but did not attend university |

(*continued*)

TABLE 5.1 (*cont.*)

| Name | Country of Ancestry | Age | Alleged Terrorist Association | Family status/ children | Occupation | Education |
|---|---|---|---|---|---|---|
| 17. Mohammed Sidique Khan[s] | Pakistan | 32 | London bombing 7/7/2005 | Married/ 1 | Ran youth programs for mosque; former elementary school mentor | College graduate, business studies |
| 18. Shahzad Tanweer[t] | Pakistan | 22 | London bombing 7/7/2005 | Single | Unemployed | College graduate, sports science |
| 19. Hasib Hussain[u] | Pakistan | 18 | London bombing 7/7/2005 | Single | Unemployed | Some high school |
| 20. Waheed Ali[v] | Bangladesh | 22 | London bombing 7/7/2005 | Single | Unknown | Some high school |
| 21. Mohammed Shakil[w] | Pakistan | 30 | London bombing 7/7/2005 | Married/ 3 | Taxi driver | Unknown |
| 22. Sadeer Saleem[x] | Pakistan | 26 | London bombing 7/7/2005 | Married/ 3 | Trustee at the Iqra bookshop[y] | Unknown |
| 23. Abdullah Ahmed Ali[z] | Pakistan | 26 | Transatlantic aircraft bomb plot | Married/ 1 | Unemployed shop worker | College graduate, computer systems engineering |
| 24. Tanvir Hussain[aa] | Pakistan | 25 | Trans-Atlantic aircraft bomb plot | Single | Temporary staff at St Anne's hospital in North London | Some college, business and computers course |
| 25. Arafat Waheed Khan[bb] | Pakistan | 25 | Transatlantic aircraft bomb plot | Single | Computer salesman | Some college, engineering |
| 26. Assad Ali Sarwar[cc] | Pakistan | 26 | Transatlantic aircraft bomb plot | Married | Unemployed; series of odd jobs | Some college, earth sciences |

| | | | | | | |
|---|---|---|---|---|---|---|
| 27. Waheed Zaman[dd] | Pakistan | 22 | Transatlantic aircraft bomb plot | Single | Biomedical science student; shop assistant at London toy store Hamleys | Some college, biomedical science |
| 28. Mohammed Usman Saddique[ee] | Pakistan | 25 | Transatlantic aircraft bomb plot | Single | Worked at pizza restaurant | Unknown |
| 29. Adam Osman Khatib[ff] | Pakistan | 20 | Transatlantic aircraft bomb plot | Unknown | unknown | Unknown |
| 30. Abdul Muneem Patel[gg] | India | 17 | Transatlantic aircraft bomb plot | Married | Office job | Some high school |
| 31. Shamin Mohammed Uddin[hh] | Pakistan | 36 | Transatlantic aircraft bomb plot | Married/ 3 | Ex-bodybuilder | Unknown |

[a] This list of terrorism suspects involves individuals charged with, but not necessarily convicted of terrorism offenses.

[b] Sheikh was sentenced to death for abducting and murdering Pearl. "Profile: Omar Saeed Sheikh," BBC News, 16 July, 2002, at http://news.bbc.co.uk/2/hi/uk_news/1804710.stm.

[c] Suicide bomber.

[d] Escaped after bomb failed to detonate. His body found in the sea days later, believed drowned.

[e] Sentenced to 20 years in prison, "Dhiren Barot's co-conspirators," *BBC News*, June 15, 2007, at 225.

For the prosecution's case against the defendants, see Metropolitan Police, London, Directorate of Public Affairs, "Operation Rhyme – Defendants." All of the conspirators were charged with the same offenses. The plot leader, Dhiren Barot, aka Abu Isa al-Hindi, was additionally charged with possessing reconnaissance plans of the Stock Exchange in New York, the IMF in Washington, the Prudential Building in New Jersey, and the Citigroup in New York and having notebooks with information on explosives, poisons, chemicals, and related matters. Rosie Cowan and Richard Norton-Taylor, "Surveillance led to terror arrests," *The Guardian*, London, August 4, 2004, at http://www.theguardian.com/uk/2004/aug/05/september11.terrorism.

[f] Sentenced to 22 years in prison.

[g] Sentenced to 18 years in prison.

[h] Sentenced to 26 years in prison.

[i] Sentenced to 15 years in prison.

[j] Sentenced to 15 years in prison.

[k] Sentenced to 20 years in prison.

[l] Amin was found guilty of conspiracy to cause explosions likely to endanger life. His appeal was rejected, and he was sentenced to life in prison. "Terror bomb plotters lose appeal," *Metro* (UK), July 23, 2008, at http://www.metro.co.uk/news/article.html?in_article_id=231348&in_page_id=34&in_a_source=.

[m] Operation Crevice refers to the counterterrorism operation launched in March 2004 against suspects in the London fertilizer truck-bomb plot.

[n] Not much is known about Abu Munthir, but according to trial testimony, he split his time between the UK and Pakistan. Munthir reportedly told Khyam that if he was really serious about jihad, he should "do something" in Britain. Abu Munthir was arrested in Pakistan in 2004. Ian Cobain and Richard Norton-Taylor, "'Because British soldiers are killing Muslims,'" *The Guardian* (UK), April 30, 2007, at http://www.guardian.co.uk/uk/2007/apr/30/terrorism.world2.

[o] American citizen of Pakistani origin. Met the Crevice group in Pakistan after September 11 and testified against them in a plea bargain with the U.S. government.

[p] Akbar was found guilty of conspiracy to cause explosions likely to endanger life. His appeal was rejected and he was sentenced to life in prison. "Terror bomb plotters lose appeal," *Metro* (UK), July 23, 2008, at http://www.metro.co.uk/news/article.html?in_article_id=231348&in_page_id=34&in_a_source=.

[q] Mahmood was found guilty of conspiracy to cause explosions likely to endanger life. His appeal was rejected and he was sentenced to life in prison. "Terror bomb plotters lose appeal."

[r] Ringleader. Khyam was found guilty of conspiracy to cause explosions likely to endanger life. His appeal was rejected and he was sentenced to life in prison. "Terror bomb plotters lose appeal."

[s] Ringleader and suicide bomber.

[t] Suicide bomber.

[u] Suicide bomber.

[v] Accused of conspiring with the 7/7 bombers and conducting reconnaissance for London terrorist attacks. The jury failed to reach a verdict in the case. Haroon Siddique and Rachel Williams, "July 7 trial jury fails to reach verdict," *Guardian* (UK), August 1, 2008, at http://www.guardian.co.uk/uk/2008/aug/01/july7.uksecurity.

[w] Accused of conspiring with the 7/7 bombers and conducting reconnaissance for London terrorist attacks. The jury failed to reach verdicts on the case. Siddique and Williams, August 1, 2008.

[x] Accused of conspiring with the 7/7 bombers and conducting reconnaissance for London terrorist attacks. The jury failed to reach verdicts on the case. Siddique and Williams, August 1, 2008.

[y] The Iqra bookshop was the alleged hub of the July 7 plot. "London terror trial – the accused," *Telegraph* (UK), April 14, 2008, at http://www.telegraph.co.uk/news/uknews/1584718/London-terror-trial---the-accused.html.

[z] Alleged ringleader. Found guilty of conspiracy to murder charges. Nico Hines, "Terror mastermind Abdulla Ahmed Ali guilty of bombing plot," *The Times* (UK), September 8, 2008, at http://www.thetimes.co.uk/tto/news/uk/crime/article1874946.ece. Found guilty of conspiracy to cause explosions on

aircraft, conspiracy to murder, conspiracy to cause explosions, and conspiracy to cause public nuisance on retrial in September 2009. "Mass murder at 30,000 feet: Islamic extremists guilty of airline bomb plot," *Times Online*, September 7, 2009, at http://www.timesonline.co.uk/tol/news/uk/crime/article6824884.ece.

[aa] Recorded martyrdom video. Found guilty of conspiracy to murder charges. Sean O'Neill, "Police in crisis after jury rejects £10m terror case," *The Times* (UK), September 9, 2008, at http://business.timesonline.co.uk/tol/business/law/public_law/article4710879.ece, Found guilty of conspiracy to cause explosions on aircraft, conspiracy to murder, conspiracy to cause explosions, and conspiracy to cause public nuisance upon retrial in September 2009. "Mass murder at 30,000 feet: Islamic extremists guilty of airline bomb plot," *Times Online*, September 7, 2009 at http://www.timesonline.co.uk/tol/news/uk/crime/article6824884.ece.

[bb] Charged with conspiracy to murder and with preparing acts of terrorism. Recorded a martyrdom video. The jury failed to reach a verdict on the charges. Sean O'Neill, "Police in crisis after jury rejects £10m terror case," *The Times* (UK), September 9, 2008, at http://business.timesonline.co.uk/tol/business/law/public_law/article4710879.ece. Found not guilty of conspiracy to cause explosions on aircraft upon retrial in September 2009 but could face retrial on more general conspiracy to murder charges because the jury could not reach a verdict. "Mass murder at 30,000 feet: Islamic extremists guilty of airline bomb plot," *Times Online*, September 7, 2009.

[cc] Recorded a martyrdom video. Found guilty of conspiracy to murder charges. Sean O'Neill, "Police in crisis after jury rejects £10m terror case," *The Times* (UK), September 9, 2008, at http://business.timesonline.co.uk/tol/business/law/public_law/article4710879.ece. Found guilty of conspiracy to cause explosions on aircraft, conspiracy to murder, conspiracy to cause explosions, and conspiracy to cause public nuisance upon retrial in September 2009. "Mass murder at 30,000 feet: Islamic extremists guilty of airline bomb plot," *Times Online*, September 7, 2009.

[dd] Charged with conspiracy to murder and with preparing acts of terrorism. Recorded a martyrdom video. The jury failed to reach a verdict on the charges. Sean O'Neill, "Police in crisis after jury rejects £10m terror case," *The Times* (UK), September 9, 2008. Found not guilty of conspiracy to cause explosions on aircraft upon retrial in September 2009, but could face retrial on more general conspiracy to murder charges because the jury could not reach a verdict. "Mass murder at 30,000 feet: Islamic extremists guilty of airline bomb plot," *Times Online*, September 7, 2009.

[ee] Charged under section 5 (1) of the Terrorism Act 2006 with preparing to smuggle parts of improvised explosive devices on to aircraft and assemble and detonate them on board.

[ff] Charged with conspiracy to murder and with preparing acts of terrorism under section 5 of the Terrorism Act 2006.

[gg] Convicted of having a terrorism-related explosives manual. Sentenced to six months in a juvenile facility. "Explosives manual teenager jailed," *BBC News*, October 26, 2007, at http://news.bbc.co.uk/2/hi/uk_news/7063727.stm.

[hh] Charged under section 5 (1) of the Terrorism Act 2006 with preparing to smuggle parts of improvised explosive devices on to aircraft and assemble and detonate them on board and under section 1 (1) of the Criminal Law Act 1977 of conspiring with other persons to murder other persons. Believed to suffer from mental illness after a violent assault that left him in a coma.

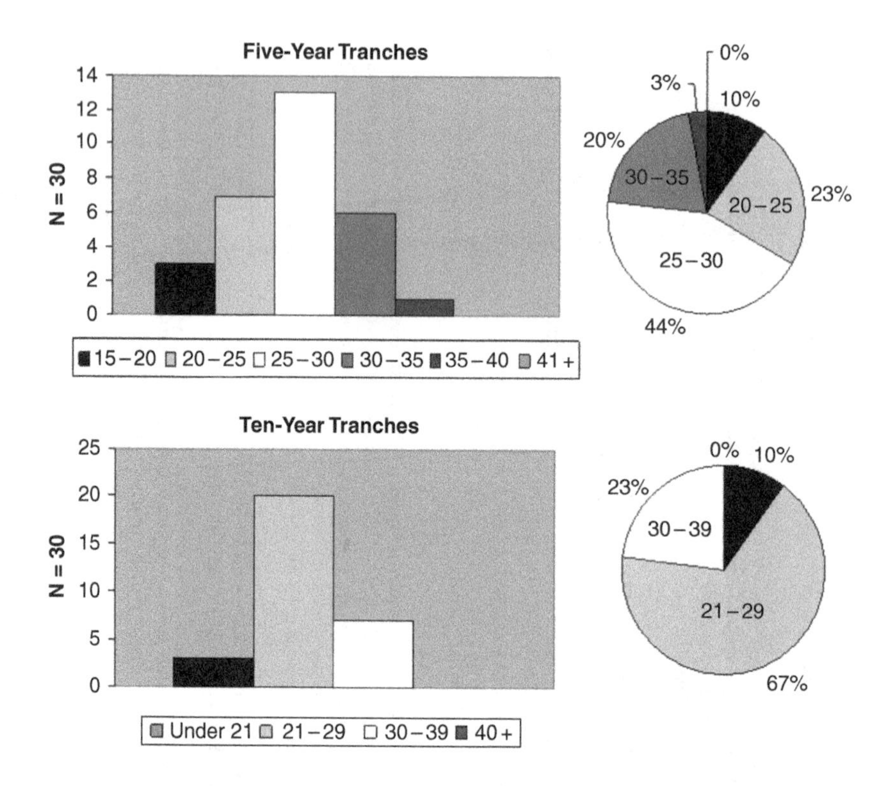


FIGURE 5.1 Age Range of Second-Generation British Terrorism Suspects of South Asian Ancestry

In terms of occupation, although most individuals tend to have some record of employment, it is difficult to determine the exact occupation of a given individual at the time of a terrorist attack or arrest. We were unable to find employment information for 3 individuals. Of the other 28, one-fifth (21 percent) were unemployed at the time of their arrest. Another 44 percent were working in unskilled jobs, and only 35 percent had skilled or professional jobs.

What emerges from these data is a substantial gap between education level (the majority had some college education) and employment (only a minority had skilled or professional jobs). This gap may have created a sense of relative deprivation among members of this population and may have been a contributing factor in their radicalization into violence.

According to Ghaffar Husain of the Quilliam Foundation, the families of British Muslim extremists are not particularly religious. The young men who

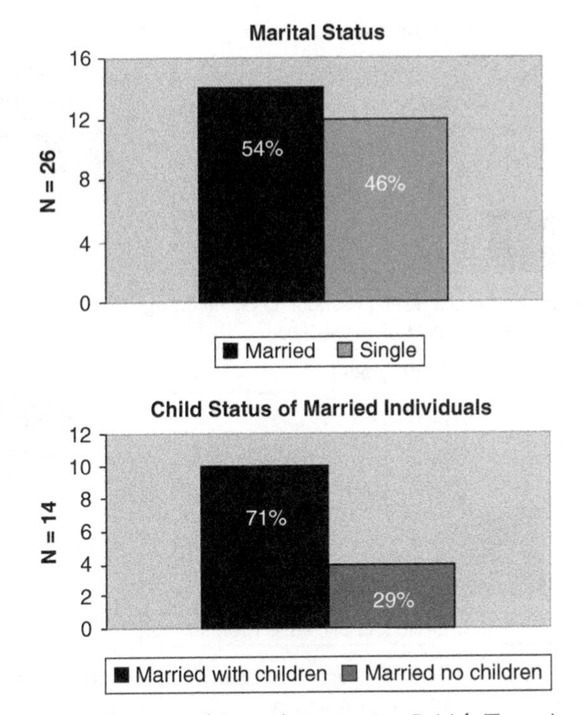


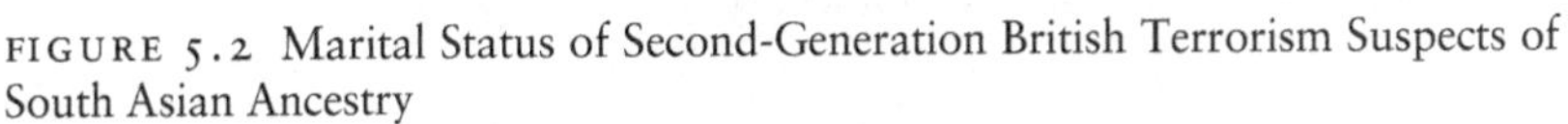

FIGURE 5.2 Marital Status of Second-Generation British Terrorism Suspects of South Asian Ancestry

become extremists – individuals associated with terrorist events are usually male – experience real or perceived discrimination and conclude that they are not really British, but not Pakistani either. They associate with people in similar circumstances, some of whom might be part of Islamist networks. It is not a matter of being recruited from the outside; rather, their social network socializes them into radicalization. Their perceptions of the world are interpreted through the prism of Islamist narratives of Western oppression of Muslims. These perceptions drive and justify the transition to violence.[10]

Approximately two-thirds of the British Muslim population of Pakistani origin trace their ancestry to the district of Mirpur in the southern part of Azad Jammu and Kashmir or to the southern part of the district of Kotli, which lies immediately to the north of Mirpur. Most settled in the north of England, in Bradford, Leeds, Blackburn, and Burnly. According to Roger Ballard, director of the Centre for Applied South Asian Studies at

[10] Interview with Ghaffar Husain, London, September 2008. See also Oliver Roy, *Globalized Islam: The Search for a New Ummah*. New York: Columbia University Press.

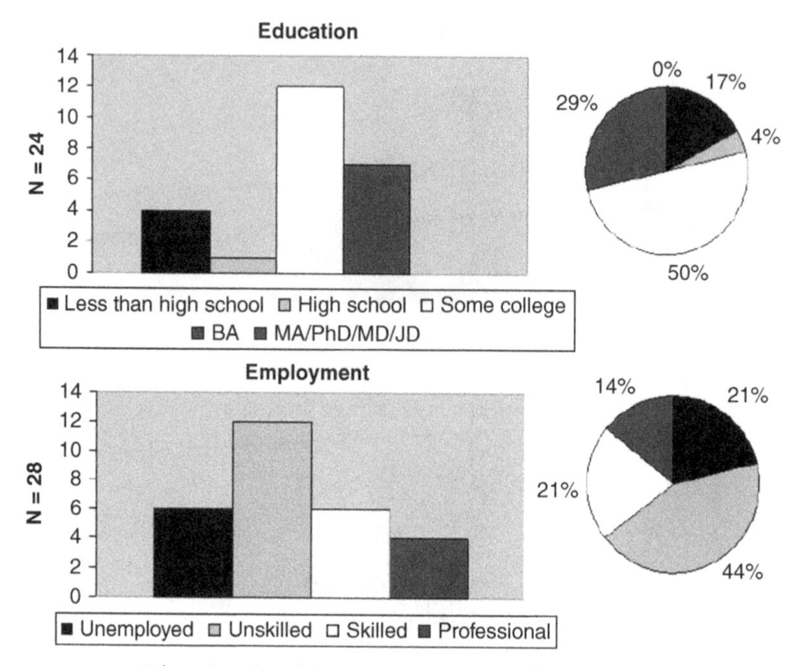


FIGURE 5.3 Educational and Occupational Status of Second-Generation British Terrorism Suspects of South Asian Ancestry

the University of Manchester, Mirpuris identify themselves as Kashmiri, not necessarily as Pakistani. Bumper stickers displaying chinar leaves[11] and the slogan "I ♥ Kashmir" are commonplace on the streets of British cities.[12] The conflict in Kashmir, therefore, resonates more strongly with this sector of the British Muslim population than it would have if migration patterns had been different. Diasporic connections, in turn, facilitate the linkage of disaffected young British Muslims of Mirpuri ancestry to Kashmiri terrorist groups.

## Profiles of Second-Generation British Muslim Terrorists

### *The Operation Crevice Conspirators*

In March 2004, eight British-born Muslims between ages 17 and 32 were arrested across southern England in a counterterrorist operation

[11] The chinar or cinar is the plane tree of Kashmir.

[12] Roger Ballard, "The Kashmir Crisis: A View from Mirpur," *Economic and Political Weekly*, 1991, pp. 513 – 517, at http://www.jstor.org/discover/10.2307/4397403?uid=3739256&uid=2129&uid=2&uid=70&uid=4&sid=21104120801917.

code-named "Operation Crevice," on intelligence that they were planning a series of massive truck-bomb attacks across London. The targets were believed to include the Ministry of Defence, the Foreign and Commonwealth Office, Downing Street, and a major shopping center in north London. The Jordanian Embassy was also named as a possible target. More than half a ton of ammonium nitrate fertilizer was seized at the same time. In addition, one man was arrested in Ottawa on suspicion of links to this group.[13] The cell's operations were disrupted through long-term surveillance of the storage unit where the fertilizer was stored and infiltration of the group "with the assistance of a foreign security service."[14]

British security leaders believed that this would have constituted the biggest terrorist attack ever in Britain had it succeeded, "capable of wreaking havoc on a huge scale and claiming hundreds of lives." British security officials stated, however, that there did not appear to be "any direct link between the arrested men and al-Qaida," and that the planning had been carried out by a group of "young radicalized Muslims who were difficult to label but viciously anti-Western."[15]

Omar Khyam, 24, considered by prosecutors to be the ringleader of the group, began his journey to extremism as a teenager in Crawley, just south of London. Khyam, a standout cricket player, planned to study electrical engineering in college; however, when he was 16, he began spending time with members of Al Muhajiroun, the extremist group led by Omar Bakri Mohammed. He subsequently attended a terrorist training camp in Pakistan. A second defendant, Salahuddin Amin, 31, believed to be the liaison between the group and militants in Pakistan, was also a member of Al Muhajiroun. He met some of the other conspirators, including Khyam and a man accused of being an al-Qaeda operative, Abu Munthir, who was visiting from Pakistan, at a prayer center in Luton, a borough in Bedfordshire 30 miles

[13] Mohammed Momin Khawaja was charged with helping a "terrorist group" in Canada and the UK from November 2003 onward; he is the first person to be charged under Canada's Anti-Terrorism Act, which came into effect in December 2001: "Canadian 'linked to British plot,'" *BBC News*, March 4, 2004, at http://news.bbc.co.uk/go/pr/fr/-/1/hi/world/americas/3587195.stm.

[14] "Terror suspects held in raids," *BBC News*, March 30, 2004, at http://news.bbc.co.uk/go/pr/fr/-/1/hi/england/3581687.stm; Rosie Cowan and Tania Branigan, "Staking out suburbia: why police moved quickly after a long watch," *The Guardian*, March 31, 2004, at http://www.theguardian.com/uk/2004/mar/31/terrorism.world; Jason Bennetto and Kim Sengupta, "How a telephone intercept led to MI5's biggest hunt for islamic terror suspects," *The Independent*, London, March 31, 2004, at http://old.cageprisoners.com/articles.php?id=1111.

[15] "MI5 agents foil bomb plot," *The Guardian*, March 31, 2004, at http://www.theguardian.com/uk/2004/mar/31/politics.september11.

northwest of London with a large population of South Asian background. In 2003, Amin, Khyam, and another man traveled to a safe house in Kohat, Pakistan, for two days of training in making fertilizer-based explosives. A key player was a Pakistani American named Mohammed Junaid Babar, who reportedly worked for the New York chapter of Al Muhajiroun. In his testimony at the trial, Babar said he moved to Pakistan in November 2001 with money and instructions from Al Muhajiroun. A year later, on a fund-raising trip to London, he first met members of what he called the "Crawley lot," including Khyam. Babar said that Khyam told him that he and other "brothers" from Crawley were not just a local operation but reported to a man called Abdul Hadi, described by Khyam as the "No. 3" in al-Qaeda.[16]

At the time, Operation Crevice was the largest counterterrorism operation conducted in the UK. It involved close cooperation and intelligence sharing among the UK, the United States, Canada, and Pakistan. The authorities moved in to make arrests when they feared that the conspirators were close to mounting their attack.[17] The trial began in March 2006 and ended in April 2007 with the conviction of five of the defendants: Omar Khyam, Jawad Akbar, Salhunddin Amin, Waheed Mahmood, and Anthony Garcia. Two other defendants were found not guilty.[18]

## The 7/7 London Bombings and the Transatlantic Aircraft Liquid Bombing Plot Conspirators

The July 7, 2005, London underground and bus bombings and the August 2006 transatlantic aircraft bombing plot exhibit the same pattern of British-born Muslims with linkages to militants in Pakistan. Three of the four perpetrators of the London bombings, Mohammed Sidique Khan, Shahzad Tanweer, and Hasib Hussain, were second-generation British Muslims of Pakistani origin. The fourth bomber, Germaine Lindsay, was a Jamaican immigrant who converted to Islam. All three of the British-born bombers appeared to have been well integrated into British society and

[16] "British Terror Trial Traces a Path to Militant Islam," *The New York Times*, November 26, 2006, at http://www.nytimes.com/2006/11/26/world/europe/26crevice.html?pagewanted=all&_r=0. Abdul Hadi was probably senior al-Qaeda operative Nashwan Abd al-Razaq abd al-Baqi, alias Abdul Hadi al-Iraqi, captured in 2006.

[17] United Kingdom, London Metropolitan Police, Operation Crevice: MPS statement, April 30, 2007, at http://content.met.police.uk/News/Operation-Crevice-MPS-statement/1260267589317/1257246745756.

[18] Royal United Services Institute, "Operation Crevice Trial Ends," at http://www.rusi.org/go.php?structureID=S4459C0DF31D9A&ref=C4638BFFA4FEC1.

came from middle-class backgrounds. Mohammed Sidique Khan, the attack group's leader, was an elementary school teacher and mentor and had studied at Leeds University. Some accounts describe him as a good family man and an exemplary member of his community; friends and acquaintances expressed disbelief that he was involved in terrorism. Other accounts described him as frustrated with his station in life (Khan left his job in December 2004, seven months before the London bombings) and increasingly drawn to radical Islamic teachings.[19]

The other terrorists appeared to fall into the categories that Petter Nesser calls "misfits" or "drifters."[20] Shahzad Tanweer, 22, was effectively unemployed, although he had received good grades at school before going on to study sports science at Leeds University. His father was a prosperous businessman who owned several small businesses in the Beeston suburb of Leeds. Hasib Hussain, 18, was unemployed. The Jamaica-born convert, Germaine Lindsay, 19, was a carpet fitter; he is believed to have met the other bombers at a gym set up by Khan as part of his youth-mentoring program.[21]

The transatlantic aircraft liquid bombing plot suspects followed uneven educational and career paths. Tanvir Hussain, Arafat Wahid Khan, Assad Ali Sarwar, and Waheed Zaman had all attended university but did not attain professional-level jobs. Tanvir Hussain worked as a temporary member of the staff at St. Anne's Hospital in north London; Assad Ali Sarwar held a variety of odd jobs; Waheed Zaman was a shop assistant at a London toy store. Mohammed Usman Saddique worked at a pizza restaurant; he belonged to street gangs before becoming devout.[22] One of the suspects, Amin Asmin Tariq, was a security worker at Heathrow airport.[23]

As is often the case, family and friends expressed shock when some of the suspects were arrested. Neighbors described Waheed Arafat Khan as thoughtful, considerate, and polite and were astonished to learn that he had been arrested over the alleged plot. A neighbor said that "he would dress

[19] Paul Tumelty, "An In-Depth Look at the London Bombers," The Jamestown Foundation, *Terrorism Monitor*, Vol. 3, Issue 15, July 28, 2005, at http://www.jamestown.org/programs/tm/single/?tx_ttnews[tt_news]=535&tx_ttnews[backPid]=180&no_cache=1#.U5JWriRBxQY.

[20] Petter Nesser's presentation, RAND Institute for Middle East Youth (IMEY) Conference on Positive Options to Deter Youth Radicalism, Washington, DC, September 22, 2005.

[21] Tumelty, "An In-Depth Look at the London Bombers."

[22] Globalsecurity.org "UK foils transatlantic bombings," at http://www.globalsecurity.org/security/profiles/uk_foils_transatlantic_bombings.htm.

[23] "Who are the 'bomb plot' suspects?," *Times Online*, August 11, 2006, at http://www.timesonline.co.uk/tol/news/uk/article1084359.ece.

in western clothes and sometimes in traditional Pakistani robes. He was clean shaven. I always thought he worked in the City." Waheed Zaman's older sister Safeena said that he was "a great believer in the importance of integration between our community and the Western world."[24]

## RADICALIZED MIDDLE EASTERN AND NORTH AFRICAN IMMIGRANTS

On the Continent, ethnic Arabs have played a far more prominent role in radical recruitment and activities than Turks or immigrants from other parts of the Muslim world. Syrians (many with links to the Syrian Muslim Brotherhood) predominated in the pre-9/11 Spanish al-Qaeda network. Of the 24 defendants in the trial of the members of the al-Qaeda cell uncovered in Madrid in 2001 and 2002, 17 were from Syria, including the alleged leader, Imad Eddin Barakat Yarkas, aka Abu Dahdah, and four were from Morocco. Six had been fighters in Bosnia, and several had traveled to Afghanistan.[25]

According to a study by Spanish terrorism analyst Fernando Reinares, 75.5 percent of those arrested on suspicion of Islamist terrorism in Spain between 2001 and 2005 were of North African origin.[26] Sarhane Ben Abdelmajid Fakhet, the leader of the cell that planned and executed the March 11, 2004, Madrid bombings was a Tunisian. He and six others blew themselves up in the apartment in the Leganés neighborhood of Madrid when the police closed in after the Madrid bombings. The others were five were Moroccans – Jamal Ahmidan, Abdennabi Kounjaa, Fouad el-Morabit Anghar, and the brothers Mohammed and Rachid Oulad Akcha; and an Algerian, Allekama Lamari. Five other suspected members of the cell were Moroccan and one was Algerian.[27]

Some of the Arab and North African immigrants who became active in Islamist terrorist networks arrived in Europe as students and economic

[24] Ibid.

[25] The trial concluded in September 2005. The cell's leader Eddin Barakat Yarkas was sentenced to 27 years in prison. Seventeen others received sentences of 6 to 11 years and six were absolved. "Quién es quién en el macrojuicio contra la célula de Al Qaeda," *El Mundo* (Spain), September 26, 2005.

[26] Reinares, "Hacia una caracterización social del terrorismo yihadista en España: implicaciones en seguridad interior y acción exterior," Real Instituto Elcano, ARI N° 34/2006 Análisis, March 14, 2006, at http://www.realinstitutoelcano.org/wps/portal/rielcano/contenido?WCM_GLOBAL_CONTEXT=/elcano/elcano_es/zonas_es/terrorismo+internacional/ari+34-2006 No. 34/2006, March 14, 2006.

[27] The Moroccans were Said Berraj, Mohammed El Hadi Chedadi, Mohamed Afalah, Hasan El Haski, and Abderrahim Zbakh. The Algerian was Daoud Ouhnane. We have not been able to determine the nationality of one suspect, Asri Rifuat Anouar.

migrants and others as asylum seekers and political refugees. The operational leaders of the Madrid bombings of March 11, 2004, were for the most part well educated and economically successful. Fakhet, the leader of the attack team, came to Spain in 1996 to study economics at the Universidad Autónoma de Madrid through a scholarship from the Spanish Cooperation Agency and later became a successful real estate agent.[28] Abderrahim Zbakh, aka "the Chemist," a Moroccan and allegedly the main participant in the assembly of the detonators and explosives, studied chemistry and physics at the University of Tetuán, Morocco, and did his postgraduate studies at the Universidad Complutense in Madrid.[29] Jamal Zougam, the owner of the telephone store where the cell phones used as detonators in the Madrid bombing were traced, owned one of the most successful businesses in Lavapiés, the working-class neighborhood in Madrid in which the terrorist cell was based.[30]

An analysis of 45 members of the Madrid terrorist network by Spanish terrorism expert Javier Jordán shows that none were born in Spain, but 37 (83 percent) were legal residents of Spain, 5 (11 percent) were nationalized Spanish citizens, and only 2 (4 percent) had what Jordán describes as an irregular residence status. The majority of the cell members (39, or 87 percent) were working class, and 4 (9 percent) were middle class. Some earned a respectable salary, while others lived at a subsistence level – a situation not dissimilar to the status of other North African immigrants living in Spain. About half (22, or 48 percent) were married, mostly to Moroccan women, and the other half (22, or 48 percent) were single. Most were 25 to 35 years old when the Madrid bombing took place. Jordán's conclusion, which is consistent with the cases of other European Islamist terrorists reviewed in this book, is that most members of the networks can be categorized as socially integrated, as measured by socioeconomic indicators, but psychologically alienated and hostile to the society in which they lived.[31]

[28] Galiacho, Juan Luis, and Irene H. Velasco, "El Egipcio viajero," *El Mundo* (Madrid), June 13, 2004, at http://www.elmundo.es/cronica/2004/452/1087216560.html.

[29] "Jamal, 'el de Tánger'," *El Mundo* (Madrid) March 21, 2004, at http://www.elmundo.es/cronica/2004/440/1079968711.html.

[30] On the other hand, in his sample of individuals imprisoned in Spain for Islamist terrorism-related offenses, Reinares found that close to 60 percent were laborers and agricultural workers, 20 percent were skilled workers or service personnel, and only 10 percent were professionals and white-collar workers. Reinares, "Hacia una caracterización social del terrorismo yihadista en España."

[31] Javier Jordán, Fernando M. Mañas, and Nicola Horsburgh, "Strengths and Weaknesses of Grassroot Jihadist Networks: The Madrid Bombings," *Studies in Conflict & Terrorism*, Vol. 31, Issue 1, January 2008.

Algerians play an inordinately important role in radical Islamist networks in Europe. Although they constitute a relatively small proportion of the population of North African origin in Spain (about 50,000 compared to an estimated 700,000 Moroccans), almost as many Algerians as Moroccans are arrested and imprisoned for terrorist-related activities. In Reinares's sample, for instance, 36.7 percent were Moroccan and 35.6 percent Algerian.[32] The trajectory of Algerian extremist organizations – in particular, their role in the Algerian civil war – explains the prominence of Algerians in Europe-based Islamist extremist and terrorist groups. After Algerians, Moroccans are also prominently represented in these groups. In their case, the existence of transnational Moroccan extremist networks facilitates the recruitment of other Moroccans into extremist groups. The Moroccan Islamic Combatant Group (*Groupe Islamique Combattant Marocain – GCIM*), with cells throughout Western Europe, has been a pole of attraction for Moroccan militants.[33]

In the Netherlands, Moroccans constituted the bulk of the membership of the Hofstad Group (see later discussion). Moroccans constitute the largest part of the North African immigrant population there, and are predominantly Berber rather than Arab; most do not even speak Arabic. Some believe that it is the historic Berber tradition of rebellion and resistance against state authority that, having become part of their collective posture, explains their greater involvement in radical activities.[34]

One explanation for the prevalence of North Africans in Islamist militant groups in Europe is that many came not as migrant workers, but as asylum seekers and refugees. Thus, they numbered among them individuals who had been politically active before and who brought their experience and in some cases their political agendas with them. Some of these extremists were able to resume their subversive activities in Europe, after having been expelled from their home countries for the very same activities. Sometimes their attention remained focused on the original agenda related to their country of origin, but in other cases, they turned against the host country and its culture, either because that country's government supported the regime they opposed or took a foreign policy stance that they viewed as inimical to Muslim interests or because they were drawn to a more global agenda while in the West.

Anecdotal evidence cited by Jonathan Githens-Mazer about individuals of North African origin named or reported as terrorist suspects or subject

[32] Reinares, "Hacia una caracterización social del terrorismo yihadista en España."
[33] Ibid.
[34] Cheryl Benard's interview with AIVD, Amsterdam, April 2005.

to Special Immigration Appeals Court hearings in the United Kingdom suggests that most were in their late teens or early 20s during the height of the conflict in Afghanistan and the most brutal stages of the Algerian civil war. Although, Githens-Mazer says, most did not participate in either conflict, these episodes provided contexts for their youth and young adulthood.[35] Similarly, in his analysis of the social characteristics of Islamist extremists imprisoned in Spain, Reinares found that most were born between 1966 and 1975; that is, they entered adolescence in the initial stages of the Iranian revolution and the Afghan war and reached a critical point in their political socialization at the time of the Soviet defeat in Afghanistan, the collapse of communism, the beginning of the Bosnian war, and the spread of Salafist ideologies throughout the Muslim world and the Muslim communities in Europe.[36]

Nizar Trabelsi, a Tunisian, was sentenced to 10 years in prison for plotting to drive a car bomb into Kleine Brogel, a NATO airbase in Belgium. A seemingly integrated immigrant, Trabelsi played professional soccer in Germany in the late 1980s and early 1990s; according to media reports, he did not embrace radical Islam until the mid-1990s after his contract with the German soccer team Fortuna Düsseldorf was canceled. Trabelsi drifted from team to team, was divorced, and he fell into a period of drug abuse and petty crime. According to Belgian authorities, Trabelsi was recruited after leaving a German prison by Islamic fundamentalists at a mosque in Dostrum, in northwestern Germany. It was a vulnerable transition period in his life from professional athlete to petty criminal. He became associated with the violent extremist group Takfir wal-Hijra. His path culminated in a trip to Afghanistan in 2000, where he met senior al-Qaeda leaders.[37] Trabelsi's story, according to Glenn Audenaert, director of the Federal Police Service in Brussels, was similar to those of other radicalized immigrants from Muslim countries: "They tried to become part of a multicultural society but, for whatever reason, they did not fit in."[38] Driven by resentment and alienation, they gravitate toward militant Islamist groups.

[35] Interview with Jonathan Githens-Mazer, London, September 2008.

[36] Reinares, "Hacia una caracterización social del terrorismo yihadista en España.

[37] Petter Nesser, *Jihad in Europe: A Survey of the Motivations for Sunni Islamist Terrorism in Post-Milennium Europe*, Norwegian Defense Research Establishment, Kjeller, Norway: FFI/RAPPORT-2004/01146, pp. 47–48, at http://www.investigativeproject.org/documents/testimony/35.pdf.

[38] Cited in Zachary K. Johnson, "Bin Laden's Striker: The case of Nizar Trabelsi," Frontline: Al Qaeda's New Front, January 25, 2005, at http://www.pbs.org/wgbh/pages/frontline/shows/front/special/cron.html.

The two main suspects in the "suitcase plot" in Germany, Youssef Mohamad el Hajdib and Jihad Hamad, made bombs from gas canisters filled with propane gas and deposited it hidden in suitcases in two German regional trains on July 31, 2006. The devices, fitted with alarm clocks for timers, failed to detonate. At first, the plot looked like an isolated incident, because Hamad said that the attack was intended as revenge for the publication of the Prophet Muhammad cartoons and because of the amateurish mistakes that the plotters made (they picked the wrong gas for the explosive device and failed to cover their tracks). But after months of investigation, the German authorities concluded that the attack had been commissioned by a man with links to al-Qaeda as a test of courage to qualify them for attacks on U.S.-led forces in Iraq. In an e-mail message from Hajdib to Hamad six weeks before the attack, Hajdib wrote that his brother in Sweden had rung and said he would come to Germany on June 29. Hajdib went on to say they would need to be patient for a little longer "until we have totally made it and passed the initiation test. Then we'll travel to Iraq together."[39]

Hajdib, a Lebanese, and Hamad, a Palestinian who grew up in a refugee camp in Lebanon, had been in Germany for a relatively short period of time (Hajdib less than three years and Hamad for about a year) when they began to plot the attack. Both Hajdib and Hamad went to Germany to pursue university studies. Hajdib's family in Lebanon was said to have close connections to Hizb ut-Tahrir. In the summer of 2003, he moved to Kiel to study Mechatronik (a combination of engineering and computer science). His German studies were progressing slowly and he had to repeat one semester.[40] Hajdib was described as highly religious. He prayed five times a day and did not socialize with fellow students. Although he was a Sunni, the door to his room was decorated with a poster of the Imam Ali mosque in Hamburg-Uhlenhorst, which was known as a meeting place for Shi'ite Hezbollah adherents.[41] In January 2006, when one of his teachers

[39] Andreas Ulrich, "Terrorism in Germany: Failed Plot Seen As Al-Qaida Initiation Test," *Spiegel Online International*, April 9, 2007, at http://www.spiegel.de/international/germany/terrorism-in-germany-failed-bomb-plot-seen-as-al-qaida-initiation-test-a-476238.html; "Punishing Failed Terror Plot: Cologne Suitcase Bombers Get Long Sentences," *Spiegel Online International*, April 9, 2007, at http://www.spiegel.de/international/germany/punishing-failed-terror-plot-cologne-suitcase-bombers-get-long-sentences-a-524134.html.

[40] "Zeitzuender im Kopf," *Die Zeit*, August 24, 2006, at http://www.zeit.de/2006/35/Kofferbomber.

[41] "Ermittler pruefen Spur zu al-Qaida," *Der Spiegel*, August 23, 2006, at http://www.spiegel.de/panorama/0,1518,433113,00.html.

wanted to discuss the Muhammad cartoons in class, Hajdib defended the use of any form of violence when the prophet was offended.

Hamad grew up in the Palestinian refugee camp Ain-al-Hilwe in Sidon. In 2003, the camp accepted al-Qaeda leaders and fighters, and some 200 al-Qaeda militants moved in and started to take charge of the camp's youth. As the Lebanese secret service later found out, Hamad was already radicalized when he went to Germany in 2005. An uncle helped him obtain a visa and took him to the Saladin mosque in Essen. His radical opinions caused trouble there and he was expelled. In late April 2006, he moved to Cologne. At this point, he and Hajdib began preparing the bombings. One of Hajdib's brothers was killed by an Israeli air strike in Tripoli on July 17, 2006, but this was not the cause of Hadjib's decision to engage in violence. Investigators with Germany's Federal Criminal Police Office (BKA) found receipts in his accomplice Hamad's Cologne apartment proving that the gas bottles used in the attempted bombing were purchased on July 4, thirteen days before the death of Hajdib's brother, and filled three days later.[42]

When the bombs that they placed in two trains leaving the Cologne station failed to explode, the two terrorists took the last flight from the Cologne/Bonn airport to Istanbul, and from there they traveled to Damascus and Lebanon. Hamad hid for a week in Southern Lebanon before visiting his family. Hajdib returned to Kiel a week later, intending to continue his studies. However, security cameras had already identified the two suspects and Hajdib saw his face on television on his arrival in Kiel. He panicked and called his father in Lebanon, who advised him to leave Germany. Lebanese military intelligence overheard the conversation and informed the German authorities. Before he could get on a train to Denmark, Hajdib was arrested. Hamad later surrendered voluntarily to Lebanese authorities and made a detailed confession.[43]

Hamad's testimony resulted in the arrest of a third 24-year-old Lebanese suspect. The Lebanese minister of the interior confirmed possible ties to al-Qaeda and data found on Hamad's laptop further supported this suspicion. According to the interrogation records, Hajdib was said to have been friends with one Abu Shaima, an Iraqi believed to have collected funds and recruited

[42] Most of the previous information is taken from *Focus Magazine* No. 35, "Aufgewachsen mit al-Qaida," August 28, 2006, p. 19ff; "Terrorism in Germany: Every Investigator's Nightmare," Spiegel Online International, August 28, 2006, at http://www.spiegel.de/international/spiegel/terrorism-in-germany-every-investigator-s-nightmare-a-433839-2.html.

[43] "Der Dritte Man," Spiegel No. 36, September 4, 2006, at http://www.spiegel.de/spiegel/print/d-48753321.html.

fighters for the Iraq insurgency. Police in Beirut arrested one of Hajdib's relatives, a cousin named Khaled, shortly after Hamad's detention. Khaled is believed to be one of the men pulling the strings of the attempted attacks and the person who introduced Hajdib to Hamad.[44]

## The Hofstad Group

Aside from the Madrid bombers, an example of a European-based network of individuals of North African origin or descent, with an admixture of converts to Islam, is the Hofstad Group, the cell with which Mohammed Bouyeri, the assassin of Dutch film maker Theo van Gogh, was associated. The Hofstad Group operated mainly in the Netherlands, but also across state boundaries, and its members maintained a number of international contacts. Individuals in the group have been linked to terrorist activities in other European countries. Investigations have revealed that in 2004, they planned to assassinate the Portuguese president-designate of the European Commission, Jose Manuel Durao Barroso, as well as other foreign guests, at a reception at the Freixo Palace.[45]

The probable founder of the Hofstad Group was a Syrian radical preacher, Ridwan al-Issar, who met Bouyeri during the latter's brief affiliation with the al-Tawheed mosque in Amsterdam. Al-Issar is described as a "radical autodidact" who developed a more and more extremist stance while waiting for his asylum application to go through a lengthy review and appeals process. Even when his claim was rejected, he reportedly continued to travel widely in Western Europe using false papers.[46]

Police investigations and interrogations following the arrest of Bouyeri did not paint the picture of a focused, cohesive structure in terms of motivation, ideology, or linkages. Rather, the grievances uniting the core members of the Hofstad Group and their sympathizers appeared as a mixture of personal and social problems attaching themselves to a mixed set of motivations derived from various domestic, national, international, and global sources, with cultural alienation at their root and a politically conceptualized religion as their overarching identifier. Danish terrorism researcher Michael Taarnby deconstructs the letter pinned to the body of

[44] "Wir lassen Blut aus euren Gesichtern fliessen," *Focus Online*, January 8, 2007, at http://www.focus.de/politik/deutschland/kofferbomber_aid_68493.html.

[45] Petter Nesser, "The Slaying of the Dutch Filmmaker – Religiously motivated violence or Islamist terrorism in the name of global jihad?" Norwegian Defense Research Establishment, Kjeller, Norway 2005, p. 19, at http://www.ffi.no/no/Rapporter/05-00376.pdf.

[46] Ibid., p. 14.

Theo Van Gogh by the assassin. According to Taarnby, the letter's content is "a juxtaposition of Qur'anic verses taken out of context, HAMAS-inspired political diatribe, obscure Talmud references and amateurish analysis of current Dutch political issues." It is, Taarnby says, "a mirror image of a marginalized community of believers who explicitly condemn Europe and Holland and who vehemently label any critics as infidels and apostates. Despite the shrill Islamist rhetoric, the terminology and concepts are rooted in an exclusively European socio-cultural context."[47]

Van Gogh's assassin, Bouyeri, was a 26-year-old second-generation immigrant, a dual citizen of the Netherlands and Morocco. He had grown up in a predominantly Muslim suburb of Amsterdam, done reasonably well in school, and gone on to attend a technical college, where he majored in computer sciences until he eventually dropped out. He at first seemed to take a constructive approach to the problems of European Muslims, working in a youth center, organizing sports events and writing for its newsletter.[48]

His path to radicalization is unclear. According to some reports, he spent seven months in jail for a violent crime. He went on welfare and attended the fundamentalist al-Tawheed mosque, but only briefly. At some point, he formed or joined a private prayer group and discussion circle. He began to take a hard-line stance at the youth center, opposing coeducational events and the serving of alcohol, causing so much discord that he was encouraged to leave. His writings and postings on the Internet provide indications of an increasingly hostile, extremist stance. The death of his mother, the influence of a radical preacher, and his failures to complete school or to find satisfactory work are a few of the factors suggested by observers to explain his trajectory toward radicalism and violence.[49]

In March 2006, a court convicted 9 of the 14 alleged members of the Hofstad Group of membership in a criminal organization with terrorist intent. The court handed down sentences of 1 to 15 years in prison. Four defendants were acquitted, and one was released because his sentence would have exceeded the 13 months he had already spent in custody. Bouyeri was convicted of Van Gogh's murder in a separate trial. In January 2008, a Dutch appeals court overturned the lower court's verdict, ruling that the Hofstad Group was not a criminal terrorist organization

[47] Michael Taarnby, "The European Battleground," *Terrorism Monitor*, The Jamestown Foundation, Vol. 2, Issue 23, May 5, 2005, at http://www.jamestown.org/single/?tx_ttnews[tt_news]=338&no_cache=1#.U5TS2yRBxQY.

[48] Glenn Frankel, "From Civic Activist to Alleged Terrorist," *The Washington Post*, November 28, 2004, at http://www.washingtonpost.com/wp-dyn/articles/A16855-2004Nov27.html.

[49] Ibid.; Nesser, "The Slaying of the Dutch Filmmaker."

"because a sustained and structured collaboration could not be established and neither could it be established there was a joint ideology." The judges acquitted the accused of charges of participating in a criminal and terrorist organization.[50]

The eight individuals who were initially convicted were Jason Walters, Ismail Akhnikh, Ahmed Hamdi, Mohammed Fahmi Boughabe, Nouredine El Fatmi, Mohammed El Morabit, Zine Labidine Aourghe, and Youssef Ettoumi.[51] Zine Labidine Aourghe did not appeal his 2006 conviction, and Samir Azzouz was convicted on separate charges of illegal possession of firearms. Ettoumi, Boughabe, El Morabit, and Hamdi had already been released from prison after serving short sentences.[52]

In October 2008, an appeals court in The Hague successfully re-convicted several of those previously acquitted on charges of membership in a terrorist organization. The appeals court agreed that "trial evidence showed they were part of a single group," adhered to a single violent belief system, engaged in weapons training, and coordinated their efforts to obtain the addresses of Dutch politicians on their hit list, including the Dutch prime minister. Samir Azzouz was sentenced to one additional year in prison; al Fatmi's four-year sentence was doubled to eight; his ex-wife, Soumaya Sahla, was sentenced to an additional year; and Mohammed Chentouf's sentence was increased by two years.[53]

Other than Bouyeri, about whom we know a fair amount, we have little individual-level information about the other members of this group. We do know that excluding the two converts (Jason Walters and Martine van den Oever) and spiritual leader Radwan al-Issar, the other accused were either first- or second-generation Dutch residents of Moroccan ancestry. Additional information is presented in Table 5.2.

Education and employment data about members of the Hofstad Group (Figure 5.4) are consistent with what we see in the sections on converts linked to terrorism and the second-generation British terrorism suspects of

[50] Agence France-Presse (North European Service), "Dutch Court Acquits Seven over Suspected Terror Links."

[51] Emerson Vermaat, "Hofstad Group – Wrong decision by Dutch appeals court," *Militant Islam Monitor*, January 31, 2008, at http://www.militantislammonitor.org/article/id/3341.

[52] Emers "The Hofstadgroep," Transnational Terrorism, Security & the Rule of Law, April 15, 2007 (revised April 2008), at http://www.transnationalterrorism.eu/tekst/publications/Hofstadgroep.pdf.

[53] Toby Sterling, "Dutch court extends prison for 4 terror plotters," Associated Press, October 2, 2008, at http://www.nrc.nl/international/article2006944.ece/Extended_prison_sentence_for_four_terror_plotters.

TABLE 5.2 *Hofstad Group*

| Name | Country of Ancestry | Age | Family status/ children | Occupation | Education |
|---|---|---|---|---|---|
| 1. Radwan al-Issar[a] | Syria | 43 | Married/1 | Preacher | College graduate, geology |
| 2. Mohammed Bouyeri[b] | Morocco | 26 | Single | Unemployed; youth mentor | 5 years postsecondary education, accounting and information technology[c] |
| 3. Samir Azzouz[d] | Morocco | 18 | Married | Supermarket worker | High school graduate (VWO) |
| 4. Ismaël Akhnikh[e] | Morocco | 22 | Single | Unknown | Expelled from high school |
| 5. Mohammed Fahmi Boughabe[f] | Morocco | 23 | Unknown | Tile layer | Unknown |
| 6. Nouredine El Fahtni[g] | Morocco | 22 | Married (possibly twice) | Worked in Schiedam Phone Center | Unknown |
| 7. Yousef Ettoumi[h] | Morocco | 27 | Married/ 2 | Unknown | Unknown; wanted to be a social worker |
| 8. Ahmed Hamdi[i] | Morocco | 26 | Divorced | Worked at UPC, a European telecom company | Unknown |
| 9. Zine Labidine Aourghe[j] | Morocco | 26 | Married/ 2 | Unemployed; borrows from friends | Unknown |
| 10. Mohamed El Morabit[k] | Morocco | 22 | Married | Unknown | Unknown |
| 11. Jason Walters, aka Jamal[l] | Netherlands; United States | 19 | Single | Unemployed | High school |
| 12. Martine van der Oeven[m] | Netherlands | 26 | Unknown | Former police officer | At least postsecondary |

[a] Suspected spiritual leader of the group. Al-Issar reportedly fled the Netherlands on the day of van Gogh's murder. He is wanted by Dutch authorities, but his whereabouts are unknown. Nessar, Peter, "The Slaying of the Dutch Filmmaker: Religiously Motivated Violence or Islamist Terrorism in the Name of Global Jihad?," *Forsvarets Forskningsinstitutt*, FFI Rapport No. 00376, 2005, pp. 14–15, http://www.ffi.no/no/Rapporter/05-00376.pdf.

[b] In 2005, Bouyeri was sentenced to life imprisonment for killing Dutch film maker Theo van Gogh the prior year, Agence France-Presse (North European Service), "Dutch Terrorism Trial of Six Alleged Muslim Radicals Starts Monday," in English, October 12, 2006.

[c] Bouyeri received a HAVO diploma. With this type of diploma, he could continue on to polytechnic schools, but not universities. Bouyeri enrolled in an HBO program but did not complete it. In the Netherlands, the HBO is a four-year tertiary-level professional education degree. "The Netherlands (Holland) – Education & Schools," Expat Focus Website, http://www.expatfocus.com/expatriate-netherlands-holland-education-schools; and Albert Benschop, "Chronicle of a Political Murder Foretold," FORUM Institute for Multicultural Development, January 6, 2014, at http://www.sociosite.org/jihad_nl_en.php.

[d] Azzouz was sentenced to eight years in prison for preparation of terrorist attacks in December 2006; Ahmet Olgun, "Samir A.'s Action Divides Prisoners," Rotterdam NRC Handelsblad (Internet Version-WWW) in Dutch, December 28, 2006. That conviction was separate from the charges related to the Hofstad Group, for which the Amsterdam appeals court sentenced him to four years for preparing terrorist attacks on government buildings in 2004. Office of the Coordinator for Counterterrorism, "Country Reports on Terrorism: Europe and Eurasia Overview," U.S. Department of State, April 30, 2008.

[e] Akhnikh was with Walters when the latter threw a grenade at police who were trying to arrest them. Initially sentenced to 13 years for membership in the Hofstad Group, possession of grenades, and as an accomplice to murder, Akhnikh's sentence was reduced to 15 months by the January 2008 appeals court. He was acquitted of being an accomplice, but the possession charges remained. Agence France-Presse (North European Service), "Dutch Court Acquits Seven over Suspected Terror Links," in English, January 23, 2008.

[f] Boughabe served 18 months in prison for membership in a terrorist organization, although he was later acquitted by an appeals court. "The 'Hofstadgroep,' a Report from Transnational Terrorism, Security, and the Rule of Law," Workpackage 3, Deliverable 5, April 15, 2007, at http://www.transnationalterrorism.eu/tekst/publications/Hofstadgroep.pdf.

[g] El Fahtni was sentenced to five years for membership in a terrorist organization and illegal possession of arms. Although he was initially acquitted of the membership charges, he was re-convicted in October 2008 and sentenced to eight years. Toby Sterling, "Dutch court extends prison for 4 terror plotters."

[h] Ettoumi served 12 months in prison for membership in a terrorist organization, although he was later acquitted by an appeals court. "The 'Hofstadgroep,' a Report from Transnational Terrorism, Security, and the Rule of Law."

[i] Hamdi served almost all of his two-year sentence for membership in a terrorist organization before being acquitted by an appeals court. "The 'Hofstadgroep,' a Report from Transnational Terrorism, Security, and the Rule of Law."

[j] In 2006, Aouraghe was sentenced to 18 months in prison for membership in a terrorist organization. He did not appeal his conviction and was, therefore, not part of the January 2008 acquittal. Emerson Vermaat, "Hofstad Group – Wrong decision by Dutch appeals court," *Militant Islam Monitor*, January 31, 2008.

[k] El Morabit served almost all of his two-year sentence for membership in a terrorist organization before being acquitted by an appeals court. "The 'Hofstadgroep,' a Report from Transnational Terrorism, Security, and the Rule of Law."

[l] Walters was sentenced to 15 years in prison for possession of four grenades and for throwing a grenade at the police who attempted to arrest him. This sentence was upheld by the January 2008 appeals court, Agence France-Presse (North European Service), "Dutch Court Acquits Seven over Suspected Terror Links," in English, January 23, 2008. Walters and van der Oeven are also listed in the matrix of biographical information on converts to Islam in Table 5.3.

[m] Identified as a member of the Hofstad Group in Olivier Roy, "al-Qaeda: A True Global Movement" in Rik Coolsaet, ed., *Jihadi Terrorism and the Radicalization Challenge in Europe*; Surrey, UK: Ashgate Publishing, 2008, pp. 111–112. Van der Oeven was arrested with Nouredine El Fahtni and his wife Soumaya Sahla in June 2005; she was released in August 2005 for "personal reasons," although police said she remained a suspect. "Dutch Muslim O. Van den released," Netherlands Elsevier (Internet Version) in Dutch, August 3, 2005, at http://www.elsevier.nl/web/nederland/nederlandsemoslimavandeno.vrijgelaten.htm.Walters and van der Oeven are also listed in the matrix of biographical information on converts to Islam in Table 5.3.

South Asian ancestry. We have education data on only half of the 12, but 5 of the 6 have less than a college degree. We have occupation data for 8 of the 12. They are evenly split between those who are either unemployed or working in unskilled jobs and those who are working in either professional or skilled positions. Three-fourths (9) of the members are between the ages of 20 and 30. We are missing marital status data for 2 of the 12 members. Of the remaining members, the majority (7) are married and 3 are single. In conclusion, as with other extremist populations, the data for the Hofstad Group do not support the stereotype of European Islamist extremists as rootless, impressionable young men.

## EAST AFRICANS

Until recently, East Africans have not been in evidence on the European jihadist scene, with the exception of the group that attempted the failed bombings of the London Underground on July 21, 2005.[54] Since 2007, however, there has been a sharp increase in radical recruitment among the Somali communities in Europe and the United States, linked to geopolitical developments in Somalia – the overthrow of the Islamic Courts Union (ICU) government and the Ethiopian occupation of Mogadishu (which ended in January 2009) and the rise of the extremist al-Shabaab insurgency.

### Recruiting the Underclass: The (Failed) July 21, 2005, London Bombers

The group that attempted the bombings of the London Underground on July 21, 2005, was composed of individuals reportedly involved in street crime who manipulated the British immigration and welfare systems.[55] At least two were unemployed, and one received housing benefits. They lived in disparate parts of London and appear to have forged their connections

[54] According to Lorenzo Vidino, Italian authorities believe that Somalis and Eritreans have established extensive networks throughout the country. Lorenzo Vidino, "Is Italy Next in Line after London?" The Jamestown Foundation, *Terrorism Monitor*, Vol. 3, Issue 18, September 21, 2005, at http://www.jamestown.org/programs/tm/single/?tx_ttnews[tt_news]=569&tx_ttnews[backPid]=180&no_cache=1#.U5ThMyRBxQY. Nevertheless, these networks are not known to have been involved in terrorist attacks.

[55] "London bomb suspects stood out as radicals," *Los Angeles Times*, August 15, 2005, at http://www.latimes.com/news/nationworld/world/la-fg-britbombs15aug15,1,2512549.story?coll=la-headlines-world.

through a gymnasium and the Finsbury Park mosque.[56] Yassin Hassan Omar, 24, arrived in the UK from Somalia in 1992 unaccompanied and lived in foster care throughout his teens. He lived in an apartment in north London with Mukhtar Said-Ibrahim, 27, the alleged ringleader of the plot. Mukhtar came to the UK from Eritrea in 1992 as a child refugee. He attended school in north London and became a naturalized British citizen. He may have been radicalized during an almost three-year period as a young offender moving from institution to institution in England. The third bomber, Ramzi Mohamed, 23, a Somali, was part of a small group at the al-Manaar Muslim Cultural Heritage Center in North Kensington that tried to recruit worshippers to radical Islam. According to the imam at the center, whom Mohamed unsuccessfully tried to have fired, Mohamed's group ran a stall in Notting Hill where they distributed radical Islamic books and pamphlets.[57] The fourth, Osman Hussain, aka Isaac Hamdi, 27, is a naturalized British citizen born in Ethiopia. He is believed to have been brought up in Italy, where his family sought asylum claiming to be Somali refugees. He was part of a group of extremists that attempted to gain control of the Stockwell mosque in south London in mid-2003. The last of the would-be bombers, Manfo Kwaku Asiedu, 32, is a British Ghanian who abandoned his bomb in a west London park. A number of other individuals including spouses and family members were arrested alongside these five and charged with supporting their activities.[58]

[56] Paul Tumelty, "Reassessing the July 21 London Bombings," The Jamestown Foundation, *Terrorism Monitor*, Vol. 3, Issue 17, September 14, 2005, at http://www.jamestown.org/programs/tm/single/?tx_ttnews[tt_news]=558&tx_ttnews[backPid]=180&no_cache=1#.U5ThoiRBxQY.

[57] "From refugee to thug to suspect in London plot," *The Washington Post*, August 4, 2005, at http://www.washingtonpost.com/wp-dyn/content/article/2005/08/03/AR2005080302073_pf.html.

[58] Ibid., *BBC News*, "In depth: London attacks: 21 July 2005 – The bombers" (no date) at http://news.bbc.co.uk/1/shared/spl/hi/uk/05/london_blasts/investigation/html/suspects.stm; Martin Bright and Tariq Panja, "Family of Briton held in Zambia fear US jail bid," *The Observer*, July 31, 2005, at www.guardian.co.uk/attackonlondon/story/0,16132,1539785,00.html; "10 face court over July 21 attacks," August 11, 2005, at www.guardian.co.uk/attackonlondon/story/0,16132,1546877,00.html; Alan Travis and Audrey Gillan, "Bomb suspect 'became a militant' in prison – background details emerge of refugee pair who grew up in Britain, amid alarm at scapegoating of asylum seekers," *The Guardian*, July 28, 2005, at www.guardian.co.uk/attackonlondon/story/0,16132,1537640,00.html; "Profiles of the five men in custody – the July 21 suspects," *The Guardian*, July 29, 2005, at http://www.theguardian.com/uk/2005/jul/30/july7.immigrationpolicy2; Audrey Gillan, "Four suspects said to have worshipped at Finsbury Park mosque," *The Guardian*, August 1, 2005, at www.guardian.co.uk/attackonlondon/story/0,16132,1540243,00.html.

After the failed attack, one of the suspects, Osman Hussain, fled to Italy and contacted associates in Rome, Brescia, and Udine.[59] This was no accident. Italian authorities believe that Somalis and Eritreans have established an extensive network throughout the country.[60] These networks might take on greater significance in the European jihadist scene as greater numbers of Europe-based Somalis become involved with al-Shabaab.

## Radicalization of Ethnic Somalis

One of the phenomena associated with the Ethiopian invasion of Mogadishu and the rise of al-Shabaab as the core of the resistance to the Ethiopians was the radicalization of sectors of the Somali Diaspora. In contrast to other Somali Islamist groups, whose objectives extend only to Greater Somalia,[61] al-Shabaab sought to link the struggle in Somalia to the global jihad. This view is given credence by al-Shabaab's links to al-Qaeda and the protection that the group extended to senior al-Qaeda figures in Somalia.[62] A video released by al-Shabaab in November 2008 featured Kenyan al-Qaeda operative Saleh Ali Saleh Nabhan, also known as Abu Yusuf (killed in a U.S. special operations raid in southern Somalia in September 2009), meeting with al-Shabaab spokesman Mukhtar Robow, alias Abu Mansur, and training fighters at a terrorist training camp. Saleh declared that the camps are open for anyone and called for Muslim youth in Africa to come to Somalia.[63]

[59] Lorenzo Vidino, "Is Italy Next in Line after London?" The Jamestown Foundation, *Terrorism Monitor*, Vol. 3, No. 18, September 21, 2005.

[60] "El Tribunal Supremo italiano da su visto bueno a la extradición a España de El Egipcio," *El Pais* (Spain), December 1, 2004, at http://elpais.com/elpais/2004/12/01/actualidad/1101892619_850215.html.

[61] Somalia proper, including Puntland and Somaliland, and the Somali-majority regions in the Ogaden and Kenya.

[62] These included Abu Talha al-Sudani (aka Tariq Abdullah) and Fazul Mohammed ("the Comoran"), both associated with the bombings of the American embassies in Kenya and Nairobi. Al-Sudani was killed in early 2007. Fazul Mohammed was reportedly appointed al-Qaeda's new leader in East Africa in November 2009, replacing Saleh Ali Saleh Nabhan. Mohammed was killed in a shootout at a checkpoint in Mogadishu in June 2011. Bill Roggio, "Senior al-Qaeda Operative Killed in Somalia," *The Long War Journal*, September 1, 2008, at http://www.longwarjournal.org/archives/2008/09/senior_al_qaeda_oper_1.php; and "Al Qaeda Names Fazul Mohammed East African Commander, November 11, 2009, at http://www.longwarjournal.org/archives/2009/11/al_qaeda_names_fazul.php.

[63] Nick Grace, "Shabaab Reaches Out to al Qaeda Senior Leaders, Announces Death al Sudani," *The Long War Journal*, September 2, 2008, at http://www.longwarjournal.org/archives/2008/09/shabab_reaches_out_t.php.

Most European Muslims joining the Shabaab come from Scandinavian countries, where there are large numbers of Somali refugees. Somali authorities reported in early 2007 that several Swedish citizens were killed during Ethiopian and Somali transitional federal government forces attacks on retreating ICU forces. Ethiopian forces arrested three other Swedish citizens in early 2007. The Ethiopians also reportedly arrested at least seven British Muslims on suspicion of aiding the ICU.[64] The role of Europe-based foreign fighters (mostly ethnic Somalis residing in the West) in the armed conflict in Somalia since 2007 is discussed in Chapter 7.

## TURKS: A TRADITIONAL COMMUNITY ON THE PATH TO RADICALIZATION?

Groups on the radical fringe of political Islam such as the Cologne-based Kalifaatstaat, better known as the Kaplan Group, headed by Cemalettin Kaplan and after his death in 1995 by his son Metin Kaplan until the latter's extradition to Turkey in 2004, had long operated in Europe. However, until recently, the Turkish community in Europe produced few Islamist terrorists.[65] The Turks generally went to Germany, the Netherlands, and Austria as migrant workers and continue to be focused on economic goals. Most came from rural areas, held traditional values, and were not particularly engaged in politics. The hierarchical pattern of Turkish families also meant that these communities had better control of their youth. Moreover, few Turks understand Arabic, which is the preferred language of jihadist discourse. However, as noted later, these barriers are beginning to crumble.

In recent years, the Turkish communities in Germany and the Netherlands have been showing a trend toward a parallel Muslim society. Some German sociologists believe they are seeing a process of de-integration, by which the third generation is less assimilated than the second and is becoming more religious and more conservative. According to Faruk Süen, director of the Center for Turkish Studies, boys and girls are increasingly defining themselves by reference to their faith. In a 2000 survey, 8 percent of immigrants of Turkish extraction said

[64] James Brandon, "Islamist Movements Recruiting in the West for the Somali Jihad," The Jamestown Foundation, *Terrorism Monitor*, Vol. 7, No. 1, January 9, 2009, at http://www.jamestown.org/programs/tm/single/?tx_ttnews[tt_news]=34321&tx_ttnews[backPid]=412&no_cache=1#.U4zPdS9woSA.

[65] We do not include in this analysis Kurdish terrorists associated with the separatist Kurdistan Workers' Party (PKK).

they were "very religious." In 2005, the figure had climbed to 28 percent. The percentage of those who believed that Muslim women should cover their hair almost doubled from 27 percent in 2000 to 47 percent five years later. A similar pattern emerged on the topics of coeducational sports classes and school trips. The proportion of those opposed to mixed-sex activities rose from 19 percent in 2000 to 30 percent in 2005. The trend toward religious conservatism was particularly strong among women and young men: 59 percent of all 18- to 30-year-olds and almost 62 percent of female respondents favored Muslim women wearing headscarves.[66]

German security officials believe that Turks may not be as resistant to radicalization as hitherto believed, but rather that they have lagged behind ethnic Arabs, who have been the principal source of Muslim extremists in Germany.[67] According to German terrorism expert Guido Steinberg, a distinct Turkish jihadist scene has developed in Turkey and among Turks in the European diaspora that has adopted a more internationalist ideology than that of their predecessors. This trend was manifested in the discovery in September 2007 of a plot by a Turkish-Kurdish-Arab-German group known as the Sauerland cell to carry out terrorist attacks against U.S. targets in Germany.

The nucleus of this group seems to have been formed in the Salafist milieu of the Multikulturhaus in Neu-Ulm. At least 10 to 20 of them went to terrorist training camps in Pakistan run by the IJU, a splinter group of the Islamic Movement of Uzbekistan (IMU). Apparently the IJU leadership wanted to influence the German debate on extending the Afghanistan mandate and bring about the withdrawal of German forces from Afghanistan.[68] Of the three individuals initially arrested in connection with this plot, two were German converts to Islam and the third, Adem Yilmaz, 28, was a German citizen of Turkish descent. Further investigation expanded the parameters of the group to some 30 individuals, most of them ethnic Turks and several converts, Azeris, Uzbeks, and an Arab.[69]

[66] Andrea Brandt and Cordula Meyer, "Religious Divisions within Germany: A Parallel Muslim Universe," *Der Spiegel*, February 20, 2007, at http://www.spiegel.de/international/religious-divisions-within-germany-a-parallel-muslim-universe-a-467360.html.

[67] Interview with German Ministry of Interior officials, Berlin, June 2008.

[68] Guido Steinberg, "The Evolving Threat from Jihadist Terrorism in Turkey," Real Instituto Elcano, February 16, 2009, at http://www.realinstitutoelcano.org/wps/portal/web/rielcano_en/contenido?WCM_GLOBAL_CONTEXT=/elcano/elcano_in/zonas_in/international+terrorism/ari26-2009#.U5TlwSRBxQY.

[69] Raffaello Pantucci, "'Fritz:' Germany's new breed of holy warrior," *HSToday*, April 4, 2008, at http://www.hstoday.us/briefings/correspondents-watch/single-article/fritz-germany-s-new-breed-of-holy-warrior/ef8871e440bc514b70f554c0867840b7.html;

The two men who operated the IJU website were Turks based in Istanbul. German authorities are concerned that the IJU plot may represent a new trend, the emergence of multiethnic extremist networks composed of Arabs, Pakistanis, Turks, and converts. This development could represent a significant escalation of the threat.[70]

A Turkish national born in Germany, Cüneyt Ciftci, aka Saad Abu Furqan, 28, drove an explosive-laden truck into a U.S. guard post in Afghanistan in the spring of 2008, killing two American soldiers. Ciftci was born in Bavaria to a family of Turkish immigrants. His father was a prominent member of the Turkish community in Ansbach, the town in Bavaria where his family had settled. Ciftci's father was described as orthodox and as a founding member of the Ansbach Milli Görüs mosque society. At the age of 12, Ciftci was sent by his father to a state-run religious school in Turkey, where he learned, among other things, to recite the Quran from memory.

After studying for three years in Turkey, Ciftci returned to Ansbach, where he spent the next period of his life trying to find his place. He is said to have encountered great difficulties adapting to secular German life. He dropped out of school and broke off a masonry apprenticeship. He worked for a while as an interior decorator and also as a McDonald's employee. In 1998, Ciftci found employment with Bosch, an international technology company. This job provided him with a dependable income, paid vacation, health insurance, and other benefits. During his employment at Bosch, he was regarded as a "normal employee" whose conduct at work was "orderly and level-headed." In 2000, Ciftci was granted an unlimited right of residence in Germany, but his application for German citizenship was repeatedly turned down. He eventually withdrew his application.[71]

According to his acquaintances, at this time Ciftci was not especially religious. Rather, he was seen as "modern" and "Western." He met a woman in a döner kebab restaurant and married her in 2001 against the will of his father. The bride came from a secular Turkish family and did not wear a headscarf. Four years after the wedding, the young family moved in

Guido Steinberg, "A Turkish al-Qaeda: The Islamic Jihad Union and the Internationalization of Uzbek Jihadism," Center for Contemporary Conflict, *Strategic Insights*, Vol. 7, Issue 2, July 2008, at http://www.ccc.nps.navy.mil/si/2008/Jul/steinbergJul08.asp.

[70] Interview with German Ministry of Interior officials, Berlin, June 2008.

[71] Stefan Meining and Ahmet Senyurt, "The Case of the Bavarian Taliban," Current Trends in Islamist Ideology, Vol. 7, The Hudson Institute, Center on Islam, Democracy and the Future of the Muslim World, November 11, 2008, at http://dev.hudson.org/content/researchattachments/attachment/1173/20081111_ct7.pdf.

with Ciftci's parents, and Ciftci's wife suddenly began to wear a headscarf. She gradually became estranged from her mother, whom Ciftci regarded as too Western. Ciftci's own outward appearance also changed, and he began wearing Islamic clothing and a beard. In April 2007, Ciftci, his wife and two children left Germany for Pakistan, after formally deregistering as a resident at the local town hall. After settling with his family in Pakistan, he proceeded to a training camp run by the IJU.[72] Ciftci, according to Bavarian security authorities, had been in contact with the transnational Islamic missionary movement Tablighi Jamaat (TJ), which has been the subject of increased scrutiny by German authorities in recent years; his recruitment into the IJU might have been through Adem Yilmaz, one of the suspects in the Sauerland plot, who seems to have facilitated Ciftci's journey to the Pakistan-Afghanistan region.[73]

Other signs of radicalization are apparent in the European Turkish community. The number of radical Islamist websites in Turkish is increasing, suggesting a growing market for radical media content.[74] German security authorities fear that converts are also a channel for the transmission of radical ideas – in German – to the Turkish community.[75] Dutch security agencies also believe that young people of Turkish descent are becoming more vulnerable to radicalization. The Dutch believe that Turkish communities are losing some of their cohesion and beginning to produce disaffected, disassociated young people ripe for recruitment into extremist groups. The second and third generations tend to be culturally conflicted, torn between the traditional values of the parent generation and the modern Western values they themselves were born into. They also tend to be economically adrift, no longer willing to perform menial jobs and manual labor but not integrated or educated enough to compete for better white-collar jobs. This is exacerbated by downturns in the European economies and the decline of sectors that formerly employed unskilled or semiskilled workers.

## CONVERTS

Reliable statistics on European converts to Islam do not exist. France's internal intelligence service, the Renseignements Généraux (RG), estimated

[72] Meining and Senyurt.

[73] Annette Ramelsberger and Matthias Sander, "Per E-Mail in den Heiligen Krieg," *Süddeutsche.de,* May 17, 2010, at http://www.sueddeutsche.de/bayern/selbstmordattentaeter-aus-ansbach-per-e-mail-in-den-heiligen-krieg-1.282642.

[74] Discussion with Guido Steinberg, Berlin, June 2008.

[75] Interview with German Ministry of Interior officials, Berlin, June 2008.

that there were 30,000 to 50,000 converts in France.[76] A German security official estimated about 20,000 to 30,000 converts in Germany.[77] In his study of British converts, Ali Köse found that the converts had become strongly critical both of their childhood religion and of the society in which they grew up. They found Christianity too morally permissive and society too secularized. Choosing Islam enabled them to more easily orient their everyday lives toward God, as Islam offered practical ways to lead a meaningful private and social life. Köse concluded that it was the dynamics of their own lives and thoughts that led them to convert. The vast majority (83 percent) reported that they had not lost their belief in God although they felt they had lost their earlier allegiance to a church. Comments by those in the sample also indicated discontent with questionable aspects of their own lifestyles. Conversion to Islam was an experience of breaking with the past in order to turn to a more real religious life.[78]

Although the majority of converts to Islam reject the extremist world-view – for instance, converts have played a leading role in moderate Muslim networks in Spain[79] – a small but growing number have been involved in extremist movements.[80] What makes some converts more likely than others to join extremist groups? A key factor appears to be the experience of conversion. Conversion through Sufism leads to a moderate dimension of Islam.[81] On the other hand, some convert directly to Salafism, within which numerous gateways to radicalization can be found.

[76] Craig Smith, "Europe fears threat from its converts to Islam," *International Herald Tribune*, July 19, 2004, at http://www.religionnewsblog.com/7916/europe-fears-threat-from-its-converts-to-islam.

[77] Interview with German Ministry of Interior officials, Berlin, June 2008.

[78] Ali Köse, "The Journey from the Secular to the Sacred: Experiences of Native British Converts to Islam," *Social Compass*, Vol. 46, No. 3, 1999, pp. 301–312, at http://scp.sagepub.com/cgi/content/abstract/46/3/301. Se also Köse, *Conversion to Islam: A Study of Native British Converts*. London and New York: Kegan Paul, 1996; Thomas Gerholm and Yngve George Litham, eds., *The New Islamic Presence in Europe*, London: Mansell, 1988; Larry Poston, *Islamic Da'wah in the West: Muslim Missionary Activity and the Dynamics of Conversion to Islam*. New York: Oxford University Press, 1992.

[79] Examples are Mansur Escudero, president of the Islamic Council (Junta Islámica) of Spain, and Yusuf Fernández, head of webislam.com, the largest Spanish and French Muslim website.

[80] With some exceptions. According to Reinares, the number of radicalized converts in his sample of 188 persons imprisoned for Islamist terrorism-related offenses in Spain is statistically insignificant. Fernando Reinares, "Hacia una caracterización social del terrorismo yihadista en España.

[81] Many Western converts to Islam are drawn to Sufism, because Sufi spirituality allows a personal relationship with God that many individuals in search of spiritual meaning find appealing.

A German security official believes that a prior criminal record – a common characteristic of a subset of converts – is a reliable predictor of radicalization.[82]

Some converts, particularly those who are poorly educated or have criminal or other troubled backgrounds, know little about Islam when they are first introduced to the religion and, therefore, are more likely to accept the interpretation that they are taught. These converts generally lack a cultural context to be able to filter out extremist rhetoric; many become educated about Islam not only through the lens of the individuals they meet but also by surfing the Internet.[83] The proliferation of Islamic extremist websites designed to attract new recruits helps guide these individuals into accepting a radical Salafist worldview.

The socioeconomic profile of European converts differs depending on the country. In a June 2005 report, the RG presented the results of a study of 1,610 French converts to Islam who had come to the attention of the police because of active proselytism, criminal activities, or links to radical groups. The converts in the RG study constitute a young population, mainly male, with a median age of 32. Seventeen percent are women. They are concentrated in urban areas with a large practicing Muslim North African population.

The converts in the RG report are disproportionately in the lower socioeconomic strata of the French population. Forty-nine percent do not have a secondary school diploma. Of those between the ages of 15 and 19, only 20 percent are students (in contrast to the national rate of 95 percent). In the 20- to 24-year-old bracket, 6 percent are in educational institutions (the national rate is 50 percent). About 50 percent of the converts are without known employment or unofficially unemployed, and 31 percent are unskilled or low-skilled workers.

About 10 percent convert to Islam while in prison. According to the RG report, Islamic proselytism in prisons sometimes takes the form of a power struggle with the prison authorities or with other prisoners. The believers ask for the installation of a prayer room, halal meals, or a Muslim chaplaincy and complain about discrimination. Once freed, nearly 17 percent

[82] Interview with German Ministry of Interior officials, Berlin, June 2008.

[83] This is consistent with Quintan Wiktorowicz's findings in his research on Al Muhajiroun. Wiktorowicz found that many members had no previous religious affiliation and little understanding of the Quran. Quintan Wiktorowicz, *Radical Islam Rising: Muslim Extremism in the West*. Lanham, MD: Rowman & Littlefield, 2005, p. 102.

of those who convert to Islam in prison join radical Islamist groups or their support networks. Overall, close to 44 percent opt for a Salafist-inspired form of Islam. Salafists, according to the study, "benefit from the wave of re-Islamization of Maghrebian youth in the suburbs, initiated by Tabligh."[84]

An examination of European converts might shed some light into the processes that lead European converts to join extremist groups. Table 5.3 summarizes the background of European converts who have been involved in incidents of Islamist terrorism.[85]

Figure 5.6 presents the educational and occupational backgrounds of the converts linked to terrorism. Ninety percent have less than a college degree. Of these, 18 percent dropped out of high school; 14 percent completed either a certificate or vocational program after high school; and 14 percent have some college coursework.[86] Consistent with the findings in the RG report, seventy-one percent of the converts were either unemployed or employed in unskilled jobs.[87] The breakdown of European nationalities in Figure 5.7 shows that the most commonly represented backgrounds in the sample are French (34 percent) and British (29 percent).

Figure 5.8 indicates the age range of the converts identified earlier. A total of 24 individuals were included in the assessment with no missing data. A majority (58 percent) of converts linked to terrorism were in their 20s at the time of their arrest or at the time when the plot was developing. Another 21 percent were in their 30s, with 13 percent older than age 35.

[84] "Les conversions à l'islam radical inquiètent la police française," *Le Monde*, July 13, 2005, at http://www.geostrategique.net/viewtopic.php?t=670&sid=274f7632a690b0a54ae206be78d06f2f.

[85] There is no comprehensive list of converts to Islam linked to terrorist incidents in Europe. This list was compiled in the course of the research for this project.

[86] Data are missing for two individuals.

[87] For our purposes, jobs were classified as "unskilled" if they required fewer than two years of training or experience. Skilled jobs required at least two years of training and experience. For example, an assembly line worker who checks that new televisions can turn on and off is in an unskilled position because he or she would be able to do the same job with little or no understanding of how a television works. In contrast, a television repair person is a skilled worker because he or she must be able to diagnose and fix the problem and, hence, understand how a television works. A profession is an occupation or career that generally involves substantial academic training, formal qualifications, and membership in a professional or regulatory body. Examples include physician, nurse, lawyer, accountant, architect, pilot, teacher, engineer, and so on.

TABLE 5.3 *Converts Linked to Terrorism*

| Name | Nationality | DOB | Age[a] | Terrorist association | Family status/ children | Occupation | Education |
|---|---|---|---|---|---|---|---|
| 1. José Luis Galán González | Spain | 1964 | 40 | Member of Yarkas cell in Spain | Married/ 2 | Call center operator for Seur | Unknown |
| 2. Baldomero Lara Sánchez | Spain | 1975 | 29 | Martyrs of Morocco | Married | Arms dealer | Unknown |
| 3. Richard Reid | UK | 1973 | 28 | al-Qaeda | Single | Unemployed | High school through age 16[b] |
| 4. Dhiren Barot aka Abu Isa al-Hindi | UK (born in India) | 1971 | 32 | al-Qaeda | Married | Reservations assistant, Air Malta | High school through age 16; certificate in tourism |
| 5. Germaine Lindsay | UK (born in Jamaica) | 1985 | 19 | 7/7/2005 London bombing | Married/ 2 | Carpet fitter (former drug dealer) | High school |
| 6. Andrew Rowe, aka Yusef Abdullah[c] | UK | 1971 | 34 | Linked to Lionel Dumont gang | Married/ 4 | Former drug dealer | High school |
| 7. Donald Stewart-Whyte, aka Abdul Waheed[d] | UK | 1986 | 21 | August 2006 TransaAtlantic airliner bomb plot | Married | Unemployed; previous work at a hairdresser's and electronics store | High school through age 16 |
| 8. Oliver Savant, aka Ibrahim Savant[e] | UK | 1980 | 26 | August 2006 transatlantic airliner bomb plot | Married/ 1 | Bookkeeper | Some college |
| 9. Brian Young, aka Umar Islam[f] | UK | 1978 | 28 | August 2006 transatlantic airliner bomb plot | Married/ 1 | Postman | General National Vocational Qualification (GNVQ) in Business[g] |

(*continued*)

TABLE 5.3 (*cont.*)

| Name | Nationality | DOB | Age[a] | Terrorist association | Family status/ children | Occupation | Education |
|---|---|---|---|---|---|---|---|
| 10. Lionel Dumont[h] | France | 1971 | 25 | Roubaix Gang | Married | Car dealer (fired) | High school |
| 11. Christophe Caze[i] | France | 1969 | 27 | Roubaix Gang | Single | Medical student | Medical school |
| 12. Pierre Richard Robert | France | 1972 | 28 | May 2003 Casablanca attacks | Married | Street vendor; petty criminal | Some high school |
| 13. David Courtailler[j] | France/UK | 1976 | 28 | American Embassy Paris bomb plot | Single | Unemployed | High school |
| 14. Jérôme Courtailler | France/UK | 1974 | 29 | American Embassy Paris bomb plot | Single | Unemployed | High school |
| 15. Johann Bonté | France | 1981 | 20 | American Embassy Paris bomb plot | Single | Series of temporary jobs | High school |
| 16. Jean-Marc Grandvisir | France | 1978 | 23 | American Embassy Paris bomb plot | Unknown | Youth counselor | Some college |
| 17. Willie Virgile Brigitte[k] | France | 1968 | 35 | al-Qaeda | Married/ 1 | Trained in marine mechanics | Bachelor's degree |
| 18. Christian Ganczarski | Germany (born in Poland) | 1966 | 36 | Bombing of Djerba synagogue, Tunisia | Married/ 3 | Trained as locksmith | Vocational |
| 19. Jason Walters, aka Jamal[l] | Netherlands | 1985 | 19 | Hofstad Group | Single | Unemployed | High school |
| 20. Martine van den Oever | Netherlands | 1979 | 26 | Hofstad Group | Unknown | Former police officer | At least vocational |

| | | | | | | | |
|---|---|---|---|---|---|---|---|
| 21. Muriel Degauque | Belgium | 1967 | 38 | Suicide bomber | Married | Unemployed; sometime café worker and homemaker | Left school at 16 |
| 22. Eric Breininger, aka Mujahid Abdul Gaffar al-Almani[m] | Germany | 1987 | 20 | Islamic Jihad Union (IJU) | Married | Unemployed; did part-time work for a package company | Dropped out of junior high and trade school |
| 23. Daniel Schneider, aka Abdullah[n] | Germany | 1985 | 21 | IJU | Single | Unemployed; welfare | High school through 11th grade |
| 24. Fritz Martin Gelowicz[o] | Germany | 1979 | 28 | IJU | Married | Unemployed; welfare | Some college |

[a] At time of arrest or terrorist incident.

[b] In the UK, compulsory education ends at age 16. This is not quite equivalent to a high school diploma, however.

[c] Sentenced to 15 years in prison on terrorism charges in September 2005. "British Muslim convert jailed for terrorism offences," *The Guardian* (UK), September 24, 2005, at http://www.guardian.co.uk/uk/2005/sep/24/terrorism.politics.

[d] Found not guilty of conspiracy to cause explosions on aircraft and conspiracy to murder but pleaded guilty to a firearms offense. "Mass murder at 30,000 feet: Islamic extremists guilty of airline bomb plot," *Times Online*, September 7, 2009 at http://www.timesonline.co.uk/tol/news/uk/crime/article6824884.ece.

[e] Found not guilty of conspiracy to cause explosions on aircraft, but could face retrial on more general conspiracy to murder charges because the jury could not reach a verdict. "Mass murder at 30,000 feet: Islamic extremists guilty of airline bomb plot," *Times Online*, September 7, 2009.

[f] Found guilty of conspiracy to murder. "Mass murder at 30,000 feet: Islamic extremists guilty of airline bomb plot," *Times Online*, September 7, 2009.

[g] Falls somewhere in between high school and college on the U.S. scale.

[h] Veteran of Bosnian war. "Trial of French Islamic Radical sheds light on converts' role," *Washington Post*, January 1, 2006, at http://www.washingtonpost.com/wp-dyn/content/article/2005/12/31/AR2005123101056_pf.html.

[i] Veteran of Bosnian war. "Trial of French Islamic Radical sheds light on converts' role," *Washington Post*, January 1, 2006.

[j] Craig H. Smith, "Europe fears Islamic converts may give cover for extremism," *New York Times*, July 19, 2004, at http://query.nytimes.com/gst/fullpage.html?res=9C06E0DD133AF93AA25754C0A9629C8B63.

[k] May have played a role in the assassination of Afghan Northern Alliance commander Ahmed Shah Massoud.

[l] Arrested in the Netherlands in November 2004 following the assassination of Theo van Gogh. Suspected of planning assassination of Dutch political figures

[m] "Eric B." is a 20-year-old German convert to Islam from Neuenkirchen in Saarland who traveled to Pakistan in 2007 and joined the IJU. See NEFA Foundation, "Islamic Jihad Union (IJU): "Interview with German Islamic Convert 'Eric B.,'" May 23, 2008. Killed by Pakistani forces in North Waziristan in April 2010.

[n] Charged in connection with IJU plot to bomb the U.S. air base at Ramstein and other targets in Germany.

[o] Charged in connection with IJU plot to bomb the U.S. air base at Ramstein and other targets in Germany.

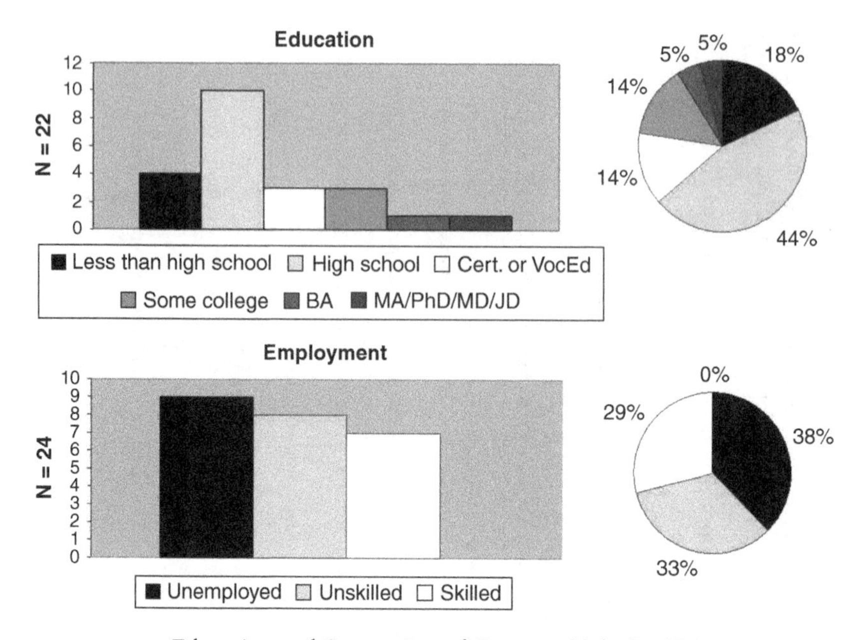


FIGURE 5.4 Education and Occupation of Converts Linked to Terrorism

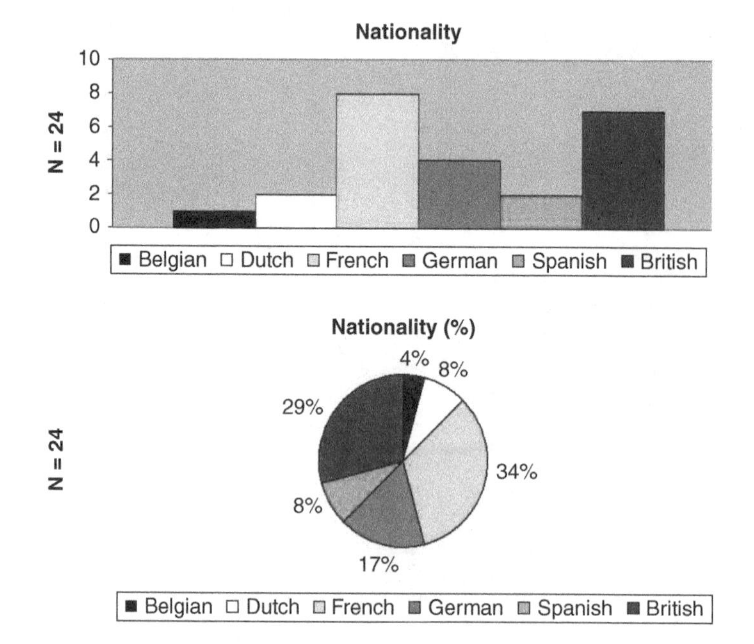


FIGURE 5.5 Nationalities of Converts Linked to Terrorism

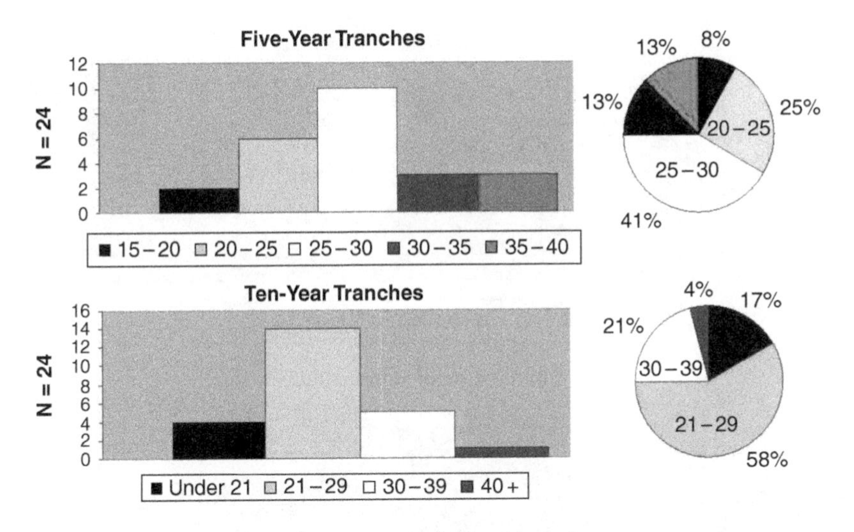


FIGURE 5.6 Age Range of Converts Linked to Terrorism

In this same group of individuals, about two-thirds were married, as shown in Figure 5.9. Among those who were married, half had children and half did not.[88] None of those who were unmarried had children.

The trial of Lionel Dumont in France sheds light on the role of converts in Islamist terrorist networks. Dumont, a former Catholic from northern France, converted to Islam in 1991. Christophe Caze, a fellow convert, persuaded Dumont to join him in a mission to Bosnia, where both enlisted in the Bosnian army's international Mujahidin battalion. After returning to France, he joined a group headed by Caze known as the Roubaix gang, which engaged in armed robberies and attempted a car-bomb attack against a G-7 summit in Lille in 1996. Caze and other gang members were killed in a shootout with police, but Dumont survived and fled to Bosnia. Over the next seven years, he traveled extensively throughout southeastern Europe and Asia using false passports. British authorities believe that when he was arrested in Munich in 2003, Dumont and an associate, a British convert of Jamaican descent named Andrew Rowe, were in the late stages of planning a terrorist attack in Europe.[89]

[88] Data are missing for four individuals.

[89] Rowe was arrested as he tried to board the English Channel tunnel train in France. "Trial of French Islamic radical sheds light on converts' role," *Washington Post*, January 1, 2006, at http://www.washingtonpost.com/wp-dyn/content/article/2005/12/31/AR2005123101056.html.

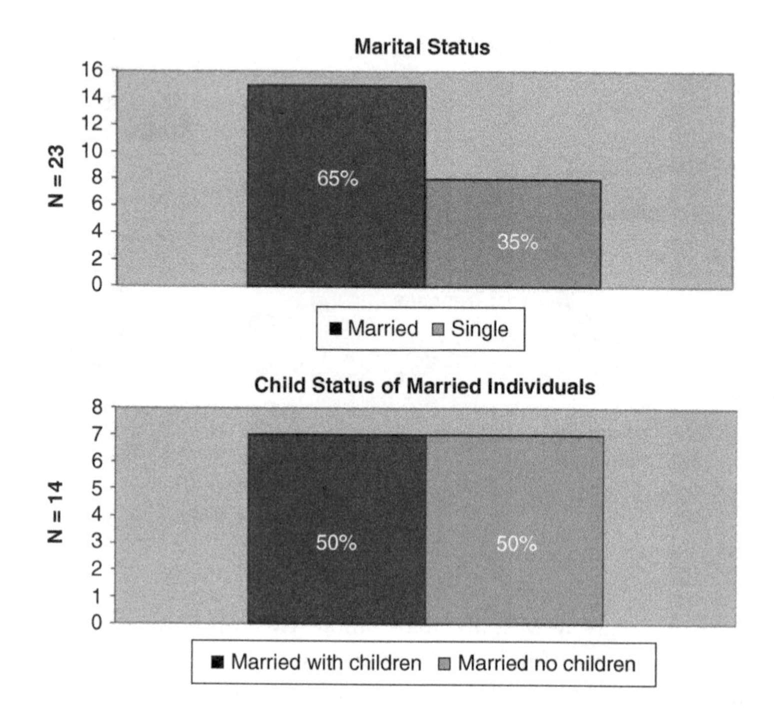


FIGURE 5.7 Marital Status of Converts Linked to Terrorism

The first European female suicide bomber was Muriel Degauque, 38. She was raised as a Catholic near the Belgian industrial city of Charleroi. She appears to have had a chaotic adolescence, used drugs, had an irregular work history, and ran away from home. She married and divorced a Belgian of Turkish ancestry and converted to Islam after becoming involved with an Algerian man. After meeting her second husband, a Moroccan named Issam Goris, she became increasingly estranged from her family. In the fall of 2004, she and her husband traveled to Iraq, apparently through Syria. In November 2004, she detonated explosives strapped to her body in an attack on an American military column near Baquba. The Belgian police believe that her husband, Goris, had fallen in with a recruiting network for al-Zarqawi's al-Qaeda in Iraq organization. U.S. soldiers subsequently killed Degauque's husband in a separate incident in Iraq.[90]

[90] Craig Smith, "Raised as Catholic in Belgium, she died as a Muslim bomber," *The New York Times*, December 6, 2005, at http://www.nytimes.com/2005/12/06/international/europe/06brussels.html?pagewanted=all.

"Shoebomber" Richard Reid and Don Stewart-Whyte, aka Abdul Waheed, one of the accused in the August 2006 transatlantic airline bombing plot, fit the same profile of troubled individuals who found an answer to their personal problems in radical Islam. Before his conversion, Reid fell into a life of petty crime and was jailed for a string of muggings, for which he served sentences in a number of prisons, including Feltham young offenders' institution in west London, where he is said to have converted to Islam.[91]

Stewart-Whyte's father was a Conservative Party agent, and he attended the prestigious Dr. Challoner's Grammar School in Chesham. He had trouble with drugs and alcohol as a teenager. He worked at a hairdresser's and a local electronics store and converted to Islam along with his sister. According to neighbors, "he said that he was converting to Islam because it all made sense and had just clicked with him ... His mother was not best pleased about it but after he converted he seemed a lot calmer and more at peace with himself."[92]

By contrast, Fritz Gelowicz, alleged to be the leader of the Sauerland group, the terrorist cell uncovered in Germany in September 2007, was not marginalized from society except in a psychological sense. His father was an engineer running a firm developing solar energy technology. His mother was a medical doctor. His parents divorced when he was a teenager. Former schoolmates say that the divorce was hard for him and that he turned to religion as a way of coping. His brother also converted to Islam but according to German authorities was never involved in extremism. Gelowicz enrolled to study engineering at Ulm University, where he became a member of an extremist Islamic study circle. He befriended Yehia Yousif, a medical doctor, who acted as imam and leader in this community. Gelowicz became increasingly absorbed into militant Islamism. He took a leave of absence from the university and enrolled in Arabic courses in Egypt and Syria and religious studies in Saudi Arabia. He also undertook the *hajj* to Mecca with the two other main suspects in the conspiracy and spent time at a training camp in the tribal areas of Pakistan run by the IJU.[93]

[91] "Who is Richard Reid?" *BBC News*, December 28, 2001, at http://news.bbc.co.uk/2/hi/uk_news/1731568.stm.

[92] "Profiling the suspects: Converts to Islam," *Time*, August 11, 2006, at http://www.time.com/time/world/article/0,8599,1225687,00.html.

[93] Petter Nesser, "Lessons Learned from the September 2007 German Terrorist Plot," *CTC Sentinel*, Vol. 1, Issue 4, 2008.

Eric Breininger, who gained notoriety as the spokesman for the German Taliban Mujahideen, is an example of the individual who had become discontented with his lifestyle and converted to Islam as a way of breaking with his past and beginning a new life. Breininger was raised by a single mother after his parents' divorce. In his alleged autobiography, *Mein Weg nach Jannah* (My way to paradise), which was released on jihadi websites after his death, he says that he had the life of a "typical Western teenager." Breininger's conversion to radical Islam may have been a function of where he lived. A Muslim colleague at his workplace in Neunkirchen, a town near Saarbrücken, introduced him to a Salafi version of Islam. There he also met Daniel Schneider, aka "Abdullah," a member of the Sauerland cell who was later sentenced to 12 years in prison on terrorism charges, and Hussain al-Malla, a Lebanese residing in Germany who provided the final inspiration for Breininger to convert.

Breininger was influenced by the Salafi precepts of *al-wala' wal-bara'* (loyalty toward Muslims and enmity toward infidels) and *fard al-'ayn* (the individual obligation of jihad). He consumed jihadist videos and the works of radical ideologues. When his original decision to participate in the armed struggle in Algeria did not work out, he traveled to Egypt to study Arabic in Cairo. There he was joined by al-Malla, who convinced him to travel to Afghanistan. They proceeded by way of Iran and Pakistan until they arrived at an IJU training camp. After three years with the IJU, Breininger helped establish a subgroup, the German Taliban Mujahideen, with other Germans who had completed training and were planning to join the Taliban. Pakistani forces in the border region with Afghanistan killed Breininger in May 2010.[94]

According to a story in the German periodical *Spiegel*, the Federal Office of Criminal Investigation (BKA) maintains a list of about 100 suspects who have gone to Afghanistan or Pakistan. These expatriates are different from an earlier generation of extremists. They are ethnically mixed and often men and women leave Germany together with their children, or even before the birth of their children, usually burning the bridges behind them. Among these were "Jan" and "Alexandra," a young convert couple from Berlin. Jan's parents noticed the first change in 2008, when their son suddenly refused to eat pork. He told his mother earlier that he had purchased a copy of the Quran. His parents were not concerned because Jan had completed high school and planned to become a career

[94] Thomas Hegghammer, "Guest Post: The Story of Eric Breininger," *Jihadica*, May 11, 2010, at http://www.jihadica.com/guest-post-the-story-of-eric-breininger/.

soldier. He and his girlfriend Alexandra, who was two years younger than him, wanted to get married. The wedding was in September. In November, the couple married again – this time in a Muslim ceremony. After that, the process of radicalization moved very quickly. By early 2009, the young couple mentioned for the first time that they would rather practice their faith undisturbed by distractions, in a country where this was still possible, such as Yemen, Somalia, or Pakistan, far away from the big cities.

A few months later, Jan and Alexandra started to secretly auction off their possessions on eBay. In September, they left supposedly on a vacation trip to celebrate their first wedding anniversary. Jan and Alexandra packed their belongings into a rental car, picked up another couple, and the four headed off into exile. One of their traveling companions was 17 years old and six months pregnant – her husband had just turned 20. Their child would not be born in Germany. The two married couples headed to Budapest, where they boarded a plane for Istanbul. Jan placed one last call to his parents from a hotel. Since then, there have been only sporadic e-mails to Jan's parents. He is living among brothers, and they can't visit him; it would be too dangerous, he said. And he could no longer imagine returning to a life among the infidels.

## CONCLUSION

The analysis in this chapter makes clear that radicalization does not advance uniformly across Europe's diverse Muslim populations. Some communities appear to be more prone to radicalization than others, for reasons peculiar to those communities. For instance, the vast majority of individuals who have been involved in episodes of Islamist extremist violence in the United Kingdom are second- or third-generation British citizens of Pakistani ancestry. Moreover, for the most part, this population traces its ancestry to districts in Pakistan adjacent to the conflict zone in Kashmir. This suggests that the diasporic connections to terrorist groups active in Kashmir may have a strong explanatory value for the radicalization into violence of sectors of the British ethnic Pakistani community. The degree of integration of these radicalized individuals, as measured in conventional terms, does not appear to have been a strong factor, although the data show a substantial gap between education level and employment, possibly generating frustration and a sense of relative deprivation.

Similar conclusions can be reached with regard to radicalized individuals of Middle Eastern and North African ancestry on the Continent. The radicalization of Algerians goes back to the internal conflict in Algeria in the 1990s and the networks that Algerian terrorist groups developed in Europe to support their struggle. There is a more recent, and very strong trend toward radicalization of Moroccans, as seen in the composition of the group that carried out the March 11, 2004, Madrid train bombings, as well as in the Hofstad Group in the Netherlands. As in the case of radicalized British Muslims, the individuals involved in the Madrid bombings and the Hofstad Group appeared to be integrated into their societies. Van Gogh's assassin Bouyeri, for instance, was a product of the Dutch educational system.

By contrast, ethnic Turks who arguably may not be as well integrated into European societies as South Asians in the United Kingdom, appear to have been remarkably resistant to radicalization (although that picture may be beginning to change, as discussed in the chapter). This may be the result of the sociological characteristics of Turkish immigrants to Central and Western Europe, but the absence of widespread terrorist networks in Turkey with the ability to reach out to diaspora communities (in contrast to Pakistan and North Africa) may also be an important factor in what could be called the terrorism lag among Turks in Europe. This points to the importance of radical Islamist networks in producing and sustaining violent radicalization among European Muslims. The role of networks is discussed in Chapter 7.

# 6

# Radicalization and Recruitment Nodes

## RADICAL MOSQUES AND SOCIAL CENTERS

Radical mosques have played an important role as venues for the dissemination of extremist ideology and have served as gateways to radical recruitment. Materials published by different extremist organizations such as books, pamphlets, audio- and videocassettes are widely distributed in mosques. Of course, although the content of the sermons and the materials distributed at a mosque may contribute to radicalization, the more interesting question concerns the social network implications of a religious meeting place. In some cases, even where the mosque leadership did not itself promote extremism, the mosques served as meeting places where like-minded radicals came together and created their social networks.

Before 9/11, mosques provided the settings where the cells involved in some of the most destructive terror attacks in Europe coalesced.[1] Mohammed Atta, Ramzi Binalshibh, Marwan Al-Shehhi, and Ziad Samir Jarrah, all involved in the 9/11 attacks, were members of the al-Quds mosque in Hamburg. The London-based extremist Abu Qatada often visited the al-Quds mosque. He also visited the Abu Baker mosque in Madrid. According to Rohan Gunaratna, "Indoctrination material including videotapes, magazines, and pamphlets from a variety of fundamentalists Islamic groups, including the GIA, Hamas, Egyptian Jihad, the

[1] Michael Taarnby, *Recruitment of Islamist Terrorists in Europe, Trends and Perspectives*, Centre for Cultural Research, University of Aarhus, Research Report for the Danish Ministry of Justice, January 14, 2005.

mujaheddin in Bosnia and Afghanistan, and announcements from Osama bin Laden were found in the Abu Baker mosque."[2]

Some of the suspects in the March 11, 2004, Madrid train bombings worshipped at the El Portillo (Toledo) mosque, whose imam was arrested in connection with the May 16, 2003, Casablanca bombings.[3] An investigation by the Spanish Guardia Civil found that an extremist network that recruited a young Algerian man named Bellil Belgacem had used the Al Forkane mosque in Vilanova i la Geltrú, in Barcelona to carry out recruitment and fund-raising activities.[4] Belgacem carried out a suicide attack against the Italian military base in Nassiriya, Iraq, on November 12, 2003, that resulted in the death of 35 persons, including 17 Italian military personnel.

According to a Spanish intelligence source, there were 750 known mosques in Spain in 2005. In 18 percent of these mosques, the Spanish authorities had detected preaching that was considered to have radical content. The same source stated that the level of acceptance of radical preaching by the congregations was growing. In the past, some members of the audience would question the radical message and even take steps to remove the imams, but this was no longer the case in some mosques.[5]

In the United Kingdom, the Finsbury Park mosque in London, formerly the base of Abu Hamza al-Masri and Omar Bakri and now known as the North London Central Mosque, is under the supervision of the Islamist-dominated but supposedly mainstream Muslim Association of Britain (MAB). Within months of the MAB's takeover of the mosque, preachers from Somalia's Islamic Courts Union were advocating armed jihad in Somalia,[6] and Hizb ut-Tahrir activists were freely using the premises to distribute literature and recruit new members.[7]

[2] Rohan Gunaratna, "Spain: An al Qaeda Hub?" UNISCI Discussion Papers, May 2004, at https://revistas.ucm.es/index.php/UNIS/article/viewFile/UNIS0404230002A/28253.

[3] Proyecto de Dictámen De la Comisión de Investigación sobre los Atentados del 11-M, June 8, 2005, p. 71. The Casablanca bombings killed 45 people, including the 12 suicide bombers. The attacks were attributed to a group that Moroccan authorities called Salafiya Jihadia, which may be a composite of Moroccan terrorist groups and the Moroccan Islamic Combat Group (GICM).

[4] Fernando Delgado, "Los reclutadores son de mediana edad y gozan de gran respeto," *Actualidad Terrorismo Yihadista*/25, at www.fundacionvt.org.

[5] Discussion with Spanish intelligence analysts, Madrid, September 2005.

[6] Jeevan Vasagar, "Somali Islamists held UK meeting to raise funds," *The Guardian*, January 13, 2007, at http://www.theguardian.com/world/2007/jan/13/alqaida.terrorism.

[7] Adam Lusher, "Islamists use raid to stir up UK Somalis," *The Telegraph*, January 14, 2007, at http://www.telegraph.co.uk/news/worldnews/1539501/Islamists-use-raid-to-stir-up-UK-Somalis.html.

The East London Mosque hosted at least 27 radical and extremist preachers over a three-year period.[8] The mosque's "End of Time" event, held on New Year's Day 2009, featured an appearance via satellite feed by the late U.S.-born, Yemen-based extremist preacher Anwar al-Awlaki, who had been linked to a number of terrorist incidents in the United States. The promotional poster for the event showed New York being destroyed by meteors. The New Year's Day 2010 event, "Dark Forces: The Enemy Within," featured Yasir Qadhi, well known as a Holocaust denier, and Hamza Andreas Tzortzis, a Muslim convert and Hizb ut-Tahrir activist who opposes secularism and freedom of speech.[9]

According to British security sources, Islamist radicalization is rife on university campuses, especially in London.[10] Three of the past four presidents of the Islamic Society at University College London (UCL) have been arrested on terrorism charges, including failed airliner bomber Umar Farouk Abdulmutallab. As president of the Islamic Society from 2006 to 2007, Abdulmutallab actively organized events featuring notorious extremists such as Abu Usama, who preaches hatred of non-Muslims and maintains that apostasy and homosexuality are punishable by death, and former Guantanamo detainee and extremist propagandist Moazzem Begg.[11] The Islamic Society at UCL has a long history of inviting radical speakers, including imam Anthony "Abdur Raheem" Green of the Regents Park mosque. Green is on record as advocating violent jihad and arguing that Islam is not compatible with democracy; the aforementioned Abu Usama; Ryad al-Huq, who urges British Muslims to seek martyrdom abroad; Taji Mustafa, media spokesman for Hizb ut-Tahrir; and extremist preacher Haitham al-Haddad.[12]

[8] Andrew Gilligan, "Inextricably linked to controversial mosque: The secret world of IFE," *The Telegraph*, February 28, 2010, at http://www.telegraph.co.uk/news/politics/labour/7333487/Inextricably-linked-to-controversial-mosque-the-secret-world-of-IFE.html.

[9] "Secularism basis refuted and proof of Quran," at https://www.youtube.com/watch?v=KOw4Mk1QK84.

[10] "Al-Qaeda 'groomed Abdulmutallab in London,'" *The Times*, December 30, 2009, at http://www.thetimes.co.uk/tto/news/uk/article1946431.ece.

[11] Patrick Sawert and David Barrett, "Detroit bomber's mentor continues to influence British mosques and universities," *Telegraph*, January 2, 2010, at http://www.theapricity.com/forum/showthread.php?12114-Detroit-bomber-s-mentor-continues-to-influence-British-mosques-and-universities.

[12] John Thorne and Hannah Stuart, *Islam on Campus*, The Centre for Social Cohesion, London, 2008; Andrew Norfolk, "The homegrown cleric who loathes the British," *The Sunday Times*, September 7, 2007, at www.timesonline.co.uk/tol/news/uk/article2402998.ece.

A 2008 study by the Centre for Social Cohesion concluded that the majority of British Muslim students have tolerant ideas, reject violence in the name of faith and support Britain's secular and democratic governance, but a significant minority supports violence in the name of Islam; endorses *shari'a*, including punishment of apostates; is intolerant of Jews, homosexuals, and atheists; and supports the establishment of an Islamic state in Britain. The study suggests that members of Islamic societies are more likely to hold intolerant views, indicating more radical attitudes than those of Muslim students at large.[13]

In Germany, the leadership of the Islamisches Informationszentrum (IIZ) in Ulm is a radical mix of Turks, Arabs, and German converts. Torga Durbin and Attila Selek, both German citizens of Turkish descent who trained in Islamic Jihad Union (IJU) camps in Pakistan, and Fritz Gelowicz, alias Abdullah, the alleged ringleader of the IJU plot to attack U.S. targets in Germany uncovered in September 2007 were active in the Shura Council, the governing body of the IIZ. Thomas Fischer, alias Hamza, a German convert who was one of the founders of the IIZ left Ulm for Chechnya and was killed by Russian special forces in November 2003.[14]

The IIZ was closely connected to the Multikultur Haus (MKH) in Neu Ulm, Bavaria, which attracted extremists from all over the country, including veterans of the Afghan war, two individuals later killed in Chechnya, and at least one al-Qaeda operative. It was founded by Dr. Aldy el-Attar, a member of Egypt's al-Gama'a al-Islamiyya, who was in close contact with Mamdouh Mahmud Salim, one of the original founders of al-Qaeda. Salim was arrested in Germany in 1998 and extradited to the United States for his involvement in the Africa Embassy bombings.[15] German authorities closed the Multikultur Haus in 2005 on charges that it propagated anti-Semitism.[16]

The Taiba (formerly al-Quds) mosque in Hamburg, the meeting place for the 9/11 hijackers, was closed by German authorities in August 2010. The mosque had been watched closely since 9/11. The mosque occasionally hosted sermons by Mamoun Darkazanli, a German-Syrian businessman on

[13] Thorne and Stuart, *Islam on Campus*.

[14] Ronald Sandee, "The Islamic Jihad Union (IJU)," The NEFA Foundation, October 14, 2008, at http://www.scribd.com/doc/11108371 5/nefaijuocto8.

[15] Ibid. Two members of the Hamburg 9/11 cell, Muhammad Atta and Ramzi Binalshib visited el-Attar and Reda Seyam, a suspected financier of the 2002 Bali bombing, in Neu-Ulm.

[16] Interview with Yassin Musharbash, *Der Spiegel*, Berlin, June 2008. See also Petter Nesser, "Lessons Learned from the September 2007 German Terrorist Plot," Combating Terrorism Center at West Point, CTC Sentinel, Vol. 1 Issue 4, March 2008.

the European Union terrorist watch list who was allegedly associated with the 9/11 hijackers. The mosque reportedly hosted Moroccans, Bosnians, Saudis, Egyptians, Muslims from the Caucasus and Pakistan, as well as a number of German converts. German authorities told local media that some of those who frequented the mosque were in touch with radicals in at least five other German cities, and that they spoke of becoming martyrs, though no specific plots were known. The mosque attracted heightened attention by the authorities in 2009, after a group of 10 Hamburg militants traveled to the Afghan-Pakistani border region. One of them, an Iranian called Shahab D., joined the Islamic Movement of Uzbekistan (IMU) there and appeared in a video under the name Abu Askar in which he called on German Muslims to join the armed struggle.[17]

The most important center of Islamist extremism in Italy is the Islamic Culture Institute (ICI) of Milan. Unlike other European mosques, which were founded by mainstream Muslims and then infiltrated by extremists, the ICI was founded in the late 1980s by extremists who were dissatisfied with the Muslim Brotherhood–linked leadership of the Islamic Center of Milan and Lombardy. The ICI cultivated connections with the Egyptian terrorist group al-Gama'a al-Islamiyya and its affiliates around the world and became a transit and logistics center for fighters going to Bosnia during the Bosnian war.[18]

After the war, the mosque continued to be a venue for Salafist preachers in Italy and extended its influence to many mosques in Lombardy and other parts of northern Italy. The ICI also became the most important al-Qaeda station in Europe and sent money and recruits to jihadist groups in North Africa and Afghanistan. More recently, the ICI played a prominent role in recruitment for the conflict in Iraq. According to Italian

[17] Björn Hengst and Christoph Scheuermann, "Hamburg Hate Preachers Lose Their Home," *Spiegel Online International*, August 9, 2010, at www.spiegel.de/international/germany/0,1518,710952,00.html; Robert Marquand, "Why Germany Closed Mosque Where 9/11 Plotters Met," *Christian Science Monitor*, August 9, 2010, at http://www.csmonitor.com/World/Europe/2010/0809/Why-Germany-closed-mosque-where-9–11-plotters-met. According to media reports, Darkazali was included on a CIA list of individuals subject to "extraordinary renditions," but the plans to seize Darkazanli were abandoned because of likely objections by the German government. John Goetz and Holger Stark, "CIA Had Secret Plan to Kidnap German-Syrian Suspect in Hamburg," *Spiegel Online International*, January 12, 2010, at www.spiegel.de/international/germany/extraordinary-rendition-plot-cia-had-secret-plan-to-kidnap-german-syrian-suspect-in-hamburg-a-671198.html.

[18] Lorenzo Vidino, "Islam, Islamism and Jihadism in Italy," *Current Trends in Islamist Ideology*, Vol. 7, Hudson Institute, 2008, at http://www.hudson.org/content/researchattachments/attachment/1173/20081111_ct7.pdf.

officials, the Milanese networks recruited no fewer than 200 militants throughout Europe, 70 of them from Italy alone. By 2004, in response to increased surveillance by the authorities, militants began to move their activities away from the ICI to other, more opaque venues. The ICI still preaches a strict Salafist ideology and operates an unauthorized school for Muslim children.[19]

Radical networks composed mostly of North African militants have been uncovered in northern Italy around mosques that had been created by or were subordinated to the ICI. One such network was developed by members of the Moroccan Islamic Fighting Group (GICM) at the mosque at Cremona. The Cremona network was active in recruiting, fund-raising, and proselytizing until 2004, when most of its members were convicted of various terrorism-related crimes. The network had also allegedly planned attacks against the Cremona cathedral and the Milan underground transit system. Most northern Italian cities, as well as some cities in central Italy, host radical mosques and networks. A common trend, according to terrorism expert Lorenzo Vidino, is the de-localization of jihadist networks, as radical clusters seem to be increasingly forming outside of mosques.[20]

Before 9/11, radical recruitment in Europe was conducted openly, and the recruits were channeled through the radical mosques to Afghanistan. To some extent, this traffic was known by the authorities, who deliberately ignored it on the assumption that the terrorists would not conduct operations on European soil. As Western Europe was believed to be a critical rear support area for terrorists, it was assumed that they would not want to jeopardize their networks by engaging in attacks there. Complaints by local Muslims infuriated by the behavior of the extremists were dismissed or treated as intra-communal disputes.

The fact that there always seems to be complaints from moderate mosque members about extremists reinforces the notion that neither the mosque nor the religious orientation embodied by the mosque's imam is the direct cause of violent radicalization, or at least that some intervening variable is at work.[21] In many cases, the more radical groups schedule their

[19] Ibid.

[20] Ibid.

[21] For instance, 7/7 London bomber Mohammed Siddique Khan's activities in the Hardy Street mosque began to draw attention in 2001. The mosque's secretary has said that Khan and some of his associates subscribed to Wahhabi views and had upset some of the mosque's community. Eventually, he was asked to leave. Paul Tumelty, "New Developments Following the London Bombings," The Jamestown Foundation, *Terrorism Monitor*, Volume 3, Issue 23, December 2, 2005.

own meetings or prayer groups to discuss their ideas outside of the broader mosque community. Members of the larger community also tend to shun the smaller group, although this does not necessarily mean that they go to the police with their suspicions of potentially violent activities.

The tendency of extremists to segregate themselves into smaller, more secretive units within the mosque community became more pronounced after the 9/11 attacks, which brought intensified monitoring by the authorities. Of course, official vigilance has not stopped these activities; rather, it has has driven them underground. Extremists continue to make contact at some open or authorized mosques, but the actual recruitment and planning of operations now takes place in underground mosques and prayer halls and other, less transparent venues. For instance, the Buttes-Chaumont cell, a group of radicalized youths of North African ancestry from the 19th arrondissement in Paris who had been recruited by a self-proclaimed imam named Farid Benyettou for suicide missions in Iraq, initially met at the Isqra mosque in the Parisian suburb of Levallois-Perret. French authorities closed the mosque after men linked to the group were killed or detained in Iraq. The remaining militants simply reconvened and began to recruit new members at the Adda'wa mosque in the 19th arrondissement, unbeknownst to the mosque's leadership.[22]

Authorities in France and other European countries are becoming less concerned about extremists in established mosques and more focused on smaller makeshift mosques located in apartments in low-income housing complexes. Radical imam Chelalli Benchellali, sentenced to five years in prison in June 2006 for his role in a plot to stage attacks in France to support fighters in Chechnya, ran the Abu Bakr mosque from the ground floor activity room of a housing complex in the Lyon suburb of Vénissieux.[23]

Nevertheless, even in the current, less permissive environment, mosques in communities with radical elements can position themselves as mainstream institutions, while actually promoting very narrow, politicized interpretations of Islam and allowing radicals and sometimes violent extremists to use their premises. Even if proselytizing and recruitment by

[22] Peter R. Neumann and Brooke Rogers, *Recruitment and Mobilisation for the Islamist Militant Movement in Europe*, The International Centre for the Study of Radicalisation and Political Violence (ICSR), King's College, London, 2008, at http://icsr.info/wp-content/uploads/2012/10/1234516791ICSREUResearchReport_Proof1.pdf; Peter Taylor, "A reason to hate," *The Guardian*, September 1, 2006, at http://www.guardian.co.uk/world/2006/sep/01/iraq.july7.

[23] Jonathan Laurence and Justin Vaisse, *Integrating Islam: Political and Religious Challenges in Contemporary France*. Washington, DC: Brookings Institution Press, 2006.

violent extremists may no longer be taking place, as the discussion of the East London Mosque shows, these mosques promote an environment conducive to violent radicalization.

## PRISONS

Prisons have become breeding grounds for extremists. For the most part, prisoners join extremist groups not for ideological reasons, but to cope with personal problems or because they are recruited by a friend or acquaintance. For petty criminals without much of a future, radical Islam offers a way to rise above their condition in life. Joining the ranks of the Islamists can give them a sense of brotherhood with a larger group of prisoners and a sense of purpose in life.[24]

Numerous individuals involved in terrorist actions in Europe served time in prison. Mukhtar Said-Ibrahim, one of the suspects in the failed London bombings of July 21, 2005, was jailed in 1996 for violent street robberies and moved around a series of young offenders' institutions in the south of England before gaining early release; he appears to have been radicalized while in prison.[25] Jamal Ahmidan, a Moroccan immigrant in Spain responsible for the logistics of the March 11, 2004, Madrid bombings (known in Spain as 3/11), had a criminal record for drug trafficking. Ahmidan was born in Tetuan, in northern Morocco, into a relatively well-off middle-class family. His father had worked in the Netherlands for several years. When he returned home, he had sufficient funds to set up a fabric business. He was a religious man and hoped that his sons would be inspired by his example, but Jamal and his elder brother Mustafa had a strained relationship with their father and both began to engage in drug trafficking. They sold hashish directly in Spain and in the Netherlands, exchanging it for cocaine and ecstasy that they then sold in Spain. After settling in Madrid (claiming to be an Algerian asylum seeker), Jamal set up a criminal network composed largely of friends and kinsmen, a common feature of many criminal and terrorist networks.[26]

[24] Zohar Neumann, "Islamists and Incarceration," The Jewish Institute for National Security Affairs, December 8, 2004, at http://archive.today/OeSRS.

[25] Paul Tumelty, "Reassessing the July 21 London Bombings," Jamestown Foundation, *Terrorism Monitor*, at http://archive.today/iZsGo

[26] Jeffrey Bale, "Jihadist Cells and 'I.E.D.' Capabilities in Europe: Assessing the Present and Future Threat to the West," Monterey Institute of International Studies, May 2009, p. 48. Bale's paper is the most complete analysis of the Madrid bombings available in English.

After his arrest for drug trafficking in 1993, Jamal was sentenced to two years in prison, where he became addicted to heroin. He sought solace in Islam in an effort to end his drug addiction. When he was released in 1995, he became increasingly religious. According to Jeffrey Bale's study of the Madrid terrorist network, his sense of victimization after successive arrests led to his radicalization. After he was arrested in 2001 with false documents, he became the de facto leader of the other prisoners and adopted an increasingly hostile attitude toward his country of residence. His fortuitous encounter with Fakhet after his release from prison in 2003 led to his taking an active role in the 3/11 plot.[27]

Ahmidan's criminal network played a critical role in financing and procuring the explosives used in the bombings. According to the then Spanish interior minister Angel Acebes, the Madrid bombing plot was financed "with the sales of hashish and ecstasy."[28] The explosive materials and detonators were obtained by a group of radicalized Moroccan petty criminals from Spanish counterparts in Asturias in exchange for drugs.[29]

Two of the individuals involved in the transaction for the explosives used in the Madrid bombings made contact at the Villabona prison in Asturias, in northwestern Spain. The thwarted plot to blow up the anti-terrorism court in Madrid in 2004 was hatched by Islamist extremists imprisoned at Topas. The plot's mastermind, an Algerian named Abderrahamane Tahiri, alias Mohamed Achraf, assembled the group that called itself "Martyrs of Morocco" while serving time in prison.[30] The Spanish authorities became so alarmed that they set up a task force to better control the spread of radical Islam in the prison system.

Prisons also produce individuals with the skills required by terrorist organizations. Radicalized prisoners are generally not educated, but they are streetwise.[31] According to Alain Grignard, a senior Belgian police authority on terrorism, the "intermingling of terrorist networks with the criminal milieu is becoming more and more important ... It's in prisons where political operatives recruit specialists whom they need to run their

[27] Ibid., pp. 48–49.
[28] "Spain says bombers drank water from Mecca and sold drugs," *New York Times*, April 15, 2004, at http://www.nytimes.com/2004/04/15/world/spain-says-bombers-drank-water-from-mecca-and-sold-drugs.html.
[29] Bale, "Jihadist Cells and 'I.E.D.' Capabilities in Europe," p. 35.
[30] See Juzgado Central de Instrucción Número Cinco de la Audiencia Nacional, Sumario 26/04-D, Madrid, March 13, 2006.
[31] Petter Nesser, Presentation, RAND IMEY Conference, September 22, 2005.

networks – specialists in fraudulent documents, arms trafficking, etc. They use concepts that justify crime, that transform it into redemption."[32]

The high proportion of Muslims in European prisons aggravates the problem of prisons as radical incubators. According to French sociologist Farhad Khosrokhavar, 50 to 80 percent of the inmates in French prisons are Muslim. This concentration of Muslims, who are sometimes housed together, facilitates radical recruitment. Ian Cuthbertson, another expert, notes that disconnected, impressionable young men and women become a captive audience for those who espouse extremist Islamic dogma.[33]

In Spain, of a total prison population of some 71,000, more than 7,000 are of North African origin. Most are charged with drug trafficking, trafficking in persons, or involvement in organized crime. About 250 have been convicted of terrorism offenses or collaboration with terrorists.[34] Muslim prisoners tend to congregate. They speak the same language and sometime come from the same towns in Morocco. Within the prison, they designate an imam, usually the prisoner who exhibits the greatest leadership qualities, education, and knowledge of the Quran. Although most of the Muslim population in Spain and about half the Muslim prison population are of Moroccan origin, the Muslim prisoners' leaders are usually Algerian. This, according to a Spanish expert on prison radicalization, is because of the prestige Algerians enjoy among Islamists because of their presumed greater experience of jihad.[35]

Muslim prisoners tend to gravitate toward Islamist groups because of the protection and services that these groups can provide. Most Maghrebi inmates in Spanish prisons are indigent, and the Islamists can provide lawyers and money and facilitate contacts with their families. When al-Qaeda figure Abu Dahdah was in prison in Spain, he had €300,000 at his disposal that he used to support the families of individuals imprisoned on terrorism charges. Islamist groups also rely on intimidation and coercion to enforce Islamic norms in prisons – for instance, morning and evening prayers and the prohibitions on alcohol, pork, and homosexual

[32] Cited in Ian M. Cuthbertson, "Prisons and the Education of Terrorists," *World Policy Journal*, Vol. 21, No. 3, Fall 2004, at http://www.jstor.org/stable/40210232.

[33] Ibid.

[34] Interview with José Antonio Gutiérrez, director of studies, ACAIP prison employees union, Madrid, September 2008. According to Fernando Reinares, as of December 31, 2008, there were 104 individuals imprisoned in Spain for terrorist activities related to al-Qaeda, associated organizations, or independent cells. Of these, 46 had been convicted, and 58 prosecuted and awaiting trial or sentences. Fernando Reinares, Presentation, International Conference on Terrorist Rehabilitation, Singapore, February 2009.

[35] Interview with Gutierrez.

relations.[36] A British prison inspectorate 2008 report on Whitemoor prison reported prison staff concerns that intimidating, "bullying" behavior was becoming a more widespread problem, reporting that staff had "noted a move away from small groups of perpetrators into 'gang culture on the wing.'" The report said that prison staff were reluctant to intervene to prevent bullying or gang behavior among Muslims and quoted an officer as saying that Muslim prisoners "policed themselves." The report also noted "a reluctance to engage with Muslim prisoners and challenge inappropriate behaviour."[37]

In the fall of 2004, after Spanish authorities realized that prisons were being used for radicalization and recruitment, the authorities responded by dispersing inmates about whom there was reason for concern throughout some 25 penitentiaries across the country. The Spanish dispersal policy was initiated in 1989 to make it more difficult for the Basque terrorist organization Euskadi Ta Askatasuna (ETA) to coerce members in prison and to facilitate their rehabilitation. Although this policy was successful with ETA members, who did not try to recruit non-Basques, dispersal only increased opportunities for Islamists to try to convert and recruit other inmates.[38]

According to a Quilliam Foundation study, about 10,000 Muslims were prisoners in England and Wales in 2009, about 12 percent of the overall prison population. Of these, about 100 were being held on charges relating to Islamist terrorism. Some of these individuals, who were mostly held in a small number of Category A (highest security) prisons, were serving their sentences after being convicted in British courts. Others were held awaiting trial or appealing deportation or extradition to face trial abroad. According to the Quilliam study, the core element of extremist recruitment, both inside and outside prison, was proactively approaching potential recruits. Once initial contact was made, extremists offered support and advice on day-to-day issues and progressively exposed potential recruits to a comprehensive politico-theological ideology that appears to explain the world around them and their place in it.[39]

In many cases, extremists casually approach new Muslim prisoners soon after they enter prison, offering them friendship and reassurance.

[36] Ibid.

[37] HM Inspectorate of Prisons, "Report on an Unannounced Full-Return Prison Inspection of H.M. Whitemoor Prison, 3–7 October 2008," cited in James Brandon, *Unlocking al-Qaeda: Islamist Extremism in British Prisons*, Quilliam, November 2009, p. 34.

[38] Reinares, International Conference on Terrorist Rehabilitation.

[39] Brandon, *Unlocking Al-Qaeda*.

The recruiter may soon begin to offer spiritual advice and to recommend reading material and indicate which fellow inmates or prison staff to trust and which to avoid. "Abu Abdullah," who was held in Belmarsh prison for several months on suspicion of financing terrorism before being acquitted, described how radicals in the prison approached him on his first day there:

> On that same day [that I arrived in prison], I went to the exercise yard. I had all these thoughts in my head: What do I do? Is anyone going to bully me? I don't know what to expect. Alhamdulillah (Praise be to Allah) I was fortunate. On that day, some brothers approached me and said that they had been expecting me. Some were brothers held without charge. There was a Palestinian brother, and an Algerian brother ... These brothers were very friendly. At first I was a bit apprehensive as to whether I should trust them or not ... But afterwards I felt comfortable. One of the brothers Masha'Allah he packed some fruit and a chocolate in a bag and handed it to me before I went back to my cell.[40]

Extremists often seek leadership of Muslim prisoners. Abdullah el-Faisal, imprisoned in Belmarsh prison between 2003 and 2007, told Jamaican television after his release and deportation that he had seen it as his duty as a cleric to lead and inspire other Muslim prisoners. On one occasion, when the prison authorities tried to stop the Muslims from Friday prayers while in the holding rooms and send them back to their cells, Faisal led a sit-in until the authorities gave in to the Muslim prisoners' demands. The incident enhanced Faisal's prestige among the inmates as a man willing to stand up to the authorities. In some cases, prison authorities empower extremists if they believe that they can help prevent outbreaks of violence. In other cases, prison authorities have empowered prisoners by allowing them to lead Friday prayers.[41]

Some well-known extremists can exercise great influence over other prisoners through the force of their personalities. Omar Khyam, a British-Pakistani convicted of planning terrorist attacks in Britain, has described the extraordinary influence over other inmates enjoyed by Rachid Ramda, a French Muslim imprisoned while fighting extradition to France, where he was later convicted of organizing the 1995 Paris metro bombings. Khyam said of Ramda, "He made me feel as if I had known him for years, such a warm personality and character, making everyone feel wanted and important, as if you are his best friend."[42] During his imprisonment while awaiting trial in the Netherlands, Van

[40] Ibid., p. 27.
[41] Ibid., pp. 30–32.
[42] Cited in ibid., p. 28.

Gogh assassin Bouyeri allegedly tried to indoctrinate two other prisoners using radical Islamist tracts. Dutch authorities, concerned that he could become a "prison prophet," curtailed his contact with other prison inmates and prohibited him from using the Internet or his mobile phone while incarcerated. Dutch law gives inmates the right to "write, publish and distribute articles" but if the texts infringe criminal law, for example when they incite hatred or sedition, the author can be prosecuted.[43]

In some countries, individuals imprisoned for terrorism offenses are kept under a strict prison regime. Their communications are monitored and they are not allowed to communicate with other prisoners, but they find ways around the restrictions through their contacts with their families, nongovernmental organizations (NGOs), and sympathetic imams.[44] In Spain, individuals imprisoned for terrorist activities are under strict control and surveillance mechanisms, resulting from inclusion in a special file, Fichero FIES. Fichero FIES was created in 1996 to track the records of inmates considered to be especially dangerous. The file was modified in 2006 to apply not only to imprisoned terrorists but also to other inmates thought to be undergoing violent radicalization.[45] Despite these measures, the language barrier and a general lack of familiarity with the prisoners' culture, customs, and religion hinder the prison authorities' ability to keep extremists under control.[46]

Since 2009, individuals convicted of terrorism offenses in Italy have been concentrated in four prisons: Asti, Macomer, Benevento, and Rossano. Three former prisoners from Guantanamo were sent to the Opera prison in Milan. They were kept in individual cells and not allowed to meet with one another. In his report on jihadist radicalization in European prisons, Sergio Bianchi says that the 80 terrorist inmates held in Italian prisons have a high degree of military training and organizational and logistical leadership skills. In Padua, a self-proclaimed imam has reportedly turned a number of Muslim inmates toward extremism. Any Muslim who walks past his cell has to show him respect, as if he were a Mafia capo. After he was transferred to prison in Udine and then to Treviso, he continued to recruit. In the Bari jails, imams Bassam Ayachi

[43] "Mohammed Bouyeri Sentenced," The Crime Library, at http://www.crimelibrary.com/notorious_murders/famous/theo_van_gogh/13.html.

[44] Interview with Gutierrez.

[45] Reinares, International Conference on Terrorist Rehabilitation.

[46] Interview with Gutierrez.

and his accomplice Raphael Gendron, a convert to Islam, arrested in 2008, continued to hatch plots. The authorities learned from eavesdropping on conversations that from inside the prison, they may have been planning attacks at Paris airports and were talking about a 9/11-style attack in Britain.[47]

The development of militant prison networks helps explain the rising connection between common criminals and terrorists. In Italy, there was a case of a member of the Camorra (Neapolitan Mafia) who converted to Islam and then facilitated the trade of arms and drugs between organized crime and Islamic radicals. The chief of France's domestic intelligence service, the Direction de la Surveillance du Territoire (DST), reported the same pattern in France.

The patterns of Islamist radicalization in prison and the behavior of Islamist inmates differ from country to country in accordance with differing legal frameworks, prison regimes, and approaches to countering radicalization in prison. Most importantly, these patterns differ by country because Muslim prison populations often reflect the makeup of national Muslim populations that differ in significant ways from one country to another. Nevertheless, as noted earlier, there are common elements: the segregation or self-segregation of Muslims from other inmates and the process of radicalization itself, which involves the socialization of the inmate into a radical worldview, changes in behavior and appearance (e.g., they adopt a more "Islamic" look, stop smoking, begin to pray regularly), and adoption of a more militant and confrontational stance toward the prison authorities.[48]

Europeans recognize the danger of prison radicalization. The Austrian Presidency of the EU launched a project in 2006, continued under the German and French Presidencies and financed by the European Commission, to address the radicalization and radical recruitment in prisons. The result of this project was a good practices manual to guide the training of field agents and prison staff, which was presented at a closed-door conference of EU security experts at the end of September 2008. Drawing from the experience of European and other security officials, including New York City police, the manual identifies outward signs of radicalization that prison authorities should watch for. The

[47] "Così l'islam recluta i carcerati in Italia," *Il Giornale*, May 24, 2010, at http://issuu.com/pietro83/docs/il-giornale-24-maggio-2010/1.

[48] Interview with Gutierrez.

specific content of the manual has not been made public to avoid alerting extremists to the warning signs listed in the manual.[49]

## THE INTERNET AND SOCIAL MEDIA

Like nearly every aspect of life in twenty-first-century "information societies," the web has profoundly influenced the practice of terrorism. The web has become a platform for extremist activity and a critical enabler of terrorism. In March 2013, German authorities banned three Salafist associations, DawaFFM, Islamische Audios, and an-Nussrah, and raided the apartments of 20 people associated with these entities, saying that the groups were involved in recruitment, fund-raising, and the distribution of propaganda through the Internet. The authorities said that the videos and propaganda circulated over the Internet by DawaFFM helped radicalize Arid Uka, a young man originally from Kosovo who killed two American airmen at Frankfurt airport in 2011.[50] Jihadist blogs provide extremists with the opportunity to operate beyond their immediate surroundings and persist in the face of increasingly sophisticated security regimes. These blogs connect networks of extremists and allow peripheral players to promote their agendas in ways that were not possible before.

One effect of the Internet is the blurring of operational theaters. An illustration is Younis Tsouli, better know as Irhabi007, a self-recruited cyberterrorist – the word *irhabi* means "terrorist" in Arabic. The IT-skilled 22-year-old son of a Moroccan tourism board official, and a resident of Shepherd's Bush in west London, was a ubiquitous figure on al-Qaeda's online activity. He administered several radical Internet sites and pioneered new tactics, techniques. and procedures in the electronic jihad. Tsouli knew well that his online activism was a far cry from actually fighting the enemy in Iraq. In one encrypted chat conversation, he openly struggled with the dilemma of matching words with deeds. "Dude," Tsouli

[49] EU, French Presidency, Seminar, "Field Agents Facing the Phenomenon of Radicalization," November 5, 2008, at http://www.ue2008.fr/PFUE/cache/offonce/lang/en/accueil/PFUE-09_2008/PFUE-29.09.2008/seminaire_les_acteurs_de_terrain_confrontes_au_phenomene_de_radicalisation;jsessionid=A1C5FD7D0E67C790A77CC188545 0DE07; "EU draws up manual to help prisons identify Muslim extremists," *Weekly Telegraph*, October 2, 2008, at http://www.telegraph.co.uk/news/worldnews/europe/france/3124378/EU-draws-up-manual-to-help-prisons-identify-Muslim-extremists.html.

[50] Melissa Eddy, "Germany arrests 4 and bans groups linked to Salafism," *New York Times*, March 13, 2013, at http://www.nytimes.com/2013/03/14/world/europe/germany-arrests-4-and-bans-groups-linked-to-salafism.html?_r=0.

complained to another online jihadist, who chose the pseudonym Abuthaabit, "my heart is in Iraq." A telling dialogue ensued:

ABUTHAABIT: How are you going to have enough to go there?
IRHABI007: I suppose someone gotta be here!
ABUTHAABIT: This media work, I am telling you, is very important. Very, very, very, very.
IRHABI007: I know, I know.
ABUTHAABIT: Because a lot of the funds the brothers are getting is because they are seeing stuff like this coming out. Imagine how many people have gone [to Iraq] after seeing the situation because of the videos. Imagine how many of them could have been *shaheed* [martyrs] as well.[51]

This brief exchange illustrates the tie between online organization and offline action. Tsouli was far away from the battlefields, in London and, like many, badly wanted to have an impact on the struggle in Iraq and Afghanistan. Yet, his was an effort to inspire other potential extremists to fight, mounted from Europe and targeting regions beyond Europe's borders.

At closer view, the interactive Internet today offers a variety of utilities and possibilities for radical extremists. Any countermeasure should focus on one particular utility, or purpose. At least six such utilities should be distinguished. First, extremists may use public information and the web to legitimize their actions. Engaging in subversive activities means taking considerable personal risk. If operatives are caught, they might face deportation; prison sentences; and depending on their country of origin, torture and even consequences for families and friends. Perpetrating extreme violent acts requires strong convictions, particularly if the killing of innocent civilians and bystanders is involved. Providing ideological orientation, stability, and defensive arguments against moderate voices is a critical enabler of terrorist activity. Closed and self-referential ideological systems, such as radical Islam, act as enablers.

Second, Internet communication may be used to justify particular operations. The demand for ideological and quasi-juridical justification or violent action is great, particularly so if an extremist is conservative at heart and appreciates established conventions and authority. One of the best-known examples is the use of fatwas and the concept of *takfir*, or excommunication, to justify the killing of civilians and, even more problematic for Muslims, the killing of fellow Muslim civilians. As

[51] Cited in "Internet jihad: A world wide web of terror," *The Economist*, July 12, 2007, at http://www.abc.net.au/mediawatch/transcripts/1317_economist.pdf.

extremists are planning specific operations and approach their execution, the need for guidance becomes more compelling.

Third, The Internet opens up a variety of organizational functions for radical groups. Doctrinal debates have been moved into the semipublic space. Media products are used for training. Subversive action requires a broad set of skills on how to gather intelligence, prepare attacks, recruit operatives, use all kinds of weapons, build explosives, administer poisons, resist interrogation, and so on. All such training has two sides, a theoretical and a practical one. Manuals and instructions are widely available electronically. One of the most comprehensive jihadist manuals is the *Mawsu'at al-I'dad*, or *Encyclopedia of Preparation*, compiled and updated during the Afghan war from 1979 to 1989. This material often comes with links to videos or directly in the form of CDs, and it includes instructional videos. Some handbooks are designed for experts and require a background in chemistry or electronics; others are written for the novice. In the absence of physical training camps, visual illustration materials facilitate the transition to practical training and execution, and thus the transition from passive sympathizer to active terrorist, although even the best videos cannot replace personal expert training and rehearsals.

Fourth, the Internet may be used to recruit operatives. Many products and channels can be used to advance the recruitment of activists, any violent movement's most essential resource: pamphlets, press articles, videos, memoirs, sermons, Internet forums, and both offline and online social networks. The logistical challenge of joining a training camp or a combat zone may also be facilitated. Skilled recruiters may even be in a position to spot talented potential recruits online and get in touch with them.

Fifth, the web may be used to raise funds. As in political campaigning, violent movements rely on targeted fund-raising efforts. Loyal groups can be tapped for smaller and mid-sized donations or wealthy individuals through trusted personal networks for larger donations. The newsletters or websites used for fund-raising can be public, semipublic, or secret.

Sixth, the interactive media facilitate networking. Anonymous and encryptable web-based applications such as discussion forums, instant messaging, Voice over Internet Protocol (VoIP), or e-mail enable a semipublic dialogue and even a near risk-free establishment of personal contact. This significantly facilitates the outreach of militant groups to sympathetic individuals and organizations such as suppliers, other radical groups, potential supporters and recruits, or even journalists.

An example of Internet radicalization is the case of Mohammed Irfan Raja and the four Bradford University students convicted and jailed for downloading and sharing terrorism-related material. Raja was born and raised in Great Britain. His grandfather had served in the British India police and had been personally decorated by Lord Mountbatten. As a teenager, Raja began to surf radical websites and made a martyr poster of himself. A man in New Jersey who called himself "Brother Ali," whom he met on the Internet, put him in touch with the Bradford Four, who were planning to go to Pakistan to train to fight in Afghanistan. When he set out on the trip to Pakistan, Raja left a note to his parents explaining that he had gone off to become a martyr. His parents informed the police immediately, fearing that their son had been brainwashed by terrorists. Raja, however, had second thoughts. He returned home and confessed everything to the police, who then arrested the entire group.

The case of Mohammed Irfan Raja and the Bradford Four is interesting because it is one of the few cases in which the radicalization and mobilization of radicalized Muslims – in this case to fight in Afghanistan – took place entirely on the Internet. It is also interesting because it represents the operation of a new type of decentralized network in which the facilitator ("Brother Ali") remains anonymous.

The brief illustration of the web's ideological, organizational, and operational functions makes clear that the online dimension of extremism and terrorism is tightly connected to its offline dimension. The problem cannot easily be described as a "war of ideas" or as something that could be easily remedied by a comprehensive countermeasure, such as a communication unit in a ministry or a public outreach program. Instead, the web should be seen as an aspect of nearly all counter-extremism or counterterrorism measures.

Paradoxically, jihadist websites have "emancipated" female activists by allowing them to communicate with male extremists without violating social and religious precepts. The Garden of Female Believers, a Francophone website, carries admonitions by Abu Musab al-Zarqawi and London-based extremist ideologue Abu Basir al-Tartusi, as well as advice on women's health and beauty.[52] Al Mujaddida, formerly known as Tajdid Sisters, is another French-language women-only blog.

The most infamous female Internet jihadist is a Belgian citizen born in Morocco, Malika El Aroud, the widow of Abdessater Dahmane, one of the men who murdered Ahmed Shah Massoud, the leader of Afghanistan's Northern Alliance, at the behest of Osama bin Laden, two days before

[52] The website lejardindescroyantes.com is no longer active. It appears to have migrated to http://www.ansar-alhaqq.net/forum/showthread.php?t=17500.

9/11. Malika was suspected by Belgian authorities of shipping to her husband electronic equipment that was used in the Massoud assassination, and she was tried with 22 others for complicity in Massoud's killing; she was acquitted for lack of evidence.

In some ways, Malika's profile resembles that of Belgian female suicide bomber Muriel Degauque. Unlike Degauque, a convert, Malika was raised in an observant Muslim family, but in her early adolescence, she seems to have distanced herself from her family and culture and then, after a personal crisis, "rediscovered" Islam in its radical manifestation. And while both Degauque's and Malika's personal trajectories were influenced by their choice of husbands, Malika had the stronger personality.

According to terrorism expert Paul Cruickshank, Malika had grown up feeling stifled and frustrated; her parents had required her to don a veil at home, but she wore miniskirts and tight jeans to school. As soon as she could, she broke free of her father's control and started hanging out in discos and nightclubs, sleeping at the apartments of random acquaintances, and showering in public restrooms. At one point, she said in an interview, she became so disgusted with herself that she wanted to die. Eventually, she got engaged to a cousin, who left her when she became pregnant. And then, a new beginning. She began her journey back to Islam when she was listening to a Moroccan radio station and heard the Arabic call of prayer. She "felt something very strong in my heart," she said. A few years later, she signed up for classes at the Centre Islamique Belge, an organization that adheres to a Salafist interpretation of Islam and was under surveillance by the Belgian intelligence service. There, she learned to wear the veil and absorbed the center's radical teachings.

Malika married twice and quickly divorced twice before she met Abdessater Dahmane, a Tunisian devoted to Osama bin Laden. Dahmane left for Afghanistan in the spring of 2000 and Malike followed in January 2001. They lived in a compound for al-Qaeda families in Jalalabad. Dahmane trained at the notorious camp at Derunta, where al-Qaeda tested poison gas on dogs. In August 2001, bin Laden sent Dahmane on a suicide mission. Posing as television reporters, he and another Tunisian named Bouraoui el-Ouaer killed Massoud with an explosive charge hidden in a camera. In an interview, Malika said that people came from far away to embrace her and congratulate her because "it is the pinnacle in Islam to be the widow of a martyr."

After the United States invaded Afghanistan, Malika made her way to Pakistan. She went to the Belgian Embassy in Islamabad and was repatriated to Belgium, where she refused to answer questions. Subsequent to her acquittal of the Massoud assassination charges, Malika met on the web and married Moez Garsalloui, a Tunisian radical several years her junior who had political refugee status in Switzerland and joined his online jihad. In 2007, she and her new husband were convicted in Switzerland of promoting violence and supporting a criminal organization. Malika received a six-month suspended sentence. She and her husband returned to Belgium, where according to authorities they recruited young men for jihadist training camps in Pakistan. As the police gathered evidence, Garsalloui fled to the Pakistan-Afghanistan border area. A message from him that Malika placed on her website stated, "You know, brothers and sisters, the solution is not fatwas. It is 'booom.'" He also reportedly conveyed instructions from the al-Qaeda organization to organize attacks in Europe. In March 2010, the authorities charged nine extremists, including Malika and her husband, in absentia, for directing a terrorist network. Malika and her husband, who is still at large, were sentenced to eight years in prison in May 2010.[53]

[53] Paul Cruickshank, "Love in the Time of Terror," *Marie Claire*, May 15, 2009, at http://www.marieclaire.com/world-reports/news/international/malika-el-aroud-female-terrorist; Elaine Sciolino and Souad Mekhennet, "Al Qaeda warrior uses Internet to rally women," *New York Times*, May 28, 2008, at http://www.nytimes.com/2008/05/28/world/europe/28terror.html?pagewanted=all; see also the interviews with Malika on CNN World's Untold Stories, "One Woman's War," February 25, 2009, at http://edition.cnn.com/2007/WORLD/europe/02/16/untold.stories/; Library of Congress, "Belgium:Terror Suspects Convicted, Sentenced," at http://www.loc.gov/lawweb/servlet/lloc_news?disp3_l205401977_text.

# 7

# Evolution of Radical Networks in Europe

There is no question that the Internet plays an increasingly important role in disseminating radical Islamist narratives. However, the transition from radicalization to terrorism almost always takes place in face-to-face encounters and very seldom on the Internet. Moreover, while individuals might become radicalized on their own or in extremist chat rooms, this kind of spontaneous radicalization may lead to discrete acts of violence, but it will be highly unlikely to generate a sustained campaign of violence in the absence of organized structures that can harness and channel the individual extremist's willingness to engage in violence.

Radical Islamist and jihadist groups in Western Europe are linked to other extremist groups in Europe and the Middle East through personal relationships and informal networks. Cases of true "lone wolf" terrorism, that is, an individual or small isolated group engaged in terrorism under the influence of a radical ideology but without external direction or connection to an organized group or network,[1] have been relatively rare in Europe (although more frequent in the United States).[2] Some European cases include those of Andrew ("Issa") Ibrahim, a young Muslim convert incarcerated in July 2009 after plotting a suicide terror attack at a shopping mall in Bristol; Roshonara

[1] The definition is from Raffaello Pantucci, "A Typology of Lone Wolves: Preliminary Analysis of Lone Islamist Terrorists," The International Centre for the Study of Radicalisation and Political Violence (ICSR), King's College London, March 2011, p. 9 at http://icsr.info/paper/a-typology-of-lone-wolves-preliminary-analysis-of-lone-islamist-terrorists.

[2] U.S. cases of lone wolf terrorism include Mir Aimal Kansi's shooting outside CIA headquarters in January 1993, Hesham Mohamed Hadayet's shooting at the El Al ticket counter in Los Angeles International Airport in July 2002, Naveed Haq's shooting at the Jewish Federation of Greater Seattle in July 2006, and Major Nidal Malik Hasan's shooting at Fort Dix in November 2009.

Choudhry, convicted of attempting to murder Member of Parliament Stephens Timms; Nicky Reilly, a Muslim convert whose device exploded prematurely in the toilet of a restaurant in Exeter; Jihad Hamad and Youssef el Hajbid, convicted of attempting to bomb two German passenger trains in July 2006; and Mohammed Game, Abdelaziz Mahmoud Kol, and Muhammad Imbaeya Israfel, convicted of setting off a bomb outside an army barracks in Milan, Italy, in October 2009.[3]

As Raffaello Pantucci warns, the term *lone wolf* is often erroneously deployed to provide easy explanations for what are often more complex terrorist attacks.[4] The Madrid bombing, for instance, appeared to have been the work of a small, independent cell but, in fact, was the work of a complicated confluence of groups inside and outside Spain, with links to the Casablanca bombing through the Moroccan Islamic Combatant Group (GICM) and to the Iraqi insurgency through Ansar al-Islam. The Hofstad Group, to which Van Gogh assassin Bouyeri belonged, had some relationship with counterparts in Italy, Spain, and Belgium and contacts with extremists in Morocco, through a member who was affiliated with the GICM.

Network connections that should be well understood by investigators also exist between violent foreign organizations and groups and individuals of interest in European countries vulnerable to terrorism. But there are also connections between violent groups and individuals and ostensibly non-violent extremist organizations, some of which operate legally.[5] Networks can be physical or virtual and defined in terms of membership (ethnic or other), scope (local, national, or international), or function (e.g., indoctrination, propaganda, recruitment, training, financing, logistics, or operations). They could be preexisting networks, such as the pre-9/11 Middle Eastern terrorist networks in Europe, or self-organized or newly created networks.

## RECENT EVOLUTION OF ISLAMIST TERRORIST NETWORKS IN EUROPE

After 9/11 and the Madrid and London bombings, Islamist terrorists in Europe have confronted and adapted to a less permissive environment. Some terrorism analysts believe that it is increasingly misleading to speak

[3] Pantucci, "A Typology of Lone Wolves," pp. 16–25.

[4] Ibid., p. 10.

[5] Diana Dunham-Scott, "Social Network Analysis of British Jihadists," Pardee RAND Graduate School 2012 (unpublished) is a good example of the use of social network analysis (SNA) to understand the linkages of Islamist extremists linked to acts of violence in the United Kingdom.

with any confidence in terms of organizations, groups, and networks. They think this depicts the Islamist terrorist scene as more orderly and more hierarchical than it is, while not reflecting the amorphous, improvised, ever-shifting nature of the threat. Javier Jordán, Fernando M. Mañas, and Nicola Horsburgh differentiate between what they call hit squads, that is, members of al-Qaeda or groups associated with al-Qaeda who enter Europe from abroad to carry out terrorist attacks; local cells belonging to al-Qaeda or other transnational terrorist groups that are autonomous at the tactical level but part of a wider hierarchical organization at the strategic and operational levels; and grassroots jihadist networks made up of individuals who accept al-Qaeda's strategic objectives and attempt to contribute to these from their country of residence, but are not part of the hierarchical structure of al-Qaeda or any other associated organization. The strengths of these grassroots networks are autonomy in operational and tactical command and control and no easily identifiable links to known terrorist organizations; their weaknesses are a lack of professionalism and reliance on local personnel and resources.[6]

What we have learned from published reports of documents seized by U.S. forces in bin Laden's hideout in Abbottabad, Pakistan, is that bin Laden was personally linked to multiple recent terrorist plots. This finding is corroborated by Diana Dunham-Scott's detailed social network analysis of British extremists linked to acts of violence in the United Kingdom. Dunham-Scott finds that in one measure of centrality in these networks, the top 20 individuals include, as would be expected, infamous clerics and propagandists Abu Hamza, Abu Izzadeen, and Abdul el-Faisal and plot leaders and their right-hand men. What is surprising, she said, is to find senior al-Qaeda leaders who did not operate physically in Britain (Osama bin Laden, for instance, is no. 4 in this measure). This may mean that these leaders were personally directing resources from afar to support terrorist activities in the United Kingdom.[7]

The death of bin Laden and the attrition of the al-Qaeda core have had two strategic-level effects. One is the diminished ability of the al-Qaeda core to perform the organizing and proselytizing functions that it previously performed as the vanguard of the global jihadist movement. The second is that the center of gravity of the global jihadist movement has

[6] Jordán, Mañas, and Horsburgh (2008), pp. 17–39.

[7] Dunham-Scott, "Social Network Analysis of British Jihadists." The measure referred to is "betweenness centrality," a measure of a node's centrality in a network equal to the number of shortest paths from all vertices to all others that pass through that node. It is a measure of the node's influence in the network, not necessarily of the number of connections.

shifted to affiliated groups and cells. As terrorism expert Bruce Hoffman has noted, the broader global jihadist movement has become stronger than its core. The greater likelihood is that terrorist attacks will be smaller and from a variety of entities in different regions. These attacks will be more difficult to predict and anticipate.[8]

In his valuable study of jihadist cells in Europe, Jeffrey Bale argues that the debate over the nature of these cells is often framed in a way as to suggest that they are either linked to and receiving direction from al-Qaeda Central or that they are fully autonomous. Bale points out that neither of these contrasting interpretations is accurate with respect to the terrorist cells actually found in Europe. The reality is much more ambiguous. Many jihadist cells, whether their members were recruited by foreign operatives or were self-recruited, had connections to terrorist groups elsewhere.[9]

Understanding the nature of the linkages among the components of the global jihadist movement is critical to understanding the Islamist terrorist threat in Europe, but it is no easy task. As Bale noted in his study, there are limitations to social network analysis, as many links and nodes that appear central from a spatial perspective (e.g., in terms of frequency of communications) may in fact play a minor functional role in the network.[10] Approaching these networks from the perspective of their structure and function would be more productive. We identify three types of nontraditional networks: decentralized, mixed, reconstituted.

## Decentralized Networks

A Spanish expert on Islamist terrorist networks explains how the new decentralized networks work. Someone could notify the members of a cell that a "brother" is coming and needs support, money, or documents. The facilitator acts as a bridge between the capabilities (the cell) and the requirements (the brother's needs). The contact could be impersonal, maybe just an e-mail address, but the recipients of the request know that behind the e-mail address is a member of the organization.[11]

A case in point is Omar Nackcha, a young man in his early 20s, the child of Moroccans who emigrated to Belgium. He was alleged to be the contact between Mohsen Khaibar, a top GICM operative based in Syria who led a

[8] Bruce Hoffman, presentation at Jamestown Foundation Fifth Annual Terrorism Conference, Washington, DC, December 8, 2011.

[9] Bale, pp. 30–31.

[10] Ibid., p. 31.

[11] Interview with Gutierrez.

network that recruited and sent fighters to Iraq, and several cells in Spain. Nackcha, who was arrested in Barcelona in October 2006, allegedly facilitated the escape from Spain of four members of the cell that carried out the Madrid train bombings.[12]

In this model of decentralized networks, one cell may include persons holding different affiliations; targeting decisions may be a result of coincidences rather than a centralized plan; groups with little prior contact may provide support to one another for a specific plot; and some cells may claim to belong to a radical network or to answer to a prominent terrorist figure, even if it is not true, just to enhance their credibility and stature.[13]

Some attacks in the United Kingdom seem to fit this pattern. The investigation of the attempted car bomb attacks in London and Glasgow in July 2007 did not uncover any indication of outside direction or connection to al-Qaeda. Two of the individuals arrested were medical doctors, Mohammed Asha, from Jordan, and Bilal Abdullah, a British citizen of Iraqi ancestry born and raised in the UK until his family returned to Iraq when he was eight years old. He returned to the UK in 2004. The "doctors' plot" was a departure in several ways from the pattern of terrorist incidents in Britain.[14] One intriguing aspect is the Iraqi connection. Although no evidence of external linkages has been uncovered, Shiraz Maher, who knew Abdullah well, believes that Abdullah was recruited by al-Qaeda in Iraq and sent back to the UK to carry out a terrorist mission. Maher said that Abdullah was the most extreme *takfiri* he ever met. As Maher points out, Abdullah spoke fluent English, was a medical doctor, and had a British passport – the profile that al-Qaeda looks for in terrorists operating in the West.[15]

This model of decentralized networks can be very effective and helps preserve the anonymity of the members, but it is potentially vulnerable to countermeasures because it can be penetrated more easily than the old hierarchical networks. The social networks of the terrorists and their supporters and the ties of kinship and friendship that are the means of

[12] Interview with Gutierrez. The four were Said Berraj, Daoud Ouhnane, Mohamed Belhadj, and Mohamed Afalah, believed to have been killed in a suicide attack in Iraq."En busca y captura," *El Mundo*, n.d., at http://www.elmundo.es/documentos/2004/03/espana/atentados11m/huidos.html.. For the flight of Afalah and Belhadj and the nexus to Belgian cell, see *Procesamiento*, pp. 1337–1340

[13] Bundesverfassungsschutzbericht 2004, p. 200.

[14] Alan Cowell and Raymond Bonner, "Britain arrests 3 more suspects in car bomb plot," *New York Times*, July 2, 2007, at http://www.nytimes.com/2007/07/02/world/europe/02cnd-britain.html?_r=0

[15] Interview with Shiraz Maher, London, September 2008.

access to the network can mitigate this vulnerability. These social networks are central to the survival of the jihadist system. Without them, the system becomes chaotic: it turns into individuals or small groups acting without a wider support structure – a true "atomization" of the terrorist threat. Radical social networks are also largely impervious to legal measures. As Spanish investigator José Antonio Gutiérrez noted, the network's support activities are often not illegal ("All I did was give a phone number to the brother")[16] and some European legal codes require proof of structure or organization before designating a group as a terrorist organization.[17]

## Mixed Networks

A second school of thought holds that the emerging environment in which Islamic militants previously part of the Armed Islamic Group (GIA), the Salafist Group for Preaching and Combat (GSPC), or other traditional networks mix with al-Qaeda logistics and operations personnel and are now operating independently of these networks. With the cooperation of radicalized European-born Muslims, militants are forming transient terrorist teams to carry out operations within Europe. In this sense, Islamist terrorism in Europe today is in a constant state of flux, with these teams simply interested in jihad against the state and its allies.[18]

This pattern – decentralized groups acting without centralized direction but in cooperation with other extremists – is explained by two trends: the dismantlement and disintegration of older terrorist networks and their consequent reconstruction from dispersed elements and the globalization of the jihad, which is overshadowing previous national priorities.[19] According to a Spanish analyst of terrorist networks, before 9/11 the North African terrorist cells in Europe were part of international networks. Cells were in contact with cells in other countries, but only

[16] Interview with Gutierrez.

[17] The argument that there was no "solid organization" was among those accepted by the Dutch Appeals Court's January 23, 2008, decision that the Hofstad Group was not a terrorist organization.

[18] RAND information. See also Petter Nesser, "The Slaying of the Dutch Filmmaker – Religiously Motivated Violence or Islamist Terrorism in the Name of Global Jihad?" Kjeller, Norway: Forsvarets Forskningsinstitutt, FFI/Rapport 2005/00376, pp. 13–19, at http://www.ffi.no/no/Rapporter/05-00376.pdf.

[19] Javier Jordán and Robert Wesley, "After 3/11: The Evolution of Jihadist Networks in Spain," *Terrorism Monitor*, The Jamestown Foundation, Vol. 4, Issue 1, January 12, 2006.

through their leaders. This arrangement facilitated coordination but was vulnerable to disruption. When a cell leader was removed, the cell's international links were broken and the regeneration of international contacts was difficult. The groups adapted to a more unforgiving counterterrorist environment by transforming the role of the cell leader. Now, individuals outside of the cell's inner leadership core have external contacts as well.

An example of a mixed network is the cell that carried out the Madrid train bombings on March 11, 2004. The Madrid cell had two components: the operational group that actually carried out the attacks and the logistical support group that acquired the explosives and detonators and provided financing, false documents, stolen cars, and other support for the operational cell. As noted earlier, several of the leading members of the 3/11 cell had linkages to Abu Dahdah's al-Qaeda cell. Bale notes that individuals linked to al-Qaeda personally and directly facilitated the transformation of the operational leader of the cell, Sarhane Ben Abdelmajid Fakhet, into an Islamist extremist. One was Ahmad Ibrahim, a Moroccan whose daughter for a time was Fakhet's fiancée. Ibrahim was arrested in 2002 on charges of being al-Qaeda's main financial operative in Spain. Another was Amer al-Azizi, a Moroccan who lived in Spain for a decade until moving to Pakistan in November 2001; he later became the adjunct to al-Qaeda's head of external operations, the Egyptian Hamza Rabia. A third was Abu Dahdah, whose network Fakhet joined before it was dismantled in November 2001. Al-Azizi and another Moroccan, Mustafa Maymouni, were also associated with the GICM. Azizi traveled from Pakistan to Spain at the end of 2003, likely to convey al-Qaeda's approval for the Madrid attacks and to finalize the preparations.[20] Because of these links, according to Spanish terrorism expert Fernando Reinares, al-Azizi ended up in positions of importance within al-Qaeda's senior leadership.[21]

[20] Jeffrey Bale, "Jihadist Cells and 'I.E.D.' Capabilities in Europe: Assessing the Present and Future Threat to the West," Monterey Institute of International Studies, May 2009, at http://www.strategicstudiesinstitute.army.mil/pubs/display.cfm?pubID=1134, p. 45. For Abu Dahdah's and al-Azizi activities prior to the dismantling of Abu Dahdah's al-Qaeda cell, see Juzgado Central de Instrucción No. 005 Madrid, Sumario (Proc. Ordinario) 0000035/2001E, September 17, 2003, pp. 63, 267–268; and Fernando Reinares, "The Evidence of Al-Qa'ida's Role in the 2004 Madrid Attack," *CTC Sentinel*, Combating Terrorism Center at West Point, March 22, 2012, at http://www.ctc.usma.edu/posts/the-evidence-of-al-qaidas-role-in-the-2004-madrid-attack.

[21] Reinares, "The Madrid Bombings and Global Jihadism."

Another key player was Maymouni. A confidential police informant reported that Maymouni had become the leader of a group known as Harakat al-Salafiyya al-Jihadiyya (a small Spain-based group, not to be confused with al-Salafiyya al-Jihadiyya that according to Moroccan authorities operated in Morocco). Members of this group joined with another militant group that had been established in Spain by Muhammad the Egyptian to form the core of the network that planned and carried out the Madrid bombings. Maymouni left Spain in early 2003 to organize jihadist cells in Morocco and was arrested by Moroccan authorities after the May 2003 Casablanca bombing. Fakhet replaced him as the leader of the group. Yet another GICM member, Yusuf al-Hajj, established a base of operations in Belgium and, among other things, helped facilitate the flight from Spain of his brother Muhammad and another militant after the attack.[22]

Another key player in the 3/11 network was Jamal Zugham, a member of Abu Dahdah's al-Qaeda cell. Zugham had extensive international terrorist connections, including the Norway-based Mullah Krekar, the leader of the Kurdish group Ansar al-Islam, and Moroccan militant groups. Zugham was well known to Spanish intelligence. In response to a request by French anti-terrorism magistrate Jean-Louis Bruguière in 2001, the police had surreptitiously entered Zougam's flat and found material relating to jihadist activity. Later, his name surfaced in relation to the May 16, 2003, Casablanca bombings.[23]

Another group that illustrates this network model is the Hofstad Group in the Netherlands. The group had some relationship with counterparts in Spain and Belgium. It also had contacts with extremists in Morocco through a member who was affiliated with the GICM. Members of the group were believed to have been working on plans to attack a nuclear power plant in the Netherlands, the parliament in The Hague, and Schiphol Airport. They had a list of potential assassination victims that included the president of the European Commission. Some sources link the group with the organization of the late Abu Musab al-Zarqawi, with al-Qaeda operative Saleh Eddine Benia, and with a Syrian active in the Iraqi insurgency.[24]

[22] Bale, "Jihadist Cells and 'I.E.D.' Capabilities in Europe," pp. 44–51.

[23] Ibid., pp. 34–35, 46–47.

[24] Robert Leiken, "Europe's Mujahedeen," p. 7; David Crawford and Keith Johnson, "New terror threat in Europe," *Wall Street Journal*, December 27, 2004, at http://online.wsj.com/news/articles/SB110409924954609595; Jean-Pierre Stroobants, "Le reseau islamiste 'Hofstad' etait solidement ancre en Europe," *Le Monde*, December 10, 2004, at http://www.lemonde.fr/recherche/?keywords=Le+réseau+islamiste+%22Hofstad%22+était+solidement+ancré+en+Europe&qt=recherche_globale.

### Reconstituted Networks

Other analysts believe that the networks have declined in significance compared to the independent cells, and that the central command structure no longer exists. However, particularly at the height of the Iraqi insurgency in 2005 and 2006, there was heightened concern that returning fighters might seek to establish a network-like structure.[25] The threat of terrorist operations in Europe linked to the Iraqi insurgency was lent credibility by reports that the late Abu Musab al-Zarqawi, then leader of al-Qaeda in Iraq, was moving to reestablish his network in Europe.[26]

In fact, the threat that returning veterans from Iraq could constitute the core of a reconstituted al-Qaeda network in Europe did not materialize, possibly because in contrast to the anti-Soviet campaign in Afghanistan – and the prestige that their successful campaign accrued to the Mujahideen – the tide of conflict in Iraq turned decisively against al-Qaeda in Iraq following the U.S. troop surge in 2007, and many of its key operatives were killed or abandoned the struggle. As discussed later, a more recent development, the participation of large numbers of European and other Western volunteers in the armed conflict in Syria, poses a much greater danger of reconstituted jihadist networks in Europe.

## THE GLOBAL DIMENSION OF EUROPE-BASED ISLAMIST TERRORISM

### Links to Syria

The civil war in Syria, where jihadists linked to al-Qaeda are playing a prominent role, has given these groups a new lease on life.[27] Syria is an appealing destination for radicalized young European Muslims not only because it is the most prominent theater of armed conflict in the Muslim world but also because of its geographic accessibility and relative ease of travel. Generally, volunteers need only drive or fly to Turkey from where they can cross the border into Syria. This allows some to thwart the attempts of the authorities in countries such as Germany to stop them by confiscating their passports when their intentions become known. As they

[25] Benard interview with Georg Witschel, Undersecretary for Combating and Preventing International Terrorism, German Ministry of Foreign Affairs, Washington, June 6, 2005.

[26] "Echoes of al-Qaeda, hints of Iraq," *Los Angeles Times*, July 8, 2005, at http://articles.latimes.com/2005/jul/08/world/fg-terror8.

[27] Aaron Y. Zelin, "al-Qaeda in Iraq enters the Syrian conflict," *al-Wasat*, March 11, 2013, at http://thewasat.wordpress.com/2013/03/11/al-qaeda-in-iraq-enters-the-syrian-conflict/.

still retain their identity cards, they can generally enter Turkey and from there reach their destination.[28]

Many extremists, including al-Zawahiri, as indicated in an audio message released in June 2013, believe that the struggle in Syria will lead to the restoration of the caliphate and the destruction of Israel.[29] The war in Syria is also linked to predictions in Islamic eschatology about the final days. Jabhat al-Nusra's media outlet is named al-Manarah al-Bayda or the White Minaret in the Ummayyad mosque of Damascus, where according to a hadith the Prophet Issa (Jesus) will descend at the end of time. Abi Mohammed al-Adnani, a Syrian jihadist leader, said in an audio recording that they would not abandon the struggle until they had surrendered the flag to Issa.[30] According to Islamic tradition, the climactic battle between the Madhi, a central figure in the Islamic narrative of the final days, and the Dajjal, or False Messiah, will be preceded by the appearance of a tyrant named the Sufyani in Damascus. The Sufyani will send an army to Mecca to depose the Madhi, but his army will be swallowed by the desert. After the Sufyani is defeated and executed under a tree in Tiberias, the Dajjal will appear. The Muslims under the Mahdi will be in Damascus, surrounded by the armies of the Dajjal. As the Mahdi and his companions prepare for prayer, the Prophet Issa will descend from the heavens, leaning on the shoulders of two angels. The battle is then joined and Issa chases the Dajjal until he catches up with him and slays him.[31]

The Islamic narration of the end of days resonates with Assad's Sunni opponents, who identify Assad with the Sufyani. The Dajjal, in this view, is a person claiming to be the Shi'ite Madhi who will be supported by the Shi'ites and will be defeated in the final battle.[32] The apocalyptic dimension of the Syrian conflict imbues it for Sunni militants with greater significance than other theaters of armed conflict, as the struggle there is linked to the final triumph of Islam.

According to a report in the German daily *Die Welt*, citing Western intelligence sources, in 2011 al-Qaeda leader al-Zawahiri sent at least three

[28] Carolin Fromm and Simon Kremer, "Junge Norddeutsche Kaempfen in Syrien," NDR.de, Sept. 4, 2013 at www.ndr.de/regional/islamistensyrien101.html.

[29] https://www.youtube.com/watch?v=z7esoE1ANLU.

[30] "al-Qaeda's internal divide grows in Syria," *Al Monitor*, August 19, 2013, at http://archive.today/ofis4#selection-1595.302-1595.888.

[31] The prophecies regarding the Sufyani, the coming of the Madhi, and the reign and defeat of the Dajjal are found in several hadith in the collections of Muslim, Bukhari, and Abu Dawud.

[32] "Bashar al-Assad is the Sufyani?" Sunni Forum, at http://www.sunniforum.com/forum/showthread.php?82916-Bashar-al-Assad-is-the-Sufyani/.

organizers to Syria to establish jihadist groups. According to these sources, al-Zawahiri's intentions were to train extremists with European passports in Egypt and Syria so that they could build terror cells in Europe and to turn Syria turn into a replica of Waziristan. Al-Zawahiri's contact in Syria was Abu Muhammad al-Julani, a Syrian formerly associated with Abu Musab al-Zarqawi's network in Iraq. After the Syrian uprising began, al-Julani (who was reported killed twice, in Iraq in 2006 and in Syria in 2008) moved to Syria and was named emir of Jabhat al-Nusra, which during the first years of the conflict was the destination of choice for many Western European volunteers.[33]

In April 2013, Abu Bakr al-Baghdadi, the leader of the Islamic State of Iraq (ISI), al-Qaeda's affiliate in Iraq, announced that al-Nusra was ISI's front in Syria and that the two organizations would henceforth be known as the Islamic State of Iraq and al-Sham (ISIS) – al-Sham being the historic Arabic term for the Levant or Greater Syria. Jabhat al-Nusra refused to acknowledge ISIS's primacy, especially when its members were ordered to swear allegiance to al-Baghdadi, and the rivalry between the two organizations soon turned violent. In May 2013, al-Zawahiri ordered ISIS to disband its Islamic state and focus its efforts inside Iraq. Both al-Baghdadi and al-Julani could continue as emirs of their respective groups, but each had to report to al-Qaeda's general command.[34]

ISIS openly defied this order; in November 2013, ISIS fighters beheaded Muhammad Fares Marroush, a commander in Ahrar al-Sham, another jihadist group with links to al-Qaeda, later claiming that it had mistaken Marroush for another man. On February 3, 2014, after several failed attempts to mediate between the two groups, al-Qaeda formally disavowed ISIS and acknowledged Jabhat al-Nusra as its official branch in Syria. Several influential jihadi ideologues, such as Sheikh Abdallah Muhammad al Muhaysini,

[33] Florian Flade and Clemens Wergin, "Has Syria become al-Qaeda's new base for terror strikes on Europe?" *Die Welt*, December 18, 2012, at http://worldcrunch.com/world-affairs/has-syria-become-al-qaeda-039-s-new-base-for-terror-strikes-on-europe-/islam-jihad-al-qaeda-bin-laden-morsi-assad/c1s10415/#.UVnYzRmiESA; Noman Benotman and Roisin Blake, "Jabhat al-Nusra li-ahl al-Sham min Mujahedi al-Sham fi Sahat al-Jihad. A Strategic Briefing," Quilliam Foundation, at http://www.quilliamfoundation.org/wp/wp-content/uploads/publications/free/jabhat-al-nusra-a-strategic-briefing.pdf; Pieter van Ostaeyen, "An Alleged Biography of Abu Muhammad al-Julani: Some Ideas," at http://pietervanostaeyen.wordpress.com/2013/12/16/an-alleged-biography-of-abu-muhammad-al-julani-some-ideas/.

[34] Thomas Joscelyn, "Analysis: Zawahiri's letter to al-Qaeda branches in Syria, Iraq," *The Long War Journal*, June 10, 2013, at http://www.longwarjournal.org/archives/2013/06/analysis_alleged_let.ph.

Abu Qatada, and Abu Muhammad al Maqdisi sided with al-Zawahiri and sharply criticized al-Baghdadi.[35] (The last two were imprisoned in Jordan; nevertheless they were able to comment on current events and provide ideological guidance. Al Maqdisi was released in June 2014; Abu Qatada was cleared by a Jordanian court of terrorism offenses related to 1998 plot, but still faces other charges.) Not too long afterward, ISIS sent two suicide bombers who assassinated Abu Khalid al-Suri, a co-founder of Ahrar al-Sham and al-Zawahiri's representative in Syria. Al-Suri had been sent to mediate the dispute between ISIS and Jabhat al-Nusra and other jihadi groups.[36]

In June 2014 ISIS scored stunning victories in Iraq, taking over a large swatch of territory in the northwestern part of the country, including Mosul, Iraq's second largest city, and has overtaken Jabhat-al-Nusra as a destination for Western jihadists. According to Peter Neumann, director of the International Centre for the Study of Radicalisation and Political Violence (ICSR), King's College London, as many as 80 percent of British foreign fighters have joined ISIS.[37] A March 2014 ICSR study found that 55 percent of the Western foreign fighters in its sample were affiliated with ISIS, while just under 14 percent were believed to belong to Jabhat al-Nusra. In interviews conducted in Turkish towns along the Syrian border the ICSR researchers found that the foreign composition of ISIS was so acute that many referred to the group as "the foreigners."[38]

Another destination of European fighters is Jaish al-Muhajireen wal-Ansar (the Army of the Emigrants and Helpers), also known as the Foreigners' Brigade, which has sworn allegiance to al-Baghdadi. The group is headed by a Chechen and contains many Turkish and Chechen fighters, in addition to Europeans. The most prominent German jihadist, the rapper Denis Cuspert, aka Deso Dogg and Abou Maleeq, belonged to

[35] Thomas Joscelyn, "Pro-al Qaeda Saudi cleric calls on ISIS members to defect," *The Long War Journal*, February 3, 2014, at http://www.longwarjournal.org/archives/2014/02/pro-al_qaeda_saudi_c.php.

[36] "Two bombers kill senior Al-Qaida fighter," *Gulf News*, February 23, 2014, at http://gulfnews.com/in-focus/syria/two-bombers-kill-senior-al-qaida-fighter-1.1294943.

[37] Peter Neumann, "How to curb the threat of homecoming jihadist fighters," *New Scientist*, June 25, 2014, at http://www.newscientist.com/article/dn25784-how-to-curb-the-threat-of-homecoming-jihadist-fighters.html#.U7H-SSRBxQY.

[38] Joseph A. Carter, Shiraz Maher, and Peter R. Neumann, "#Greenbirds: Measuring Importance and Influence in Syrian Foreign Fighter Networks," International Centre for the Study of Radicalisation and Political Violence (ICSR), King's College London, 2014, p. 11, at http://icsr.info/wp-content/uploads/2014/04/ICSR-Report-Greenbirds-Measuring-Importance-and-Influence-in-Syrian-Foreign-Fighter-Networks.pdf.

this brigade; he was recently injured and there were reports that he was killed, though denials later appeared on the social media.[39]

Reports have indicated that facilitation networks that were established to send foreign fighters to Iraq have been reactivated to recruit and assist foreign extremists to join the fight in Syria. The German newspaper *Sueddeutsche* reports on quasi-charities that have been established in Germany to funnel money and supplies to Syrian jihadists, and it cites incidents in which German police intercepted trucks with military equipment destined for radical fighters.[40] The would-be foreign jihadists are met at the airport in Istanbul and transported to the Syrian border. One such facilitator, "Abu Hussein the Russian," a native Syrian who had been living in Ukraine, was interviewed by a Western journalist:

> When I met him in Akçakale – a Turkish town on the border with Syria – he whipped out his passport. "Want to see this?" he asked. Page after page was covered in Turkish entry and exit stamps, each of them representing a foreign fighter that he had helped to bring into his country. He escorted them one by one, travelling up to Istanbul by plane from the border region of Hatay, and then travelling back down by bus to avoid the attentions of the security services. At the border he would deliver his new companion to another contact, who would then smuggle them in over the border. The whole journey, there and back, took less than 24 hours.[41]

As of June 2012, an estimated 700 to 1,400 foreign fighters were in Syria, mostly from neighboring countries and North Africa.[42] By December 2013, the number of foreign fighters in Syria was estimated to have increased to more than 8,500 from 74 countries. The number of Western Europeans more than tripled from 600 in April 2013 to 1,900 in December 2013. Western Europeans represented almost one-fifth of the total number of foreign fighters in Syria. The largest contingents come from France, the United Kingdom, Belgium, Germany, and the Netherlands.[43]

[39] Jan Bielicki, "Per Billigflug in den 'Heiligen Krieg,'" *Sueddeutsche Zeitung*, December 17, 2013, at http://www.sueddeutsche.de/politik/deutsche-dschihadisten-per-billigflug-in-den-heiligen-krieg-1.1845516; "Chechen-led group swears allegiance to head of Islamic State of Iraq and Sham," *The Long War Journal*, November 27, 2013, at http://www.longwarjournal.org/archives/2013/11/muhajireen_army_swea.php.

[40] Bielicki, "Per Billigflug in den 'Heiligen Krieg.'"

[41] Hannah Lucinda Smith, "The Man Who Drives British Fighters to Jihad," Vice Media Inc., January 31, 2014, at http://www.vice.com/en_uk/read/meeting-the-jihadi-transporter.

[42] Aaron Y. Zelin, "Foreign Fighters Trickle into the Syrian Rebellion," The Washington Institute for Near East Policy, June 11, 2012, at http://www.washingtoninstitute.org/policy-analysis/view/foreign-fighters-trickle-into-the-syrian-rebellion.

[43] Aaron Y. Zelin, "Up to 11,000 Foreign Fighters in Syria; Steep Rise among Western Europeans," International Centre for the Study of Radicalisation and Political Violence,

The head of MI-5, the British domestic intelligence service, told a parliamentary committee in November 2013 that the number of British militants who had gone to fight in Syria was in the low hundreds.[44] British and Dutch journalists who had been held by a group of militants in Syria reported on their release that almost a dozen British jihadists were in the group, nine of whom had "London accents," including a National Health Service trainee doctor. The trainee doctor in question, Shajul Islam, was arrested on his return to the UK and, together with an accomplice, charged for his role in kidnapping the journalists.[45]

According to French press reports, the security services had identified about 440 persons who had gone or wanted to go to Syria to fight against the Assad regime.[46] A careful estimate of European fighters in Syria by the International Centre for the Study of Radicalisation and Political Violence, King's College London, put the number of French fighters in Syria at between 63 and 413 as of December 2013.[47] According to the German National Security Agency, the Bundesverfassungsschutz, at least 220 prospective fighters departed Germany for Syria in 2012; more than half of these held German citizenship.[48] The largest number of recruits comes from North Rhine–Westphalia, followed by Hesse, Berlin, Bavaria, and Hamburg. Apparently, the German recruits live together in a dedicated "German camp" for German recruits.[49]

Dutch militants from different backgrounds – Moroccans, Turks, Kurds, Somalis, and converts – have traveled to Syria since mid-2012. According to an analysis of Dutch fighters in Syria, it would be reasonable to expect to find up to 200 Dutch volunteers fighting in Syria. The fighters were recruited by preachers associated with radical groups such as Sharia4Holland, Behind Bars, Straat Dawah (Dawah Street), and Waarheid (the Truth). The first

King's College London, December 17, 2013, at http://icsr.info/2013/12/icsr-insight-11000-foreign-fighters-syria-steep-rise-among-western-europeans/.

[44] "Hundreds of Britons fighting in Syria – MI-5 chief," *BBC News*, November 7, 2013, at http://www.bbc.co.uk/news/world-middle-east-24856553.

[45] Raffaello Pantucci, "British Fighters Joining the War in Syria," *CTC Sentinel*, Vol. 6, Issue 2, February 2013, at http://www.ctc.usma.edu/wp-content/uploads/2013/02/CTCSentinel-Vol6Iss22.pdf.

[46] "Une filière djihadiste vers la Syrie," *Le Monde*, November 26, 2013, at http://www.lemonde.fr/societe/article/2013/11/26/filiere-djihadiste-vers-la-syrie-une-arrestation-dans-le-nord-de-la-france_3520789_3224.html.

[47] Zelin, "Up to 11,000 Foreign Fighters in Syria."

[48] Hans Georg Maassen, head of the Bundesverfassungsschutz, in an interview cited in Sabine Siebold and Alexandra Hudson, "Syria conflict draws rising numbers of German jihadists," Reuters, Berlin, November 13, 2013, at http://uk.reuters.com/article/2013/11/13/uk-syria-crisis-germany-idUKBRE9AC0NA20131113.

[49] Kersten Knipp, "Jihad and back: German fighters in Syria." *DW.DE*, October 22, 2013, at http://www.dw.de/jihad-and-back-german-fighters-in-syria/a-17174394.

Dutch volunteers traveled to Syria by way of Egypt until other routes by way of Germany and Turkey opened up. Most of the volunteers receive their basic training in Syria before they are deployed to the battlefield. If they do well, they may be picked to join Jabhat al-Nusra. If they do not do well enough to join al-Nusra, they are handed to other Islamist groups fighting in Syria. They are fighting in the north of Syria, in Aleppo, Idlib, and Latakia province. Based on their own postings on social media, it appears that some of them have been involved in the execution of prisoners.[50]

Belgium also provides one of the largest numbers of European recruits. According to the Belgian daily *De Standaard*, the Sharia4Belgium group, which was officially disbanded at the end of 2012, played an important role in the recruitment of young militants in Belgium to fight in Syria.[51] Sweden's secret police service Säpo considers Swedes traveling abroad, especially to Syria, to take part in military training the greatest potential threat. The Säpo estimates that at least 75 people have traveled from Sweden to Syria.[52]

Most of the Spaniards are Muslims from the city of Ceuta, the Spanish enclave in North Africa across the Strait of Gibraltar. Except for three, or perhaps four, cases, none of the Spanish fighters had any significant jihadist record predating the Syrian conflict. At least two of them, however, were already taking part in extremist proselytizing meetings that had been held regularly since 2008 in Ceuta and in the southern province of Cádiz. One important exception was the Syrian-born Mouhannad Almallah Dabas, a naturalized Spanish citizen and former member of the al-Qaeda cell established in Spain in the mid-1990s led by Abu Dahdah. Almallah Dabas was indicted in the 2004 Madrid train-bombings case and first convicted at the National Court but later absolved by a Supreme Court ruling. He then went to Syria, where he was placed in charge of the logistic activities of Jabhat al-Nusra.[53]

[50] Ronald Sandee and Michael S. Smith II, "Inside the Jihad: Dutch Fighters in Syria," Kronos Advisory, October 24, 2013, at http://www.kronosadvisory.com/Kronos_DUTCH.FIGHTERS.IN.SYRIA.pdf.

[51] "Syria: A training ground for European jihadists," PressEurop, VOXeurop, March 25, 2013, at http://www.voxeurop.eu/en/content/news-brief/3587521-training-ground-european-jihadists.

[52] "Islamic extremism on the rse in Sweden: Study," *The Local*, February 1, 2014, at http://www.thelocal.se/20140131/sweden-sees-increased-threat-from-islamic-extremists.

[53] Fernando Reinares and Carola García-Calvo, "Jihadists from Spain in Syria: Facts and Figures," Real Instituto Elcano, December 12, 2013, at http://www.realinstitutoelcano.org/wps/portal/rielcano/contenido?WCM_GLOBAL_CONTEXT=/elcano/elcano_in/zonas_in/international+terrorism/reinares-garcia-calvo-jihadists-from-spain-in-syria.

A number of Europe-based militants have been killed fighting in Syria. Among these were two Britons of Algerian ancestry who died in a firefight with Syrian government forces in March 2012;[54] a Briton of Palestinian descent and a Britain-raised Libyan;[55] six or possibly seven Dutch volunteers;[56] nine French residents;[57] two Spanish citizens from Ceuta;[58] two Danes, one a convert to Islam and the other the offspring of a Danish mother and an Algerian father who had spent two years in U.S. custody at the Guantanamo detention facility in Cuba;[59] and a young Swedish man who traveled first to Turkey and then joined the Free Syrian Army. According to a video transcription, he left the FSA soon after and joined a jihadist group that fights alongside Jabhat al-Nusra, where he felt "right at home with the group that consisted of brothers who came to fight for the sake of Allah from around the world."[60]

European counterterrorism authorities believe that Syria could turn into a safe haven for terrorists and that European militants fighting in Syria could pose a threat to European societies on their return.[61] British Foreign Secretary William Hague said in a speech in London in February 2013 that Syria was now the number one destination for jihadists anywhere in the world, and he warned that the longer the Syria conflict goes on, the greater the risk of an attack on the UK by ideologically hardened jihadists with battle experience.[62]

[54] Initial reports indicated that the two were journalists, but subsequent information suggests otherwise. See Pantucci, "British Fighters Joining the War in Syria."

[55] Shiv Malik and Haroon Siddique, "Briton killed fighting in Syria civil war," *The Guardian*, November 20, 2013, at http://www.theguardian.com/world/2013/nov/20/briton-killed-syria-civil-war-mohammed-el-araj-london.

[56] "Sandee and Smith, "Inside the Jihad," pp. 22–24.

[57] "Syrie: neuf djihadistes français tués," *L'Express*, September 4, 2013, at http://www.lexpress.fr/actualite/indiscrets/syrie-neuf-djihadistes-francais-tues_1278641.html.

[58] José María Irujo, "Muere otro yihadista ceutí en Siria," *El País*, July 18, 2012, at http://politica.elpais.com/politica/2012/07/17/actualidad/1342559055_659472.html.

[59] Soeren Kern, "European Jihadists: The Latest Export," Gatestone Institute, March 21, 2013, at http://www.gatestoneinstitute.org/3634/european-jihadists.

[60] Lisa Lundquist, "Recent videos show international makeup of Syrian jihad," *Long War Journal/Threat Matrix*, March 20, 2013, at http://www.longwarjournal.org/threat-matrix/archives/2013/03/recent_videos_show_internation.php?utm_source=twitterfeed&utm_medium=twitter.

[61] Statement by EU Counter-Terrorism Coordinator Gilles de Kerchove, 9th European Day in Remembrance of Victims of Terrorism, Brussels, March 11, 2013, at http://www.consilium.europa.eu/uedocs/cms_data/docs/pressdata/en/jha/135943.pdf.

[62] Tom Whitehead, "Threat of UK attack by British jihadists in Syria growing, Hague warns," *The Telegram*, February 14, 2013, at http://www.telegraph.co.uk/news/worldnews/middleeast/syria/9870619/Threat-of-UK-attack-by-British-jihadists-in-Syria-growing-Hague-warns.html.

If there is uncertainty regarding the number of Europe-based fighters in Syria, their actual utility on the battlefield, the effect their experiences will have on them, and the possible consequences for the security threat that they pose on their return, it seems clear is that having gone to Syria – however briefly – is a status item for young would-be jihadists. Torsten Voss, deputy director of the Hamburg Regional Security Agency, has found that the motives for going to Syria are often mixed and subject to change. For example, someone may initially intend to assist with a humanitarian effort but might then be drawn into a combat role. One consequence is that while the conflict in the Pakistani-Afghan theater tended to attract hard-core Islamists who already were known to the security agencies, the conflict in Syria speaks to a much broader base.[63]

The typical German jihadist is a young man just out of school, from a lower-middle-class or ghetto environment, often a gang member; a German television documentary also uncovered repeated links to individuals associated with Hizb ut-Tahrir. This young person often departs for Syria out of conviction but partially also to establish his street credentials and raise his standing on his return. This is evidenced by Facebook postings and blog entries in which the individual poses dramatically with a weapon.[64]

German authorities have mixed assessments of the potential consequences of this development. On the one hand, they are alarmed by the prospect that individuals who can freely move in German society will return not only further radicalized but also equipped with battle experience and new ties to extremist networks. But on the other hand, some experts comfort themselves with the thought that the experience in Syria might be sobering for many of these young enthusiasts. Compared to other foreign fighters, they bring little to the table in terms of battle experience. Language obstacles may cause them to feel marginalized. The camp situation itself may be different from what a young person accustomed to life in the West might expect. They are frequent targets of attack and the infrastructure is rudimentary. Moreover, the bitter divisiveness inside the Syrian opposition might be disenchanting for at least the more thoughtful among the recruits.

However, previous experience indicates that even unskilled and socially or mentally inept individuals can serve a useful purpose to extremist organizations, at a minimum as cannon fodder in suicide missions. European volunteers, whether converts or Diaspora Muslims or native-born Europeans from

[63] Fromm and Kremer, "Junge Norddeutsche Kaempfen in Syrien."
[64] Ibid.

immigrant families are knowledgeable about their home countries and can blend into European societies, and they will be seen as assets in radicalization and proselytizing effort as well as in future potential terrorist plots. Also, there are ample noncombat functions that a Western-educated person with fluency in European languages can perform, and the radical Islamist movement will certainly tap into this resource base.

The government of the German state of Baden-Württemberg reports with concern about the intensive online activities of German jihadists in Syria. One social media cell run by a group known as Jund al-Sham (the Army of Syria) maintains the "Sham-Center," which manages a website; a Youtube presence; and Facebook, Twitter, and Google+ accounts. They describe their activities as their contribution to a "social jihad." Their intent, they say, is to provide information about the battle for Syria, remind Muslims everywhere of their obligation to support this and the global jihad, and to recruit supporters and inspire financial donations. The group further claims to also be participating in active combat in the area around Latakia in partnership with experienced fighters, among them a number of Chechens who head up their combat wing.

Hesse's minister of the interior has developed a "Jihadist Early Warning" system that he wants the state to adopt. The system would consist of a telephone hotline and advisory offices where parents and citizens can report "extremist youths." This would allow interventions and potentially even permit the authorities to ban travel by those individuals. The minister believes that communities and families are sensitive to early signs of behavior change that indicate radicalization, and that this is a resource that should be used. Germany has applied a similar approach to counteract right-wing radicalization of youths.[65]

About 25 to 30 Dutch fighters have returned to the Netherlands. Some of the returnees indicated that the situation in Syria was more complex than they expected and that it was not simply a fight against Assad. Rather, there were many players in the conflict and they were ordered to fight against other Muslims. Although many of those who returned were disillusioned, others wanted to continue to fight their jihad in the West.[66]

The Dutch government raised its alert level for terrorist attacks from "limited" to "substantial" in March 2013. The national coordinator for

[65] "Hessen Plant Frühwarnsystem Gegen Dschihad-Trips Nach Syrien," *Spiegel Online*, December 3, 2013, at http://www.spiegel.de/politik/deutschland/hessen-plant-fruehwarn system-gegen-dschihad-trips-nach-syrien-a-936868.html.

[66] Sandee and Smith, "Inside the Jihad," p. 25.

security and counterterrorism explained that the chances of an attack in the Netherlands or against Dutch interests abroad had risen because close to a hundred individuals had recently left the Netherlands for various countries in Africa and the Middle East, especially Syria.[67]

For European governments – the French and British in particular – that support the opposition to the Assad regime, it is difficult to reconcile their political goals in Syria with preventing a jihadist blowback. French anti-terrorism judge Marc Trévidic told *Le Figaro* that the presence of so many French jihadists in Syria presents French authorities with an uncomfortable paradox. Because France officially supports the effort to overthrow the Assad regime – France was the first Western country to recognize the National Syrian Coalition as the only legitimate representative of the Syrian people – it is difficult for the French government to oppose those who are fighting the regime.[68]

## Links to Pakistan

Many of the terrorist incidents in Europe reveal linkages to al-Qaeda or associated groups in Pakistan. What the examination of these incidents shows is not just the radicalization of European Muslims but their incorporation into broad-ranging international conspiracies, some stretching over three continents.

According to EU Counter-Terrorism Coordinator Gilles van de Kerckhove in 2008, a component of the Islamist terrorist threat to Europe is connected to al-Qaeda in the Federally Administered Tribal Areas (FATA) of Pakistan. More people were seen moving between Europe and Pakistan, and there appeared to be an increasingly Pakistani dimension to terrorist plots in Europe.[69] European jihadist entrepreneurs such as Rashid Rauf, a British-Pakistani operative arrested in Pakistan in connection with the 2006 transatlantic airline liquid bomb plot; Belgian female Internet jihadist Malika El Aroud; and Mevlüt Kar, a Turkish citizen accused of helping four Islamist extremists on trial in Germany to obtain detonators for car bombings, have been involved in connecting

[67] Kern, "European Jihadists."

[68] "Plus de 50 djihadistes français en Syrie," *Le Figaro*, March 13, 2013, at http://www.lefigaro.fr/international/2013/03/12/01003-20130312ARTFIG00564-plus-de-50-djihadistes-francais-en-syrie.php.

[69] Interview with Gilles van de Kerckhove, Brussels, September 2008. According to van de Kerckhove, other components of the Islamist terrorist threat to Europe include groups associated with or inspired by al-Qaeda, such as al-Qaeda in the Islamic Maghreb, which has logistical cells in Europe, and homegrown terrorists.

European terrorist networks to Pakistan and in some cases directly participated in planning terrorist attacks.[70]

British and American officials believe that at least one and possibly two of the 7/7 London bombers traveled to Pakistan, joined a training camp, and may have sought out al-Qaeda. Zeeshan Siddique, a British national of Pakistani origin arrested in northwest Pakistan in May 2005 reportedly told Pakistani interrogators that he had trained at a terrorist camp in Pakistan with one of the London bombers and had met there with two senior leaders of al-Qaeda. After being deported to the United Kingdom, Siddique denied any links to al-Qaeda and alleged that his Pakistani interrogators had tried to extract a false confession from him.[71] An intriguing connection involves Mohammed Junaid Babar, a Pakistani-American linked to the 2003 London fertilizer bombing plot and Mohammed Sidique Khan, the ringleader of the 7/7 London bombings. After the 7/7 attacks, Babar admitted knowing Mohammed Sidique Khan and identified him from photographs shown to him.[72]

Although one of the July 21, 2007, would-be London bombers stated openly that his cell "never had any contact with the Pakistanis," it was reported that at the end of 2004, the group's leader Mukhtar Said-Ibrahim traveled from Britain to Saudi Arabia and on to Pakistan, putting him in Pakistan at the same time as two of the 7/7 bombers.[73] Said-Ibrahim had no known family connections in Pakistan.[74] Some investigators believe it possible that both cells were recruited and directed by one individual.[75]

The link to Pakistan is clearer in the failed August 2006 transatlantic airline bombing plot.[76] At least one of the plotters attended a terrorist

[70] Lorenzo Vidino, *Radicalization, Linkage, and Diversity: Current Trends in Terrorism in Europe*. Santa Monica, CA: RAND Corporation, 2011, p. 23.

[71] "Accounts after 2005 London bombings Point to al-Qaeda role from Pakistan," *New York Times*, August 13, 2006, at http://travel.nytimes.com/2006/08/13/world/europe/13qaeda.html?n=Top%2fReference%2fTimes%20Topics%2fOrganizations%2fA%2fAl%20Qaeda%20.

[72] "Bomber's link to al-Qaeda 'grass,'" *Scotland on Sunday*, July 17, 2005, at http://scotlandonsunday.scotsman.com/index.cfm?id=1640612005.

[73] "July 21 bomb suspects also linked to Pakistan," MSNBC News, August 1, 2005, at http://www.msnbc.msn.com/id/8791099/#storyContinued.

[74] "Did alleged leader of 21/7 meet 7/7 bombers in Pakistan?" *The Times*, August 3, 2005, at http://www.thetimes.co.uk/tto/news/uk/article1936371.ece.

[75] Tony Thompson et al., "Terror suspect gives first account of London attack," *The Observer*, July 31, 2005 at www.guardian.co.uk/attackonlondon/story/0,16132,1539851,00.html.

[76] "Bojinka II: The Transatlantic Liquid Bomb Plot," *NEFA Foundation*, April 2008, at http://narcosphere.narconews.com/userfiles/70/Bojinka2LiquidBombs.pdf; "Jury begins

training camp in Pakistan. Pakistani officials said that a senior al-Qaeda leader in Afghanistan masterminded the foiled plot. The aforementioned Rashid Rauf, a former resident of Birmingham who had fled to Pakistan in 2002 after allegedly having been involved in the murder of his uncle in a dispute over an arranged marriage, was said to be the middleman between al-Qaeda and the bombers. New information has revealed that Rauf played a key role as an intermediary not only in the 7/7 London attack but also in the failed 7/21 plot.

Rauf contacted two of the 7/7 bombers, Mohammed Siddique Khan and Shehzad Tanweer, and put them in touch with an al-Qaeda operative in the tribal areas of Pakistan identified as Haji, who persuaded the two men to undertake a suicide bombing in the United Kingdom. Rauf accompanied the two men around the tribal regions to get explosives training, record their suicide videos, and instruct them on targets. Once they had returned to the United Kingdom, he continued to handle them using Yahoo messenger, e-mails, and mobile phones. Rauf played an analogous role with Muktar Said-Ibrahim, the alleged ringleader of the 7/21 plot but apparently did not spend as much with Said-Ibrahim and his associates (two of whom were killed in an accident during explosives training) and was not able to communicate directly with him after the latter returned to the United Kingdom.[77] Rauf was reportedly killed in a U.S. missile strike in North Waziristan in November 2008.[78]

According to the Danish authorities, some of the individuals arrested in September 2007 on charges of plotting a terrorist attack in Denmark had links to high-ranking al-Qaeda leaders. One of the defendants, Hammad Khuershid, a Danish citizen of Pakistani origin, convicted of preparing a terrorist attack, had spent time in Waziristan. Investigators found handwritten bomb-making manuals that prosecutors said Khuershid had copied at the extremist Red Mosque in Islamabad.[79]

All of the individuals arrested in Germany in connection with the Islamic Jihad Union (IJU) plot had been to Pakistan and had connections with senior

deliberation in trans-Atlantic airliner bomb plot case," *International Herald Tribune Europe*, July 28, 2008, at http://www.highbeam.com/doc/1A1-D926SPMGo.html.

77 Raffaello Pantucci, "A Biography of Rashid Rauf: Al-Qa`ida's British Operative," *CTC Sentinel*, July 24, 2012, Combating Terrorism Center at West Point, at http://www.ctc.usma.edu/posts/a-biography-of-rashid-rauf-al-qaidas-british-operative.

78 "Bojinka II: The Transatlantic Liquid Bomb Plot"; "The life and death of Rashid Rauf," *The Independent*, November 23, 2008, at http://www.independent.co.uk/news/world/asia/the-life-and-death-of-rashid-rauf-1031217.html.

79 "2 convicted in Denmark of preparing terror attack," AP, October 21, 2008, at http://seattletimes.com/html/nationworld/2008292294_webdenmarkterror21.html.

al-Qaeda leaders in Iran and the al-Qaeda core leadership through Abu Laith al-Libi, al-Qaeda's military chief.[80] Captured German al-Qaeda recruit Ahmed Siddiqui reportedly told interrogators that Osama bin Laden had personally approved a plot to attack multiple European targets uncovered in October 2010. A second captured German terrorist recruit and "other sources" verified Siddiqui's claims, according to U.S. and German officials.[81]

The Barcelona plot of January 2008, which led to the arrest of 12 Pakistanis and 2 Indians suspected of planning a suicide bomb attack on the city's public transport system, was hatched in Pakistan. A Pakistani Taliban group linked to al-Qaeda, Tehrik-i-Taliban Pakistan, claimed responsibility for the foiled attack, which a Taliban spokesman said was planned because of Spain's participation in the NATO mission in Afghanistan.[82] It is worth noting that Baitullah Mehsud, the notorious Pakistani Taliban leader alleged to have orchestrated the assassination of Benazir Bhutto, taped a video warning Spain of consequences for its military presence in Afghanistan. The video was supposed to have been released prior to the foiled Barcelona attack, but it arrived at *al-Jazeera* four days after the arrest of the terrorists.[83]

## Links to Central Asia

The most interesting, if baffling, connection between violent European Islamists and non-European organizations is that between the German converts and ethnic Turks in Germany and Central Asian militants. Two court cases in Germany highlight this connection. The first is a case in Koblenz that involved Ahmad Wali Siddiqui, a German Afghan who was captured in July 2010 by American forces in Kabul. After moving to Germany in 1990 at the age of 16, Siddiqui achieved little in life beyond failing at business before encountering Mounir al-Motassadeq while they both worked at Hamburg airport in 1997. Al-Motassadeq is a Moroccan who was later convicted in Germany of supporting the 9/11 cell. In 2009, Siddiqui joined a contingent of eleven Germans (nine men and two of their wives) who traveled to Pakistan to join the jihad in Waziristan. There, the

[80] Interview with senior German security official, Berlin, June 2008.

[81] Troy McMullen and Anna Schecter, "German Terror Connection Grows; 45 More Suspects Being Tracked," *ABC News*, Oct. 7, 2010, at http://abcnews.go.com/Blotter/ahmed-siddiqui-german-terror-connection/story?id=11760048#.T74UGlIpmzU.

[82] "TTP claims responsibility for foiled terror plan in Barcelona," *Dawn Internet Edition*, September 19, 2008, at http://www.dawn.com/2008/09/19/top13.htm.

[83] Interview with Fernando Reinares, Madrid, September 2008.

group pledged allegiance to Tahir Yuldashev, the leader of the Islamic Movement of Uzbekistan (IMU) and trained at an IMU camp. At this camp, Siddiqui and a friend from Hamburg, Rami Makanesi, a German jihadist of Syrian ancestry, met Yunis al-Mauretani, an al-Qaeda commander who told them about a plot being planned with cells in Italy, France, and the UK to launch Mumbai-style assaults on European cities. Al-Mauretani wanted the Germans to return to Germany to act as contacts.

Instead, Makanesi decided to turn himself in to the German Embassy in Islamabad. The German Embassy alerted Pakistani authorities who arrested Makanesi in northwest Pakistan, as he was trying to leave the tribal areas disguised in a *burqa*. Siddiqui was captured in Kabul on his way back to Germany.[84] During his interrogation, Siddiqui said that he had been told that Osama bin Laden was privy to the plot. Siddiqui also reportedly had contact with Ilyas Kashmiri, who was in charge of the planning of al-Qaeda's foreign operations. Kashmiri had been in touch with the perpetrators of the Mumbai attacks as well as other terrorists who had allegedly planned attacks in the United States and Europe.[85] (Kashmiri was reportedly killed in a drone strike in June 2011 but was spotted at a meeting with the Pakistani Taliban in 2012.) Mohammed Merah, the French jihadist who killed three French soldiers and three Jewish children and a teacher in a shooting spree in the south of France in March 2012, might have been part of this plot. Merah had been involved with the ringleader of a group accused of sending young French jihadists to Iraq and traveled to Pakistan and Afghanistan in 2010 and 2011.[86]

The second case involves Yusuf Ocak and Maqsood Lodin who traveled to Waziristan with a group of young German extremists a few months

[84] Raffaello Pantucci, "German Trials Highlight the Role of the IMU as a Feeder for al-Qaeda Operations in Europe," *Terrorism Monitor*, Vol. 10, Issue 9, May 4, 2012, at http://www.jamestown.org/single/?no_cache=1&tx_ttnews[tt_news]=39332; Marcel Rosenbach and Holger Stark, "German Jihad: Homegrown Terror Takes on New Dimensions," *Spiegel Online*, May 9, 2011, at http://www.spiegel.de/international/germany/german-jihad-homegrown-terror-takes-on-new-dimensions-a-761391.html.

[85] Yassin Musharbash, "'Euro Plot': Al-Qaida Said To Be Planning European Hostage-Takings, Part 2: German Jihadists with Al-Qaida Ties" *Spiegel Online*, October 27, 2010, at http://www.spiegel.de/international/europe/euro-plot-al-qaida-said-to-be-planning-european-hostage-takings-a-725618-2.html; Florian Flade, "al-Qaeda's Euro-Plot – What to make of it?" Jih@d, September 30, 2010, at http://ojihad.wordpress.com/2010/09/30/al-qaeda%C2%B4s-euro-plot-what-to-make-of-it/.

[86] Pascale Combelles Siegel, "French Counterterrorism Policy in the Wake of Mohammed Merah's Attack," *CTC Sentinel*, Combating Terrorism Center at West Point, April 23, 2012, at http://www.ctc.usma.edu/posts/french-counterterrorism-policy-in-the-wake-of-mohammed-merahs-attack.

after Siddiqui's group to join the German Taliban Mujahideen. The German Taliban Mujahideen and a closely related Turkish group, Taifatul Mansura (the Victorious Sect), were established by the IJU, an offshoot of the IMU in 2009 to accommodate the increasing number of Germans arriving in Waziristan. The group disintegrated after the death of its founding emir, Ahmed Manavbasi, a Turkish Kurd, in 2010.[87]

Apparently Ocak and Lodin wanted to remain in Waziristan where, according to Ocak, they wanted to live following *shari'a* law and waging jihad; however, after the death of Manavbasi, they were recruited by al-Qaeda and ordered to return to Europe to support al-Qaeda networks there. The two left Pakistan in early 2011, traveling via Iran and Turkey to Budapest where they were tasked with raising funds and establishing networks of suicide bombers that could be used in future al-Qaeda operations. Ocak appeared in a video where he threatened Germany with attacks, leaving an audio trail that German investigators were able to trace, leading to his capture.[88] Lodin, an Austrian citizen, was arrested by the German police and extradited to Austria. Pornographic videos seized from Lodin, on closer examination, contained encrypted al-Qaeda documents with plans for terror attacks in Europe.[89]

Other prominent German jihadists have been killed in Afghanistan and Pakistan. Bekkay Harrach, also known as Al-Hafidh Abu Talha al Almani (the German), was killed while leading an assault on Bagram Airbase in May 2010. Harrach led a team of 20 fighters made up from the ranks of al-Qaeda, the Pakistani Taliban, and the IMU, according to his martyrdom statement. Before his death, Harrach produced propaganda for al-Qaeda in which he threatened attacks on Germany. "Abdullah from Essen," a German citizen from Afghanistan who was known as Miqdad, was killed while fighting U.S. forces in Baghlan province, northern Afghanistan in March 2011. Gazavat Media, a jihadist propaganda website belonging to the Taifatul Mansura, posted in October 2011 that Abdul Fettah al Almani, identified as the head of the so-called German Taliban Mujahideen, was killed in a U.S. airstrike. Several other Germans were reported to have been killed by U.S. Predator strikes in the Mir Ali area of North Waziristan. The

[87] Raffaello Pantucci, "Terror in Germany: An Interview with Guido Steinberg," The International Centre for the Study of Radicalisation (ICSR), March 16, 2011, at http://icsr.info/2011/03/terror-in-germany-an-interview-with-guido-steinberg/.

[88] Pantucci, "German Trials Highlight the Role of the IMU."

[89] "Maqsoon Lodin," *Global Jihad*, June 22, 2011, at http://www.globaljihad.net/view_page.asp?id=2118.

Germans were thought to be training for attacks in Europe.[90] The death of about a dozen militants, the constant danger of U.S. drone attacks, and the harsh living conditions in Waziristan have brought about a reversal of the trend. According to a 2012 *Spiegel* report, the number of German volunteers going to Waziristan is declining, while the number of those going back home is growing.[91]

Three of the four individuals sentenced in connection with the Sauerland plot, Fritz Gelowicz, Daniel Schneider, and Adem Yilmaz, had trained at an IJU camp in the tribal areas of Pakistan. The group returned to Germany and prosecutors detailed how the suspects maintained contact with IJU operatives and frequented Internet cafes to communicate with their handlers. They acquired hydrogen peroxide and equipment, including fuses that were hidden in shoes, delivered from Turkey by Atilla Selek, born in Germany to a family of Turkish descent.[92] There is, of course, an ethnic connection between Turks and Uzbeks, and perhaps more. The two men who operated the IJU website were Turks based in Istanbul and the website was in Turkish. What concerns counterterrorism authorities is that the IJU cannot be regarded as solely an Uzbek organization. It has a global agenda consistent with that of al-Qaeda.[93]

## Links to Yemen and East Africa

There are emergent links between Europe-based extremists and terrorist sanctuaries in Yemen and Somalia. In 2009, Yemen emerged as a major center of gravity of global Islamist terrorism as a result of two related developments. One was the reconstitution of al-Qaeda in the Arabian Peninsula (AQAP). AQAP launched a major terrorist campaign in Saudi Arabia in 2003, but by 2005, the group had been decimated by effective Saudi counterterrorist operations. The remnants of AQAP retreated to areas

[90] Bill Roggio, "IMU Announces Death of German Jihadist," *The Long War Journal*, November 8, 2011 at http://www.longwarjournal.org/archives/2011/11/imu_announces_death.php; "'German Taliban Mujahideen Thought Killed in US Airstrike," October 4, 2011, at http://www.longwarjournal.org/archives/2011/10/german_taliban_mujah.php.

[91] Oezlem Gezer and Holger Stark, "More Pistols than Pampers: Disillusioned German Islamists Abandoning Jihad," *Spiegel Online*, July 18, 2012, at http://www.spiegel.de/international/world/disillusioned-german-islamists-returning-home-to-germany-a-844799.html.

[92] Patrick Donahue, "German Trial of Anti-U.S. Terrorist Suspects Begins," Bloomberg, April 22, 2009, at http://www.bloomberg.com/apps/news?pid=newsarchive&sid=ahS4hwfsNq.k&refer=germany.

[93] Discussion with Yassin Musharbash, *Der Spiegel*, Berlin, June 2008.

in Yemen over which the Yemeni government exercised tenuous, if any, control and merged with the Yemeni branch of al-Qaeda.[94] The second development was the movement of al-Qaeda personnel from the border region of Pakistan to Yemen because the intensified counterterrorism operations had made it more difficult for them to operate in Pakistan.[95]

AQAP is the only one of al-Qaeda's regional branches to attempt high-profile attacks against the U.S. homeland: the attempt of underwear bomber Umar Farouk Abdulmutallab to destroy a U.S. airliner over Detroit on Christmas Day, 2009, and the failed parcel bombs plot of October 2010 – AQAP's plot to down Western cargo planes with bombs hidden in a laser printer and a printer cartridge. These incidents were linked to the late U.S.-born cleric Anwar al-Awlaki, AQAP's head of foreign operations.[96]

The importance of al-Awlaki, a former imam at the Dar al-Hijrah mosque in Falls Church, Virginia, and Muslim chaplain at George Washington University in Washington, DC, who was killed in a U.S. missile strike in northern Yemen on September 30, 2011, derived from his fluent English and knowledge of the United States, which enabled AQAP to convey its messages more effectively to audiences in the West. Al-Awlaki's sermons (one of which has been viewed more than 40,000 times on YouTube) explained to followers why the West is evil and that the only just war is one fought for Islam in American English peppered with references to pop culture.[97]

In addition to his role as an ideologue and propagandist, al-Awlaki assumed operational responsibilities in AQAP's Foreign Operations Unit, which specializes in international operations and keeps a certain distance from the rest of the organization. The unit is staffed by individuals familiar with Western societies and expert bomb makers. Al-Awlaki himself had been in direct e-mail contact with a number of people charged with or convicted of terrorism-related charges in the West, such as Fort Hood shooter Nidal Malik Hassan; failed Times Square bomber Faisal

[94] Thomas Hegghammer, "Saudi and Yemeni Branches of al-Qaida Unite," Jihadica, January 24, 2009, at http://www.jihadica.com/saudi-and-yemeni-branches-of-al-qaida-unite/.

[95] Ben Quinn, "To Rein in al-Qaeda in Yemen, Britain Taps its Colonial Past," *Christian Science Monitor*, January 5, 2010, at http://www.csmonitor.com/World/Europe/2010/0105/To-rein-in-al-Qaeda-in-Yemen-Britain-taps-its-colonial-past.

[96] Thomas Hegghammer, "The Case for Chasing al-Awlaki," The Middle East Channel, *Foreign Policy*, November 24, 2010, at http://mideast.foreignpolicy.com/posts/2010/11/24/the_case_for_chasing_al_awlaki.

[97] Aamer Madhani, "What makes cleric al-Awlaki so dangerous," *USA Today*, August 25, 2010, at http://www.usatoday.com/printedition/news/20100825/1a_awlaki25_cv.art.htm.

Shahzad; Alaska resident Paul Rockwood, who pleaded guilty to assembling a hit list of 15 targets for assassination or bomb attacks in the United States; Zachary Chesser, a Virginia resident charged with attempting to travel to Somalia to join al-Shabaab; Texas resident Barry Bujol, accused of trying to provide terrorists with global positioning instruments, cell phones, and a restricted publication on U.S. military weapons in Afghanistan; and Sharif Mobley, an American charged with murder in Yemen.[98]

Three cells plotting attacks in Britain have been linked to al-Awlaki. The men, from London, Stoke, and Cardiff, were inspired by al-Awlaki and used AQAP's English-language magazine *Inspire* as a guide. According to media reports, meetings took place in November and December 2010 at which the defendants planned to use explosive devices to attack significant locations in London and around the country. The Stoke group members have their origins in Pakistan, while those in the London and Cardiff groups were originally from Bangladesh. The ringleader of the London group was Mohammed Chowdhury, 21. He and Shah Rahman, 29, were under surveillance as they toured central London casing potential attack sites. Abdul Miah, 25, said to be at the center of the Cardiff gang, and his brother Omar Latif, 28, pleaded guilty to taking part in a plot to bomb the Stock Exchange. Gurukanth Desai, 30, pleaded guilty to attending meetings of the group. Mohibur Rahman, 27, from Stoke pleaded guilty to possession of a document containing information useful to a person preparing an act of terrorism. Usman Khan, 20; Mohammed Shahjahan, 27; and Nazam Hussain, 26, all from Stoke pleaded guilty to preparing acts of terrorism. At Khan's home in Stoke, police officers recovered a document that bore notes of the structure, roles, and responsibilities of individuals in a terrorist cell.[99]

Yemen has also become a destination for Western would-be jihadists. According to a British government source, about 20 British nationals traveled to Yemen in 2009 to join AQAP training camps.[100] The breakdown of authority in Yemen brought about by the uprising against the government of President Ali Abdullah Saleh and the armed conflict that followed meant that AQAP had enhanced opportunities to network with

[98] Hegghammer, "The Case for Chasing al-Awlaki."

[99] Duncan Gardham, "Terrorists admit plot to bomb London Stock Exchange and US Embassy," *The Telegraph*, February 1, 2012, at http://www.telegraph.co.uk/news/uknews/terrorism-in-the-uk/9053681/Terrorists-admit-plot-to-bomb-London-Stock-Exchange-and-US-Embassy.html.

[100] "Detroit terror attack: Britain sends counter-terrorist forces to Yemen," *Sunday Telegraph*, January 3, 2010, at http://www.telegraph.co.uk/news/worldnews/middleeast/yemen/6924502/Detroit-terror-attack-Britain-sends-counter-terrorist-forces-to-Yemen.html.

other regional Islamist extremist groups and to expand its international links.[101]

East Africa has been a sanctuary and base for Islamist terrorist operations since the early 1990s and remains a priority area in al-Qaeda's global strategy. al-Qaeda's military chief, Ali al-Rashidi, aka Abu Ubadiah al-Banshiri, drowned in Lake Victoria in May 1996 while preparing for the bombings of American embassies in East Africa.[102] Planning for African operations continued after al-Banshiri's death and al-Qaeda's expulsion from Sudan in 1996. In August 1998, al-Qaeda carried out two of its most spectacular pre-9/11 terrorist attacks: the suicide bombings of the American embassies in Nairobi, Kenya, and Dar es Salaam, Tanzania. In November 2002, al-Qaeda conducted two nearly simultaneous attacks in Kenya: the car bombing of the Paradise Hotel and the failed surface-to-air missile attack on an Israeli charter aircraft taking off from Mombasa airport.

Geographic proximity and social, cultural, and religious affinities between East Africa and the Arabian Peninsula make East Africa vulnerable to infiltration by militants and ideologies from the Middle East. The chaos in Somalia created opportunities that were exploited by radical groups with links to al-Qaeda, in particular Harakat al-Shabaab al-Mujahideen, commonly known as al-Shabaab (the youth), a radical militia currently engaged in an armed struggle against the Transitional Federal Government of Somalia and the forces of the African Union Mission to Somalia (AMISOM). This is not to suggest that East Africa is necessarily fertile soil for radical Islamism. Although Salafism has made inroads among the educated elites, traditional and Sufi practices continue to predominate among the mass of the Muslim populations in the region.

Al-Shabaab was the strongest and most radical of the militias backing the Islamic Courts Union (ICU), a group of *shari'a* courts that took control of Mogadishu and most of southern Somalia in 2006. Ethiopia's perception of the threat that the ICU government presented to its vital interests, including the ICU's backing of secessionists in the Ogaden, its ties to Ethiopia's arch-enemy Eritrea, and concern that an Islamist government in Somalia might stimulate the radicalization of its own Muslim population, led to the decision to invade ICU-controlled territory and seize

[101] See Michael Horton, "al-Qaeda in the Arabian Peninsula: Challenges and Opportunities in Revolutionary Yemen," *Terrorism Monitor*, Jamestown Foundation, Vol. 9, Issue 16, April 22, 2011, at http://www.jamestown.org/single/?no_cache=1&tx_ttnews%5Btt_news%5D=37828#.U5CJcl44QpE.

[102] Rohan Gunaratna, *Inside al-Qaeda: Global Network of Terror*. New York: Columbia University Press, 2002, p. 26.

Mogadishu in December 2006. Although driven out by the Ethiopian invasion, al-Shabaab remained intact and was able to maintain a base in southern Somalia, centered in the port city of Kismaayo.[103]

The group's stated goals were to expel foreign forces from Somalia and to turn Somalia into a state run in accordance with its interpretation of Islamic law. Following the Ethiopians' withdrawal from Mogadishu in 2009, al-Shabaab's discourse morphed from one of the Somali nationalist struggle to one more firmly grounded in radical Islamist principles – the enforcement of the group's conception of *shari'a* and the establishment of a global caliphate.[104]

Some important aspects of the globalization of the armed struggle in Somalia include the presence in Somalia of large numbers of foreign fighters; an upsurge in suicide bombings, a tactic associated with al-Qaeda and associated groups, but previously unknown in Somalia; and the development of linkages to the Somali Diaspora in Europe and North America. The majority of Somali foreign fighters have been recruited in the United Kingdom and Scandinavia, with others coming from the United States, Canada, and the Netherlands. These include an estimated 100 from Britain, up to 50 from Denmark and 20 from Sweden. Malmö and Göteborg, in Sweden, are centers of radicalization and recruitment among young Somalis. Al-Shabaab's largest community online, www.alqimmah.net, distributes press releases for al Shabaab in English and Arabic and is based in Göteborg.[105]

Some Western foreign fighters rose to high positions in al-Shabaab. Bilal al-Berjawi, a British citizen born in Lebanon, rose through the ranks of al-Shabaab and the foreign fighter cell linked to al-Qaeda to become second only to the head of al-Qaeda's East Africa operations, Fazul Abdullah Mohammad. He was killed in a drone strike in January 2012. Samantha Lewthwaite, also known as the White Widow, the convert wife of London bomber Jermaine Lindsay, remains at large in East Africa and is said to be a key figure in al-Shabaab cells outside Somalia.[106] Omar Hammami, better

[103] For the evolution of al-Shabaab before and after the Ethiopian invasion, see Angel Rabasa, *Radical Islam in East Africa*. RAND: Santa Monica, 2009.

[104] Cody Curran, "Global Ambitions: An Analysis of al Shabaab's Evolving Rhetoric," AEI Critical Threats, February 17, 2011, at http://www.criticalthreats.org/somalia/global-ambitions-analysis-al-shabaabs-evolving-rhetoric-february-17-2011.

[105] Rob W. Kurz, "Europe's Somali Diaspora: Both a Vulnerability and a Strength," The Foreign Military Studies Office (FMSO)/U.S. European Command (EUCOM), pp. 4–6, at http://fmso.leavenworth.army.mil/Collaboration/COCOM/EUCOM/Diaspora.pdf.

[106] Raffaello Pantucci, "Bilal al-Berjawi and the Shifting Fortunes of Foreign Fighters in Somalia," *CTC Sentinel*, Combating Terrorism Center at West Point, September 24,

known as Abu Mansour al-Amriki, was an American who rose to prominence as a spokesman in the group's propaganda videos. Al-Amriki was killed in a battle between al-Shabaab factions together with a British citizen of Pakistani origin, Osama al-Britani, in September 2013.[107]

A number of suicide attacks in Somalia appear to have been carried out by ethnic Somalis residing in the West who traveled to Somalia to participate in the fighting. The suicide bomber who disguised himself as a woman and killed 22 people, including four cabinet ministers of the Somali Transitional Federal Government at the graduation ceremony of the Benadir University Medical School in Mogadishu – the most destructive terrorist act in Somalia – was a Copenhagen resident in his early 20s who came to Denmark at the age of five.[108] A 21-year-old British Somali blew himself up at a military checkpoint in Baidoa, killing up to 20 soldiers. The man recorded a martyrdom video before his trip to Somalia imploring fellow British Somalis to follow his example.[109] One of the two suicide bombers who penetrated security at an AMISOM base in Mogadishu and killed 21 people, including the deputy AMISOM commander and 16 other peacekeepers, was later confirmed to be an American citizen recruited by al-Shabaab in Minneapolis.[110] A Norwegian citizen of Somali origin was reported to be one of the participants in the siege of the Westgate mall in Nairobi in September 2013. He was said to be an acquaintance of al-Shabaab's external operations chief, Abdukadir Mohamed Abdukadir, also known as Ikrima. Ikrima had spent time in Norway and applied for political asylum in 2004. He departed Norway in 2008 without having received a decision on his asylum application.[111]

The development of networks in Europe, Canada, and the United States has potentially given al-Shabaab the capability to mount terrorist attacks

2013, at http://www.ctc.usma.edu/posts/bilal-al-berjawi-and-the-shifting-fortunes-of-foreign-fighters-in-somalia.

107 "Al-Amriki and al-Britani: Militants 'Killed' in Somalia," BBC News, September 12, 2013, at http://www.bbc.co.uk/news/world-africa-24060558.

108 "Mogadishu hotel bomber identified as a Danish citizen," *Somalilandpress*, December 9, 2009, at http://somalilandpress.com/mogadishu-hotel-bomber-came-from-denmark-10012.

109 "Revealed: British Muslim student killed 20 in suicide attack in Somalia," *Daily Mail*, February 16, 2009, at http://www.dailymail.co.uk/news/article-1146290/Revealed-British-Muslim-student-killed-20-suicide-bomb-attack-Somalia.html.

110 Bill Roggio, "Shabaab Suicide Bomber Kills Seven at Mogadishu Medical Clinic," *The Long War Journal*, January 26, 2010, at http://www.longwarjournal.org/archives/2010/01/shabaab_suicide_bomb.php.

111 Lisa Lundquist, "Norwegian Authorities Looking for Westgate Massacre Suspect," *The Long War Journal*, October 10, 2013, at http://www.longwarjournal.org/archives/2013/10/norwegian_authoritie.php.

in the West. So far, al-Shabaab's leadership does not appear to have made a decision to attack Western nations. The main foreign targets of its attacks have been the countries participating in AMISOM. Al-Shabaab's deadliest attacks outside of Somalia's borders were the bombings during the 2010 FIFA World Cup Final in Kampala, Uganda, in July 2010 and the terror attack on the Westgate mall in Nairobi. Nevertheless, given the decentralized nature of jihadi networks, the very existence of mixed or affiliated networks based in the West constitutes a latent threat that could at any time be activated.[112]

The situation of foreign fighters in Somalia became much more precarious in 2013 as a consequence of a violent rift within al-Shabaab. In June of that year, al-Shabaab's emir Ahmed Abdi Godane, who goes by the *nom de guerre* Abu Zubeir staged a purge of his critics within the leadership. Ibrahim al-Afghani, his former deputy and one of the co-founders of al-Shabaab, was killed, and others driven out, including Muktar Robow, the group's former spokesman. Two months before, al-Afghani had written an open letter to al-Zawahiri, the leader of al-Qaeda, in which he criticized Godane for targeting foreign jihadists, imprisoning them in secret detention centers, and even killing them. There were even reports that al-Qaeda had asked al-Shabaab to appoint al-Afghani as its emir but Godane had managed to block al-Qaeda's instruction.[113]

Eliminating competitors was nothing new to Godane. The al-Shabaab emir had been linked to the death of Fazul Abdullah Mohammed, al-Qaeda's leader in East Africa, who was killed in June 2011 when his convoy was directed by al-Shabaab fighters, allegedly under Godane's instructions, to drive straight into an AMISOM security checkpoint in Mogadishu. According to Omar Ali Roble, former minister for disarmament and reintegration of militias in Somalia, foreign fighters linked to al-Qaeda represented a threat to Godane's authority.[114]

112 See Hussein Solomon, "Beyond Despondency: Taking the Fight to al-Shabaab in Somalia," International Centre for the Study of Radicalisation (ICSR), February 11, 2011, at http://icsr.info/2011/02/beyond-despondency-taking-the-fight-to-al-shabaab-in-somalia/.

113 Hassan M. Abukar, "Somalia: The Godane Coup and the Unraveling of Al-Shabaab," *African Arguments*, July 2, 2013, at http://africanarguments.org/2013/07/02/somalia-the-godane-coup-and-the-unraveling-of-al-shabaab-%E2%80%93-by-hassan-m-abukar/.

114 Majid Ahmed, "Al-Amriki and foreign fighters in showdown with al-Shabaab leader," *Sabahi*, April 30, 2013, at http://sabahionline.com/en_GB/articles/hoa/articles/features/2013/04/30/feature-01.

# 8

# Terrorist Operations and Tactics

## THE EUROPEAN ENVIRONMENT

Islamist extremists and terrorists have found a number of facilitating factors in Europe. They can utilize geographic, demographic, political, and social features of the host countries to promote their agenda and achieve their operational goals.

### Favorable Legal Regimes

Extremists in Europe attempt to take advantage of Western values and highly developed legal systems. Conceptions of privacy and civil liberties, asylum laws, stringent rules of evidence, and other legal protections not available in most countries in the Muslim world, all lend themselves to manipulation by extremists. Over the past decades, European asylum policies admitted not only the unjustly persecuted but also a slew of radicals banished from their home countries – and even some other European countries – for inciting violence and destruction. For instance, members of the Frankfurt cell later convicted of plotting to bomb Strasbourg's Christmas market sought refuge in London from French counterterrorist authorities.[1] Elaborate judicial procedures and legal protections enabled foreign extremists to remain active through a seemingly endless series of hearings and appeals, building up their organizations and acquiring followers.

[1] See Stephen Ulph, "Londonistan," *Terrorism Monitor*, Vol. 2, Issue 4, February 26, 2004, at http://www.jamestown.org/terrorism/news/article.php?articleid=23565.

After protracted legal proceedings, the British government succeeded in deporting two of the most notorious extremists in the United Kingdom, Abu Hamza al-Masri and Abu Qatada, but efforts by the Norwegian government to deport Mullah Krekar, founder of the terrorist Ansar al-Islam organization and declared by the Norwegian government to be "a threat to national security," to Iraq have been thwarted by legal proscriptions that prohibit extradition of refugees to countries where they may be at risk of death or torture. Radwan Al-Issar, considered to be the spiritual leader of the Hofstad Group, to which Van Gogh's assassin belonged, was able to continue to operate in Germany and the Netherlands for years and to travel between the two countries despite repeated expulsions and detentions. In Germany, it took the courts decades to finally expel the Turkish extremist leader Metin Kaplan, the leader of the radical Islamist movement Kalifatsstaat (Caliphate State). The French, by contrast, have regularly expelled radical imams.

After the upsurge of Islamist terrorism within Europe with the Madrid bombing of March 11, 2004, several European governments attempted to develop stricter counterterrorism legislation, as well as broader approaches designed to engage European Muslim communities to discourage support for extremists. These new European approaches are discussed later in this chapter.

## Operational Access and Target-Rich Environment

From a terrorist's standpoint, an ideal operating environment is not just one that provides opportunities for concealment and support but also one that provides reasonably easy access to desired attack venues. These targets could take the form of Western populations or infrastructure, diplomatic missions and military facilities, banks and businesses, and political and cultural symbols. The Schengen agreement on the free movement of EU citizens across national borders has essentially eliminated border control among its 28 members. This enhances what in a RAND study was called operational access – the terrorists' ability to reach and attack their targets.[2]

The lack of infrastructure generally associated with traditional terrorist sanctuaries in ungoverned territories and the lack of lucrative targets in these territories make it relatively difficult, or at least more laborious, for terrorists based there to mount attacks beyond their immediate environs. Europe

[2] Angel Rabasa et al., *Ungoverned Territories.*

offers a target-rich environment as well as free movement and abundant and easy transportation. While steps can be taken to defend key government facilities or symbolic sites, European mass transportation systems have proven vulnerable to terrorist attack from within. The Madrid train bombings and the London bombings exposed this vulnerability, but these were not the only attempts to attack European transportations systems; there were plans in various degrees of maturity on the part of jihadist groups to attack Heathrow Airport, Frankfurt airport, the Milan railroad station, and trains in Germany (the "suitcase plot").

On the other side of the ledger, Europe has well-developed and efficient law enforcement and intelligence agencies that render terrorist operations more difficult. The success of European counterterrorism is measured by the fact that, with the exception of far-right terrorist Anders Breivik's mass shooting at a Workers' Youth League camp in Norway in July 2011, there have been no mass casualty terrorist attacks in Europe since the London bombings of July 7, 2005. During this period, the European security services have foiled major plots in several countries, which indicates that Europe remains under a severe terrorism threat.

## ATTACKS ON COMMERCIAL AVIATION

Terrorist targeting in Europe has focused on commercial aviation and ground transportation systems. The al-Hindi group had "meticulous details" of Heathrow in its surveillance materials, including photographs of terminal buildings, the airport's fuel farm and tunnels used by passengers and freight companies inside the security perimeter, how long traffic lights remain on red around the Heathrow perimeter and inside the security cordon, traffic flows on roads to Heathrow, and details of escape routes.[3] Khalid Sheikh Mohammed reportedly told his interrogators that bin Laden had ordered an attack against Heathrow soon after 9/11. Sheikh Mohammed said that he gave an al-Qaeda team money to undertake surveillance of Heathrow, "assessing its weak points and finding locations from which planes might be shot down." Sheikh Mohammed claims that the operation he knew of "never advanced

[3] "Manhunt as five al-Qaeda militants evade police: Police suspect plan to attack Heathrow with huge lorry bomb," *Times Online*, August 6, 2004, at http://www.thetimes.co.uk/tto/news/uk/article1927424.ece; "Eyewitness: Terror suspects in court," BBC News, August 18, 2004, at http://news.bbc.co.uk/2/hi/uk_news/3577710.stm; Metropolitan Police Service, "Anti-terrorist charges," *Bulletin 2004/0111*.

beyond surveillance," blaming communications interruptions following the overthrow of the Taliban.[4]

Although terrorists have not been able to successfully penetrate airport security in Europe, there have been continued attempts to carry out acts of terrorism against aircraft. "Shoe bomber" Richard Reid was overpowered by flight attendants and passengers aboard American Airlines Flight 63 from Paris to Miami on December 23, 2001, while he was attempting to light the fuse to an explosive device concealed in his shoes. The devise contained about 50 grams of the highly explosive chemical pentaerythritol tetranitrate or PETN, which would have been enough to blow a hole in the side of an airliner. A Venezuelan national, Rahaman Alan Hazil Mohammed, was arrested at Gatwick Airport on February 13, 2002, after flying on a British Airways flight from Caracas with a live grenade in his luggage; he was later charged with terrorism offenses.[5] In November 2006, German authorities arrested six men with foreign passports. The suspects were of Lebanese, Kuwaiti, and Iraqi origin. The six were accused of having planned an attack on an airplane of the Israeli airline El Al.[6]

"Underwear bomber" Umar Abdulmutallab tried to blow up Northwest Airlines Flight 253 from Amsterdam to Detroit on Christmas Day 2009 at the behest of al-Qaeda in the Arabian Peninsula. Abdulmutallab had about 80 grams of PETN sewn into his underwear. The detonator, acid in a syringe, caused a fire in Abdulmutallab's briefs but did not make contact with the PETN. The device went undetected by airport security at Lagos, his port of origin, and Amsterdam.[7]

The most potentially destructive terrorist plot against aircraft since 9/11 was the transatlantic airliner liquid bomb plot of August 2006 in Great Britain, discussed in Chapter 5. Although it was unsuccessful, this plot illustrated terrorist adaptation and innovation and the terrorists' ability to identify and seek to exploit weaknesses in counterterrorism measures in the heavily defended air transportation sector. The plotters had planned to target simultaneously up to ten aircraft from three U.S. carriers flying from

[4] Christina Lamb, "al-Qaeda leader says: Heathrow our target," *Sunday Times*, London, March 28, 2004, at http://www.freerepublic.com/focus/news/1106699/posts.

[5] "Would-be bomber born of privilege," BBC News, April 5, 2005, at http://news.bbc.co.uk/1/hi/uk/4413379.stm.

[6] Martin Lutz, "El-Al-Maschine entgeht Bombenanschlag," *Die Welt*, November 21, 2006, at http://www.welt.de/print-welt/article95977/El-Al-Maschine-entgeht-Bombenanschlag.html.

[7] Richard Esposito and Brian Ross, "Exclusive: Photos of the Northwest Airlines Flight 253 Bomb," ABC News, December 28, 2009, at http://abcnews.go.com/Blotter/northwest-airlines-flight-253-bomb-photos-exclusive/story?id=9436297&page=2.

Britain to North America by smuggling onboard a peroxide-based solution disguised as beverages or other liquid or gel products that could ignite when sparked by a camera flash or another electronic device. The terrorists planned to carry the liquid explosive ingredients into the planes in factory-sealed sports drink bottles modified with false bottoms. Two conspirators intended to bring their baby on board and hide explosives in the infant's bottle.[8] Some of the final destinations reported by the British media included New York, Washington DC, Boston, Miami, Los Angeles, and San Francisco. At the trial of the conspirators, it was revealed that the bombers also planned to target Air Canada flights bound for Toronto and Montreal. According to British and U.S. reports, the conspirators had assembled bomb-making equipment and materials and were in the final stages of planning when the plot was discovered. Several had recorded martyrdom videos. The plot unraveled when Pakistani authorities arrested a key plotter, reported al-Qaeda operative Rashid Rauf.[9]

Al-Qaeda's continued fixation on attacks on civil aviation is striking because the hardening of civil aviation infrastructure against terrorist attacks since 9/11 has made attacks on airports and civil aircraft increasingly difficult. In response to countermeasures, terrorists have continued to adapt and search for weak points in the defenses. The use of Man-portable air defense systems (MANPADS) would appear to be an option for terrorists seeking to attack civilian aircraft.

Nevertheless, with the exception of the failed missile attack on the Israeli aircraft in Mombasa in November 2002, the shooting down of an IL-76 cargo plane in Somalia in March 2007, and a thwarted attack on an aircraft at Mogadishu international airport in October 2008,[10] Islamist terrorists have not been known to attempt to use MANPADS against civil

[8] "Bojinka II: The Transatlantic Liquid Bomb Plot," NEFA Foundation, April 2008, at http://narcosphere.narconews.com/userfiles/70/Bojinka2LiquidBombs.pdf. Some have questioned whether the operatives possessed the necessary technical skills to succeed in their mission. However, tests conducted at Sandia National Laboratory confirmed that the explosives formula the suspects were utilizing was viable and capable of causing a "large explosion." There is also a report that the conspirators tested the mixture in Pakistan. Ibid.

[9] "Details emerge on alleged plot to bomb airliners," NBC News, August 10, 2006, at http://www.msnbc.msn.com/id/14278216. NEFA Foundation, "Bojinka II: The Transatlantic Liquid Bomb Plot."

[10] The IL-76, belonging to Transaviaexport, a Belarusian company, was shot down after an SA-18 missile fired by al-Shabaab fighters hit the left wing. The missile was reported to be part of a consignment of six SA-18s that had been delivered by Eritrea to Somali militants. Report of the Monitoring Group on Somalia pursuant to Security Council resolution 1724 (2006), S/2007/436, July 18, 2007, at http://www.un.org/ga/search/view_doc.asp?symbol=S/2007/436.

aviation. This is surprising because MANPADS are believed to be widely available, and their relatively low cost compared to the high cost of protecting civilian aircraft makes them an attractive weapons for terrorists.[11] In Mogadishu alone, as of 2011, there were at least ten 1970s Soviet-made SA-7s in the hands of militants or arms dealers (although they may not be operable – the batteries have a life expectancy of about 20 years).[12]

Luggage or package bombs are other vectors for terrorist attacks on civil aviation. A luggage bomb was used in the destruction of Pan Am Flight 103 over Lockerbie, Scotland, on December 21, 1988, and in other attacks on civilian aircraft in the 1980s. However, this terrorist technique was not attempted by al-Qaeda until October 2010, when a bomb inside a printer cartridge sent from Yemen to a synagogue in Chicago was found aboard a UPS cargo plane in Britain. The bomb contained 300 grams of PETN and was only detected because the Saudis alerted British authorities about which package to look for. The bomb was set to go off as the plane was over the eastern seaboard of the United States. A similar device was found on a FedEx plane at Dubai International Airport, also intended to detonate over the United States.[13]

## ATTACKS ON GROUND MASS TRANSPORTATION SYSTEMS

While steps can be taken to defend commercial airlines, key government facilities, or symbolic sites, European ground mass transportation systems have proven vulnerable to terrorist attack. The March 2004 Madrid train bombings and the July 2005 London Underground and bus bombings exposed this vulnerability.

The Madrid bombings of March 11, 2004, were the most devastating attacks on European soil since the Pan Am Lockerbie bombing in 1988 and the ones with the most far-reaching political consequences. The first bombs

[11] See Jean Luc Marret, "From Lockerbie to Umar Farouk Abdul-Mutallab: Assessing the Destruction of Civilian Aircrafts by Terrorism," Fondation pour la Recherche Stratégique, Transatlantic Security Paper No. 1, April 2010 at www.frstrategie.org/barreCompetences/terrorisme/doc/tsp.pdf.

[12] Information from member of United Nations Somalia & Eritrea Monitoring Group, Washington, DC, July 2011.

[13] Some terrorism experts believe that given the uncertainties of cargo timetables, it was impossible for the plotters to know where the bombs would have detonated. Vikram Dodd, Richard Norton-Taylor, and Paul Harris, "Cargo plane bomb found in Britain was primed to blow up over US," *The Guardian*, November 10, 2010, at http://www.guardian.co.uk/world/2010/nov/10/cargo-plane-bomb-us-alqaida.

went off on a train carrying blue-collar commuters outside of the Atocha station in the center of Madrid. Quickly following the first explosion at 7:38 a.m., four other bombs were detonated on another train also near the Atocha station. If the bombs had detonated inside the station, several thousand more people would likely have fallen victim to the explosions. By the time emergency responders started to arrive on the scene, two more bombs exploded at 7:42 a.m. at a station three miles from the Atocha station. The last bombs to explode were at the Santa Eugenia station in the suburbs of Madrid. The four bombings resulted in 191 fatalities and more than 1,600 injuries.[14]

The Spanish government immediately attributed the attacks to the Basque terrorist group Euzkadi Ta Azkatasuna (ETA). In 1995, the ETA attempted to assassinate Prime Minister José María Aznar with a car bomb. The Aznar government, in turn, moved proactively to dismantle the ETA organization. The bombings, however, did not reflect the historical ETA practice of issuing warnings before the explosions and avoiding attacks on the "working class." In their scale and targeting of civilians, the Madrid bombings resembled the Casablanca attacks of May 2003, with the difference that the Casablanca attacks were carried out by suicide bombers, whereas in Madrid the bombs were placed in backpacks and detonated by the use of cellular phones. A stolen van found in the town of Alcalá Henares, from which the trains had left for Madrid contained detonators and Quranic verses. The discovery of a sports bag containing 22 pounds of explosives connected to a cellular phone detonator led the police away from ETA operatives and to a network of North African immigrants. Further, the police learned that the phone was sold and activated by Jamal Zougam, a Moroccan immigrant who had been under surveillance because of his associations with extremists.[15]

Following the bombings, police began an intensive search for potential bombing suspects in immigrant neighborhoods. Door-to-door searches led to the apartment in the Madrid working-class neighborhood of Leganés where police found seven men, most of them Moroccans. During the confrontation, the men made several attempts to call

[14] For a detailed reconstruction of the Madrid bombings, see Lawrence Wright, "The Terror Web," *The New Yorker,"* August 2, 2004, at http://www.newyorker.com/archive/2004/08/02/040802fa_fact.

[15] Petter Nesser, *Jihad in Europe: A Survey of the Motivations for Sunni Islamist Terrorism in post-Milennium Europe*. Kjeller, Norway: FFI/RAPPORT-2004/01146.

Abu Qatada, the alleged spiritual leader of al-Qaeda in Europe, then in the Belmarsh Prison in London. When the police finally stormed the apartment, an explosion demolished the apartment killing all of the seven men who were inside and a police officer. In the apartment, the police found 22 pounds of Goma-2 explosives and 200 copper detonators similar to those used in the train bombings. The police also found a tape stating that the group called themselves "the brigade situated in Al Andalus" and that they would "continue [their] jihad until martyrdom in the land of Tariq ibn Ziyad" (i.e., Spain).[16]

The July 7, 2005, London transport network bombing was the first successful attack by Islamist terrorists in Britain. The attack consisted of four simultaneous suicide bombings, three on the Tube (Underground) and one on a London bus, all during the morning rush hour. With 56 people killed (including the four suicide bombers) and 750 injured, it was the worst terrorist atrocity in the United Kingdom's modern history.[17] The explosive used by the bombers was composed of flour powder mixed with liquid hydrogen peroxide, detonated by a booster charge. The bombers' intention was apparently to cause four explosions on the Underground, forming a cross of fire with arms in the four cardinal directions, but one of the bombers was unable to access the Northern Line and instead detonated his device in a bus.

While the July 7 attacks were still being investigated and London was on its highest state of alert in modern times, four more bombers attempted to strike the London transportation network on July 21. All four bombs failed to detonate, indicating a deficiency in technical skills; while it appeared that all four bombers were intent on suicide bombings, replicating the July 7 attacks – some manually set off the detonators – all fled when the bombs failed to explode and were subsequently arrested (three in Great Britain and one in Italy). Also arrested was a fifth bomber who had abandoned his mission before the other four attacked, and nine other alleged accomplices or supporters.[18]

[16] Wright, "The Terror Web."

[17] The worst terrorist atrocity in modern British history, before the London bombings of July 7, 2005, was the car-bomb attack carried out by the Real IRA (a splinter faction from the Provisional IRA, which rejected the PIRA ceasefire and Northern Ireland peace process) in Omagh, Northern Ireland, on August 15, 1998, that killed 29 and injured 220 persons.

[18] The full story of the extraordinary investigation and arrests surrounding the July 21 attacks can be found at Jason Burke et al., "Run to ground: The biggest police operation in British history reached a dramatic climax on live television," *The Observer*, July 31, 2005, at http://www.theguardian.com/uk/2005/jul/31/july7.uksecurity.

A foiled attack with potentially devastating consequences was the 2006 "suitcase plot" in Germany. Unlike other Islamist terrorist events, the attempted attack was not a suicide bombing. The plan of the would-be perpetrators, Youssef Mohamad el Hajdib and Jihad Hamad, was to leave bombs in two trains timed to explode after they got off. Hajdib and Hamad packed two 11-liter containers of a propane-gas-oxygen mixture in two suitcases. The two bombs were supposed to go off in two regional trains departing the Cologne station. The timers were set for the same time – it is unclear whether or not they were supposed to go off while the trains were in a station. Had the explosion taken place in a station, the number of potential victims would have been much larger. The two terrorists placed the suitcases on the trains and got off at the next station. The timers went off but the bombs did not explode because there was not enough oxygen in the containers.[19]

## JIHADIST ADAPTATION

After 9/11, al-Qaeda and associated groups stepped up efforts to recruit American, British, and other foreign nationals who can more easily penetrate the heightened post-9/11 security measures. At the end of 2003 and into February 2004, several British Airways flights – between London and Washington and London and Riyadh – were canceled because of intelligence received by the United States and passed on to the British that terrorists using British, American, or European passports were targeting these flights for destruction. The concern over the use of "clean" passports was based on reported intelligence of conversations between terrorists that "We need foreigners. We have Albanians, Swiss, and English ... all that is important is that they are of a high cultural level ... businessmen, professors, engineers, doctors, and teachers".[20] Numerous reports indicate that al-Qaeda has used stolen passports from

[19] Josef Hufelschulte,"Knapp am Tod vorbei," *Focus Magazin* No. 34, August 21, 2006, at http://www.focus.de/politik/deutschland/anschlag-knapp-am-tod-vorbei_aid_214199.html.

[20] British Airways Flight 223 from London to Washington was canceled numerous times and intercepted by U.S. fighter jets outside the continental United States owing to this intelligence; when eventually allowed to fly again, the first flight back was delayed by more than three hours as all 268 passengers were individually checked, searched, and personally escorted onto the plane one at a time. Peter Beaumont and Anthony Barnett, "Hunt for UK terror cell: Hijack gang 'have British passports,'" *The Observer*, January 3, 2004, at http://www.theguardian.com/business/2004/jan/04/theairlineindustry.terrorism2.

Albania, South Africa, and other countries to disguise the movements, identities, and backgrounds of operatives.[21] The counterterrorism challenge of extremists with Western passports has been magnified by the armed conflict in Syria, where the number of Western fighters is larger by far than in any previous conflict in a Muslim country.

## THE JIHADISTS' SEARCH FOR WEAPONS OF MASS DESTRUCTION

Al-Qaeda and supporters of the global jihad have made no effort to disguise their interest in acquiring and using chemical, biological, radiological, or nuclear (CBRN) weapons. Bin Laden told an interviewer in 1999, "It would be a sin for Muslims not to try and possess the weapons that would prevent the infidels from inflicting harm on Muslims."[22] According to bin Laden, "the United States is the biggest mischief maker, terrorist, and rogue in the world ... it is the duty of every Muslim to struggle for its annihilation."[23] So far, a nuclear attack on the West has been beyond al-Qaeda's capabilities, although, as discussed later, there have been unsuccessful attempts by Islamist terrorists in Europe to acquire and deploy chemical and radiological weapons.

Nevertheless, the possibility that a terrorist group, particularly one that shares al-Qaeda's view of the global jihad and methodology of mass casualty attacks, might come into possession of nuclear weapons or materials defines the upper end of the scale of terrorist threats. That possibility alone has defining consequences for Western societies. In *Will Terrorists Go Nuclear?* Brian Jenkins distinguishes between nuclear terrorism, something that has never occurred, and nuclear terror, the state of societal fear that is induced by the prospect that terrorists could acquire and use nuclear weapons. Jihadists, like all those who use terror to advance political goals, have sought to exploit this fear.[24]

[21] South African passports have been found in a number of arrests in the UK and at the U.S.-Mexican border. In 1998, the London *Sunday Telegraph* reported that more than 1,000 Albanian passports had been stolen from Tirana during riots in 1997. Bill Gertz, "Airline hijackers connected to Albanian terrorist cell," *Washington Times*, September 18, 2001, at http://www.freerepublic.com/focus/f-news/526234/posts?q=1&;page=151. "How al-Qaeda get their hands on your passport," IOL News, July 30, 2004, at http://www.iol.co.za/news/world/how-al-qaeda-get-their-hands-on-your-passport-1.218474#.U5i19SRBxQY.

[22] Rahimulla Yusufzai, "Conversation with Terror," *Time*, January 11, 1999, at http://content.time.com/time/magazine/article/0,9171,17676,00.html.

[23] "Interview with Usama Bin Laden Reported," *Al-Akhbar* (Islamabad), March 31, 1998, FBIS, p. 61, at http://www.fas.org/irp/world/para/ubl-fbis.pdf.

[24] Brian Michael Jenkins, *Will Terrorists Go Nuclear?* Amherst, NY: Prometheus Books, 2008.

Islamist terrorists, however, require a religious justification for their violence, and the lawfulness of the use of weapons of mass destruction (WMD) is highly contested by Islamic scholars.[25] Theological justification for a WMD attack against civilian targets was provided by a young Saudi cleric, Nasir bin Hamid al-Fahd, in a 25-page document, *Risalah fi hukm istikhdam aslihat al-damar al-shamel didh al-kuffar* (a treatise on the legal status of using weapons of mass destruction against infidels).[26] First, al-Fahd argues, "Proscription [of weapons of mass destruction] Belongs to God Almighty, and to None Other Than He, such as Humans." Terms such as "weapons of mass destruction" or "internationally banned weapons" have no standing in Islamic law, he says, "because God Almighty has reserved judgment and legislation to Himself."

Second, al-Fahd justifies use of WMD on the basis of reciprocity: "Some brothers have totaled the number of Muslims killed directly or indirectly by their weapons and come up with a figure of nearly 10 million." Therefore, an attack against America that would take an equal number of lives is permissible: "If a bomb that killed ten million of them and burned as much of their land as they have burned Muslims' land were dropped on them, it would be permissible, with no need to mention any other argument. We might need other arguments if we wanted to annihilate more than this number of them."

Al-Fahd argues that large civilian casualties are acceptable if they result from an attack meant to defeat an enemy, and not an attack aimed only at killing the innocent:

> The messenger of God commanded an attack on the enemy. In many traditions, he attacked others ... He was not prevented from this by what we know, namely that he knew that women and children would not be safe from harm. He allowed the

[25] Mainstream Muslim views on the possession and use of WMDs, especially nuclear weapons, are ambivalent. According to al-Azhar University in Cairo, the Muslim world's most authoritative center of Islamic studies, as long as the enemies of the Muslims have nuclear weapons, Muslims have an obligation to acquire them. A Muslim regime that does not do this may be guilty of corruption on earth. The aim of having these weapons is to "make the enemies of the Muslim tremble," presumably to deter attacks against Muslims. The issue of actual use of nuclear weapons is more complicated. According to some scholars, if nuclear weapons are used against Muslims, then Muslims are allowed to retaliate in kind. On the other hand, there is a view that they cannot be used at all because they kill indiscriminately and therefore would kill certain protected categories of people that Allah has forbidden to kill. See Shmuel Bar, *Warrants for Terror: The Fatwas of Radical Islam and the Duty to Jihad*. Lanham, MD: Rowman & Littlefield Publishers, 2006.

[26] Cited in Michael Scheuer, *Imperial Hubris: Why the West is Losing the War on Terror*. Washington, DC: Brassey's, 2004, pp. 154–156.

attack because the intent of the attackers was not to harm them ... Thus the situation in this regard is that if those engaged in jihad establish that the evil of the infidels can be repelled only by attacking them at night with weapons of mass destruction, they may be used even if they annihilate the infidels.

During the 1990s, bin Laden made a protracted and apparently fruitless effort to acquire WMD. After his relocation from Sudan to Afghanistan in 1996, bin Laden received advice from Pakistani nuclear scientists.[27] At a laboratory in Darunta, al-Qaeda developed a crude form of cyanide gas, which was tested on a dog in December 1999 (and recorded on videotape). After the fall of the Taliban regime in late 2001, technical manuals found in Khost, Kabul, and other areas confirmed al-Qaeda's interest in nuclear, radiological, chemical, and biological weapons.[28] Accounts during this period indicate that bin Laden also attempted to purchase nuclear weapons in the former Soviet Union with the help of Russian and Chechen crime syndicates.[29]

Jihadist have attempted to mount WMD attacks in the West, but none of them reached the operational stage.[30] Jose Padilla, a former Chicago gang member who had converted to Islam, was arrested at O'Hare Airport in May 2002 and charged with taking part in an al-Qaeda plot to detonate a radioactive "dirty bomb" within the United States, but the plan apparently did not advance past the conceptual phase. Padilla's indictment in November 2005 made no mention of a dirty bomb.[31]

[27] Anonymous [Michael Scheuer], *Through Our Enemies' Eyes*. Washington, DC: Potomac Books, 2006, p. 188; and Peter Baker, "Pakistani scientist who Met Bin Laden failed polygraphs, renewing suspicions," *Washington Post*, March 3, 2002, at http://www.highbeam.com/doc/1P2-332382.html.

[28] Jason Burke, *Al-Qaeda: Casting a Shadow of Terror*. London: I.B. Tauris, 2003, p. 187; and Mike Boettcher and Ingrid Arnesen, "al-Qaeda Documents Outline Serious Weapon Program," January 25, 2002, CNN.com at http://edition.cnn.com/2002/US/01/24/inv.al.qaeda.documents/.

[29] "Al Qaeda network may have transported nuclear, biological, and chemical weapons to the United States," *The Frontier Post* (Peshawar), November 20, 2001, at http://www.freerepublic.com/focus/f-news/568104/posts.

[30] One analyst offers three reasons why al-Qaeda has not yet launched an attack with CBRN weapons: (1) disruption of al-Qaeda's efforts through stepped-up counterterrorism operations after 9/11; (2) deterrence, that is, fear that an attack on the West with CBRN weapons would trigger an invasion of al-Qaeda's sanctuary in the tribal areas of Pakistan; and (3) al-Qaeda may be waiting for the right time to launch a CBRN attack. Chris Quillen, "Three Explanations for al-Qaeda's Lack of a CBRN Attack," *Terrorism Monitor*, Vol. 5, Issue 3, February 21, 2007, at http://www.jamestown.org/programs/gta/single/?tx_ttnews%5Btt_news%5D=1015&tx_ttnews%5BbackPid%5D=182&no_cache=1.

[31] "Jose Padilla," Times Topics, *The New York Times*, updated March 6, 2009, at http://topics.nytimes.com/topics/reference/timestopics/people/p/jose_padilla/index.html.

Four reported incidents occurred in Europe: Dhiren Barot's "dirty bomb" plot, Salahuddin Amin's attempt to purchase radiological materials, the 2003 ricin plot, all in the United Kingdom, and the Lyon cell plan for a chemical attack on the Russian embassy in Paris. Dhiren Barot aka Abu Isa al-Hindi was arrested in August 2004 in north London on suspicion of terrorist activities. Subsequent investigations revealed him to be one of al-Qaeda's leading operatives in Great Britain and heavily involved in al-Qaeda intelligence-collection activities globally. Born in 1972 in Nairobi to parents from Gujarat, India, he converted from Hinduism to Islam at the age of 20.[32] In the 1990s, he fought in Kashmir, subsequently returning to the United Kingdom for a period, before traveling to Afghanistan to become an instructor in an al-Qaeda camp.[33] He is believed to have been subsequently handpicked by Khalid Sheikh Mohammed and bin Laden for his subsequent intelligence-led targeting activities because of his fluency in English, Arabic, Farsi, and Urdu, and because of his British passport.

Barot allegedly conducted extensive surveillance of financial centers in New York and New Jersey, as possible terror targets while posing as a student in New Jersey prior to 9/11, which led directly to the U.S. alerts in August 2004. Barot's documents were found among a trove of papers, computer files, sketches, and photographs recovered during mid-July 2004 raids in Pakistan at the home of al-Qaeda computers and communications expert Muhammad Naeem Noor Khan. British authorities disclosed that Barot had developed a document known as the "Final Presentation." It outlined his research on the production of dirty bombs, which he characterized as designed to "cause injury, fear, terror and chaos" rather than to kill. In a separate British police operation in 2004, British authorities arrested British national Salahuddin Amin and six others on terrorism-related charges. Amin was accused of making inquiries about buying a radioisotope bomb from the Russian mafia in Belgium. Nothing appeared to have come from his inquiries, according to British

[32] Al-Hindi's parents, a respected Kenyan Asian couple, Manubhai (Manu) and Bhartiyaben Dhiren (Bhartia) Barot, migrated to the UK from Nairobi in 1973; they bought a house in northwest London where al-Hindi grew-up. He is believed to have married a Thai woman whom he met while under the tutelage of former Jemaah Islamiyah operations chief Riduan Isamuddin, aka Hambali in Thailand.

[33] Al-Hindi authored the book *The Army of Madinah in Kashmir* (published in Birmingham), seen by Western counterterrorism officials as a jihad recruitment book – exhorting martyrs to join the worldwide jihad with "stealthy modern-day war stratagems," including "germ warfare."

prosecutors. Neither Barot nor Amin had the opportunity to carry his plans forward to an operational stage.[34]

In January 2003, six Algerians, one of whom was alleged to have undergone training in al-Qaeda's Afghan camps, and one Ethiopian were arrested in north London. Most had arrived in the United Kingdom shortly before their arrest. Subsequent police raids in Bournemouth (south England), Manchester, and London resulted in the arrest of nine more foreign nationals.[35] Later in the month, Spanish authorities arrested sixteen suspected terrorists in Catalonia connected to those arrested in Britain and France.[36]

The plan, had it not been disrupted by British anti-terrorist authorities, was alleged to have involved the production of a ricin-based paste that the plotters would have smeared, in small quantities, on some of the most prominent public surfaces in London including the doors of taxicabs and the metallic poles on tube trains and buses.[37] Four of five defendants were acquitted in 2005 of conspiracy to commit murder and conspiracy to cause a public nuisance in relation to the ricin plot; one of the defendants, Kamel Bourgass, was convicted of conspiracy to cause a public nuisance, but the jury failed to reach a verdict on the conspiracy to commit murder charge. Bourgass had earlier been convicted of murdering a police officer who took part in a raid on a flat in Manchester where he was staying.[38]

The 2004 incident in France involved eight Chechens, most of whom were relatives of Menad Benchellali, the son of a radical imam in the Lyon suburb of Venisseux. Menad trained in an al-Qaeda camp in Afghanistan and left Afghanistan in early 2001. His brother Mourad and a friend,

[34] U.S. Nuclear Regulatory Commission, "Fact Sheet on Dirty Bombs," December 2012, at http://www.nrc.gov/reading-rm/doc-collections/fact-sheets/fs-dirty-bombs.html.

[35] Nick Hopkins, "Four remanded on ricin terror charges as six more arrested," *The Guardian*, January 13, 2003, at http://www.theguardian.com/uk/2003/jan/14/september11.world; Jason Burke and Martin Bright, "Britain faces fresh peril from the 'clean-skinned' terrorists," *The Observer*, January 11, 2003, at http://www.theguardian.com/uk/2003/jan/12/terrorism.alqaida.

[36] Spanish authorities allegedly discovered substantial quantities of ricin (reported as "two barrels") as well as bomb detonators and a number of false passports and credit cards, while Italian police arrested five Moroccans, equipped with Semtex and believed to be planning to carry out an attack on central London. Dan McDougall, "Arrests foil new ricin poison plot," *The Scotsman*, January 25, 2003, at http://news.scotsman.com/topics.cfm?tid=322&id=95762003; "Operación policial en Cataluña contra la infraestructura europea de al-Qaeda," *El País*, January 25, 2003, at http://elpais.com/diario/2003/01/25/espana/1043449201_850215.html.

[37] RAND interviews, senior UK counterterrorist officials, London, May 2004.

[38] "The Ricin case timeline," BBC News, April 13, 2005, at http://news.bbc.co.uk/2/hi/uk_news/4433459.stm.

Nizar Sassi, remained in Afghanistan, where they were captured by U.S. forces and were held for a few years in the U.S. detention facility at Guantanamo before being returned to France. After spending a short time in France, Murad and other militants from France traveled to the Pankisi Gorge, in northeastern Georgia, where they had joined other foreign volunteers in helping anti-Russian Chechen warlord Ruslav Gelayev rebuild his force. There they allegedly met with associates of Abu Musab al-Zarkawi, who at the time was running an independent jihadi group, Jund al-Sham. Menad and most the senior members of the cell were under surveillance after they returned to France in March 2002. Menad had trained in poison-making skills in Afghanistan, and was attempting to produce a botulism toxin as well as ricin. He had tested his chemicals on animals and was believed to have been planning suicide bomb attacks on Russian interests in Paris, including the Russian embassy.[39] There are allegations that a quantity of the ricin was sent to Kamel Bourgass in Britain.[40] In December 2002, four senior activists, including Menad Benchelalli and Merouane Benhamed, described later by the French court as the cell's leader, were arrested in connection with the plot. In January 2004, other cell members were arrested. A total of 27 people stood trial in the Lyon cell case. The senior offenders, Menad Benchelalli, Merouane Benhamed, Said Arif, and Nouredine Merabet described as the cell's financier, were sentenced to 10 years in prison.

[39] Craig S. Smith, "French court sentences 25 Islamic extremists," *The New York Times*, June 14, 2006, at http://www.nytimes.com/2006/06/14/world/europe/14iht-france.1974917.html?_r=0; "Menad Benchelalli, *Global Jihad*, September 24, 2007 at http://www.globaljihad.net/view_page.asp?id=447.

[40] "Lyon Cell," *Global Jihad*, September 23, 2007, at http://globaljihad.net/view_page.asp?id=442.

# 9

# New European Approaches

European approaches to counter-radicalization vary considerably from country to country. However, the European Union has sought to create an overarching counter-radicalization structure – the EU Strategy for Combating Radicalization and Recruitment to Terrorism – within its Counter-Terrorism Strategy, which is to serve as a strategic template.[1] Alongside these institutional efforts, an informal consensus has also emerged, with an emphasis on the attempt to work in conjunction with mainstream Muslim organizations to prevent, in particular, the radicalization of the younger generation and the veering into extremism on the part of overzealous individual converts. It is generally thought by European governments that, ideology aside, Muslim organizations and Western governments can agree that these two outcomes need to be prevented, and that Muslim organizations – nongovernmental organizations (NGOs), mosques, community associations, and the like – are best positioned to notice any radical activity early on.

Supporting Muslim NGOs that have, in the view of European governments, sufficient credibility within the Muslim community to mitigate the risk of radicalization and that, or so they hope, can be trusted also accommodates the difficulty otherwise faced by secular Western

[1] Council of the European Union, *The European Union Counter-Terrorism Strategy*, Brussels, November 30, 2005, p. 3, at http://register.consilium.europa.eu/doc/srv?l=EN&f=ST%2014469%202005%20REV%204. The discussion in this chapter has been informed by the research on European counter-radicalization in Angel Rabasa, Stacie L. Pettyjohn, Jeremy J. Ghez, and Christopher Boucek, *Deradicalizing Islamist Extremists*, Santa Monica, CA: RAND Corporation, 2010.

governments in directly addressing the religious and ideological components of Islamist radicalization.

The perhaps more fully articulated European counter-radicalization approach is the Prevent component in the British government's counter-terrorism strategy, the Central Counter-Terrorism Strategy (CONTEST). The strategy consists of four components – Prevent (preventing terrorism by addressing the factors that produce radicalization), Pursue (pursuing terrorists and their sponsors), Protect (protecting the British public and government), and Prepare (preparing for the consequences of a terrorist attack).[2] Initially, CONTEST's emphasis was on the last three Ps. In the 2009 iteration of the strategy, referred to as CONTEST-2, greater emphasis was placed on a more proactive approach predicated on Prevent. The Prevent strand of CONTEST focused on combating radicalization in the United Kingdom by partnering with the police, local governments, and NGOs to challenge radical Islamism, disrupt those who promote violent extremism, support individuals who are vulnerable to radicalization or who have begun to radicalize, increase the capacity of communities to resist violent extremism, and address grievances that violent extremists exploit.[3]

The first strand of Prevent aims to counter radical Islamism and bolster those who espouse a moderate Islamic ideology. After the 2005 London bombings, the government organized seven working groups of prominent Muslims tasked with recommending how the government could stop the spread of violent extremism in the country. Called Preventing Extremism Together, these committees submitted their list of proposals to the British government in September 2005. Their recommendations included creating a mosques' and imams' national advisory board, a traveling scholars' road show called the Radical Middle Way, and forums discussing Islamophobia and extremism.[4]

The second component of Prevent seeks to impede the efforts of those trying to radicalize others in places such as mosques, schools, prisons, and

[2] HM Government, *Countering International Terrorism: The United Kingdom's Strategy*, London, July 2006, pp. 1–2.

[3] HM Government, *The Prevent Strategy: A Guide for Local Partners in England*, June 2008, at http://webarchive.nationalarchives.gov.uk/20130401151715/http://www.education.gov.uk/publications/eOrderingDownload/Prevent_Strategy.pdf.

[4] For the working groups' recommendations see "*Preventing Extremism Together*" *Working Groups, August–October 2005*, London: UK Home Office, October 2005. See also Michael Whine, "The Radicalization of Diasporas and Terrorism: United Kingdom," in Doron Zimmermann and William Rosenau, eds., *The Radicalization of Diasporas and Terrorism*. Zurich: Center for Security Studies, ETH Zurich, 2009, pp. 31–33.

community centers and on the Internet. Efforts in this area include criminalizing actions that support terrorism so that individuals who promote and assist terrorists can be prosecuted, obtaining intelligence about imprisoned radicals, and raising the standards in mosques.[5]

The third element of Prevent is supporting vulnerable individuals. It consists of providing mentoring programs and training opportunities for young Muslim leaders so that they have the knowledge and skills to counter radicalism.[6] The government wanted to avoid imprisoning at-risk individuals as part of this effort; instead, the authorities sought to help those who were moving toward violent extremism but had not yet broken the law by organizing local interventions. Toward this end, the British instituted the Channel Project, a local, community-based program that relies on the police, local authorities, and local communities to identify individuals who are radicalizing and then help them to return to the right path. Community partners refer to the authorities those individuals who are exhibiting alarming behavior, such as visiting terrorist websites, discussing and promoting violence, or other behavior indicating movement toward radicalization.

The Channel Project assesses referred individuals to determine whether they are likely to become involved in violent extremism and whether they have influence over others. The project's focus "is on preventing radical beliefs escalating to violent extremism and not on preventing individuals, groups or places from expressing radical or extreme views or behaviour."[7] If the project determines that an individual is moving toward violent radicalism, local partners and authorities decide how to stage an intervention, which may include the individual's family, the police, and local imams. Guidance provided to local partners recommends that the Channel Project's interventions deal with many of the factors that lead to radicalization, not just ideology.[8]

[5] HM Government, *Pursue Prevent Protect Prepare: The United Kingdom's Strategy for Countering International Terrorism*, London, March 2009, pp. 88–89.

[6] HM Government *The Prevent Strategy: A Guide for Local Partners in England*, 2008, pp. 27–29; HM Government, *Pursue Prevent Protect Prepare* 2009, pp. 89–90.

[7] Audit Commission, *Preventing Violent Extremism: Learning and Developing Exercise*. London, October 2008, p. 46, at http://archive.audit-commission.gov.uk/auditcommission/subwebs/publications/corporate/publicationPDF/NEW1083.pdf.

[8] HM Government, *The Prevent Strategy: A Guide for Local Partners in England*, 2008, pp. 28–29. Annex I of *The Prevent Strategy* identifies factors that make individuals vulnerable to radicalization, including personal crisis, a changed situation or circumstances, underemployment, links to criminality, identity, social exclusion, grievances, and a lack of trust in political structures and civil society. See also HM Government, *Channel: Supporting Individuals Vulnerable to Recruitment by Violent Extremists*," London, March 2010a.

The fourth strand of Prevent involves increasing local communities' resilience to violent extremism by strengthening moderate Muslim leaders and empowering young Muslim men and women.[9] For instance, Leeds created the Bringing Communities Together project. This seven-month plan aimed to help young Muslims resist and confront extremism and was operated by a local charity, the Hamara Healthy Living Centre, and a number of other local Muslim NGOs. The program included a poster campaign designed by young Muslims from Leeds that challenged common stereotypes. Bringing Communities Together also offered training courses for young Muslims to help them discredit extremism and Islamophobia.[10]

The fifth and final component of Prevent aims to address grievances that extremists use to mobilize support by reducing discrimination and inequality. In addition, the British government promotes discussion about its foreign policy so that it can explain and rebut extremists' criticisms.[11]

Effective communication with target audiences is a key part of the British counterterrorism approach. The Research, Information, and Communications Unit (RICU), composed of personnel from the Home Office, the Foreign and Commonwealth Office, and the Department of Communities and Local Government, is the organization charged with developing a single interdepartmental approach to implementing the strategic communication component of CONTEST-2. To fine-tune the government's message, RICU is trying to understand audiences in more detail, both in terms of demographics and attitudes. It created questionnaires about attitudes toward violence, the state, extremism, and media consumption and has developed methodologies to identify which channels are most effective to reach audiences with the government's message and to evaluate the effect on the intended audiences.[12]

[9] HM Government, *Pursue Prevent Protect Prepare*, 2009, pp. 90–91.

[10] UK Department for Communities and Local Government, *Building Community Resilience: Prevent Case Studies*, London, December 2009, pp. 5–7. Some of the London 7/7 suicide bombers had frequented the center, however. According to a British media report, a concerned worker at the center notified the police of his suspicions that it had been exploited as a front for the radicalization of young Muslims (Russell Jenkins, "Killers may have been recruited at Youth Centre," *The Times*, July 16, 2005, at http://www.thetimes.co.uk/tto/news/uk/article1935564.ece).

[11] HM Government, *Pursue Prevent Protect Prepare*, 2009, p. 91.

[12] Interview with head of research and knowledge management, RICU, London, November 2009.

The goal of the communication strategy is to engage target audiences on issues that are relevant to them and to try to influence attitudes based on a shared starting point. For instance, what should the authorities be saying to reach these audiences most effectively? And what are the most effective channels to deliver these messages? These channels need not be exclusively media; the government could also engage local practitioners and trusted parties in the communities.

The Cameron government's review of Prevent, issued in June 2011, recognizes that the ideology of extremism lies at the root of terrorism. Consequently, the British government will not work with organizations that oppose values of universal human rights, equality before the law, democracy, and full participation in society. The government announced that it will build on the successful Channel program that identifies and provides support for people at risk of radicalization and work with sectors and institutions in which risks of radicalization exist – in particular, education and health care providers, faith groups, charities, and the wider criminal justice system. The government also recognized the challenge of radicalization on the Internet and at universities.[13]

The 2011 iteration of Prevent was predictably criticized by the left for pursuing those who hold ideological opinions that the government does not approve of and shifting the blame for terrorism to the Muslim community and its values.[14] *The Guardian* complained that doctors and other health professionals will now be asked to identify people who are vulnerable to being drawn into terrorism.[15] Anti-Islamist organizations and analysts have welcomed the new Prevent strategy as a step in the right direction, but they have cautioned that key terms such as extremism or Islamism are poorly defined, too broadly in some cases, and too narrowly in others. Nevertheless, as Shiraz Maher of Kings College's International Centre for the Study of Radicalisation and Political Violence wrote, what is most striking is the new commitment to due diligence, the greater emphasis placed on the promotion of liberal democratic British values, and the commitment not to allow extremism to go unchallenged. There is

[13] HM Government, Home Office, "Protecting the UK against Terrorism," Updated March 13, 2013, at https://www.gov.uk/government/policies/protecting-the-uk-against-terrorism/supporting-pages/prevent.

[14] "Prevent: Welcome to Totalitarian Britain," *New Civilisation*, June 11, 2008, at http://www.newcivilisation.com/home/uk-europe/prevent-welcome-to-totalitarian-britain.

[15] "Doctors asked to identify potential terrorists under Government plans," *The Guardian*, June 6, 2011, at http://www.guardian.co.uk/politics/2011/jun/06/doctors-identify-potential-terrorists-plans.

agreement that success will depend on implementation. To this end, the Quilliam Foundation recommended the appointment of a Prevent overseer in Downing Street.[16]

## "ILLEGAL" VS. "SUBVERSIVE" ACTIVITIES: THE DIVIDE IN EUROPEAN THREAT ASSESSMENT

The debate on Prevent in the United Kingdom reflects a significant split within the European debate on terrorism that has emerged over the issue of where to draw the line between terrorism and subversion: how large is the threat posed by illegal and violent activities carried out by Islamist extremists and their sympathizers? What is the role of movements and ideologies that seek to undermine modern Western societies and values – a goal that extremists pursue through both violent and nonviolent, illegal and legal means? How does a state committed to the rule of law defend itself against actions that have a subversive intent but remain within the bounds of legality? In other words, European states are running up against "the problem of the democratic paradox: how to deal in a democracy with movements that wish to put an end to democracy."[17]

Obviously, this question is not just of philosophical interest. The answer will inform the actions of the police, prosecutors, legislatures, and nearly every other agency of the state. Do the authorities wait until a group engages in overtly illegal or violent activities, considering everything short of these to be a legitimate exercise in free political expression? Or are there political goals and values that even if they are pursued by legal means, nonetheless can be considered out of bounds and actionable by a liberal society dedicated to personal and political freedom?

As the evolution of the British Prevent strategy shows, Europeans increasingly recognize the importance of addressing the ideological component of radicalization that, while not involving actual violence, fosters and justifies the violence. The Dutch, in particular, pioneered work in the

[16] See Shiraz Maher, "Summary of Revised Prevent Strategy," International Centre for the Study of Radicalisation and Political Violence (ICSR), June 10 at http://www.icsr.info/news/icsr-insight---summary-of-revised-prevent-strategy; and Quilliam Foundation, "Quilliam Response to UK Government's New 'Prevent' Policy," June 7, 2011, at http://www.quilliamfoundation.org/press-releases/quilliams-response-to-uk-governments-new-prevent-policy/.

[17] Algemene Inlichtingen- en Veiligheidsdienst (AIVD), *From Dawa to Jihad: The Various Threats from Radical Islam to the Democratic Legal Order*, General Intelligence and Security Service, Ministry of the Interior and Kingdom Relations of the Netherlands, The Hague: December 2004, p. 37, at http://www.fas.org/irp/world/netherlands/dawa.pdf.

field of terrorist counter-strategies that incorporates the ideological dimension of terrorism. Two years before Van Gogh's assassination, the Dutch General Intelligence and Security Service (AIVD) concluded that "other, not directly violent forms of radicalization may also be extremely harmful to the democratic legal order, like intentionally stirring up hatred, demonizing other groups in society (e.g. anti-Semitism) or the pursuit of extreme social isolationism."[18]

The AIVD further developed this concept in *From Dawa to Jihad: The Various Threats from Radical Islam to the Democratic Legal Order*. The main point of the study is that there is much more to the threat posed by radical Islam than terrorism. There is a need to address the initial ideological aspect of radicalization. The problem is how to deal with an ideological threat in view of the commitment to freedom of expression and freedom of religion in the Netherlands and other European countries. One way is legislation to criminalize incitement to hatred. Germany has outlawed anti-Semitic or *volksverhetzende* (hatred-inciting) propaganda, for obvious historical reasons. Enforcement, however, is a problem with Arabic- and Turkish-language publications.

Beyond sanctions, Europeans are also engaging in what we might call cultural adaptations intended to cope with the threat of radicalization and subversion. One has been the linking of residency rights to the acceptance of basic Western values – for example, through legislation that requires permit seekers to pass tests of competency in the national language as well as basic laws and values.

Germany, for example, passed a law in 2007 requiring individuals wishing to travel to Germany to join a spouse who is already a German resident or citizen to first pass a German-language competency test. The law was contested from many directions for many reasons, but it was judged constitutional in 2011. Its proponents defended it as a tool not only for improved integration but also as a liberating tool for Muslim women who otherwise often lived in isolation and complete dependence on male family members.[19] In Austria, people are given an integration grace period. They have three years to pass the language and values test. After

[18] AIVD Annual Report 2003, Ministry of the Interior and Kingdom Relations of the Netherlands, at http://www.fas.org/irp/world/netherlands/aivd2003-eng.pdf.

[19] Opponents of the law argued that the rights of spouses and families to live together should not be subjected to any preconditions. Others argued simply that the test itself was too difficult, requiring potentially years of study during which wives and children were forcibly kept apart from husbands and fathers. Supporters counterclaimed that the test required a vocabulary of only 300 words and that the benefits to all parties and the principle of

three years, if they fail the test, they must pay a fine, and after four years, they can be denied residence and required to leave the country.

This represents a significant development not just vis-à-vis the immigrants but also in regard to national and European identity, a shift from a self-perception that for many decades was largely, if tacitly, based on race and birth, to one that is based on values. On the surface, these laws seem directed toward the immigrants, but in the long run, they may have an effect on how European countries see and define themselves. However, important pieces of this effort are still missing, in particular, a focus on civic education for the young and on the development of national narratives that include the newcomers from other cultures.

It is worth noting that popular culture is distinctly ahead of European governments in this regard. Online forums, rap and hip-hop music, and street culture reflect the emergence of new multicultural identities with a leaning toward Western liberal values. For example, the newspaper *Die Welt* hosts an online forum called *politik de*, dedicated to "Information. Diskussion. Interaktion." Here, we find the collaborative efforts of German and Turkish-German bloggers in mock integration tests to purportedly measure an immigrant's ability to fit into the Berlin scene. Questions include "what is the best kebab place in Berlin?" but also the edgier "how would you go about collecting welfare payments under two different names?"[20] Given that rap and hip-hop are not generally considered establishment venues, a surprising number of young rappers and hip-hop artists have emerged with unabashedly pro-integration messages. The rapper Harris, for example, has texts such as "Du kannst nicht hier leben und alles schlecht reden"– "it's not right to live well here and talk this country down." These are promising, culturally organic developments that bear watching and encouragement.

The Netherlands has taken one of the more forward-leaning stances in identifying the ideological and cultural dimensions of Islamist radicalism as intrinsic to Islamist terrorism. The Dutch Ministry of the Interior, through its security agency (AIVD), formulated and publicized a holistic approach. The policy is noteworthy in two regards. First, it aggressively addresses both illegal activities and such activities as are legal but have a subversive intent. Second, it then attempts to begin building the sort of multi-faceted approach it believes to be necessary to master the problem in its entirety.

collective peace outweighed any disadvantages. See for example Migration News, http://migration-asyl.de/public1.

[20] http://www.welt.de/politik/deutschland.

The AIVD document sees radical Islamism as seeking to eliminate the existing legal order and to replace it with an Islamic order. Along the way to that goal, there may be several interim steps. These can include the sharpening of discord and separation between Muslims and the rest of the population; inciting civil disobedience; gradually building up a parallel society within the host country that holds opposing values and a different legal and ethical code; infiltrating state institutions, such as local administrations and schools; spreading rumors and conspiracy theories; fostering anti-Semitism; and more.[21]

Individual steps toward the larger goal of a separate Islamic identity within the majority society can appear to be harmless and even trivial. For example, the demand that Muslim girls should not be required to participate in physical education classes or to go on class outings can be interpreted as a minor accommodation to people with a different set of cultural values, or it can be seen as one small step in the gradual erosion of Western cultural norms and an acknowledgment of the principle that Muslims are entitled to a separate set of rules.

The AIVD document charts eight types of threats from radical Islam, of which half are nonviolent. It attempts to graph the relationship between legal but expansionist activities ("dawa") on the one hand with aggressive, illegal, and violent actions ("jihad") on the other. On the basis of that analysis, the document attempts to fashion a differentiated but interrelated set of responses. Obviously, legal but undesirable activities call for a different reaction than do illegal activities. The first category falls more into the domain of integration, dialogue, social work, and the mobilization of moderate forces within the Muslim communities.[22]

Germany has been quicker to ban extremist groups than have some of the other European states. It outlawed the Kaplan Group (Kalifatstaat), a radical group seeking to overthrow the Turkish state, in 2001, and Hizb ut-Tahrir in 2003. This reflects Germany's official stance against groups that pursue subversive agendas, not just groups that directly use violence. As an illustration of preemptive action against those who have an objectionable agenda, even if they cannot be directly linked to acts of violence, authorities in Berlin banned a conference scheduled for early October 2004, the "First Arab-Islamic Congress in Europe," which had the declared purposes of supporting the Palestinian resistance and the Iraqi insurgency. German authorities took the position that this

[21] AIVD, *From Dawa to Jihad*, pp. 37–43.

[22] Ibid., p. 36.

amounted to an endorsement of terrorism and denied permission for the conference to be held. One of the organizers had his temporary residence permit withdrawn and was expelled to Lebanon; three others were accused of seeking to "recruit members and supporters for a terrorist organization."[23]

The strategy of interdiction is showing some results, at least in drawing a line between sympathizers and activists. Followers and sympathizers have, German authorities believe, been discouraged by the state's actions against the group and have tended to drop away. Some are pursuing the reinstatement of their group through legal channels, while others have relocated to other European countries. According to the Federal Office for the Protection of the Constitution (Bundesamt für Bundesverfassungsschutz – BfV) 2004 report, "The prohibition of the Kalifatstaat organization and its 36 affiliated associations has had a deterrent effect on a large number of its followers. Police actions carried out subsequently additionally disconcerted the former members of that movement and have led to a further decline in their attempted activities."[24]

If that depiction is correct, we could surmise that extremist groups with a nonviolent focus attract individuals who, while they may hold or be drawn by radical positions, are nonetheless essentially mainstream in their posture and do not want to confront the law or the state authorities. If true, a tentative conclusion of greater import also follows: that criminalizing the activity of a movement about which there are justified suspicions will not necessarily lead to greater radicalization. Instead, it may drive away or at least strongly discourage the majority of essentially law-abiding people. Further study seems advisable to identify variables that can help distinguish situations where banning of extremist groups leads to radicalization from those where suppression leads to a decline in the appeal of these groups.

As in the Netherlands, the security services in Germany were ahead of other state institutions in focusing on Islamist extremism as a serious emerging threat. Already in 1995, the BfV had come to the conclusion that left-wing terrorism was waning in importance and being replaced by Islamist extremism as the most significant danger to German internal security.[25] The 2011 BfV report (*Bundesverfassungsschutzbericht*)

[23] *Bundesverfassungsschutz, Jahresbericht* 2004, p. 187.

[24] Ibid., p. 211.

[25] "German Intelligence Service: Islamic Fundamentalists Main Security Threat," *Junge Welt*, January 12, 1995, cited by FECL, Sweden, February 1995, at www.fecl.org/circular/3107.htm.

identified three categories of radical Islamist activity within Germany that pose a danger to the state: efforts to undermine the state and its values through legal activities, support to international Islamist extremists through such activities as fund-raising or dissemination of recruitment materials online, and Salafism. Salafism is seen as having two streams. One stream is focused on undermining the German state to eliminate the German constitution, its laws, and its way of life through a range of actions intended to create disloyalty and social instability and unrest. These are destructive and dangerous but not necessarily illegal. The second stream is focused on violent action including terrorism. One concern cited in the report is the apparent increase in networking among the groups as well as between these groups and larger international extremist movements. What German authorities find worrisome is that travel of known Salafists between Germany and Afghanistan and Pakistan has been on the increase, and they believe that this travel is related to terrorist training. There has also been very significant growth in Internet activity – websites, chat rooms, and other forums intended to attract, recruit, and influence susceptible individuals.[26]

## REACHING OUT TO MUSLIM COMMUNITIES

A major component of the new European approaches involves reaching to Muslim communities. European governments agree on the need to engage interlocutors in the Muslim communities. The debate is over who these interlocutors should be. One standard of moderation consists of some form of opposition to violence – worth supporting against the undesirable alternative of violent radicalism. As noted earlier, an underlying assumption in this approach is that Salafis and conservative Muslims are more likely to have greater credibility with young extremists and, therefore, might be more successful than mainstream or liberal Muslims in dissuading these young men from transitioning to violence. This approach is favored by some political sectors and by the police and security services that measure success by preventing acts of terror. Robert Lambert, former head of the Muslim Contact Unit at New Scotland Yard, for instance, points out that the young West Indian Salafis who gained control of the

[26] *Bundesverfassungsschutzbericht*, 2011, at http://www.verfassungsschutz.de/de/download-manager/_vsbericht-2011.pdf; Bundesamt für Verfassungsschutz, "Salafistische Bestrebungen in Deutschland," Köln, April 2012, at http://www.verfassungsschutz.de/de/oeffentlichkeitsarbeit/publikationen/pb-islamismus/broschuere-1204-salafistische-bestrebungen.

Brixton mosque in London in the 1990s fought Abu Qatada's efforts to establish a position of influence at the mosque.[27]

The counterargument is that that there are only weak firewalls between violent and nonviolent tactics. Most Salafis are equivocal on the issue of terrorism. They justify it in areas where Muslims are allegedly under attack.[28] For violent extremists, the meaning of "defensive" extends to striking at the enemies of God wherever they are. They see themselves as a vanguard who are willing to fulfill the religious obligation of jihad, even if other Muslims do not.[29]

Although working with Islamist organizations might produce results over the short run, over the long term, it legitimizes Islamists as spokesmen for the European Muslim communities and abets their efforts to create parallel societies separate from the broader national community. It follows, as British authorities have come to recognize, that governments should work with Muslim organizations that support Western values and institutions and believe that Muslims need to become full members of European societies and of Western modernity.

Until recently, the British government had been willing to work with Islamists, in particular with the Islamist-influenced Muslim Council of Britain (MCB), an organization that claims to represent the largest body of Muslim groups in Britain, but whose moderate credentials have been questioned.[30] In a report on honor killings, the United Kingdom's Centre for Social Cohesion noted that the MCB has sought to block legislation

[27] Interview with Robert Lambert, London, September 2008.

[28] For instance, asked his opinion about a jihad to defend Muslims under attack in the Moluccas, Yemeni Salafi Sheikh Muqbil bin Hadi al-Wadi laid down the following conditions: (1) that Muslims have the capacity to fight the kafirs, (2) that the jihad not lead to conflicts within the Muslim community, (3) that mobilization for the jihad be based purely on religion,(4) that the jihad be based on Salafi principles and not be conducted under *hizbiyyah* [party] flags, (5) that it not distract Muslims from studying the true religion, and (6) that it not be used for personal gain or to obtain political positions. International Crisis Group (ICG), "Indonesia Backgrounder: Why Salafism and Terrorism Don't Mix," ICG Asia Report No. 83, September 13, 2004.

[29] An intriguing case in point is the social network of Kafeel Ahmed, the driver of the vehicle used in the failed terrorist attack on Glasgow Airport on June 30, 2007. Kafeel was an Indian Muslim, raised in Saudi Arabia, who was studying for a doctorate in physics at Cambridge University. At Cambridge, Kafeel shared a row house with the regional commander of Hizb ut-Tahrir. Although Kafeel was not a member, Shiraz Maher, a then member of Hizb ut-Tahrir who lived in a row house across the street, believes that Kafeel's whole social network reinforced the idea of the oppression of Muslims and facilitated his descent into violence. Interview with Shiraz Maher, London, 2007.

[30] For instance, the Muslim Council of Britain has a history of defending radical Islamists who come under political attack, such as the Hizb ut-Tahrir when the Blair government

aimed at ending honor-based violence against women. As a result of MCB pressure, the report states, the British government halted its plans to criminalize forced marriages and made them a civil offense instead.[31]

More recently, there has been a noticeable shift in thinking on this second approach. Under the Labour government, the lead agency for engaging the Muslim community, the Department of Communities and Local Government, sought to refocus the government's engagement with the Muslim community away from traditional gatekeepers such as the MCB to non-Salafist groups.[32] The Department of Communities and Local Government has created a Preventing Violent Extremism Pathfinder Fund (PVEPF) that supports a wide range of local initiatives to build resilience against extremism and promote common values.[33]

A number of nongovernmental institutions have emerged in the context of these initiatives. The Radical Middle Way aims to present a mainstream view of Islam by disseminating the sermons and articles of leading British Islamic scholars.[34] The British Muslim Forum provides counter-narratives of Islam and peace in a mosque setting for Diaspora Muslims. The Quilliam Foundation, a London-based Muslim counter-extremism think tank established by former members of Hizb ut-Tahrir, carries out research, training, and outreach activities to advance its agenda of providing an alternative of Islamism and encouraging Islamists to return to mainstream Islam.[35]

## BUILDING EFFECTIVE ANTI-TERRORISM LEGAL TOOLS

Western European countries have long experience in dealing with terrorism: Great Britain with the IRA, Spain with Basque separatists, France with Corsican separatists and Algerian terrorists, Italy with the Red Brigades, Germany with the Baader-Meinhof organization. Nevertheless, the magnitude of the threat posed by Islamist terrorism after 9/11 and the

announced its intention to ban the organization. See http://mcbwatch.blogspot.com/2005/08/mcb-and-hizb-ut-tahrir.html.

[31] James Brandon and Salam Hafez, "Crimes of the Community: Honour-Based Violence in the UK," London: Centre for Social Cohesion, 2008, p. 111, at http://www.civitas.org.uk/pdf/CrimesOfTheCommunity.pdf.

[32] Interview with Michael Whine, London, September 2008.

[33] Department of Communities and Local Government, United Kingdom, "Preventing Violent Extremism Pathfinder Fund: Mapping of Project Activities 2007/2008," December 10, 2008, UK Government Web Archive, doc. 1098036 at http://www.communities.gov.uk/documents/communities/doc/1098036.doc.

[34] http://www.radicalmiddleway.org/

[35] Quilliam Foundation, "About Us," at http://www.quilliamfoundation.org/about-us.html/.

onset of Islamist terrorist attacks in Europe prompted efforts in several European countries to expand anti-terrorist legislation. These efforts have predictably generated tensions with civil libertarians and sectors of the legal establishment. The dilemma faced by European governments is how to balance the need for legal tools to address the new and difficult challenges posed by amorphous Islamist terrorist networks with the protection of individual rights.

After years of heated debate, in December 2006 the German Bundestag passed a new anti-terror law designed to promote communication and sharing of information between federal and state security services. It also includes the creation of a controversial national security database and increased surveillance powers for the police and intelligence agencies. The idea behind the database was that all police and intelligence agencies, at the federal and national levels, would gather information about terror suspects and terrorist organizations in a central database that would be accessible to all security agencies. Since 2006, the Federal Criminal Police Office (BKA) has controlled the anti-terrorism database. It contains information about individuals that can be recorded and accessed by 38 German security authorities – the BKA, the Federal Police, the Secret Service, the Military Counterintelligence Service, the Federal Intelligence Service, the state prosecutors offices, the Customs Office and the Offices of Criminal Investigation, and intelligence agencies of the federal states. It collects core data about people, information about their training and occupation, and their phone numbers and bank details. Photos and lists of special physical characteristics, details of places visited and so-called terrorism-related skills are also stored. The database is used to conduct investigations, arrests, and raids against suspected persons. In April 2013, the Constitutional Court in Karlsruhe found that the law governing the anti-terrorism database was fundamentally compatible with the constitution.[36]

As well as approving the creation of the anti-terror database, the Bundestag expanded and extended the anti-terror laws that came into

[36] Deutsche Welle, Germany Approves Anti-Terror Database, December 1, 2006, at http://www.dw-world.de/dw/article/0,2144,2256390,00.html; Federal Constitutional Court, Judgment of 24 April, 2013, "Counter-Terrorism Database in its Fundamental Structures Compatible with the Basic Law, but not Regarding Specific Aspects of its Design," at http://www.bundesverfassungsgericht.de/pressemitteilungen/bvg13-031en.html; Johannes Stern, "Germany: Federal Constitutional Court legitimises anti-terrorism database," April 27, 2013, World Socialist Website, at http://www.wsws.org/en/articles/2013/04/27/germ-a27.html.

being in the wake of 9/11. One of the most controversial pieces of legislation involved granting the intelligence services the authority to monitor the computers of suspected terrorists and their sympathizers. The surveillance technique, which involved sending e-mails with so-called Trojan horses to a suspect's computer, was challenged before the Constitutional Court, which ruled that the authorities could monitor the computers of suspected terrorists only if there is sufficient evidence of pending danger. On the other hand, shortly after, the same court limited the government's ability to collect data from telecommunications companies and Internet providers.[37]

A major change is that the Federal Office for the Protection of the Constitution can now use its intelligence resources to fight counter-constitutional activities that are currently not yet registered if these activities promote the use of violence. These could be hate speech activities by the extreme right or Islamists. It will not matter anymore whether the hate speech activities are aimed at other countries or ethnicities or people of different religious affiliations in Germany. The revisions also make it easier for the Federal Office for the Protection of the Constitution to gain access to travel data of suspect persons from airlines. In early 2007, the Ministry of Interior also created the *Gemeinsame Internet-Zentrum* (GIZ) in Berlin, a common Internet center, to supervise extremist online activity in Germany and beyond.[38]

However, the emphasis remains on prevention, improved intelligence, and community vigilance at the local level. This is reflected, for example, in the Prevention Summit convened by Minister of the Interior Hans-Peter Friedrich in June 2011, intended to create a more effective security partnership between the government, mosques, and Islamic organizations. Its purpose was to identify early on those individuals – especially youths and converts – who were expressing disaffection and seemed to be veering toward extremist religious postures.[39] The idea, however, was not uncontroversial and received considerable pushback from Muslim organizations.

[37] Gad J. Bensinger, "Law Enforcement and Counterterrorism in Post-9/11 Germany," *Pakistan Journal of Criminology*, Vol. 2. No. 1, January 2010, at http://www.cjimagazine.com/content/view/226/2/http://www.cjimagazine.com/content/view/226/2/.

[38] Discussion with Markus Kerber, Berlin, June 2008; Bundesministerium des Innern, "Das Gemeinsame Internetzentrum," July 2011, at http://www.bmi.bund.de/SharedDocs/Downloads/DE/Themen/Sicherheit/Terrorismus/giz.pdf?__blob=publicationFile.

[39] http://www.zeit.de/politik/deutschland/2011-06/praeventionsgipfel-friedrich-muslime.

In the United Kingdom, the Terrorism Act of 2006 introduced the offense of encouraging terrorism, pursuant to Article 5 of the Council of Europe Convention on the Prevention of Terrorism, which requires states to have an offense of "public provocation to commit a terrorist act." Under the act, it is an offense to make a statement that glorifies the commission or preparation of acts of terrorism or Council of Europe Convention offenses.[40] The act introduced two new offenses to the statute book: to prepare a terrorist act or to train for terrorism.[41]

Some features of the act, glorification of terrorism and the detention of a suspect for 28 days without charge (although any detention for longer than 48 hours requires judicial oversight), drew substantial criticism from Conservative, Liberal Democrats, and some Labour members of Parliament, on the grounds that "glorification" was defined too broadly and detention for 28 days too draconian.[42]

Several continental countries, notably France and Spain, have special anti-terrorism courts and magistrates. The French anti-terrorism legal regime is by far the strictest. French anti-terrorism laws lay out a regime of exception, a "regulated derogation from the common practice," which treats not only terrorist acts but the intention to commit them as offenses carrying some of the longest penalties in the French legal system (up to 30 years imprisonment). This judicial compact is built on two main pieces of legislation: the Terrorism Act of September 9, 1986, which established the centralized prosecution of all terrorist acts,[43] and the Terrorism Act of July 22, 1996, which criminalized actions based on the intent to commit terrorism and gave the law enforcement community broader powers to investigate and detain suspects through a special and harsher legal procedure.[44]

The 1986 law created a body of investigative magistrates within the central judicial administration, the Section Anti-Terroriste du Parquet de

[40] The act makes it clear that the offense is committed only if "members of the public could reasonably be expected to infer that what is being glorified is being glorified as conduct that should be emulated by them in existing circumstances." When determining how the statement is likely to be understood by the public, it is necessary to look at the contents of the statement as a whole as well as the circumstances and manner of its publication.

[41] Isaac Kfir, "British Middle East Policy: The Counterterrorism Dimension," *MERIA Journal*, Vol. 10, No. 4, December 2006.

[42] Ibid.

[43] Terrorism is defined in the law as "an infraction committed by an individual, or a group of individuals, aimed at seriously disrupting public order through intimidation or terror."

[44] Both pieces of legislation were voted after major waves of foreign terrorism had struck France.

Paris, entirely dedicated to directing all terrorism investigations and prosecutions anywhere in France. Since then, this small (six judges) but extremely powerful unit, headed by Jean-Louis Bruguière until 2007, directed more than 300 terrorism investigations and collectively amassed what probably amounts to the one of the most comprehensive pools of expertise on terrorism anywhere. As the main judicial authority for terrorism-related investigations, the Section Anti-Terroriste also weaved close ties to Direction de la Surveillance du Territoire (DST), and the Division Nationale Anti-terroriste (DNAT), two services responsible for monitoring and investigating terrorist threats, both of which depend on the authority granted to them by the anti-terrorist magistrates.[45]

The second piece of legislation, approved in 1996, established a truly unique concept in the anti-terrorism legal ethos: the "criminal association in relation to a terrorist venture."[46] This notion, which has no equivalent anywhere else in Europe, puts forward the concept that anything that happens before a terrorist act is already terrorism. By allowing the investigating magistrates to truly integrate prevention and suppression, this capability opened a vast field for proactive policing against the entire spectrum of the threat, from the terrorist groups' logistical and financial networks to their operational capabilities and formed the basis of nearly all anti-terrorism investigations since 1996.[47]

Since 9/11, France has sought to further strengthen and update this legal regime to respond to an increasingly amorphous and multinational terrorist threat. The French government introduced several pieces of legislation such as the Law on Everyday Security (Loi sur la Securité Quotidienne, March 2003), which broadened the search powers of the security services and strengthened legislation concerning the financing of terrorism. At the end of 2005, by large majorities the National Assembly and Senate passed one of the strictest anti-terrorism laws in Europe, which allows the police to obtain communication data from telephone operators, Internet services providers, and Internet cafes.[48] In a major reorganization in July 2008, the domestic intelligence agency, the DST, was merged with the police surveillance agency Renseignements Generaux (RG) into a new

[45] The investigative judge, or magistrates, oversees investigations into crimes. He or she does not hear cases but hands them over to a trial judge once the investigation is finished.

[46] Also sometimes translated as "conspiracy to commit terrorist crimes."

[47] It allowed the DST to conduct very large sweeps to build the fullest possible picture of a network and thus improve its knowledge of continually evolving networks.

[48] "France adopts anti-terrorism law," EDRI, January 18, 2006, at http://edri.org/edrigram number4-1frenchlaw/.

agency, the Direction Centrale du Renseignement Intérieur (DCRI), charged with overseeing counterterrorism, industrial espionage, cyber crime, and threats to domestic order.

Mohammed Merah's shooting spree in March 2012, the first successful terrorist attack in 16 years in France, prompted pointed public criticisms of the authorities' failure to prevent the attacks, the eight-day delay in identifying Merah as the assailant, and the police's inability to capture him alive. In response, the Ministry of Interior initiated a crackdown on radical Islamists. The authorities deported five radical clerics and arrested 13 members of Forsane Alizza (the Knights of Pride), a small radical Salafist group that was ordered dissolved in January 2012 as a threat to the republican system, on charges that they were planning to kidnap a Jewish judge. The government announced two legislative initiatives to strengthen the legal arsenal against would-be terrorists: one to curtail access to jihadist websites and the other designed to criminalize traveling to "insurrectionary countries."[49]

The report of the General Inspectorate of the National Police (Inspection générale de la police nationale – IGPN), released in October 2012, highlighted the "objective failure" of the police in monitoring and investigating Merah. It attributed this failure to a combination of omissions and errors of judgment, problems of management and organization of the security services, and the divisions still present between domestic intelligence and police, as well as to "an incredible failure of the intelligence services." The report concluded that there was no question that the DCRI needed better coordination and that the merger of the DST and the RG had not been completely achieved. The report recommended creating a liaison office among all the services (internal intelligence, judicial police, national police, Gendarmerie, Compagnies Républicaines de Sécurité (CRS) special mobile police,[50] and border police) and a new tool for auditing and inspecting domestic intelligence.[51]

[49] Siegel, "French Counterterrorism Policy in the Wake of Mohammed Merah's Attack "French Islamic Militants Planned to Kidnap Jewish Judge," JTA, April 3, 2012, at http://www.jta.org/2012/04/03/news-opinion/world/french-islamic-militants-planned-to-kidnap-jewish-judge.

[50] A unit within the National Police used mostly for riot control and assisting in maintaining public order as needed.

[51] Laurent Borredon, "Le rapport sévère de la «police des polices» sur l'affaire Merah," M Blogs, October 23, 2012, at http://delinquance.blog.lemonde.fr/2012/10/23/le-rapport-severe-de-la-police-des-polices-sur-laffaire-merah/.

The Spanish approach to combating terrorism combines a specialized legal regime, with the investigation and prosecution of terrorist crimes falling within the jurisdiction of anti-terrorist magistrates in the Audiencia Nacional, Spain's highest criminal court. Within the executive departments, the second-ranking official in the Ministry of Interior, the secretary of state for security, coordinates the government's overall counterterrorism posture. The secretary of state for security supervises the Centro Nacional de Coordinación Anti-Terrorista (CNCA), an interagency analytical fusion unit established after the 3/11 attack to coordinate and analyze information from the various security agencies and to develop threat assessments and strategies to respond to terrorist threats. The CNCA is composed of personnel from the National Police, the Civil Guard, and the Centro Nacional de Inteligencia (National Intelligence Center), Spain's intelligence agency, which is part of the Ministry of Defense.[52]

As in the French and Italian legal systems, a specialized cadre of anti-terrorism magistrates and prosecutors within the Audiencia Nacional play a key role in Spain's fight against terrorism. The Audiencia Nacional has jurisdiction over terrorism, drug trafficking, human trafficking, money counterfeiting, and universal jurisdiction crimes.[53] This system was put in place as the result of the state's need to confront the challenge of Basque terrorism. The need to protect local judges from intimidation or retaliation by the Basque terrorist group Euskadi Ta Askatasuna (ETA) prompted the consolidation of terrorism cases in the Audiencia Nacional, which has jurisdiction over all of Spain, unlike most of the courts that have territorially defined jurisdiction.

The Audiencia Nacional is composed of several courts, one of which, the Penal Court, investigates and prosecutes terrorism and organized crime. The examining magistrate *(juez de instrucción)* oversees the investigation with the help of police investigators assigned to him or her for that purpose. The examining magistrate prepares the proceedings (*sumario*), which contains the state's case against the accused. When the *juez de instrucción* completes the investigation, he or she then remands the case to the appropriate chamber for trial.[54]

[52] Gobierno de España, Consejo de Ministros, "Creado el Centro nacional de coordinación antiterrorista," at http://www.lamoncloa.gob.es/ConsejodeMinistros/Referencias/_2004/c2805040.htm#CNCoordAntiterrorista

[53] Organic Law 4/1988 of May 25, 1988, reforming the Code of Criminal Procedure.

[54] See Spanish Legal System, in Human Rights Watch, "Setting an Example? Counter-Terrorism Measures in Spain," January 2005, at http://hrw.org/reports/2005/spain0105/5.htm.

The most notable case of Islamist terrorism to come before the Audiencia Nacional prior to 3/11 was the prosecution of alleged members of the al-Qaeda cell uncovered in Spain in between November 2001 and July 2002. Judge Baltasar Garzón, known internationally for his indictment of former Chilean strongman Augusto Pinochet, indicted 24 suspects in the proceedings against suspected cell members.[55] Judge Garzón concluded the investigative phase of the process on June 15, 2004; 19 of the defendants were convicted of belonging to or cooperating with al-Qaeda.[56] Judge Garzón also conducted a separate inquiry into the Casablanca bombings of May 16, 2003, which killed 45 people, including four Spanish citizens.

A terrorist plot to attack the Audiencia Nacional with a truck bomb was thwarted in the fall of 2004. The leader was Mohamed Achraf, the recruiter of the Martyrs of Morocco cell (see Chapter 6). According to Judge Garzón, Achraf had made arrangements to acquire 1,000 kilograms of Goma-2 explosives and use at least 500 kilograms in a truck that the terrorists were planning to ram into the court building. The terrorists' goal was to kill the people inside and destroy the court's terrorism records.[57]

## ENHANCED COOPERATION WITHIN THE EU

Europeans increasingly see the threat of violent Islamism as a region-wide, if not global, problem not entirely amenable to national solutions. Nevertheless, European cooperation on counterterrorism has been hampered by the fact that despite the creation of the position of EU anti-terrorism coordinator, counterterrorism policy remains a national responsibility and by what a member of a European intelligence service in a discussion with the author called a "substratum of distrust" among national intelligence agencies that face different problems, use different methods, and respond to different national interests.

The problem of lack of interoperability among the European justice systems is illustrated by the case of the German national of Syrian descent Mamoum Darkazanli, a suspected al-Qaeda operative since the 1990s.

[55] Proceeding 35/2001.

[56] "Quién es quién en el macrojuicio contra célula de al-Qaeda," *El Mundo*, September 26, 2005, at http://www.elmundo.es/elmundo/2005/04/21/espana/1114107834.html.

[57] Kathryn Haahr, "Algerian Salafists and the New Face of Terrorism in Spain," *Terrorism Monitor*, Jamestown Foundation, Vol. 2, Issue 21, May 9, 2005, at http://www.jamestown.org/programs/tm/single/?tx_ttnews[tt_news]=346&tx_ttnews[backPid]=179&no_cache=1#.U5ywCCRBxQY.

After the Madrid bombing, Spanish anti-terrorism magistrate Garzón issued a European arrest warrant for Darkazanli as an "interlocutor and assistant" of Osama bin Laden and his network. In his warrant, Garzón laid out Darkazanli's association with his fellow Syrian, Abu Dahdah, the leader of al-Qaeda's Madrid cell. Darkazanli and Abu Dahdah had lived together in Jordan for a time before settling in Germany and Spain, respectively. However, the Germans took the view that the evidence linking Darkazanli to a specific al-Qaeda attack was insufficient. In July 2005, Germany's constitutional court ruled that Darkazanli could not be extradited to Spain. The judges found that the German legislation approving the European arrest warrant was inconsistent with the German constitution because it deprived suspects of a chance to challenge their deportation. The decision froze the implementation of the European arrest warrant in Germany. Then Justice Minister Brigitte Zypries regarded the court decision as a "blow to the government in its fight against terrorism."[58]

At the EU level, the core of the problem is the lack of an executive mandate for the EU to lead the struggle against terrorism in Europe. The EU's role is limited to promoting consultation and coordination of the counterterrorism activities of member states. The EU lacks the mandate to devise and implement a coherent counterterrorism policy. These limitations are inherent in the structure of the EU.[59]

Within these constraints, a concerted effort has been made to develop instruments and measures to combat terrorism. The implementation of the Conceptual Framework on the European Security and Defense Policy Dimension in the Fight Against Terrorism, including preventive aspects, constitutes a significant step toward the integration of the EU's counterterrorism efforts. The Conceptual Framework specifically states that terrorism can be addressed only by applying the full spectrum of instruments at the disposal of the European Union and its member states. In a departure from the general predisposition in Europe to treat terrorism as largely an intelligence and law enforcement matter, the document lists four scenarios in which military force may be used against terrorism:

[58] Derek Henry Flood, "Germany's Imam Mamoun Darkazanli: al-Qaeda's Alleged Financier and Logistician," *Intelligence Quarterly*,, August 30, 2010, at http://www.intelligencequarterly.com/2010/08/germany%E2%80%99s-imam-mamoun-darkazanli-al-qaedas-alleged-financier-and-logistician/; "The Fight within," *The Economist*, July 21, 2005, at http://www.economist.com/node/4198532.

[59] See Doron Zimmermann, "The European Union and Post-9/11 Counterterrorism: A Reappraisal," *Studies in Conflict and Terrorism*, Vol. 29, No. 2, March-April 2006, for a detailed analysis of EU counterterrorism.

prevention of a looming terrorist attack, using military personnel to protect key civilian targets and the troops themselves, response to attacks, and support to third countries fighting terrorism. Moreover, the Conceptual Framework instructs EU military authorities to include these scenarios in their force planning.[60]

EU-level counterterrorism initiatives include the development of an autonomous intelligence analysis and assessment capability within the Council's Secretariat, the decision to implement the European Arrest Warrant, and the Framework Decision on Joint Investigation Teams, which allow member states to investigate across borders. The implementation of the Framework Decision on Combating Terrorism provides the first common definition of a terrorism offense and provides minimum penalties for terrorism offenses in the EU. In the law enforcement area, the 2004 EU Plan of Action on Combating Terrorism establishes a linkage between Europol,[61] national intelligence agencies, and the European Council's Joint Situation Center (SITCEN). Other initiatives in the Plan of Action include providing the Police Chiefs Task Force (PCTF) with greater operational capability with a focus on proactive intelligence and connecting databases such as the second-generation Schengen Information System (SIS II) with the Visa Information System (VIS) and the European fingerprint database Eurodac.[62] There are still gaps in the lack of biometric identification tools and in comprehensive access to databases by asylum and police authorities, and, of course, concerns still exist about the compatibility of these measures with human rights and data protection considerations.

Intelligence coordination is a critical dimension of counterterrorism. At the intergovernmental level, Madrid was an inflection point, the first successful mass-casualty Islamist terrorist attack in Western Europe. Before Madrid, the response to a request for information from one European intelligence service to another may have been slow and no better than "sufficient" – that is, the cooperating service would provide the information requested but would not volunteer other intelligence. After Madrid, the tendency became to respond more rapidly and interpret the request more expansively to include information that may not have been

[60] European Council, "Conceptual framework on the ESDP dimension of the fight against terrorism," November 2004, at http://www.consilium.europa.eu/uedocs/cmsUpload/14797Conceptual_Framework_ESDP.pdf.

[61] Europol is the European Union law enforcement organization that handles criminal intelligence.

[62] Zimmermann, "The European Union and Post-9/11 Counterterrorism," p. 129.

requested but that, in the view of the cooperating agency, may be helpful to the requesting agency.[63]

At the EU level, the Plan of Action proposes to solicit the support of member states' defense intelligence organizations for the EU's Joint Situation Centre (SITCEN). The EU envisages developing a counterterrorism intelligence capability. To enhance SITCEN's operational role, a proposal has been made to give it a mandate to develop country threat assessments to assist the relevant EU entities with the formulation of policy.[64] At the same time, Brussels encouraged member states to take the lead in some key areas: Spain in the training of religious leaders, Sweden in community policing, Germany in the role of the Internet in radicalization, the Netherlands in the role of local authorities, and the United Kingdom in media and communication strategies.[65]

[63] Rabasa's discussions with Spanish intelligence analysts, 2005.

[64] Zimmermann, "The European Union and Post-9/11 Counterterrorism," pp. 129–130; European Union, "EU Plan of Action on Combating Terrorism – Update," at https://www.legislationline.org/plan/of/action/on/combating/terrorism-update/3cb43d452b2b5f00fc2d367d80d7.pdf.

[65] Interview with EU Anti-Terrorism Coordinator Gilles van de Kerckhove, Brussels, September 2008.

10

# Key Judgments

Europe will continue to face an Islamist terrorist threat for the foreseeable future. However, radical Islamism has important weaknesses, in particular that its appeal is limited to a radicalized fringe of Europe's Muslim communities. It is, therefore, self-limiting but also stable and probably more difficult to eradicate than the violence rooted in Middle East politics that affected Europe in the 1990s.

The risk of radicalization is only weakly related to the integration deficit of Muslim communities in Europe. The first, and least integrated, generation of Muslim residing in Europe produced few Islamist extremists. Many of those involved in violent Islamist extremism were individuals born and educated in Europe or long-term residents of European countries who on the surface appeared to be well integrated but turned against the countries where they resided.

Violent extremists are extreme exceptions among Europe's Muslims. For the minority who become radicalized, the trajectories toward extremism and violence begin with a condition of disaffection or alienation. The circumstances that generated these feelings of disaffection and a search for identity provide a cognitive opening for radical ideas. Extreme Salafi ideologies offer a new identity that allows the individual to identify with an imagined worldwide Muslim community.

The grievances that propel radicalization and violence are largely vicarious in nature. The motivating factors need not be, and often are not, part of the personal experience of the individual. More frequently, radicalization is fostered by narratives of Muslim oppression in areas of conflict outside of Europe. Radicalized European Muslims turn against their countries of birth or residence, which they see as parties to a perceived global conflict between the secular West and Islam.

Networks are critical to the progression from radicalization to terrorism. Radicalization of individuals may lead to discrete acts of violence, but it will be highly unlikely to lead to a sustained campaign of violence in the absence of organized structures that can harness and channel the individual extremist's propensity for violence.

Radical networks are sustained by ideology. While radicalization often involves a combination of factors, including cognitive and environment factors, ideology plays a key role in the construction, maintenance, and dissemination of the radical extremist worldview.

Within the broader European Muslims communities, certain populations appear to be more vulnerable than others to radicalization and recruitment into terrorist groups: second- and third-generation British Muslims of Pakistani ancestry, first- or second-generation North Africans settled on the Continent, and converts. Turks are a traditional community that appears to be undergoing a process of radicalization. Since about 2007, links have developed between Somalis residing in Europe and extremist groups in Somalia. In all of these communities, young men are particularly vulnerable to radicalization and recruitment into terrorist groups. The armed conflict in Syria presents a clear and present danger to Europe, as well as to the United States and Canada as a source of radicalization and recruitment of Western residents into transnational terrorist networks.

The radicalization of second- and third-generation Muslims in countries with established Muslim communities is of particular concern not only because it signals a profound rejection of societal values by individuals raised and educated in the West but also because these individuals present a difficult counterterrorism challenge. This development also represents a global threat, to the extent that Europe becomes a vector of terrorist attacks in other regions.

Although there is no question that the Internet plays an increasingly important role in disseminating radical Islamist narratives, the transition from radicalization to terrorism almost always takes place in face-to-face encounters and very seldom on the Internet, although the first contact may be made online.

After 9/11 and the Madrid and London bombings, Islamist terrorists in Europe have confronted and adapted to a less permissive environment. One emerging pattern is the development of new kinds of networks, including decentralized and mixed networks in which militants previously part of traditional networks mix with al-Qaeda logistics and operations personnel.

The new decentralized networks can be effective in maintaining the anonymity of its members, but they can be potentially vulnerable because they can be penetrated more easily than the old hierarchical networks. The social networks of the terrorists and their supporters can mitigate this vulnerability. These social networks are central to the survival of the jihadist system.

Islamist terrorism has an important global dimension. Many of the terrorist incidents described as cases of homegrown terrorism turn out, on closer examination, to have linkages to al-Qaeda or associated groups in Pakistan, the Middle East, Central Asia, and East Africa. What the examination of these incidents shows is not just the radicalization of European Muslims but their incorporation into broad-ranging international conspiracies.

European governments and publics have reacted to the escalation of Islamist terrorist attacks in Europe with greater vigilance, enhanced international cooperation, reduced tolerance of overt extremist activity, and attempts (with varying degrees of success) to strengthen domestic counterterrorist legislation. At the core of the new European approaches are efforts to move beyond police and security approaches by addressing the factors that encourage and facilitate recruitment into terrorist groups. Some European governments have also begun to encourage and support deradicalization initiatives – that is, programs to facilitate the exit of militants from extremist groups.

European societies have important social resources, some of them still underutilized, to reduce the risk of radicalization. Moderate Muslim organizations and Muslim intellectuals and community leaders who are well acquainted with and supportive of liberal Western values and institutions are one. An emerging multicultural youth culture in Muslim communities is another. Although as noted earlier, there is no simple relationship between the integration deficit in Muslim communities in Europe and radicalization; over the long term, more cohesive societies would present fewer risks of radicalization. Reaching this point will require difficult adjustments on the part of both the Muslim communities expected to adjust to the norms and values of their countries of residence and the societies that regarded them in the first place as immigrants and strangers.[1]

## EUROPE'S LESSONS FOR THE UNITED STATES

By any measure, the United States has been successful in integrating its Muslim population. Part of the reason is the structure of the Muslim population in the United States, which is quite different from that in Europe. The

[1] Sociology of Islam list, Conversation: Muslims in Europe, January 13, 2010, at http://www.lists.pdx.edu/lists/listinfo/sociology_of_islam.

size of the Muslim American population is difficult to measure because the U.S. census does not track religious affiliation. Estimates vary widely from 2 million to 7 million. The Muslim American population has been growing rapidly as a result of immigration, a high birthrate, and conversions.[2] Though heavily concentrated in metropolitan areas, a enumeration of religious bodies by counties found Muslims present in all 50 states and the District of Columbia.[3] U.S. Muslims are well educated – a majority are college graduates – and have annual incomes above $50,000.[4] The opportunities for economic, educational, and social advancement available in the United States go a long way in explaining the relative absence (in comparison to Europe), until 2009, of Islamist terrorist plots and attacks in the United States.

Since 2009, the tempo of these plots and attacks appeared to have intensified. These included the Fort Hood shooting by Maj. Nidal Malik Hasan, which left 13 dead and 30 injured; the June 1, 2009, shooting by Muslim convert Abdulhakim Mujahid Muhammed, formerly known as Carlos Bledsoe, at a U.S. Army/Navy recruiting center in Little Rock, Arkansas, which left one person dead; Najibullah Zazi's Denver/New York City plot allegedly to attack commuter trains with improvised explosive devices;[5] the attempt to attack the Paul Findley Federal Building in Springfield, Illinois, with what would-be bomber Michael Finton, aka Talib Islam, believed to be one ton of explosives packed in a van;[6] the North Carolina cell's plan to attack the U.S. Marine base at Quantico, Virginia;[7] the plot by four Muslim converts to attack Jewish centers in the Bronx and to shoot down an Air

[2] Embassy of the United States Baghdad, "Muslims in America – a statistical portrait," at http://iraq.usembassy.gov/resources/information/current/american/statistical.html.

[3] Dale E. Jones, Sherri Doty, Clifford Grammich, James E. Horsch, Richard Houseal, Mac Lynn, John P. Marcum, Kenneth M. Sanchagrin, and Richard H. Taylor, *Religious Congregations and Membership in the United States, 2000*. Nashville, TN: Glenmary Research Center, 2002.

[4] Project MAPS and Zogby International, *American Muslim Poll 2004*, October 2004, online at http://www.cippusa.com/wp-content/uploads/2013/10/MAPS-Shifting-political-winds.pdf.

[5] Zazi has been charged with conspiracy to use weapons of mass destruction.

[6] Madeleine Gruen,"Attempt to Attack the Paul Findley Federal Building in Springfield, Illinois," NEFA Foundation Report #23 in "Target America" Series, December 17, 2009, at http://www.defenddemocracy.org/media-hit/attempt-to-attack-the-paul-findley-federal-building-in-springfield-illinois/.

[7] Eight individuals were charged with conspiracy to provide material support to terrorists, as well as conspiracy to murder persons abroad. Some face additional charges. They are Daniel Patrick Boyd (aka "Saifullah"), 39, a U.S. citizen and North Carolina resident; Zakariya Boyd (aka "Zak"), 20, a U.S. citizen and North Carolina resident and Daniel Boyd's son; Dylan Boyd, 22, a U.S. citizen and North Carolina resident and Daniel Boyd's son; Hysen Sherifi, 24, a native of Kosovo and a U.S. legal permanent resident living in North Carolina; Anes Subasic, 33, a naturalized U.S. citizen and North Carolina resident; Mohammad Omar Aly Hassan, 22, a U.S. citizen and North Carolina resident; Ziyad Yaghi, 21, a U.S. citizen and North Carolina resident; and Jude Kenan Mohammad, 21, a U.S. citizen believed to be in Pakistan. "The

National Guard aircraft in Newburgh, New York, using a surface-to-air missile (SAM); the discovery of explosive materials in the trunk of a car in Goose Creek, South Carolina, driven by two Egyptian nationals who were studying engineering at the University of South Florida, and most deadly of all, the Boston marathon bombing of April 15, 2013, and the subsequent shootings, which resulted in 5 killed and 280 injured people.

This spike in terrorist plots and attacks suggests that the United States faces many of the same challenges as Europe in preventing Islamist terrorism. As the Hudson Institute's Hillel Fradkin noted, the American Muslim community, like other minority Muslim communities, is at risk of having the radicals define the framework for the interpretation of Islam. Some among the American Muslims, like their European counterparts, feel uprooted from their traditional way of life and are in search of a new identity. Radicals are happy to offer this in their vision of a unified and defiant global *umma*.[8]

This risk is enhanced by the presence in American society of some of the same features that facilitate the spread of Islamist extremism in Europe and by externalities such as the external funding of mosques and Islamic schools and institutions in the United States. A Freedom House study documented the continued propagation of intolerant ideology in a dozen American mosques and Islamic study centers.[9] The European experience so far may be instructive in confronting this danger. The United States and Europe can learn from the successes and failures of their respective approaches, and a more effective approach might emerge from the critical examination of the U.S. and European experiences. Although some aspects of counter-terrorism legislation in European states are not applicable to the United States, with its very different legal system and political culture, the United States could explore the European model of a special counter-terrorist legal regime as an alternative to federal courts, military commissions, or indefinite detentions of suspected foreign terrorists. The bottom line is that, as is largely understood in Europe, terrorists are neither criminals nor legal combatants, but a distinct category of threat, and that there may be experiences in the European's adaptation of their legal frameworks to deal with terrorist threats that may be of value to the United States as Americans struggle to adapt their legal system to the realities of global terrorism.

North Carolina Jihad Cell and the Quantico Marine Base Plot," NEFA Foundation, November 2009, at http://www.orgsites.com/va/asis151/QuanticoJihadCellPlot.pdf.

[8] Hillel Fradkin, "America in Islam," *The Public Interest*, Spring 2004.

[9] Freedom House, Center for Religious Freedom, "Saudi Publications on Hate Ideology Fill American Mosques," 2005, at http://www.freedomhouse.org/sites/default/files/inline_images/Saudi%20Publications%20on%20Hate%20Ideology%20Invade%20American%20Mosques.pdf.

# Bibliography


Aaron, David, *In Their Own Words: Voices of Jihad*. Santa Monica, CA: RAND Corporation, MG-602-RC, 2008.

Abadie, Alberto, "Poverty, Political Freedom, and the Roots of Terrorism," *The American Economic Review*, Vol. 96, No. 2, May 2006.

Abedin, Mahan, "Al-Muhajiroun in the UK: An Interview with Sheikh Omar Bakri Mohammed," *Spotlight on Terror*, The Jamestown Foundation, Vol. 2, No. 5, March 23, 2004.

"Inside Hizb ut-Tahrir: An Interview with Jalaluddin Patel, Leader of Hizb ut-Tahrir in the UK," *Spotlight on Terror*, The Jamestown Foundation Vol. 2, No. 8, August 11, 2004.

Aboul-Enein, Youssef H. and Sherifa Zuhur, "Islamic Rulings on Warfare," Strategic Studies Institute (SSI), Army War College, October 2004.

"Abu Musab al-Suri's Final 'Message to the British and the Europeans,'" August 2005, Global Terror Alert, at http://www.globalterroralert.com.

Agenzia Fides, "Spain and Islam," at http://www.fides.org/eng/dossier/2005/espana_islamo5.html.

Ahmad, Iftikhar, "Broken Britain," London School of Islamics, March 21, 2010, at www.politic.co.uk/15667-broken-britain.html.

Ahmed, Houriya and Hanna Stuart, "Hizb ut-Tahrir: Ideology and Strategy," The Centre for Social Cohesion, London, 2009.

"Al-Qaeda 'groomed Abdulmutallab in London'" *The Times*, December 30, 2009.

Algemene Inlichtingen- en Veiligheidsdienst (AIVD), General Intelligence and Security Service, Ministry of the Interior and Kingdom Relations of the Netherlands, "From Dawa to Jihad: The Various Threats from Radical Islam to the Democratic Legal Order," The Hague: December 2004.

"Recruitment for the Jihad in the Netherlands – from Incident to Trend," The Hague: December 2002.

Allen, Charles E., Assistant Secretary for Intelligence and Analysis/Chief Intelligence Officer, Department of Homeland Security, "Threat of Islamic Radicalization to the Homeland," Written testimony to the U.S. Senate

Committee on Homeland Security and Governmental Affairs, March 14, 2007.
"Al-Qaradhawi Speaks in Favor of Suicide Operations at an Islamic Conference in Sweden," MEMRI Special Dispatch Series, No. 542, July 24, 2003, at http://www.memri.org/bin/articles.cgi?Area=sd&ID=SP54203.
Amghar, Samir, "Les Salafistes Français: une Nouvelle Aristocratie Religieuse?" *Maghreb-Machrek*, No. 183, Spring 2005.
Anonymous [Michael Scheuer], *Imperial Hubris: Why the West Is Losing the War on Terror*. Washington, DC: Brassey's Inc., 2004.
*Through Our Enemies' Eyes, Osama Bin Laden, Radical Islam and the Future of America*. London: Brassey's Inc., 2002.
Athena Intelligence, Movimientos musulmanes y prevención del yihadismo en España: La Yama'a Al-Tabligh Al-Da'wa," Athena Paper, Vol. 2 No. 1, Artículo 4, March 27, 2007, at www.athenaintelligence.org.
Atran, Scott, "Mishandling Suicide Terrorism," *The Washington Quarterly*, Vol. 27, No. 3, 2004.
Aust, Stefan, *The Baader-Meinhof Group: The Inside Story of a Phenomenon*, translated by Anthea Bell. Topsfield, MA: The Bodley Head/Salem House, 1988.
Auster, Lawrence, "The Search for Moderate Islam," *Front Page Magazine*, January 28, 2005. As of December 29, 2008, at http://www.frontpagemag.com/Articles/Read.aspx?GUID=5F4D7BB5-CA89-4C09-986B-67CF241C2098.
Bakker, Edwin, "Jihadi Terrorists in Europe: Their Characteristics and the Circumstances in Which They Joined the Jihad: An Exploratory Study," The Hague: Netherlands Institute of International Relations Clingendael, December 2006.
Bale, Jeffrey, "Jihadist Cells and 'I.E.D.' Capabilities in Europe: Assessing the Present and Future Threat to the West," Monterey, CA: Monterey Institute of International Studies, May 2009.
"Hiding in Plain Sight in Londonistan," in Michael A. Innes, ed., *Denial of Sanctuary: Understanding Terrorist Safe Havens*, New York: Praeger, 2007.
Bandura, Albert, *Aggression: A Social Learning Analysis*. New York: Prentice Hall, 1973.
"Mechanisms of Moral Disengagement," in Walter Reich, ed., *Origins of Terrorism: Psychologies, Ideologies, Theologies, States of Mind*, Washington, D.C.: Woodrow Wilson Center Press, 1998.
*Social Foundations of Thought and Action: A Social Cognitive Theory*. Englewood Cliffs, NJ: Prentice-Hall, 1986.
Bar, Shmuel, *Warrants for Terror: The Fatwas of Radical Islam and the Duty to Jihad*. Lanham, MD: Rowman & Littlefield Publishers, 2006.
Bensinger, Gad J., "Law Enforcement and Counterterrorism in Post-9/11 Germany," *Crime and Justice International Magazine*, Sam Houston University, at http://www.cjimagazine.com/content/view/226/2/.
Berlin-Institut für Bevölkerung und Entwicklung, "Ungenutzte Potenziale," January 2008, at http://www.berlin-institut.org/studien/ungenutzte-potenziale.html.
Bjørgo, Tore, ed., *Root Causes of Terrorism: Myths, Reality and Ways Forward*. London: Routledge, 2005.

Blomberg, S. Brock, Gregory D. Hess, and Akila Weerapana, "An Economic Model of Terrorism," *Conflict Management and Peace Science*, Vol. 21, 2004.
Bloom, Mia, *Dying to Kill: Allure of Suicide Terror*. New York: Columbia University Press, 2005.
"Bosnian War Crimes Defendant Blames Al-Qaeda," October 6, 2008, at http://www.ww4report.com/node/6122.
Boucek, Christopher, "Extremist Reeducation and Rehabilitation in Saudi Arabia," *Terrorism Monitor*, Vol. 5, No. 16, August 16, 2007
Brandon, James, *Unlocking Al-Qaeda: Islamist Extremism in British Prisons*. London: Quilliam Foundation, November 2009.
*Virtual Caliphate: Islamic Extremists and Their Websites*. London: Centre for Social Cohesion, 2008.
Brandon, James, and Salam Hafez, *Crimes of the Community: Honour-Based Violence in the UK*. London: Centre for Social Cohesion, at http://www.socialcohesion.co.uk./files/1228233433_1.pdf.
Brandt, Andrea, and Cordula Meyer, "Muslim Parallel Society Develops in Germany," *Der Spiegel*, February 24, 2007.
Brettfeld, Katrin, and Peter Wetzels, *Muslime in Deutschland: Integration, Integrationsbarrieren, Religion sowie Einstellungen zu Demokratie, Rechtsstaat und politisch-religiös motivierter Gewalt*, Berlin: Bundesministerium des Innern, 2007
"British Muslim Convert Jailed for Terrorism Offences," *The Guardian* (UK), September 24, 2005, at http://www.guardian.co.uk/uk/2005/sep/24/terrorism.politics.
Brodeur, Jean-Paul, "High Policing and Low Policing: Remarks about the Policing of Political Activities," *Social Problems*, Vol. 30, 1983, pp. 507–520.
Brouwer, Marina, "Ethnic Divide in Dutch Schools," *Current Affairs*, August 28, 2003.
Bruguière, Jean-Louis, "The US and Europe: Confronting Terrorism," January 28, 2009, at http://ambafrance-us.org/spip.php?article1244.
Bundesministerium des Innern (Germany), *Extremismus in Deutschland. Erscheinungsformen und aktuelle Bestandsaufnahme*, 2004.
Burke, Jason, et al., "Run to Ground: The Biggest Police Operation in British History Reached a Dramatic Climax on Live Television," *The Observer*, July 31, 2005, at www.guardian.co.uk/print/0,3858,5252149-117079,00.html.
Byman, Daniel, *The Five Front War: The Better Way to Fight Global Jihad*. Hoboken, NJ: John Wiley & Sons, 2008.
Caldwell, Christopher, "The Dutch Rethink Multiculturalism," *The Weekly Standard*, December 27, 2004.
Callaway, Rhonda L., and Julie Harrelson-Stephens, "Toward a Theory of Terrorism: Human Security as a Determinant of Terrorism," *Studies in Conflict & Terrorism*, Vol. 29, 2006.
Chai, Sun-Ki, "An Organizational Economics Theory of Antigovernment Violence," *Comparative Politics*, Vol. 26, No. 1, October 1993.
Chalk, Peter, and William Rosenau, *Confronting the "Enemy Within" Security Intelligence, the Police, and Counterterrorism in Four Democracies*. Santa Monica, CA: RAND Corporation, MG-100-RC, 2004.

Chenoweth, Erica, "Why It Matters that Bin Laden Was Behind Recent Terrorist Plots," May 7, 2011, at http://themonkeycage.org.

Combs, Cindy C., *Terrorism in the 21st Century*. Upper Saddle River, NJ: Prentice Hall, 2003.

Comisión de Investigación sobre los Atentados del 11-M, Proyecto de Dictámen, June 8, 2005.

Council of Europe, Parliamentary Assembly, Political Affairs Committee, "European Muslim Communities Confronted with Extremism," Doc. 11540, March 27, 2008, at http://assembly.coe.int/Main.asp?link=/Documents/WorkingDocs/Doc08/EDOC11540.htm.

Cragin, Kim, and Peter Chalk, *Terrorism and Development: Using Social and Economic Development to Inhibit a Resurgence of Terrorism*. Santa Monica, CA: RAND Corporation, 2003.

Crenshaw, Martha, "The Debate over 'New' vs. 'Old' Terrorism," paper presented at the Annual Meeting of the American Political Science Association, Chicago, August 30–September 2, 2007.

"The Logic of Terrorism: Terrorist Behavior as a Product of Strategic Choice," in Walter Reich, ed., *Origins of Terrorism: Psychologies, Ideologies, Theologies, States of Mind*. Washington, DC: Woodrow Wilson Center Press, 1998a.

"Questions to Be Answered, Research to Be Done, Knowledge to Be Applied," in Walter Reich, ed., *Origins of Terrorism: Psychologies, Ideologies, Theologies, States of Mind*. Washington, DC: Woodrow Wilson Center Press, 1998b.

Crenshaw, Martha, ed., *Terrorism in Context*, 2nd ed., University Park: Pennsylvania State University Press, 2001.

Cronin, Audrey Kurth, *How Terrorism Ends: Understanding the Decline and Demise of Terrorist Campaigns*. Princeton: Princeton University Press, 2009.

Cruickshank, Paul, "Love in the Time of Terror," *Marie Claire*, May 15, 2009, at http://www.marieclaire.com/world-reports/news/international/malika-el-aroud-female-terrorist.

Cuthbertson, Ian M., "Prisons and the Education of Terrorists," *World Policy Journal*, Vol. 21, No. 3, Fall 2004, at http://www.worldpolicy.org/journal/articles/wpj04-3/Cuthbertson.html.

Dalrymple, Theodore, "Why Theo Van Gogh Was Murdered," *City Journal*, November 15, 2004, at http://www.city-journal.org/html/eon_11_1504td.html.

Dassa Kaye, Dalia, Frederic Wehrey, Audra K. Grant, and Dale Stahl, *More Freedom, Less Terror? Liberalization and Political Violence in the Arab World*, Santa Monica, CA: RAND Corporation, 2008.

Delgado, Fernando, "Los reclutadores son de mediana edad y gozan de gran respeto," *Actualidad Terrorismo Yihadista*/25, at www.fundacionvt.org.

Della Porta, Donatella, "Recruitment Processes in Clandestine Political Organizations: Italian Left-Wing Terrorism," *International Social Movement Research*, Vol. 1, 1988.

*Social Movements, Political Violence, & the State*. Cambridge, UK: Cambridge University Press, 1995.

Dia, Guido, "Diese Macho Türken, Hintergründe eines Kulturphänomens," *CUS*, 1996, at http://homepages.teuto.net/cus/Dia.html.

"Doctors Asked to Identify Potential Terrorists under Government Plans," *The Guardian*, June 6, 2011, at http://www.guardian.co.uk/politics/2011/jun/06/doctors-identify-potential-terrorists-plans.

Dodd, Vikram, Richard Norton-Taylor, and Paul Harris, "Cargo Plane Bomb Found in Britain Was Primed to Blow Up over US," *The Guardian*, November 10, 2010, at http://www.guardian.co.uk/world/2010/nov/10/cargo-plane-bomb-us-alqaida.

Donadieu, Gerard, "Vers un Marché du Religieux, le Nouveau Paysage du Croire," *Futuribles*, No. 260, January 2001.

Dunham Scott, Diana, "Social Network Analysis of British Jihadists," Pardee RAND Graduate School, Santa Monica, CA, 2012 (unpublished).

Dworkin, Anthony, "The London Terror Bombs: Were They a Crime or Act of War?" *Crimes of War Project*, July 11, 2005, at http://www.crimesofwar.org/onnews/news-london.html.

Ehrlich, Paul R., and Jianguo Liu, "Some Roots of Terrorism," *Population and Environment*, Vol. 24, No. 2, November 2002.

Engene, Jan Oskar, *Patterns of Terrorism in Western Europe, 1950–95*, Ph.D. thesis, 1998, Bergen, Norway: University of Bergen.

Escobar Stemmann, Juan José, "El Salafismo en Europa," *Política Exterior*, Vol. 19, No. 105, May/June 2005.

Eubank, William Lee, and Leonard Weinberg, "Does Democracy Encourage Terrorism?" *Terrorism and Political Violence*, Vol. 6, No. 4, 1994.

Eubank, William Lee, and Leonard Weinberg, "Terrorism and Democracy: What Recent Events Disclose," *Terrorism and Political Violence*, Vol. 10, No. 1, 1998.

Eubank, William Lee, and Leonard Weinberg, "Terrorism and Democracy: Perpetrators and Victims," *Terrorism and Political Violence*, Vol. 13, No. 1, 2001.

Eyerman, Joe, "Terrorism and Democratic States: Soft Targets or Accessible Systems?" *International Interactions*, Vol. 24, No. 2, 1998.

Farouky, Jumana, "Profiling the Suspects: Converts to Islam," *Time*, August 11, 2006, at http://www.time.com/time/world/article/0,8599,1225687,00.html.

Federal Republic of Germany, Federal Statistical Office, 2005, at http://www.destatis.de/basis/e/bevoe/bev_bsp_t3.htm.

Fernández, Haizam Amirah, "El M-11 en la estrategia yihadista," *Real Instituto Elcano* (Madrid), Publicaciones, July 15, 2004, at http://www.realinstitutoelcano.org/default.asp.

Fernandez, Roberto, and Doug McAdam, "Multiorganizational Fields and Recruitment to Social Movements," in Bert Klandermans, ed., *Organizing for Change: Social Movement Organizations in Europe and the United States*, Greenwich, Conn.: JAI Press, 1989.

"Field Agents Facing the Phenomenon of Radicalization," EU French Presidency Seminar, November 5, 2008, at http://www.ue2008.fr/PFUE/cache/offonce/lang/en/accueil/PFUE-09_2008/PFUE-29.09.2008/seminaire_les_acteurs_de_terrain_confrontes_au_phenomene_de_radicalisation;jsessionid=A1C5FD7D0E67C790A77CC188545oDE07.

Flood, Derek Henry, "Germany's Imam Mamoun Darkazanli: Al-Qaeda's Alleged Financier and Logistician," Jamestown Foundation, August 27, 2010

Fouda, Yosri, and Nick Fielding, *Masterminds of Terror: The Truth Behind the Most Devastating Terrorist Attack the World Has Ever Seen*. London: Mainstream Publishing, 2003.

Fradkin, Hillel, "America in Islam," *The Public Interest*, Spring 2004.

Friedman, Thomas, "An Islamic Reformation," *New York Times*, December 4, 2002, at http://query.nytimes.com/gst/fullpage.html?res=9D05EED7173BF937A357 51C1A9649C8B63.

Fromm, Rainer, and Frank Wolfgang Sonntag, "Radikale Islamisten in Deutschland," FAKT, *MDR Magazin*, November 24, 2003.

Fuchs, Dale, "Spain Days Bombers Drank Water from Mecca and Sold Drugs," *New York Times*, April 15, 2004, at http://query.nytimes.com/gst/fullpage.html ?res=9C02E6DB143BF936A25757C0A9629C8B63.

Galiacho, Juan Luis, "Mohamed El Egipcio, El Pintor De La Brocha Gorda," *E-Defensor*, June 2004, at http://www.e-defensor.com/secciones/firmas/galia cho/junio04/firma(21-06).asp

Gelvin, James L., "Al-Qaeda and Anarchism: A Historian's Reply to Terrorology," 2007, at http://www.international.ucla.edu/cms/files/JamesGelvin.pdf.

Gennadi, Jewstafjew, "Aufgabe Nicht Erfullt, Al Kaida Besteht Weiter," at http:// russlandonline.ru/

Gerholm, Thomas, and Yngve George Litham, eds., *The New Islamic Presence in Europe*. London: Mansell, 1988.

Gillan, Audrey, "Four suspects said to have worshipped at Finsbury Park Mosque," *Guardian.co.uk*, August 1, 2005, at www.guardian.co.uk/attack onlondon/story/0,16132,1540243,00.html.

Gilligan, Andrew, "Inextricably Linked to Controversial Mosque: The Secret World of IFE," *The Telegraph*, February 28, 2010.

Goetz John, and Holger Stark, "CIA Had Secret Plan to Kidnap German-Syrian Suspect in Hamburg," *Spiegel Online International*, January 12, 2010.

Gruen, Arno, *Der Kampf um die Demokratie, Der Extremismus, die Gewalt und der Terror*. Stuttgart: Klett-Cotta, 2002.

Grupo Parlamentario Socialista, Proyecto de Dictamen de la Comisión de Investigación Sobre los Atentados del 11-M, Madrid, June 8, 2005.

Gunaratna, Rohan, *Inside Al Qaeda: Global Network of Terror*. New York: Columbia University Press, 2002.

"Spain: An al Qaeda Hub?" UNISCI Discussion Papers, May 2004, at http:// www.ucm.es/info/unisci/Rohan2.pdf.

"Strategic Counter-Terrorism: Getting Ahead of Terrorism, Part II: The Ideological Response," The Jebsen Center for Counter-Terrorism Studies Research Briefing Series, Vol. 2, No. 2, November 2007.

Gupta, Dipak K., *The Economics of Political Violence: The Effect of Political Instability on Economic Growth*. New York: Praeger Publishers, 1990.

*Socio-Economic Costs of Unemployment and Income Inequality: A Cross National Study, 1948–67*, Ph.D. thesis, University of Pittsburgh.

"Accounting for the Waves of International Terrorism," *Perspectives on Terrorism*, Vol. 2, Issue 11, August 2008.

*Understanding Terrorism and Political Violence*, London and New York: Routledge, 2008.

Gurr, Ted Robert, "Terrorism in Democracies: Its Social and Political Biases," in Walter Reich, ed., *Origins of Terrorism: Psychologies, Ideologies, Theologies, States of Mind*, Washington, DC: Woodrow Wilson Center Press, 1998.

"Terrorism in Democracies: When It Occurs, Why It Fails," in Charles W. Kegley Jr., ed., *The New Global Terrorism: Characteristics, Causes, Controls*, Upper Saddle River, NJ: Prentice Hall, 2003.

*Why Men Rebel*. Princeton, NJ: Princeton University Press, 1970.

Gutiérrez, José Antonio, Javier Jordán, and Humberto Trujillo, "Prevención de la radicalización yihadista en las prisiones españolas," *Athena Intelligence Journal*, Vol. 3, No. 1, 2008, at www.adecaf.com/altres/mespres/mespres/islamprisiones.pdf"

Haahr-Escolano, Kathryn, "Algerian Salafists and the New Face of Terrorism in Spain," *Terrorism Monitor*, Jamestown Foundation, Vol. 2, Issue 21, November 4, 2004, at http://www.jamestown.org/terrorism/news/article.php?issue_id=3131

"GSPC in Italy: The Forward Base of Jihad in Europe," *Terrorism Monitor*, The Jamestown Foundation, Vol. 4, Issue 3, February 9, 2006.

Haddad, Yvonne Yazbeck, and Michael J. Balz, "Taming the Imams: European Governments and Islamic Preachers since 9/11," *Islam and Christian-Muslim Relations*, Vol. 19, No. 2, 2008.

Hashmi, Sohail H., ed., *Islamic Political Ethics: Civil Society, Pluralism, and Conflict*. Princeton, NJ: Princeton University Press, 2002.

Hegghammer, Thomas, "The Case for Chasing al-Awlaki," The Middle East Channel, *Foreign Policy*, November 24, 2010, at http://mideast.foreignpolicy.com/posts/2010/11/24/the_case_for_chasing_al_awlaki.

"Guest Post: The Story of Eric Breininger," *Jihadica*, May 11, 2010.

"Saudi and Yemeni Branches of al-Qaida Unite," *Jihadica*, January 24, 2009, at http://www.jihadica.com/saudi-and-yemeni-branches-of-al-qaida-unite/.

Heitmeyer, Wilhelm, Joachim Müller, and Helmut Schröder, *Verlockender Fundamentalismus: Türkische Jugendliche in Deutschland*. Frankfurt: Suhrkamp, 1997.

Helqvist, Iben, and Elizabeth Sebian, "Islam in Denmark," at www.euro-islam.info/country-profiles/denmark/.

Helsinki Federation for Human Rights, "Europa: Bericht zur Diskriminierung von Muslimen nach dem 11. September 2001," Newsletter Migration und Bevoelkerung April 2005. Online at http://www.network-migration.org/miginfo/migration_und_bevoelkerung_artikel/0503.

Hengst, Björn, and Christoph Scheuermann, "Hamburg Hate Preachers Lose Their Home," *Spiegel Online International*, August 9, 2010, at www.spiegel.de/international/germany/0,1518,710952,00.html.

Hennessy, Patrick, and Melissa Kite, "Poll reveals 40pc of Muslims want sharia law in UK," *Daily Telegraph*, February 20, 2006, at http://www.telegraph.co.uk/news/main.jhtml?xml=/news/2006/02/19/nsharia19.xml.

HM Government, *Countering International Terrorism: The United Kingdom's Strategy*. London, July 2006.

*Pursue Prevent Protect Prepare: The United Kingdom's Strategy for Countering International Terrorism*. London, March 2009.

*Channel: Supporting Individuals Vulnerable to Recruitment by Violent Extremists*. London, March 2010.

HM Government, Department for Communities and Local Government, *Building Community Resilience: Prevent Case Studies*. London, December 2009.

HM Government, Home Office, Prevent Strategy 2011, at www.homeoffice.gov.uk/counter-terrorism/.

HM Inspectorate of Constabulary, Audit Commission, "Preventing Violent Extremism, Learning and Development Exercise: Report to the Home Office and Communities and Local Government," London, October 2008.

Hoffman, Bruce, *Inside Terrorism*. New York: Columbia University Press, 1998.

"The Myth of Grass-Roots Terrorism: Why Osama Bin Laden Still Matters," *Foreign Affairs*, May/June 2008.

Hoffman, Bruce, and Gordon H. McCormick, "Terrorism, Signaling, and Suicide Attack," *Studies in Conflict & Terrorism*, Vol. 27, No. 4, 2004.

Horgan, John, "Understanding Terrorist Motivation: A Socio-Psychological Perspective," in Magnus Ranstorp, ed., *Mapping Terrorism Research: State of the Art, Gaps and Future Direction*. London and New York: Routledge, 2007.

Horton, Michael, "Al-Qaeda in the Arabian Peninsula: Challenges and Opportunities in Revolutionary Yemen," *Terrorism Monitor*, Jamestown Foundation, Vol. 9, Issue 16, April 12, 2011.

Human Rights Watch, "Setting an Example? Counter-Terrorism Measures in Spain," Spanish Legal System in Human Rights Watch, January 26, 2005, at http://www.hrw.org/en/reports/2005/01/26/setting-example-0.

Hunter, Shireen, ed., *Islam, Europe's Second Religion*. Westport, CT, and London: Praeger, 2002.

Iannaccone, Laurance, "Vodoo Economics? Reviewing the Rational Choice Approach to Religion," *Journal for the Scientific Study of Religion*, Vol. 34, No. 1, 1995.

Institut de Relations Internationales et Stratégiques (IRIS), "Actes de colloque: l'Europe face au terrorisme,'" March 8, 2005, at http://www.iris-france.org/docs/pdf/actes/livre-terrorisme-FR.pdf.

Institut National de la Statistique et des Études Économiques (INSEE), "Recensement de la Population: Mar 1999 Les Resultats," March 1999, at http://www.recensement.insee.fr:8081/CSV/A464.zip.

"Recensement de la Population: Mar 1999 Les Resultats: Table NAT2," March 1999, at http://www.recensement.insee.fr/EN/ST_ANA/F2/NATALLNAT2ANAT2A2F2EN.html.

"Recensement de la Population: Mar 1999 Les Resultats: Table NAT3," March 1999, at http://www.recensement.insee.fr/EN/ST_ANA/F2/NATALLNAT3ANAT3A4F2EN.html.

*Etude de l'Histoire Familiale*, 1999.

"Islamisten Planten Anschläge in Deutschland," *DPA*, July 28, 2005, at http://www.nordaktuell.de/dpa/html/politik-in/43Islamisten_planten_Anschlaege_in_Deutschlan.shtml.

Jenkins, Brian Michael, *Countering al Qaeda: An Appreciation of the Situation and Suggestions for Strategy*. Santa Monica, CA: RAND Corporation, 2002.

*Unconquerable Nation: Knowing Our Enemy, Strengthening Ourselves*. Santa Monica, CA: RAND Corporation, 2006.

*Will Terrorists Go Nuclear?* Amherst, NY: Prometheus Books, 2008.

Jensen, Michael Taarnby, "Jihad in Denmark: An Overview and Analysis of Jihadi Activity in Denmark 1990–2006," DIIS Working Papers, Vol. 2006, Issue 35. Copenhagen, Denmark: Danish Institute for International Studies (DIIS), November 2006.

Johnson, James Turner, "Jihad and Just War," *First Things*, Vol. 124 (June/ July 2002).

Jones, Seth, and Martin C. Libicki, *How Terrorist Groups End: Lessons for Countering al Qa'ida*, RAND Corporation, MG741, Santa Monica, CA: RAND Corporation, 2008.

Jordán, Javier, "Las redes de terrorismo islamista en España y perspectives de futuro," Real Instituto Elcano (Madrid), ARI No. 119, 2003.

"El terrorismo yihadista en España: evolución después del 11-M," Real Instituto Elcano (Madrid), Documento de Trabajo No. 7/2009.

Jordán, Javier, and Robert Wesley, "After 3/11: The Evolution of Jihadist Networks in Spain," *Terrorism Monitor*, The Jamestown Foundation, Vol. 4, Issue 1, January 12, 2006.

Jordán, Javier, and Nicola Horsburgh, "Spain and Islamist Terrorism: Analysis of the Threat and Response 1995–2005," *Mediterranean Politics*, Vol. 11, No. 2, 2006.

Jordán, Javier, Fernando M. Mañas, and Nicola Horsburgh, "Strengths and Weaknesses of Grassroot Jihadist Networks: The Madrid Bombings," *Studies in Conflict & Terrorism*, Vol. 31, No. 1, 2008.

Juergensmeyer, Mark, *Terror in the Mind of God: The Global Rise of Religious Violence*. Berkeley, CA: University of California Press, 2003.

Juzgado Central de Instrucción No. 005, Madrid, Sumario (Proc. Ordinario) 0000035/2001E.

Karstedt-Henke, Sabine, "Theorien zur Erklärung terroristischer Bewegungen," in E. Blankenberg, ed., *Politik der inneren Sicherheit*, 1980.

Kaye, Dalia Dassa, Frederic Wehrey, Audra K. Grant, and Dale Stahl, *More Freedom, Less Terror? Liberalization and Political Violence in the Arab World*, Santa Monica: RAND Corporation, 2008.

Kegley, Charles W., *The New Global Terrorism: Characteristics, Causes, Controls*. Englewood Cliffs, NJ: Prentice Hall, 2002.

Kepel, Gilles, and Anthony Roberts, *Jihad: The Trail of Political Islam*, Cambridge, MA: Belknap Press, 2003.

Kfir, Isaac, "British Middle East Policy: The Counterterrorism Dimension," *MERIA Journal*, Vol. 10, No. 4, December 2006.

Khan, Mohammed, and Carlotta Gall, "Accounts after 2005 London bombings point to Al Qaeda role from Pakistan," *New York Times*, August 13, 2006, at http://travel.nytimes.com/2006/08/13/world/europe/13qaeda.html?n=Top%2fReference%2fTimes%20Topics%2fOrganizations%2fA%2fAl%20Qaeda%20.

Khosrokhavar, Farhad, *Suicide Bombers: Allah's New Martyrs*. London: Pluto Press, 2005.

Kickasola, Joseph N., "The Clash of Civilizations within Islam: The Struggle over the Qu'ran between Muslim Democrats and Theocrats," The Center for Vision and Values, Grove City College, August 18, 2006.

Klausen, Jytte, "Counterterrorism and the Integration of Islam in Europe," Foreign Policy Research Institute, *Watch on the West*, Vol. 7, No. 1, July 2006.

Kohlmann, Evan F., *Al-Qaida's Jihad in Europe*. Oxford and New York: Berg, 2004.

Koopmans, Ruud, "The Dynamics of Protest Waves: West Germany, 1965 to 1989," *American Sociological Review*, Vol. 58, October 1993.

"Protest in Time and Space: The Evolution of Waves of Contention," in David A. Snow, Sarah A. Soule, and Hanspeter Kriesi, eds., *The Blackwell Companion to Social Movements*. Oxford: Blackwell Publishing, 2004.

Köse, Ali, *Conversion to Islam: A Study of Native British Converts*. London and New York: Kegan Paul, 1996.

"The Journey from the Secular to the Sacred: Experiences of Native British Converts to Islam," *Social Compass*, Vol. 46, No. 3, 1999, at http://scp.sagepub.com/cgi/content/abstract/46/3/301.

Kristof, Nicholas, "What Does and Doesn't Fuel Terrorism," *The International Herald Tribune* May 8, 2002.

Krueger, Alan B., and David D. Laitin, "Kto Kogo? A Cross-Country Study of the Origins and Targets of Terrorism," in Philip Keefer and Norman Loayza, eds., *Terrorism and Economic Development*. New York: Cambridge University Press, 2008.

Krueger, Alan B., and Jitka Maleckova, "Education, Poverty and Terrorism: Is There a Causal Connection?" *Journal of Economic Perspectives*, Vol. 17, No. 4, Fall 2003.

Lambert, Robert, "Empowering Salafis and Islamists against al-Qaeda: A London Counterterrorism Case Study," *Political Science & Politics*, Vol. 41, 2008, at http://journals.cambridge.org/action/displayAbstract?fromPage=online&aid=1631068.

Laurence, Jonathan, and Justin Vaisse, *Integrating Islam: Political and Religious Challenges in Contemporary France*. Washington, DC: Brookings Institution Press, 2006.

Leiken, Robert, "Europe's Angry Muslims," *Foreign Affairs*, July/August 2005.

"Europe's Mujahedeen, Where Mass Immigration Meets Global Terrorism," Center for Immigration Studies, April 2005, at http://www.cis.org/articles/2005/back405.html.

"Islamist Threat in and from Europe," presentation at the Washington Institute for Near East Studies 2005 Weinberg Founders Conference, Panel III, September 24, 2005.

"Les conversions à l'islam radical inquiètent la police française," *Le Monde*, July 13, 2005, at http://www.geostrategique.net/viewtopic.php?t=670&sid=274f7632a690b0a54ae206be78d06f2f.

Levine, Robert, *Assimilating Immigrants: Why America Can and France Cannot*. Santa Monica, CA: RAND Corporation, OP-132-RC, 2004.

Lewis, Bernard, *What Went Wrong: Western Impact and Middle Eastern Response*. New York: Oxford University Press, 2002.

Li, Quan, "Does Democracy Promote or Reduce Transnational Terrorist Incidents?" *Journal of Conflict Resolution*, Vol. 49, No. 2, 2005.

Li, Quan, and Drew Schaub, "Economic Globalization and Transnational Terrorism: A Pooled Time-Series Analysis," *Journal of Conflict Resolution*, Vol. 48, No. 2, April 2004.

Lia, Brynjar, *Architect of Global Jihad: The Life of Al Qaeda Strategist Abu Mus'ab al-Suri*. New York: Columbia University Press, 2008.

Lia, Brynjar, and Thomas Hegghammer, "FFI Explains Al-Qaida Document." Kjeller, Norway: FFI, 2004.

Lia, Brynjar, and Katja H-W Skjolberg, "Causes of Terrorism: An Expanded and Updated Review of the Literature." Kjeller, Norway: FFI 10307, 2004.

Linke, Junge, "Handbuch gegen Ueberwachung und Ausgrenzung. Freiheit Strirbt mit Sicherheit," *Beitraege zur radikaldemokratischen Diskussion*, Vol. 22, 2001.

L'Istituto Nazionale di Statistica, "La Populazione Straniera Residente nell'Italia," January 1, 2004, at http://www.istat.it/salastampa/comunicati/non_calendario/20050324_00/stranieri_2004.pdf.

Lusher, Adam, "Islamists Use Raid to Stir Up UK Somalis," *The Telegraph*, January 14, 2007.

Lutz, Dieter, *Zukunft des Terrorismus und des Friedens-Menschenrechte, Gewalt, offene Gesellschaft*. Hamburg, 2002.

Lutz, Schnedelbach, "Aktionsraum Deutschland," *Berliner Zeitung*, July 14, 2005.

Madhani, Aamer, "What Makes Cleric al-Awlaki So Dangerous," *USA Today*, August 25, 2010, at http://www.usatoday.com/printedition/news/20100825/1a_awlaki25_cv.art.htm.

Magouirk, Justin, Scott Atran, and Marc Sageman, "Connecting Terrorist Networks," *Studies in Conflict & Terrorism*, Vol. 31, No. 1, January 2008.

Maher, Shiraz, "Summary of Revised Prevent Strategy," International Centre for the Study of Radicalisation and Political Violence (ICSR), June 10, 2011, at http://www.icsr.info/news/icsr-insight---summary-of-revised-prevent-strategy.

Malik, Shiv, "NS Profile – Omar Sharif," *New Statesman*, April 24, 2006, at http://www.newstatesman.com/200604240017.

Manji, Irshad, *The Trouble with Islam: A Muslim's Call for Reform in Her Faith*. New York: St. Martin's Press, 2004.

Marquand, Robert, "Why Germany Closed Mosque Where 9/11 Plotters Met," *Christian Science Monitor*, August 9, 2010, at http://www.csmonitor.com/World/Europe/2010/0809/Why-Germany-closed-mosque-where-9-11-plotters-met.

Marret, Jean Luc, "From Lockerbie to Umar Farouk Abdul-Mutallab: Assessing the Destruction of Civilian Aircrafts by Terrorism," Fondation pour la Recherche Stratégique, Transatlantic Security Paper No. 1, April 2010, at www.frstrategie.org/barreCompetences/terrorisme/doc/tsp.pdf.

Martin, Klaus-Peter, "Fundamentalismus türkischer Jugendlicher–ist die Multikulturelle Gesellschaft gescheitert?" at www.oeko-net.de/kommune/kommune7-97/ZZMARTIN.html.

Martinez, Luis, *The Algerian Civil War, 1990–1998*, translated by Jonathan Derrick. New York: Columbia University Press, 1998.
Massey, Douglas S., "The Age of Extremes: Concentrated Affluence and Poverty in the Twenty-First Century," *Demography*, Vol. 33, No. 4, 1996.
Maurus, Hans Juergen, "Die grosse Gefahr der kleinen Zellen," *ARD*, at http://www.tagesschau.de/aktuell/meldungen/0,1185,OID4508858,00.html.
MacEoin, Denis, *The Hijacking of British Islam: How Extremist Literature Is Subverting Mosques in the UK*. London: Policy Exchange, 2007.
McAdam, Doug, "'Initiator' and 'Spin-off' Movements: Diffusion Processes in Protest Cycles," in Mark Traugott, ed., *Repertoires and Cycles of Collective Action*. Durham, NC: Duke University Press, 1994.
McCauley, Clark, ed., *Terrorism and Public Policy*. London: Frank Cass, 1991.
McGrory, Daniel, "Did Alleged Leader of 21/7 Meet 7/7 Bombers in Pakistan?" *TimesOnline*, August 3, 2005, at http://www.timesonline.co.uk/article/0,,22989-1718984,00.html.
Meesmann, Florian, and Ahmet Senyurt, "Ansar al Islam: Terror in Deutschland?" *MDR Magazine*, December 13, 2004, at http://www.mdr.de/fakt/aktuell/1733098.html.
Meining, Stefan, and Ahmet Senyurt, "The Case of the Bavarian Taliban," The Hudson Institute, Center on Islam, Democracy and the Future of the Muslim World, November 11, 2008, at http://www.futureofmuslimworld.com/research/pubID.92/pub_detail.asp.
Metropolitan Police Service (London), "Anti-terrorist Charges" *Bulletin 2004/0111*, August 17, 2004, at www.met.police.uk/pns/DisplayPN.cgi?pn_id=2004_0111.
Meyer, David S., "Protest and Political Opportunities," *Annual Review of Sociology*, Vol. 30, 2004.
"Migration and Major Cities Policy in Rotterdam," *Metropolis International*, at www.international.metropolis.net/research-policy/rott/chapt1.html.
"Militante Gruppierungen in arabischen und islamischen Ländern," *Informationsprojekt des Orientalischen Instituts Leipzig*, at http://www.stura.uni.leipzig.de.
Mirza, Munira, Abi Senthilkumaran, and Zein Ja'far, *Living Apart Together: British Muslims and the Paradox of Multiculturalism*. London: Policy Exchange, 2007.
"MI5 Report Challenges Views on Terrorism in Britain," *The Guardian*, August 21 2008, at http://www.guardian.co.uk/uk/2008/aug/20/uksecurity.terrorism1/print.
Moghadam, Assaf, "Suicide Terrorism, Occupation, and the Globalization of Martyrdom: A Critique of Dying to Win," *Studies in Conflict & Terrorism*, Vol. 29, 2006.
Moniquet, Claude, "The Radicalization of Muslim Youth in Europe: The Reality and the Scale of the Threat," Testimony before the Subcommittee on Europe and Emerging Threats, Committee on International Relations, U.S. House of Representatives, April 27, 2005.
Moreras, Jordi, "Musulmanes en España," Fundació CIDOB (Barcelona, Spain), at http://www.flwi.ugent.be/cie/moreras2.htm.

Motadel, David, "Islam in Austria," at http://www.euro-islam.info/country-profiles/austria/.

Mousseau, Michael, "Market Civilization and Its Clash with Terror," *International Security*, Vol. 27, No. 3, 2002.

Musharbash, Yassin, Marcel Rosenbach, and Holger Stark, "German Jihad Colonies Sprout Up in Waziristan," *SpiegelOnline*, April 4, 2010.

"Mustafa Setmariam Nasar Thought to Have Masterminded Attacks in Spain," *Global News Wire by BBC Monitoring International Reports*, May 2, 2004.

National Research Council, *Making the Nation Safer: The Role of Science and Technology in Countering Terrorism*. Washington, DC: National Academy Press, 2002.

NEFA Foundation, "Bojinka II: The Transatlantic Liquid Bomb Plot," April 2008, at http://www.nefafoundation.org.

"Islamic Jihad Union (IJU): Interview with German Islamic Convert 'Eric B.,'" May 23, 2008, at http://www.nefafoundation.org.

"Video of German Suicide Bomber in Afghanistan Cuneyt Ciftci," March 28, 2008, at http://www.nefafoundation.org/multimedia-prop.html.

Nesser, Petter, *Jihad in Europe: A Survey of the Motivations for Sunni Islamist Terrorism in Post-Milennium Europe*. Kjeller, Norway: FFI/RAPPORT-2004/01146.

"Lessons Learned from the September 2007 German Terrorist Plot," Combating Terrorism Center at West Point, *CTC Sentinel*, Vol. 1, Issue 4, March 2008.

Presentation, RAND Institute for Middle East Youth (IMEY) *Conference on Positive Options to Deter Youth Radicalism*. Washington, DC, September 22, 2005.

"The Slaying of the Dutch Filmmaker – Religiously Motivated Violence or Islamist Terrorism in the Name of Global Jihad?" Kjeller, Norway: FFI, 2005.

"Netherlands Islamic Community to Hit 1 Million In 2006," *Expatica as found on ReligionNewsBlog*, Netherlands: September 20, 2004, at http://www.religionnewsblog.com/8727.

Neumann, Peter R., *Joining Al-Qaeda: Jihadist Recruitment in Europe*, International Institute for Strategic Studies, Adelphi Paper No. 399, 2008.

Neumann, Peter R. and Brooke Rogers, "Recruitment and Mobilisation for the Islamist Movement in Europe," The International Centre for the Study of Radicalisation and Political Violence (ICSR), King's College, London, 2008.

Neumann, Zohar, "Islamists and Incarceration," The Jewish Institute for National Security Affairs, December 8, 2004, at http://www.jinsa.org/articles/articles.html/function/view/categoryid/165/documentid/2753/history/3,2360,655,165,2753.

Newman, Edward, "Exploring the 'Root Causes' of Terrorism," *Studies in Conflict & Terrorism*, Vol. 29, 2006.

Nikka, Roya, and Andrew Alderson, "Inside This Building, a Terror Suspect Ran a London University's Islamic group. Was It also a Recruiting Ground for 'holy war'?" *The Telegraph*, June 27, 2011.

Norfolk, Andrew, "Muslim Group behind 'mega-mosque' Seeks to Convert All Britain," *The Times Online*, September 10, 2007.

Open Society Institute, "Muslims in the EU: Cities Report," 2007.

Österreich, Statistik Austria 2002, *Volkszählung, Hauptergebnisse I*, at http://www.statistik.at/pub/neuerscheinungen/vzaustriaweb.pdf.

Palfrey, John, and Urs Gasser, *Born Digital: Understanding the First Generation of Digital Natives*. New York: Basic Books, 2008.

Pantucci, Raffaello, "Doctor's Plot" Trial Examines Unexpected Source for UK Terrorist Attacks," *Terrorism Focus*, Jamestown Foundation, Vol. 5 Issue 36, October 22, 2008, at http://www.jamestown.org/single/?no_cache=1&tx_ttnews%5Btt_news%5D=5226.

"'Fritz:' Germany's New Breed of Holy Warrior," HSToday, April 4, 2008, at http://www.hstoday.us/index.php?option=com_content&task=view&id=2766&Itemid=152.

"A Typology of Lone Wolves: Preliminary Analysis of Lone Islamist Terrorists," The International Centre for the Study of Radicalisation and Political Violence (ICSR), King's College London, March 2011, at http://icsr.info/paper/a-typology-of-lone-wolves-preliminary-analysis-of-lone-islamist-terrorists.

Pape, Robert A., *Dying to Win: The Strategic Logic of Suicide Terrorism*. New York: Random House, 2005.

Paxson, Christina, "Comment on Alan Krueger and Jitka Maleckova, 'Education, Poverty, and Terrorism: Is There a Causal Connection?'" Princeton University, Research Program in Development Studies Working Paper No. 207, 2002, at http://www.princeton.edu/rpds/papers/pdfs/paxson_krueger_comment.pdf.

Paz, Reuven, "From Madrid to London: Al-Qaeda Exports the War in Iraq to Europe," GLORIA/PRISM, Occasional Papers, Vol. 3 No. 3, July 2005.

Pelletier, Eric, and Jean-Marie Pontaut, "Ucla: La Vigie de L'antiterrorisme," *L'Express*, April 12, 2004.

Phillips, Melanie, *Londonistan*. New York: Enconter Book, 2006.

Piazza, James A., "A Supply-Side View of Suicide Terrorism: A Cross-National Study," *The Journal of Politics*, Vol. 70, 2008.

Piven, Frances Fox, and Richard A. Cloward, *Poor People's Movements: Why They Succeed, How They Fail*. New York: Pantheon Books, 1979.

Post, Jerrold M., *The Mind of the Terrorist: The Psychology of Terrorism from the IRA to al-Qaeda*. New York: Palgrave Macmillan, 2007.

Post, Jerrold M., Keven G. Ruby, and Eric D. Shaw, "The Radical Group in Context: 2. Identification of Critical Elements in the Analysis of Risk for Terrorism by Radical Group Type," *Studies in Conflict & Terrorism*, Vol. 25, 2002.

Poston, Larry, *Islamic Da'wah in the West: Muslim Missionary Activity and the Dynamics of Conversion to Islam*. New York: Oxford University Press, 1992.

"Preachers to the Converted: Reforming Jihadists," *The Economist*, December 13, 2007, at http://www.economist.com/world/international/displayStory.cfm?story_id=10286811&fsrc=nwlgafree.

"Prevent: Welcome to Totalitarian Britain," *New Civilisation*, June 11, 2008, at http://www.newcivilisation.com/home/uk-europe/prevent-welcome-to-totalitarian-britain.

"Quién es Quién en el Macrojuicio Contra La Célula de Al Qaeda," *El Mundo* (Spain), September 26, 2005.

Quilliam Foundation, "Quilliam Response to UK's Government's New 'Prevent' Policy," June 7, 2011, at http://www.quilliamfoundation.org/images/stories/pdfs/prevent7june2011.pdf.

Quinn, Patrick, "Study Gives Info on Foreign Fighters in Iraq," *The Associated Press*, March 17, at http://www.marinecorpstimes.com/news/2008/03/ap_detaineestudy_031508/.

Rabasa, Angel, "Al Qaeda Terrorism and Islamist Extremism in East Africa," Real Instituto Elcano, July 5, 2009, at http://www.realinstitutoelcano.org/wps/portal/rielcano_eng/Content?WCM_GLOBAL_CONTEXT=/elcano/elcano_in/zonas_in/international+terrorism/ari96-2009.

Rabasa, Angel et al., *Beyond al-Qaeda*, Vol. 1: *The Global Jihadist Movement*. Santa Monica, CA: RAND Corporation, MG-429-AF, 2006.

*The Muslim World After 9/11*. Santa Monica, CA: RAND Corporation, MG-246-AF, 2004.

Rabasa, Angel, Cheryl Benard, Lowell Schwart, and Peter Sickle, *Building Moderate Muslim Networks*. Santa Monica, CA: RAND Corporation, 2007.

RAND Institute for Middle East Youth (IMEY), *Conference on Positive Options to Deter Youth Radicalism*. Washington, DC, September 22, 2005.

Rapoport, David C., "The Fourth Wave: September 11 in the History of Terrorism," *Current History*, Vol. 100, December 2001.

Rapoport, David C., and Leonard Weinberg, eds., *The Democratic Experience and Political Violence*. Portland, OR: Frank Cass Publishers, 2001.

Reader, Ian, *Religious Violence in Contemporary Japan: The Case of Aum Shinrikyo*. Honolulu, Hawaii: University of Hawai'i Press, 2000.

"Recent Immigration Developments in Germany: Lessons and Implications for the U.S.," American Institute for Contemporary German Studies, March 1995, at http://migration.ucdavis.edu/cc/3_95.htm.

Reich, Walter, ed., *Origins of Terrorism: Psychologies, Ideologies, Theologies, States of Mind*. Washington, DC: Woodrow Wilson Center Press, 1998.

Reinares, Fernando, "¿Estamos Más Seguros Frente a Al-Qaeda? Reformas de la Seguridad Interior Española y Prevención del Terrorismo Global, 2004–2008," Documento de Trabajo No. 40/2008. Madrid: Real Instituto Elcano, October 9, 2008.

"Hacia una caracterización social del terrorismo yihadista en España: implicaciones en seguridad interior y acción exterior," Real Instituto Elcano, ARI N° 34/2006 Análisis, March 14, 2006, at http://www.realinstitutoelcano.org/analisis/929.asp.

"The Madrid Bombings and Global Jihadism," *Survival*, Vol. 52 No. 2, April-May 2010.

Presentation at Terrorist Threats in Europe Panel, International Institute for Counter-Terrorism, 8th Annual International Conference, Herzliya, Israel, September 10, 2008.

Reischl, Gerald, *Unter Kontrolle: Die fatalen Folgen der staatlichen Ueberwachung fuer Wirtschaft und Gesellschaft*. Ueberreuter Verlag: 2002.

République Française, *Observatoire National des Zones Urbaines Sensibles, Rapport 2005*, at http://www.ville.gouv.fr/pdf/editions/observatoire-ZUS-rapport-2005.pdf.

Reynolds, Paul, "The Last Days of Londonistan," BBC News, July 27, 2005, at http://news.bbc.co.uk/2/hi/uk_news/politics/4720603.stm.

Rid, Thomas, and Marc Hecker, *War 2.0: Irregular Warfare in the Information Age*. Westport, CT: Praeger, 2009.

Robison, Kristopher K., Edward M. Crenshaw, and Craig J. Jenkins, "Ideologies of Violence: The Social Origins of Islamist and Leftist Transnational Terrorism," *Social Forces*, Vol. 84, No. 4, June 2006.

Roggio, Bill, "Senior al-Qaeda Operative Killed in Somalia," *The Long War Journal*, September 1, 2008, at http://www.longwarjournal.org/archives/2008/09/senior_al_qaeda_oper_1.php.

Roy, Oliver, *Globalized Islam: The Search for a New Ummah*. New York: Columbia University Press, 2006.

Royal United Services Institute, "Operation Crevice Trial Ends," at http://www.rusi.org/go.php?structureID=S4459CoDF31D9A&ref=C4638BFFA4FEC1.

Sageman, Marc, *Understanding Terror Networks*. Philadelphia: University of Pennsylvania Press, 2004.

*Leaderles Jihad: Terror Networks in the Twenty-First Century*. Philadelphia: University of Pennsylvania Press, 2008.

Samuel, Henry, "EU Draws Up Manual to Help Prisons Identify Muslim Extremists," *Telegraph.co.uk*, October 2, 2008, at http://www.telegraph.co.uk/news/worldnews/europe/france/3124378/EU-draws-up-manual-to-help-prisons-identify-Muslim-extremists.html.

Sandee, Ronald, "The Islamic Jihad Union (IJU)," The NEFA Foundation, October 14, 2008, at www.nefafoundation.org.

Sandler, Todd, "On the Relationship between Democracy and Terrorism," *Terrorism and Political Violence*, Vol. 7, No. 4, 1995.

Savage, Timothy M., "Europe and Islam: Crescent Waxing, Cultures Clashing," *The Washington Quarterly*, Summer 2004.

Sawert, Patrick, and David Barrett, "Detroit Bomber's Mentor Continues to Influence British Mosques and Universities," *Telegraph*, January 2, 2010.

Schachter, Jonathan, *The Eye of the Believer: Psychological Influences on Counter-Terrorism Policy-Making*, RAND Dissertation Series, Santa Monica, CA: RAND Corporation, 2002, at http://www.rand.org/pubs/rgs_dissertations/RGSD166/index.html.

Scheuer, Michael, *Through Our Enemies' Eyes: Osama Bin Laden, Radical Islam and the Future of America*, 2nd ed. Washington, DC: Potomac Books, 2006.

Schmid, Alex P., "Terrorism and Democracy," *Terrorism and Political Violence*, Vol. 4, No. 4, 1992.

Schmid, George O., "Muslime in Europa Zwischen Integration und Fundamentalismus," *Evangelische Informationsstelle*, 1998, at http://www.ref.ch/zh/infoksr/usuliya.html.

Schwarzer, Alice, ed., *Die Gotteskrieger und die Falsche Toleranz*. Kiepenheuer und Witsch: 2002.

Sciolino, Elaine, and Souad Mekhennet, "Al Qaeda Warrior Uses Internet to Rally Women," *New York Times*, May 28, 2008.

"Secularism Based Refuted and Proof of Quran," at http://www.hizb.org.uk/hizb/in-the-community/community-events/event-hamza-tzortzis-speaks-on-refutation-of-secular-beliefs-and-proof-of-quran-in-central-london.html.

Sedgwick, Mark, "Al-Qaeda and the Nature of Religious Terrorism," *Terrorism and Political Violence*, Vol. 16, 2004.

Sendagorta, Fidel, "El trasfondo ideológico y geopolítico del 11-M," *Política Exterior*, Vol. 19, No. 104, March/April 2005.

Shapiro, Jeremy, and Suzan Bénédicte, "The French Experience of Counter-Terrorism," *Survival*, Vol. 45, No. 1, Spring 2003.

Silke, Andrew, "Holy Warriors: Exploring the Psychological Processes of Jihadi Radicalization," *European Journal of Criminology*, Vol. 5, 2008

Simon, Jeffrey D., *The Terrorist Trap: America's Experience with Terrorism*. Bloomington: Indiana University Press, 1994.

Slootman, Marieke, and Jean Tillie, *Processes of Radicalisation*. Amsterdam: University of Amsterdam, 2006.

Smelser, Neil J., and Faith Mitchell, eds., *Discouraging Terrorism: Some Implications of 9/11*, Washington, DC: National Academies Press, 2002, at http://www.nap.edu/openbook.php?isbn=0309085306&page=R1.

Smith, Craig S., "Europe Fears Converts May Aid Extremism," *New York Times*, July 19, 2004, at http://www.nytimes.com/2004/07/19/international/europe/19CONV.html?ex=1247889600&en=7210d68d25e849bd&ei=5090&partner=rssuserland.

Snow, David A., Louis A. Zurcher Jr., and Sheldon Ekland-Olson, "Social Networks and Social Movements: Microstructural Approach," *American Sociological Review*, Vol. 45, 1980.

Solomon, Hussein, "Beyond Despondency: Taking the Fight to al-Shabaab in Somalia," International Centre for the Study of Radicalisation (ICSR), February 11, 2011, at icsr.info/blog-archive.php?tag=al-Shabaab.

Speckhard, Anne, and Khapta Akhmedova, "The New Chechen Jihad: Militant Wahhabism as a Radical Movement and a Source of Suicide Terrorism in Post-War Chechen Society," *Democracy & Security*, Vol. 2, 2006.

Sprinzak, Ehud, "Extreme Left Terrorism in a Democracy," in Walter Reich, ed., *Origins of Terrorism: Psychologies, Ideologies, Theologies, States of Mind*. Washington, DC: Woodrow Wilson Center Press, 1990.

Statistics Austria, Volkszählung, Hauptergebnisse I, 2002 at www.statistik.at/pub/neuerscheinungen/vzaustriaweb.pdf.

Statistics Netherlands, "Statline," 2005, at http://www.cbs.nl/en-gb/menu/themas/mens-maatschappij/bevolking/publicaties/artikelen/2005-1759-wm.htm.

Steinberg, Guido, "Counter-Terrorism and German-American Relations: A German Perspective," *American Institute for Contemporary German Studies*, Issue Brief 26, October 2008.

"The Evolving Threat from Jihadist Terrorism in Turkey," Real Instituto Elcano, February 16, 2009, at http://www.realinstitutoelcano.org/wps/portal/rielcano_eng/Content?WCM_GLOBAL_CONTEXT=/elcano/elcano_in/zonas_in/international+terrorism/ari26-2009.

"The Threat of Jihadist Terrorism in Germany," Real Instituto Elcano, June 11, 2008 at http://www.realinstitutoelcano.org/wps/portal/rielcano_eng/Content?WCM_GLOBAL_CONTEXT=/elcano/elcano_in/zonas_in/international+terrorism/ari142-2008.

"A Turkish al-Qaeda: The Islamic Jihad Union and the Internationalization of Uzbek Jihadism," Center for Contemporary Conflict, *Strategic Insights*, Vol. 7, Issue 2, July 2008, at http://www.ccc.nps.navy.mil/si/2008/Jul/steinbergJul08.asp.

Stern, Jessica, *Terror in the Name of God: Why Religious Militants Kill.* New York: Ecco/Harper Collins Publishers, 2003.

Stolz, Rolf, Kommt der Islam*: Die Fundamentalisten vor den Toren Europas.* Munich: Herbig, 2001.

Stroobants, Jean-Pierre, "Le Reseau Islamiste 'Hofstad' Etait Solidement Ancre en Europe," *Le Monde*, December 9, 2004.

Swiss Federal Statistical Office, "Resident Population by Religion," at http://www.bfs.admin.ch/bfs/portal/en/index/themen/bevoelkerung/sprachen__religionen/blank/kennzahleno/religionen.html.

Swiss Federal Statistical Office, 2004, *Ausländerinnen und Ausländer in der Schweiz*, at http://www.bfs.admin.ch/bfs/portal/de/index/dienstleistungen/publikationen_statistik/publikationskatalog.Document.50762.html.

Syal Rajeev, and Chris Hastings, "Al Qa'eda Terror Trio Linked to London School of 'Extremists," *Daily Telegraph*, January 27, 2002.

Taarnby, Michael, "The European Battleground," *Terrorism Monitor*, The Jamestown Foundation, Vol. 2, Issue 23, December 2, 2004.

Research Report for the Danish Ministry of Justice, Centre for Cultural Research, University of Aarhus Recruitment of Islamist Terrorists in Europe, Trends and Perspectives, January 14, 2005.

Tarrow, Sidney, *Democracy and Disorder*. Oxford: Oxford University Press, 1989.

*Power in Movement: Social Movements, Collective Action and Politics.* Cambridge: Cambridge University Press, 1994.

Taylor, Peter, "A Reason to Hate," *The Guardian*, September 1, 2006, at http://www.guardian.co.uk/world/2006/sep/01/iraq.july7.

Thies, Jochen, "El Renacimiento de los Servicios Secretos," *Política Exterior* (Spain), Vol. 18, No. 1, September-October 2004.

Thorne, John, and Hannah Stuart, *Islam on Campus: A Survey of UK Student Opinions*. London: The Centre for Social Cohesion, 2008.

"Threat of Islamic Radicalization to the Homeland," written testimony of Charles E. Allen, Assistant Secretary for Intelligence and Analysis/Chief Intelligence Officer, Department of Homeland Security to the U.S. Senate Committee on Homeland Security and Governmental Affairs, March 14, 2007.

Tilly, Charles, *From Mobilization to Revolution*. Reading, MA: Addison-Wesley, 1978.

Travis, Alan, "MI5 Report Challenges Views on Terrorism in Britain," *The Guardian*, August 21, 2008, at http://www.guardian.co.uk/uk/2008/aug/20/uksecurity.terrorism1/print.

"The Making of an Extremist," *The Guardian*, August 20, 2008, at http://www.guardian.co.uk/uk/2008/aug/20/uksecurity.terrorism.

"Trial of French Islamic Radical Sheds Light on Converts' Role," *Washington Post*, January 1, 2006, at http://www.washingtonpost.com/wp-dyn/content/article/2005/12/31/AR2005123101056_pf.html.

Tribalat, Michèle, "Le Nombre de Musulmans en France: Qu'en Sait-on?" *Cités*, July 2003.
"TTP Claims Responsibility for Foiled Terror Plan in Barcelona," *Dawn Internet Edition*, September 19, 2008, at http://www.dawn.com/2008/09/19/top13.htm.
Tumelty, Paul, "An In-Depth Look at the London Bombers," *Terrorism Monitor*, The Jamestown Foundation, Vol. 2, Issue 15, July 28, 2005.
"New Developments Following the London Bombings," *Terrorism Monitor*, The Jamestown Foundation, Vol. 3, Issue 23, December 2, 2005.
"Reassessing the July 21 London Bombings," *Terrorism Monitor*, The Jamestown Foundation, Vol. 3, Issue 17, September 8, 2005.
Ulfkotte, Udo, *Der Krieg in Unseren Staedten, Wie Radikale Islamisten Deutschland Unterwandern*, June 2003.
*Propheten des Terrors, Das geheime Netzwerk der Islamisten*, Munich: 2001.
Ulph, Stephen, "Londonistan," *Terrorism Monitor*, Vol. 2, Issue 4, February 26, 2004.
"Un Juicio, Cuatro Huidos y Ocho Enigmas," *Noticias de Gipuzkoa* (Spain), October 31, 2007, at http://www.noticiasdegipuzkoa.com/ediciones/2007/10/31/politica/espana-mundo/d31esp21.789977.php.
United Kingdom, Home Office, Prevention of Terrorism Act 2005,"Anti-Terrorism Crime and Security Act 2001 (ATCSA) – Part 4 Powers," at www.homeoffice.gov.uk/terrorism/govprotect/legislation/atcsa.html.
United Kingdom, London Metropolitan Police, "Operation Crevice: MPS statement," April 30, 2007, at http://cms.met.police.uk/news/convictions/terrorism/operation_crevice_mps_statement.
United Kingdom, Office for National Statistics (ONS), "Muslim Families Most Likely to Have Children," *2001 Census*, at http://www.statistics.gov.uk/CCI/nugget.asp?ID=1168&Pos=1&ColRank=1&Rank=326.
United Kingdom, Office for National Statistics (ONS), "Population: Ethnicity & Religion," *2001 Census*, at www.statistics.gov.uk/cci/nugget.asp?id=395.
United Kingdom, Office for National Statistics (ONS), "Religion, 2001: Regional Trends 38," *2001 Census*, at www.statistics.gov.uk/STATBASE/ssdataset.asp?vlnk=7681.
United Kingdom, Office of Public Sector Information: Civil Contingencies Act, 2004, at http://www.legislation.hmso.gov.uk/acts/acts2004/20040036.htm.
United States Department of State, *International Religious Freedom Report 2003, Netherlands*, at http://www.state.gov/g/drl/rls/irf/2003/index.htm.
Urban, Johannes, *Die Bekämpfung des Internationalen Islamistischen Terrorismus*. Wiesbaden: Verlag für Sozialwissenschaften, 2006.
Van Reenen, Saskia, "Integrate or Suffer," *Current Affairs*, June 22, 2004.
Vasagar, Jeevan, "Somali Islamists held UK meeting to raise funds," *The Guardian*, January 13, 2007.
Vermaat, Emerson, "Mustafa Setmarian Nasar – A Close Friend of Bin Laden's and Al-Zarqawi's," *Militant Islam Monitor*, December 4, 2005, at http://www.militantislammonitor.org/article/id/135.
Victoroff, Jeff, "The Mind of the Terrorist: A Review and Critique of Psychological Approaches," *Journal of Conflict Resolution*, Vol. 49, No. 1, 2005.

Vidino, Lorenzo, *Al Qaeda in Europe: The New Battleground of International Jihad*. Amherst, NY: Prometheus Books, 2005.

"The Hofstad Group: The New Face of Terrorist Networks in Europe," *Studies in Conflict & Terrorism*, Vol. 30, No. 7, 2007.

"Is Italy Next in Line after London?" *Terrorism Monitor*, The Jamestown Foundation, Vol. 3, Issue 18, September 21, 2005, at http://www.jamestown.org/terrorism/news/article.php?articleid=2369788.

"Islam, Islamism and Jihadism in Italy," Hudson Institute, Center on Islam, Democracy and the Future of the Muslim World, August 4, 2008, at http://www.futureofmuslimworld.com/research/pubID.88/pub_detail.asp.

"The Muslim Brotherhood's Conquest of Europe," *The Middle East Quarterly*, Vol. 12, No. 1, 2005.

"Radicalization, Linkage, and Diversity: Current Trends in Terrorism in Europe," Occasional Paper, OP-333-OSD, Santa Monica, CA: RAND Corporation, 2011.

Wade, Sara Jackson, and Dan Reiter, "Does Democracy Matter: Regime Type and Suicide Terrorism," *Journal of Conflict Resolution*, Vol. 51, No. 2, April 2007.

Weinberg, Leonard, "Turning to Terror: The Conditions under Which Political Parties Turn to Terrorist Activities," *Comparative Politics*, Vol. 23, No. 4, 1991.

Weinberg, Leonard, and Ami Pedahzur, *Political Parties and Terrorist Groups*. New York: Routledge, 2003.

Weinberg, Leonard, Ami Pedahzur, and Arie Perlinger, *Political Parties and Terrorist Groups*, 2nd ed. New York: Routledge, 2008.

Wilkinson, Paul, *Political Terrorism*. London: Macmillan, 1974.

*Terrorism versus Democracy: The Liberal State Response*. London and Portland, OR: Frank Cass, 2001.

Wiktorowicz, Quintan, *Radical Islam Rising: Muslim Extremism in the West*. Oxford: Rowman & Littlefield, 2005.

Wright, Lawrence, "The Terror Web: Were the Madrid Bombings Part of a New, Far-Reaching Jihad Being Plotted on the Internet?" *The New Yorker*, August 2, 2004.

"Xénophobie en France," Rapport de la Commission des Droits de l'Homme de l'ONU, Document E/CN.4/1996/72/Add.3, at http://www.jura.uni-sb.de/france/Law-France/xeno.htm.

Zavis, Alexandra, "A Profile of Iraq's Foreign Insurgents: Interrogations of Fighters in U.S. Custody Yield a Portrait of Young, Lonely Recruits Who Crave Recognition," *Los Angeles Times*, March 17, 2008.

Zimmermann, Doron, "The European Union and Post-9/11 Counterterrorism: A Reappraisal," *Studies in Conflict and Terrorism*, Vol. 29, No. 2, March-April 2006.

Zimmermann, Doron, and William Rosenau, eds., *The Radicalization of Diasporas and Terrorism*. Zurich: Center for Security Studies, ETH Zurich, 2009.

# Index


Abderrahman, Hamed, 51
Abduh, Muhammad, 24
Abdulkadir, Abdulkadir Mohamed (aka Ikrima), 152
Abdullah, Abu, 114
Abdullah, Bilal, 127
Abdulmutallab, Umar Farouk, 105, 157
abrogation (*naskh*), and Salafism, 30
Abu Baker mosque (Spain), 103
Acebes, Angel, 111
Achraf, Mohamed, 188
Afalah, Mohamed, 72n27, 127n12
Afghani, Ibrahim al-, 153
Afghani, Jamal al-Din al-, 24
Africa. *See* Central Africa; East Africa; North Africa; South Africa; Sub-Saharan Africa
African Union Mission to Somalia (AMISOM), 150, 152, 153
age range: of converts to Islam, 91, 92, *93–5*, *97*; of Hostad Group, *81*, 83; of Muslim population of France, 10–11; of second-generation British Muslims implicated in terrorism, 59, *60–3*, *66*. *See also* generational distinctions
Ahmad, Iftikhar, 34
Ahmed, Kafeel, 51, 180n29
Ahmed, Rabei Osman Sayed (El Egipcio), 38–9, 49
Ahmidan, Jamal, 72, 110–11
Ahmidan, Mustafa, 110
Ain-al-Hilwe (Palestinian refugee camp), 77
aircraft bombings: Al-Qaeda and failed plots in 2009–2010, 148; terrorist attacks on commercial aviation and environment for Islamic radicalization in Europe, 156–9; and terrorist plots in United States, 195–6; and transatlantic flight plot in 2006, 71–2, 142–3, 157–8
Air France, and hijacking in 1994, 42
AIVD. *See* Netherlands
Akbar, Jawad, 53, *61*, 70
Akeha, Mohammed, 72
Akeha, Rachid Oulad, 72
Akhnikh, Ismail, 80, *81*
Al-Andalus, 39
*Al Ansar* (magazine), 49
Albania, 13, 163n22
Alevis, and Muslim population of Germany
Al Forkane mosque (Spain), 104
Algeria: importance of immigrants from to radical Islamist networks in Europe, 74; and Muslim population of France, 9–10, 11; and radical Islamic networks in France, 41–2, 43. *See also* North Africa
Ali, Abdullah Ahmed, 51, *62*
Ali, Waheed, *62*
Al-Jihad (organization), 26
Almallah Dabas, Mouhannad, 137
Al-Manaar Muslim Cultural Heritage Center (United Kingdom), 84
Al Muhajiroun (the Emigrants), 53–4
Al Mujaddida, 120
Al-Qaeda: focus of on attacks on civil aviation, 158; as ideological reference

point for second-generation immigrants to Europe, 57; and Madrid bombings, 129; operations of in Spain, 39; organizational structure of in Europe, 125; and origins of radical Islamic networks in Europe, 43, 47; and Salafism, 26, 27, 28, 35–6; search of for weapons of mass destruction, 163; and terrorist attacks in East Africa, 150
Al-Qaeda in the Arabian Peninsula (AQAP), 147–50
Al-Quds mosque (London), 103
Al-Shabaab (Somalia), 85–6, 150
Amin, Salahuddin, 53, *61*, 69–70, 166
AMISOM. *See* African Union Mission to Somalia
Anghar, Fouad el-Morabit, 72
an-Nussrah, 117
Anouar, Asri Rifuat, 72n27
anti-Semitism, and legal system of Germany, 175
Aourghe, Zine Labidine, 80, *81*
apostasy, and Salafism, 31, 32. *See also takfir*
Arif, Said, 168
*Army of Madinah in Kashmir, The* (al-Hindi), 166n33
Arwar, Assad, 51
Asha, Mohammed, 127
Asiedu, Manfo Kwaku, 84
Askar, Abu (Shahab D.), 107
Assad, Bashar, 132
asylum seekers: and legal regimes in Europe, 154; and Muslim population of the Netherlands, 17; and North African immigrants to Europe, 74
Atta, Mohammed, 48, 103, 106n15
Attachés for Religious Affairs (Turkish consulates in Germany), 13
Attar, Aldy el-, 106
Audenaert, Glenn, 75
Audiencia Nacional (Spain), 187–8
Austria, 19, 21, 175–6
Awlaki, Anwar al-, 105, 148–9
Ayachi, Bassam, 115–16
Al-Azhar University (Egypt), 164n25
Aziz, Abu Abd al-, 39
Azizi, Amer al-, 48, 129
Aznar, José María, 160
Azzouz, Samir, 80, *81*
Babar, Mohammed Junaid, 54, *61*, 70, 142
Baghdadi, Abu Bakr al-, 133
Bahiah, Mohamed, 49
Bakri, Aziz el-, 51–2
Bakri, Omar Mohammed, 32, 53, 54, 69
Bale, Jeffrey, 110n26, 111, 126, 129
Ballard, Roger, 67–8
Bangladesh, 16, 22n60
Banna, Hasan al-, 25
Bar, Shmuel, 33, 164n25
"Barbarossa" (jihadi website), 39
Barcelona plot of January 2008, 144
Barnett, Anthony, 162n20
Barot, Dhiren (Abu Isa al-Hindi), 59, *93*, 166–7
Basques (Spain), 38, 113, 160, 187
Beaumont, Peter, 162n20
Begg, Moazzem, 105
Beghal, Djamel, 43
Behbehani, Sayyid Abdullah, 25n5
Belfatmi, Mohammed, 48n23
Belgacem, Bellil, 104
Belgium: civil war in Syria and recruits from, 137; immigrants from North Africa and Islamic extremism in, 75; Muslim population of, 19, 20; origins of radical Islamic networks in, 48; recruitment for radical Islamists groups in, 122. *See also* Europe
Belhadj, Mohamed, 127n12
Benchellali, Chelalli, 109
Benchellali, Menad, 167–8
Benchellali, Mourad, 167–8
Benhamed, Merouane, 168
Bensakhria, Mohamed, 43
Benyettou, Farid, 109
Berbers, 74
Berjawi, Bilal al-, 151
Berraj, Said, 72n27, 127n12
Bhatti, Mohammed Naveed, *60*
Bhutto, Benazir, 144
Bianchi, Sergio, 115
Binalshibh, Ramzi, 48, 103, 106n15
bin Laden, Osama, 50, 120, 125, 144, 163, 165
*Bitter Harvest* (al-Zawahiri), 27
blogs, and networks of extremists, 117
Bonté, Johann, 94
Bosnia, 13, 97, 107. *See also* Yugoslavia
Boston marathon bombing (2013), 196
botulinum toxin, 168

Boucek, Christopher, 169n1
Boughabe, Mohammed Fahmi, 80, *81*
Bourgass, Kamel, 167, 168
Bouyeri, Muhammad, 2, 54, 58, 78, 79, *81*, 115
Boyd, Daniel Patrick (aka "Saifullah"), 196n7
Boyd, Dylan, 196n7
Boyd, Zakariya (aka "Zak"), 196n7
Bradford Four, 119–20
Breininger, Eric (aka Mujahid Abdul Gaffar al-Almani), *95*, 100
Breivik, Anders, 156
Brigitte, Willie Virgile, *94*
Bringing Communities Together project (United Kingdom), 172
British Muslim Forum, 181
Bruguière, Jean-Louis, 130, 185
Bujol, Barry, 149
Bulgaria, 13
Burke, Jason, 161n18
*burqa*, proposals to ban in European countries, 34. *See also* headscarves

Casablanca bombings (2003), 46, 50, 104, 160, 188
Caze, Christophe, *94*, *97*
Center for Studies in Islamism and Radicalization (Aarhus University), 2
Central Asia, and global dimension of Europe-based Islamist terrorism, 144–7
Central Counter-Terrorism Strategy (CONTEST), 170–4
Centre Islamique Belge, 121
Centre for Social Cohesion (United Kingdom), 53, 55, 106, 180
Centro Nacional de Coordinación Anti-Terrorista (CNCA), 187
Channel Project (United Kingdom), 171
Chebli, Driss, 48n23
Checens, and terrorist incident in France, 167–8
Chedadi, Mohammed El Hadi, 72n27
chemical, biological, radiological, or nuclear (CBRN) weapons, 163, 165n30
Chentouf, Mohammed, 80
Chesser, Zachary, 149
Choudary, Anjem, 35, 54
Choudhry, Roshonara, 123–4
Chowdhury, Mohammed, 149
Ciftci, Cüneyt (aka Saad Abu Furqan), 88–9
citizenship: and identity of Muslim youth in Germany, 14; Muslim population of the Netherlands and dual, 17
civil war: in Algeria, 74, 75; in Syria, 131–41
commercial aviation. *See* aircraft bombings
Compagnies Républicaines de Sécurité (CRS), 186
Comte, Auguste, 24
Conceptual Framework on the European Security and Defense Policy Dimension in the Fight Against Terrorism, 189–90
converts, to Islam and patterns of Islamic radicalization in Europe, 6–7, 89–101
corruption, of Western societies as theme in radical Islam, 34
Council of Europe Convention on the Prevention of Terrorism (United Kingdom), 184
counterterrorism: and Algerian terrorist networks in France, 42; and enhanced cooperation within European Union, 188–91; "illegal" vs. "subversive" activities and divide in assessments of threat in Europe, 174–9; legal systems and legislation on in Europe, 155, 181–8; and Operation Crevice in United Kingdom, 70; overview of European approaches to, 169–74; reaching out to Muslim communities as strategy for in Europe, 179–81
Courtailler, David, *94*
"criminal association," in French anti-terrorism law, 185
Cruikshank, Paul, 121
Crul, Maurice, 17n38
culture, and counterterrorism strategies in Netherlands, 176–7. *See also* Islamic Culture Institute
"culture of violence," and radical groups, 5
Cusbert, Denis (aka Deso Dogg and Abou Maleeq), 134
Cuthbertson, Ian, 112
cyberterrorism, 117

Dahdah, Abu, 47–50, 51, 72, 112, 129, 189
Dahlen, Haji Ahmad, 25n5
Dahmane, Abdessater, 120, 121
Dajjal (Islamic tradition), 132
Danesh, Ahmad Makhdum, 25n5
Darkazanli, Mamoum, 48, 106–107, 188–9
Da Vanzo, Julie, 8n1

DawaFFM, 117
*Da'wat al-Muqawamah al-Islamiya al-'Alamiya* (al-Suri), 34, 49
decentralized networks, 126–8
"defensive," meaning of for jihadists, 31
Degauque, Muriel, *95*, 98, 121
deintegration, of Turkish communities in Europe, 86
Delić, Rasim, 45–6
democracy, view of in radical Islamism, 27
demographics, Muslim populations in Europe and trends in, 21–2. *See also* age range; education; marital status; occupation
Denmark, 21, 138, 143
Denver/New York City plot (2009), 195
Department of Communities and Local Government (United Kingdom), 181
Desai, Gurukanth, 149
*De Standaard* (newspaper), 137
*Die Welt* (newspaper), 132, 176
"digital natives," and Internet, 5
Direction Centrale du Renseignement Intérieur (DCRI), 186
Direction de la Surveillance du Territoire (DST), 185–6
"dirty bombs," 165, 166
Division Nationale Anti-terroriste (DNAT), 185
Diyanet İşleri Başkanliği (Directorate of Religious Affairs), 13
Djerba synagogue bombing (Tunisia 2002), 50
"doctors' plot" (United Kingdom 2007), 3, 127
Donadieu, Gérard, 23n1
Dumont, Lionel, 94, 97
Dunham-Scott, Diana, 124n5, 125
Durao Barroso, Jose Manuel, 78
Durbin, Torga, 106

East Africa, and global dimension of Europe-based Islamist terrorism, 150–3. *See also* Ethiopia; Kenya; Somalia
East London Mosque, 105
economic crisis, in Spain, 18
education: of converts to Islam, 91, 92, *93–5*, *96;* of Hofstad Group, *81*, 83; of second-generation British Muslims implicated in terrorism, 59, *60–3*, 66, *68*
El Aroud, Malika, 120–2, 141
El Fahtni, Nouredine, 80, *81*
El Haski, Hasan, 72n27
El Morabit, Mohammed, 80, *81*
El Portillo mosque (Spain), 104
Elyas, Nadeem, 32
employment. *See* occupation; unemployment
Escudero, Mansur, 90n78
ETA. *See* Euskadi Ta Askatasuna
Ethiopia, 86, 150
ethnicity, and use of term "Muslim" in Europe, 8
Ettoumi, Youssef, 80, *81*
Eurodac, 190
Europe: contemporary status of Muslim populations in, 8–9; converts to Islam and patterns of radicalization in, 89–101; ethnic Somalis and patterns of Islamic radicalization in, 85–6; evolution of radical Islamism in, 26–7; East Africans and patterns of Islamic radicalization in, 83–6; global dimension of Islamist terrorism in, 131–53; Hofstad Group and patterns of Islamic radicalization in, 78–83; Islamic radicalization and integration of Muslim populations into societies of, 1–7; and jihadists' search for weapons of mass destruction, 163–8; legal systems and counterterrorism strategies in, 154–5, 181–8; lessons for United States from experience of with Islamic radicalization, 195–6; operational access and target-rich environment for Islamist terrorism in, 155–6; origins of radical Islamist networks in, 41–55; overview of approaches to counterterrorism in, 169–74; reaching out to Muslim communities as counterterrorism strategy in, 179–81; recent evolution of Islamic terrorist networks in, 124–31; recruitment methods for radical Islamic organizations in, 103–22; second-generation Muslim immigrants and Islamic extremist movements in, 56–72; strategy of Salafism in, 35–40; summary of discussion of radical Islamism in, 192–4; and terrorist attacks on commercial aviation, 156–9; and terrorist attacks on mass transportation systems, 159–62; terrorist threat assessment and distinction between "illegal" and "subversive" activities, 174–9; Turkish communities and radical

fringe of political Islam in, 86–9. *See also* Austria, Belgium, Denmark, European Union, France, Germany, Italy, Netherlands, Norway, Spain, Sweden, Switzerland, United Kingdom
European Arrest Warrant, 190
European Union (EU), and counterterrorism, 169–70, 188–91
Euskadi Ta Askatasuna (ETA), 38, 113, 160, 187
EU Strategy for Combating Radicalization and Recruitment to Terrorism, 169–70

Fagih, Saad al-, 45
Fahd, Nasir bin Hamid al-, 164
Faisal, Abdul el-, 125
Faisal, Abdullah, 35, 114
Fakhet, Sarhane Ben Abdelmajid, 72, 73, 129, 130
Faraj, Muhammad abd al-Salam, 26
*fard ayn* (personal duty), 34
fatwas, and ideology of jihad, 33, 118
Federal Office for the Protection of the Constitution (Germany), 178–9, 183
Fernández, Yusuf, 90n78
Feroze, Junade, 60
fertility rates, and Muslim populations in Europe, 22
Fichero FIES, 115
FIFA World Cup Final (Uganda 2010), 153
Finsbury Park mosque (London), 104
Finton, Michael (aka Talib Islam), 195
Fischer, Thomas (alias Hamza), 106
"First Arab-Islamic Congress in Europe" (2004), 177–8
Forsane Alizza (the Knights of Pride), 186
*Forsvarets Forskningstitutt* (FFI), 37–8
Fort Hood shooting (2009), 195
Forum on Religion & Public Life (Pew Research Center), 17n35, 18n44
Fradkin, Hillel, 196
Framework Decision on Combating Terrorism (EU), 190
France: anti-terrorism and legal regime of, 184–6; civil war in Syria and militants from, 138, 141; converts to Islam and radicalism in, 89–90, 91; mosques as recruitment nodes for radical Islamism in, 109; Muslim population of, 9–12, 22; origins of radical Islamic networks in, 41–2, 43; prisons and recruitment for radical Islamic groups in, 116; and Salafism, 36, 39. *See also* Europe
Franco, Francisco, 19n46
Frankfurt cell, 44
freedom, radical Salafism and concept of, 29
Freedom House, 196
Free Syrian Army (FSA), 138
*From Dawa to Jihad: The Various Threats from Radical Islam to the Democratic Legal Order* (AIVD 2003), 175
fund-raising, and Internet, 119

Gama'a al-Islamiyya al- (Egypt), 107
Game, Mohammed, 124
Ganczarski, Christian, 32, 94
Garcia, Anthony, 53, 70
Garden of Female Believers, 120
Garsallaoui, Moez, 51, 122
Garzón, Baltazar, 57, 188, 189
Gazavat Media, 146
Gelayev, Ruslav, 168
Gelowicz, Fritz Martin (alias Abdullah), 95, 99, 106, 147
*Gemeinsame Internet-Zentrum* (GIZ), 183
gender, and Muslim population of France, 11. *See also* women
Gendron, Raphael, 116
generational distinctions: in patterns of Islamic radicalization and terrorism in Europe, 6; second-generation Muslim immigrants and Islamic extremist movements in Europe, 56–72, 193; third-generation Turkish communities and problem of deintegration, 86. *See also* age range
Georgia, 168
Germany: and anti-terror legislation, 182–3; banning of Hizb ut-Tahrir in, 52–3; civil war in Syria and militants from, 136, 139–40; converts to Islam in, 90; counterterrorism strategies of, 175, 177–9; immigrants from Middle East and North Africa and patterns of Islamic extremism in, 76–8; legal system of, 155, 182–3; mosques as recruitment nodes for radical Islamism in, 106–107; Muslim population of, 12–15; Pakistan and Islamic terrorism in, 143–4; Turkish communities in, 12, 13–14, 86. *See also* Europe
Ghez, Jeremy J., 169n1
Githens-Mazer, Jonathan, 74–5

globalism and globalization: and Europe-based Islamist terrorism, 131–53, 194; and jihadist movement, 125–6
Godane, Ahmed Abdi (Abu Zubeir), 153
González, José Luis Galán, 47, *93*
Goris, Issam, 98
Grammich, Clifford, 8n1
Grandvisir, Jean-Marc, 94
Green, Anthony "Abdur Raheem," 105
Grignard, Alain, 111–12
*Groupe Islamique Armé*(GIA), 41–2
*Groupe Islamique Combattant Marocain* (GICM). *See* Moroccan Islamic Combatant Group
Group for Preaching and Combat (GSPC), 43
*Guardian, The* (newspaper), 173
guest workers, in Germany, 12
Gunaratna, Rohan, 103–104
Gutiérrez, José Antonio, 128

Hadayet, Mesham Mohamed, 123n2
Haddad, Haitham al-, 105
Hadjbid, Youssef el, 124
Hague, William, 138
Hajdib, Yousef Mohamad el, 76–8, 162
Hajj, Yusuf al-, 130
Hajji, Said al-, 48
Hamad, Jihad, 76–8, 124, 162
Hamara Healthy Living Centre, 172
Hamdi, Ahmed, 80, *81*
Hamdi, Isaac. *See* Osman Hussain
Hammami, Omar (aka Abu Mansour al-Amriki), 151–2
Hamza, Abu, 125
Hanif, Asif Mohammed, 53, *60*
Haq, Naveed, 123n2
Harrach, Bekkay (aka Al-Hafidh Abu Talha al Almani), 146
Harris (rapper), 176
Hasan, Nidal Malik, 123n2, 148, 195
Hassan, Mohammad Omar Aly, 196n7
headscarves, and Turkish communities in Europe, 87, 89. *See also burqa*
Heering, Liesbeth, 17n38
Hekmatyar, Gulbaddin, 42
HELP Foundation, 44
Hezb-e-Islami, 42
Hezbollah, 44
Hindi, Abu Isa al-. *See* Barot, Dhiren
*hizbiyya*, and Salafism, 24n2
Hizb ut-Tahrir (HuT), 44, 52–4, 104, 139, 180–1n30
Hoffman, Bruce, 126
Hofstad Group, 74, 78–83, 128n17, 130
homosexuality, as theme in radical Islamism, 34
Horsburgh, Nicola, 125
*House of War: Islamic Radicalization in Denmark* (Goli & Rezari 2010), 2
Huq, Ryad al-, 105
Husain, Ghaffar, 66–7
Hussain, Hasib, 62, 70–1
Hussain, Nazam, 149
Hussain, Osman (aka Isaac Hamdi), 84, 85
Hussain, Tanvir, 62, 71
"Hussein, Abu (the Russian)," 135

Iannaccone, Laurence, 23n1
Ibn Taymiyya, 28
Ibrahim, Ahmad, 129
Ibrahim, Andrew ("Issa"), 123
Ibrahim, Muktar Said, 143
*Idarat al-Tawahhush* (Naji), 34
identity: and counterterrorism, 176, 177; Islam as key source of in European Muslim communities, 8; and naturalization of Muslim youth in Germany, 14; and second-generation Muslims in Europe, 58; *umma* as alternative source of for Salafis, 29
ideology: of Al-Qaeda as reference point for second-generation Muslim immigrants to Europe, 57; and counterterrorism strategies in Netherlands, 176–7; and Internet, 118–19, 120; and radical Islamist networks, 193; of Salafism, 23–6
IJU. *See* Islamic Jihad Union
immigration: and demographic trends in Muslim populations of Europe, 21–2; and Muslim population of France, 9–10; and Muslim population of Spain, 18. *See also* asylum seekers; generational distinctions; guest workers; refugees; *specific countries of origin*
India, 16
Indonesia, 47
Inspection générale de la police nationale (IGPN), 186
*Inspire* (magazine), 149
Institut National d'Etudes Démographiques (INED), 9

Institut National de la Statistique et des Études Économiques (INSEE), 9
integration, of Muslim communities into European societies, 1–7
intelligence agencies, and counterterrorism in Europe, 156
International Centre for the Study of Radicalisation and Political Violence (ICSR), 134, 136
International Criminal Tribunal, for Yugoslavian war crimes, 45–6
Internet: and counterterrorism in Germany, 183; and recruitment for radical Islamic groups, 117–22; role of in Islamic radicalization process, 5–6, 193
IRA. *See* Irish Republican Army
Iraq, 39, 131, 134
Irish Republican Army (IRA), 161n17
Isamuddin, Riduan (aka Hambali), 166n32
Islam: contemporary status of Muslim populations in Europe, 8–22; liberal Muslims and effort to construct "European" form of, 23; reaching out to Muslim communities as counterterrorism strategy in Europe, 179–81; and religious justification for use of weapons of mass destruction, 164–5; Syria and traditional narrative on end of days, 132. *See also* Alevis; converts; Islamic radicalization; mosques; Salafism; Shit'ites; Sunni
Islam, Shajul, 136
Islamic Center of Aachen, 32
Islamic Combatant Group. *See* Moroccan Islamic Combatant Group (GICM)
Islamic Conflict Studies Bureau, 49
Islamic Courts Union (Somalia), 104, 150–1
Islamic Culture Institute (ICI), 45, 107–108
Islam4UK, 54
Islamic Jihad Union (IJU), 58, 87–8, 89, 106, 143
Islamic Movement of Uzbekistan (IMU), 87, 107, 145
Islamic radicalization (radical Islamism): converts to Islam and patterns of in Europe, 89–101; East Africans and patterns of in Europe, 83–6; ethnic Somalis and patterns of in Europe, 85–6; evolution of in Europe, 26–7; and global dimension of Europe-based terrorism, 131–53; and immigrants to Europe from Middle East and North Africa, 72–83; Hofstad group and patterns of in Europe, 78–83; and integration of Muslim populations into European societies, 1–7; legal systems of Europe and environment for, 154–5; lessons for United States from European experience with, 195–6; operational access and target-rich environment in Europe for, 155–6; and origins of networks in Europe, 41–55; and recent evolution of terrorist networks in, 124–31; recruitment nodes for in Europe, 103–22; and second-generation Muslim immigrants to Europe, 56–72; summary of discussion on status of in Europe, 192–4; and terrorist attacks on commercial aviation, 156–9; and terrorist attacks on mass transportation systems in Europe, 159–61; and Turkish community in Germany, 15. *See also* counterterrorism; jihad; Salafism
Islamic Republic of Iran, 24
Islamic Salvation Front (FIS), 41
Islamic State of Iraq and al-Sham (ISIS), 133–4
Islamic University of Medina, 32
Islamische Audios, 117
Islamisches Informationszentrum (IIZ), 106
Isqra mosque (France), 109
Israfel, Muhammad Imbaeya, 124
Issa (prophet), 132
Issar, Radwan al-, 78, 80, *81*, 155
Italy: mosques as recruitment nodes for radical Islam in, 107–108; Muslim population of, 19–20; origins of radical Islamic networks in, 45, 46; recruitment by radical Islamic groups in prisons of, 115–16
Ittihad-e-Islami, 42
Izzadeen, Abu, 125

Jaish al-Muhajireen wal-Ansar (Army of the Emigrants and Helpers), 134–5
Jalaluddin, Muhammad Tahir, 25n5
Jalil, Abdul Aziz, *60*
Jamaat-i-Islami, 24
Jarrah, Ziad Samir, 103
Jawziyya, Ibn al-Qayyim al-, 33
Jenkins, Brian, 163
jihad: as global movement, 125–6; Salafism and ideology of, 27–33; and search for weapons of mass destruction, 163–8; themes and messages of, 33–5. *See also* Al-Jihad; Islamic Jihad Union; Islamic radicalization

"Jihadist Early Warning" system, 140
*Jihad: The Neglected Obligation* (Faraj), 26
Jihadiyya, Harakat al-Salafiyya al-, 130
Joint Situation Centre (SITCEN), 190, 191
Jordán, Javier, 50, 73, 125
Juergensmeyer, Mark, 5
Julani, Abu Muhammad, al-, 133
Jund al-Sham (Army of Syria), 140, 168

Kalifatsstaat. *See* Kaplan Group
Kamel, Fateh, 46
Kandel, Johannes, 2–3
Kansi, Mir Aimal, 123n2
Kaplan, Cemalettin, 86
Kaplan, Metin, 86, 155
Kaplan Group (Kalifatstaat), 86, 155, 177, 178
Kar, Mevlüt, 141
Kashmir, 56, 67–8, 101
Kashmiri, Ilyas, 145
Kenya, 150
Kerchove, Gilles van de, 141
Khaibar, Mohsen, 126–7
Khan, Arafat Wahid, 62, 71
Khan, Mohammed Siddique, 51, 53, 54, 57, 58, 62, 70–1, 108n21, 142, 143
Khan, Usman, 149
Kharijites, 31
Khatib, Adam Osman, 63
Khawaja, Mohammed Momin, 69n13
Khemais, Essid Sami Ben, 43
Khosrokhavar, Farhad, 112
Khuershid, Hammad, 143
Khyam, Omar, 53, 54, 61, 69–70, 114
Kickasola, Joseph, 30
Klausen, Jytte, 8
Kohlmann, Evan, 46
Kol, Abdelaziz Mahmoud, 124
Köse, Ali, 90
Kounjaa, Abdennabi, 72
Krekar, Mullah, 130, 155
Kurdistan Workers' Party (PKK), 86n65
Kurds, and Muslim population of Germany, 12, 15

Lamari, Allekama, 72
Lambert, Robert, 179–80
Laoudi, Rachid, 51
Latif, Omar, 149
Lauziére, Henri, 25n6
law enforcement, and environment for terrorism in Europe, 156. *See also* counterterrorism; legal systems
Lebanese Welfare Committee (LWC), 44
Lebanon, 76
legal systems, and legislation: and counterterrorism strategies in Europe, 174–9, 181–8; and favorable environment for Islamic radicalization in Europe, 154–5. *See also* law enforcement
Leiken, Robert, 58n5
Lewthwaite, Samantha, 151–2
Libi, Laith al-, 144
Lindh, John Walker, 51
Lindsay, Germaine, 70–1, 93, 151
Little Rock, Arkansas shootings (2009), 195
Lockerbie, Scotland aircraft bombing (1988), 159
Lodin, Maqsood, 145–6
London bombings (July 7, 2005), 2, 35, 39, 57n2, 70–1, 83–5, 142, 159, 161
London School of Islamics, 34
*lone wolf*, use of term in context of terrorist attacks, 124

Ma'ali, Abu el-, 46
Maarufi, Tariq al-, 48
Madrid bombings (2004), 2, 38, 50, 72–3, 104, 129, 159–61
Mahdi (Islamic tradition), 132
Maher, Shiraz, 127, 173, 180n29
Mahmood, Waheed, 53, 61, 70
Makanesi, Rami, 145
Malla, Hussain al-, 100
Manarah al-Bayda al- (White Minaret), 132
Mañas, Fernando M., 125
Manavbasi, Ahmed, 146
Man-portable air defense systems (MANPADS), 158–9
Maqdisi, Abu Muhammad al-, 31, 134
marital status: of converts to Islam, 93–5, 97, 98; of Hofstad Group, 81, 83; of second-generation British Muslims involved in terrorist acts, 59, 60–3, 67
Marjani, Sihab al-Din, 25n5
Marroush, Muhammad Fares, 133
martyrdom, and ideology of jihad, 33
Martyrs of Morocco cell (Spain), 188
Masri, Abu Hamza al-, 44, 155
Massari, Muhammad al-, 45

Massoud, Ahmed Shah, 120, 121
mass transportation systems, terrorist attacks on in Europe, 159–62
Mauetani, Yunis al-, 145
*Mawsu'at al-I'dad* (*Encyclopedia of Preparation*), 119
Maymouni, Mustafa, 129, 130
McDougall, Dan, 167n36
Mehsud, Baitullah, 144
*Mein Weg nach Jannah* (Breininger), 100
Meliani cell, 43
Merabet, Nouredine, 168
Merah, Mohammed, 145, 186
Middle East. *See* Lebanon; Palestinians; Syria; Turkey
*Milestones Along the Road* (Qutb), 26
mixed networks, 128–30
Mobley, Sharif, 149
modernity, and Salafism, 24
Mohamed, Ramzi, 84
Mohammad, Jude Kenan, 196n7
Mohammed, Fazul Abdallah, 85n62, 151, 153
Mohammed, Rahaman Alan Hazil, 157
Moroccan Islamic Combatant Group (GICM), 46, 74, 108
Morocco: and Muslim population of Belgium, 20; and Muslim population of France, 9n5, 11; and Muslim population of Germany, 13; and Muslim population of the Netherlands, 17; and Muslim population of Spain, 18, 19. *See also* Casablanca bombings; North Africa
mosques, as recruitment nodes, 103–10
Motassadeq, Mounir al-, 144
Moussaoui, Zacarias, 48
Movement for Islamic Reform in Arabia (MIRA), 44
Muhajiroun, Al, 69, 70
Muhammed, Abdulhakim Mujahid (Carlos Bledsoe), 195
Multikultur Haus (Germany), 87, 106
Munthir, Abu, *61*, 69
Muslim(s). *See* Islam
Muslim Brotherhood, 24, 26, 47
Muslim Council of Britain (MCB), 104, 180–1
Mustafa, Shukri, 26–7
Mustafa, Taji, 105
Nabhan, Saleh Ali Saleh (aka Abu Yusuf), 85
Nackcha, Omar, 126–7
Naji, Abu Bakir, 34
Nali, Mohamed Srifi, 52
Nasar, Mustafa Setmariam, 49
National Syrian Coalition, 141
Nesser, Petter, 58, 71
Netherlands: civil war in Syria and militants from, 136–7, 138, 140–1; and counterterrorism strategies, 174–5, 176–7; and Hofstad Group, 74; legal system of, 155; Muslim population of, 17; prisons and recruitment for radical Islamic groups in, 115; Turkish communities in, 86, 89. *See also* Europe
networks, and Islamic radicalization: and Internet, 119; origins and establishment of in Europe, 41–55, 193–4; terrorism and recent evolution of in Europe, 124–31. *See also* social networking
Neumann, Peter, 134
9/11 Commission, 1
Noricks, Darcy, 2n1
North Africa: and Muslim population of France, 9, 10; and Muslim population of Germany, 13; and Muslim population of Spain, 18; and Muslim population of Switzerland, 21; and Muslim population of United Kingdom, 16; patterns of radicalization in immigrants to Europe from, 72–83. *See also* Algeria; Morocco; Tunisia
North Carolina cell, 195–6
Northern Ireland, 161n17
North London Central Mosque, 104
Norway, 21, 155
nuclear weapons, 163, 164n25, 165
Nusra, Jabhat al-, 132, 133, 137

Ocak, Yusuf, 145
occupation: of converts to Islam, 91, 92, *93–5*, *96;* of Hofstad Group, *81*, 83; and Muslim population of France, 11–12; of second-generation British Muslims involved in terrorist acts, *60–3*, 66, *68*. *See also* unemployment
Oever, Martine van den, 80, *81*, *94*
Omar, Yassin Hassan, 84
operational access, and environment for Islamic radicalization in Europe, 155–6
Operation Crevice (2004), 68–70

organizational function, of Internet, 119, 120
Ouaer, Bouraoui el-, 121
Ouhnane, Daoud, 72n27, 127n12

Padilla, José, 51, 165
Pakistan: and global dimension of Europe-based Islamist terrorism, 141–4; and Muslim population in United Kingdom, 15, 22, 56. *See also* Kashmir
Palestinians: and Muslim population of Spain, 19; and refugee camps in Lebanon, 76–7
Pantucci, Raffaello, 124
paradise, and ideology of jihad, 33
Patel, Abdul Muneem, *63*
Paul Findley Federal Building (Illinois), 195
Pearl, Daniel, 53, 59
Pettyjohn, Stacie L., 169n1
Pew Research Center, 8n3, 9n4, 17n35, 18n44
Police Chiefs Task Force (PCTF), 190
popular culture, and emergence of new multicultural identities, 176
Prevent component, of United Kingdom's counterterrorism strategy, 170–4
Preventing Violent Extremism Pathfinder Fund (PVEPF), 181
Prevention Summit (Germany 2011), 183
prisons: Islamic proselytism and conversions to Islam in, 91–2; as recruitment nodes for Islamic radicalization in Europe, 110–17

Qadhi, Yasir, 105
Qaradawi, Yusuf al-, 33n28
Qatada, Abu, 44–5, 103, 134, 155
Quarn, and Salafism, 30
Quillen, Chris, 165n30
Quilliam Foundation, 66–7, 113, 174, 181
Qutb, Sayyid, 26

Rabasa, Angel, 151n103, 169n1, 191n63
radical Islamism. *See* Islamic radicalization
Radical Middle Way (Prevent strategy), 170, 181
Rahman, Mohibur, 149
Rahman, Shah, 149
Raja, Mohammed Irfan, 119–20
Ramda, Rachid, 42, 114
RAND Corporation, 8n1, 9n4, 155
Rashidi, Ali al- (aka Abu Ubadiah al-Banshiri), 150
Rauf, Rashid, 141, 143, 158
Real Instituto Elcano, 50
reciprocity, as justification for use of weapons of mass destruction, 1 64
reconstituted networks, 131
recruitment, for radical Islamic groups: on internet and social media, 117–22; in mosques, 103–10; in prisons, 110–17
refugees, and North African immigrants to Europe, 74. *See also* asylum seekers
Rehman, Omar, *61*
Reid, Richard, *93*, *99*, 157
Reilly, Nicky, 124
Reinares, Fernando, 72, 73n30, 74, 75, 90n79, 112n34, 129
relative deprivation, involvement in terrorism and psychology of, 3
Renseignements Genereaux (RG), 185
Research, Information, and Communications Unit (RICU), 172
Ressam, Ahmed, 42
ricin, and weapons of mass destruction, 167, 168
Rida, Muhammad Rashid, 25
riots (France 2005), 10, 11
Robert, Pierre Richard, *94*
Roble, Omar Ali, 153
Robow, Muktar (alias Abu Mansur), 85, 153
Rockwood, Paul, 149
Roubaix gang, 42, 97
Rowe, Andrew (aka Yuef Abdullah), *93*, 97
Roy, Olivier, 4, 23–4n1

Saddique, Mohammed Usman, *63*, 71–2
Sahla, Soumaya, 80
Said-Ibrahim, Mukhtar, 84, 110, 142
Salafism: and converts to Islam, 90, 92; and counterterrorism in Germany, 179; description of ideology of, 23–6; and jihadist ideology, 27–33; strategy of in Europe, 35–40; themes and messages of, 33–5
Salafiya Jihadia, 104n3
Salah, Chej, 47
Saleem, Sadeer, *62*
Saleh, Ali Abdullah, 149
Salim, Mamdouh Mahmud, 106
Sánchez, Baldomero Lara, *93*

Sandia National Laboratory, 158n8
Sarwar, Assad Ali, *62*, 71–2
Sassi, Nizar, 168
Sauerland cell, 87, 99
Savant, Oliver (aka Ibrahim Savant), *93*
Saved Sect, The, 54
Saudi Arabia, 25–6
Sayyid, Abdul Rasul, 42
Schengen Information System (SIS II), 155, 190
Schneider, Daniel (aka Abdullah), *95*, 100, 147
Selek, Attila, 106, 147
self-radicalization, and Internet, 5–6
Shabaan, Anwar, 45, 46
Shaffi, Qaisar, *61*
Shahjahan, Mohammed, 149
Shahzad, Faisal, 148–9
Sharia4Belgium, 137
Shima, Abu, 77–8
Shakil, Mohammed, *62*
Sharif, Omar Khan, 53, *60*
Shehhi, Marwan al-, 103
Sheikh, Ahmed Omar, 53, 59, *60*
Sheikh Mohammed, Khalid, 156–7
Sherifi, Hysen, 196n7
Shit'ites, and Muslim population of Germany, 13
"shoebomber." *See* Richard Reid
Siddique, Zeeshan, 142
Siddiqui, Ahmed, 144–5
smartphones, 5
social network analysis (SNA), 124n5, 125, 126
social networking, and role of Internet in radicalization, 5. *See also* networks
socioeconomic status, and converts to Islam in France, 91. *See also* education; occupation
Somalia: and global dimension of Europe-base Islamist terrorism, 150; and patterns of Islamic radicalization in Europe, 85–6; and recruitment for radical Islamist groups at mosques in United Kingdom, 104; and terrorist attacks on commercial aviation, 158
South Africa, 163n22
South Asia: and Muslim population in United Kingdom, 15–16, 22; second-generation British Muslims and Islamic extremism, 58–68. *See also* India; Pakistan
Spain: civil war in Syria and militants from, 137, 138; counterterrorism and legal regime of, 187–8; converts to Islam and radical networks in, 90; immigrants from North Africa and Islamist terrorism in, 72–4; mosques as recruitment nodes for radical Islamism in, 104; Muslim population of, 18–19; origins of radical Islamic networks in, 46–50, 51–2; and prisons as recruitment nodes for radical Islamism, 112–13, 115; and Salafism, 38, 39. *See also* Europe; Madrid bombings
Spanish Civil War, 19n46
Special Immigration Appeals Commission (SIAC), 44–5
*Spiegel* (German periodical), 100
Steinberg, Guido, 87
Stewart-Whyte, Donald (aka Abdul Waheed), *93*, *99*
Subasic, Anes, 196n7
Sub-Saharan Africa: and Muslim population of France, 9; and Muslim population of Spain, 18. *See also* East Africa, South Africa
suburbs, and Muslim population of France, 11
Sudani, Abu Talha (aka Tariq Abdullah) al-, 85n62
*Sueddeutsche* (newspaper), 135
Süen, Faruk, 86
Sufism, and converts to Islam, 90
Sufyani (Islamic tradition), 132
suicide, and radical Islamism, 33n28
"suitcase plot" (Germany 2006), 76, 162
Sukati, Ahmad, 25n5
Sunnis: and Muslim population of Germany, 13; and Muslim population of Italy, 20; and Quran, 30; and Salafism, 24
"support," Muslim communities and concept of, 55
Suri, Abu Khalid al-, 134
Suri, Abu Mus'ab al-, 34, 36–7, 40
Suriname, 17
Sweden, 21, 137, 138
Switzerland, 19, 20–1, 122
Sword Verses, and Quran, 30
Syria: civil war in and Europe-based Islamist terrorism, 131–41; immigrants from and patterns of Islamic radicalization in Europe, 72; and Muslim population of Spain, 19
Syrian Muslim Brotherhood, 47

Taarnby, Michael, 78–9
Tabataba'I, Sayyid Muhammad, 25n5
Tablighi Jamaat (TJ), 50–2, 89
Taha, Mahmoud, 30n20
Tahiri, Abderrahamane (alias Mohamed Achraf), 111
Tahtawi, Rifa'at Rafi al-, 25n5
Taiba mosque (Germany), 106
Taifatul Mansura (Victorious Sect), 146
*takfir* (excommunication), 31, 32, 118
Takfir wal-Hijra, 43, 44, 75
Taliban Mujahideen (Germany), 34–5, 100, 146
Tanweer, Shehzad, 33, 51, *62*, 70–1, 143
Tariq, Amin Asmin, 71–2
Tarmohammed, Nadeem, *61*
Tartusi, Abu Bashir al-, 35, 120
*tawhid* (unity of God), and Salafism, 29
Tehrik-i-Taliban Pakistan, 144
Tel Aviv nightclub suicide bombing (2003), 59
terrorism, definition of in French law, 184n43. *See also* aircraft bombings; Casablanca bombings; counterterrorism; cyberterrorism; Islamic radicalization; London bombings; Madrid bombings
*Thirtieth Letter on Cautioning Against Excesses in Rendering the Verdict of Unbelief, The* (al-Maqdisi), 31
tolerance, for extremism in Muslim communities, 55
Touboul, Deborah, 6n13
Trabelsi, Nizar, 75
training, and Internet, 119
Transaviaexport, 158n10
Tribalat, Michèle, 10
Tsouli, Younis, 117–18
Tunisia, 9n5, 11. *See also* Djerba synagogue bombing; North Africa
Turkey: ethnic connection between Uzbeks and, 147; and Muslim population of Austria, 21; and Muslim population of Belgium, 20; and Muslim population of France, 11; and Muslim population of Germany, 12, 13–14; and Muslim population of the Netherlands, 17; and Muslim population of Switzerland, 20–1; Turkish communities in Europe and radical fringe of political Islam, 86–9
Turkish-Islamic Union for Religious Affairs (DITIB), 13
Tzortzis, Hamza Andreas, 105

Uddin, Shamin Mohammed, *63*
Uka, Arid, 117
ul-Haq, Zia, *60*
Ulph, Stephen, 27–8
*umma*, as unifying vision of radical Islam, 29
unbelievers (*kuffar*), and ideology of jihad, 32
"underwear bomber," 148, 157
unemployment: and Muslim population of France, 11; and Muslim population of Germany, 12. *See also* occupation
Union of Muslim Communities in Spain (UCIDE), 18
United Kingdom: civil war in Syria and militants from, 136, 138, 141; counterterrorism and legal system of, 155, 184; decentralized networks and terrorist attacks in, 127; and Hizb ut-Tahrir, 52; Kashmir and Muslim militants in, 56; mosques as recruitment nodes for radical Islamism in, 104; Muslim population of, 15–16, 22; origins of radical Islamic networks in, 43–5; positive attitudes toward extremism by Muslim communities in, 55; Prevent component of counterterrorism strategy of, 170–4; prisons as recruitment nodes for radical Islamism in, 113–15; reaching out to Muslim communities as counterterrorism strategy in, 180–1; and Salafism, 36, 39; second-generation Muslim and Islamic extremism in, 58–68; universities and Islamic radicalization in, 105–106. *See also* Europe; London bombings
United States: and lessons from European experience with Islamic radicalization, 195–6; and Salafism, 35–6, 37
universities, and Islamist radicalization in United Kingdom, 105–106
University College London (UCL), 105
Usama, Abu, 105
Uzbekistan, 147

Vaisse, Justin, 22n61
values, radicalization and European system of, 3–4
Van Gogh, Theo, 2, 54, 78, 79
Vidino, Lorenzo, 83n54, 108

Visa Information System (VIS), 190
Voss, Torsten, 139

Wadi, Muqbil bin Hadi al-, 31n21, 180n28
Wahhab, Muhammad ibn Abd al-, 25
Wahhabism, and Salafism, 25–6
Walters, Jason (aka Jamal), 80, *81*, *94*
war, and jihadist ideology, 33
Waziristan, 145–6, 147
weapons of mass destruction, search by jihadists in Europe for, 163–8
Westgate mall terrorism attack (Nairobi 2010), 153
Wiktorowicz, Quintan, 91n82
*Will Terrorists Go Nuclear?* (Jenkins), 163
Wright, Lawrence, 160n14
women: and Islamic groups on Internet, 120; and religious conservatism in Turkish communities of Europe, 87; and themes in radical Islamism, 34–5. *See also burqa*; gender; headscarves

Yaghi, Ziyad, 196n7
Yarkas, Imad Eddin Barakat. *See* Abu Dahdah
Yemen, 147–50
Yilmaz, Adem, 87, 89, 147
Young, Brian (aka Umar Islam), *93*
Yousif, Yehia, 99
Yugoslavia, 21, 45–6. *See also* Bosnia
Yuldashev, Tahir, 145

Zaman, Safeena, 72
Zaman, Waheed, *63*, 71–2
Zammar, Haydar, 48
Zarqawi, Abu Musab al-, 31, 48, 120, 131, 168
Zawahiri, Ayman al-, 27, 39, 57n2, 132–3
Zazi, Najibullah, 195
Zbakh, Abderrahim, 72n27, 73
Zougam, Jamal, 73, 130, 160
Zypries, Brigitte, 189